VOLUMES 1-12

the naked lawyer®

RIP to XXX

How to Market, Brand and Sell YOU!

Globe Law and Business

Author
Chrissie Lightfoot

Published by
Globe Law and Business Ltd
3 Mylor Close
Horsell
Woking
Surrey GU21 4DD
United Kingdom
Tel: +44 20 3745 4770
www.globelawandbusiness.com

ISBN: 978-1-90778-730-0
A catalogue record for this book is available from the British Library

contents

preface

HI THERE! I'd like to take this opportunity to provide you with a whistle-stop tour of *the naked lawyer*.

We're living in the digital age. Everything seems topsy-turvy and uncertain. We're all fighting to find *space* in the battle to win more business (sales) and to achieve personal fulfilment.

The global recession and the self reliance human economy, combined with the Legal Services Act 2007 and alternative business structures, mean that increased competition from client-centric major players, 'DIY free legal documents providers' via the internet, virtual law firms and virtual lawyering, will all challenge the legal profession's established engagement model.

Throw into the mix the enlightened consumer – who is more demanding and discerning with increased levels of expectation, responsible for setting new higher standards in customer service – together with the disruptive technologies of the past few years along with future anticipated technological advances, and what have we got? Our traditional way of lawyering under threat, juxtaposed with an opportunity to mould a brighter future, if we dare to choose, change and take control.

The legal world (law law land), inevitably, is experiencing an unprecedented transitional period, the likes of which it has never so far experienced.

I wholeheartedly believe and advocate that we need to welcome innovation, embrace radical change, reinvent customer service and work harder and smarter in light of the inevitable commoditisation and evolution of legal provision.

It's because of the present and future trend, in which the buyers of legal advice, services and provision (entrepreneurs/ business people) can choose who, where, what, why, when and how they wish to purchase legal products and services, that we lawyers need to arm ourselves with 'soft skills' in order to prepare and position ourselves for the evolution, and arguably revolution, of an outdated profession.

To survive and thrive in the years to come, I propose that a paradigm shift is required in our mindset (thinking), behaviour, actions, focus and expectations by the law firm (partners/owners/directors), existing practising lawyers and next generation lawyers.

But, in law law land, we have a problem...

Entrepreneurs are from Venus and lawyers are from Mars. Accordingly I suggest that we lawyers need to become more entrepreneurial and to 'get naked'.

Hopefully, as entrepreneurs (legal service buyers) and we lawyers increase our understanding of each other and improve 'the relationship' between us, both parties will be happy with the outcome – improved cost effective and time efficient legal provision which creates value for both the entrepreneur (buyer) and the lawyer (seller).

Traditional lawyers, entrepreneurial lawyers and the next generation have a wonderful opportunity in this enlightened, consumer-led digital era to become 'super lawyers'.

I propose that extraordinary relationships and customer service will be the holy grail at the heart of the successful super lawyer. Building an enduring value relationship with the consumer, utilising 'fluffy soft-skills stuff' combined with a total consumer-centric focus, is where the real value will be for the lawyer, law firm and consumer of today and the future.

Enter 'soft-skilling' – the requirement for us lawyers to be able to truly relate, ROAR (Reach Out And Relate) style – in a bid to become extraordinary rainmaker lawyers, of the naked kind.

From my experience, knowledge and understanding, I believe there are opportunities to significantly enhance YOUR career prospects and options, add value and income to the company you serve and possibly even increase your own income (whatever stage you are at in your career), sense of achievement and personal fulfilment, by following the proven blueprint sales development ROAR model contained in this book.

If you need, want or desire to get more clients, sales, referrals, income, value, growth and success (any or all of these) as an individual or as an entity, then *the naked lawyer* will show you how. It will help you make those difficult choices, the necessary changes and to take control of your career, lifestyle and life through learning and knowing how to market, brand and sell YOU!

It also provides an insight into the legal profession, present and future. Whether you are a lawyer or not, if you have had dealings with the legal profession, or if you simply wish to try some refreshingly new ways of marketing, branding and selling yourself with a view to achieving more choice, change and control in your career and life, then this book will hit the spot.

It's more than a marketing, branding and sales blueprint. It's a manual for your life.

the naked lawyer is a real-life, totally transparent, brutally honest and detailed tale of my rainmaking activities, achievements and experiences (both positive and negative) in the legal profession/industry during 2008-09 when, throughout my final year as a trainee solicitor and since founding EntrepreneurLawyer Limited (a period of a little over a year during the 2009 recession), I generated £562,000 of new client legal work enquiries which I referred to practising solicitors.

Whilst I deal with serious matters by providing serious messages, solutions, material and ideas throughout the book, I take an idiosyncratic approach which may or may not be to your taste.

However, I promise you this: *the naked lawyer* is certainly a new, informative, fun and sexy way of my sharing (teaching) and you learning. It is a reflection of what it preaches. It's innovative. And, I reckon you're more likely to engage, remember the key points and messages and actively do something as a result of reading it.

In the volumes which follow you will note that there is an 'adult' element and theme throughout. But that's OK, I reckon. We're all adults. And of course, you have the choice as to whether you wish to read any further.

Choice, change and control are ultimately the undercurrent flowing throughout *the naked lawyer* as you discover and decide how to market, brand and sell yourself in order to survive and thrive in the years to come. Ergo, how to become a lawyer of tomorrow, today.

I share my real-life story with you throughout *the naked lawyer* in the guise of an imaginary prancing, private dancing 'Naked Lawyer' in law law land.

It's a story, a sales blueprint and a workbook all wrapped up into one neat little package; feel free to check the EntrepreneurLawyer website (http://entrepreneurlawyer.co.uk) to find out whether CPD accreditation (or an alternative) is available should you carry out the 'after dark activities'.

Volume 1 sets the scene and provides you with the background detailing what the problem is, why I have written *the naked lawyer*, what you're about to experience in reading the book, what you can expect to learn and how to get the best out of the whole thing.

Volume 2 introduces you to the first element of the ROAR model – emotional intelligence (EI), aka, self-awareness. It focuses on awakening your inner YOU and laying the foundations for everything else which follows.

In Volume 3, I show you why and how to research, establish and develop your niche, identify target market(s) and sort your positioning and differentiation so that you are ready to develop your personal brand.

In Volume 4, I reveal why and how to devise your personal brand and align it with your firm brand – your 'Brand,Me' and 'Brand,Firm'.

Throughout Volume 5, I share with you why and how to establish and build a raving referral network fast, to last, by bringing your EI, niche and 'Brand,Me' into play. It is one of the first real *doing* elements in applying the 'how to market, brand and sell YOU!' based on the preparatory *thinking* foundations in relation to your reading and carrying out the activities in Volumes 1 through to 4.

In Volume 6, we line dance, hip hop, flamenco, jazz and swing together as I share with you how to use social media and social networking to positively waltz your way into being a socially savvy, happily naked, rainmaker lawyer.

During Volume 7, we begin to look more closely at the sales process. I introduce you to the concept of nurturing fuzz to get more buzz. I focus your attention on establishing and building extraordinary *relationships* of value by looking at relationship marketing, unsales and fuzz. We look at how YOU can add value to your referrers, clients, firm and those whom you serve, due to your 'Brand, You' and relationship building, leveraging and sustaining activities. The essence of this volume lies in the mantra, 'Ask not what your referrers or clients can do for you, but what you can do for your referrers and clients.'

Volume 8 is dedicated to the subject of communication and behaviour, a fundamental element of the ROAR model, and how YOU add value as both a stand-alone individual and within a dynamic team, through communicating your messages by capitalising on your strengths, talents, knowledge, experience, skills and 'Brand, You'. I introduce you to The Focus Lifestyle and the SRO communication module.

In Volume 9, I share with you what I believe is 'extraordinary customer service'. It's another fundamental element of the ROAR model, and how YOU will set your stall out as a truly extraordinary rainmaker lawyer. I introduce you to 'the ROAR unsales egg-timer'. It's a sales, customer service and referral process that I devised (in my own time), and used (and still do) whilst a trainee solicitor, which embraces all of the elements of the ROAR model. It's how referrers, prospects and clients go from not knowing anything about you to being ready to give you (and 'the firm') their business, or more of their business, on an ongoing basis.

Volume 10 is dedicated to the subject of innovation. Innovation is why you will continually stimulate and arouse curiosity in your referrers, prospects and clients. It is the element that makes the ROAR model timeless and is fundamental to your continual personal and professional development. It's what will make YOU exciting to know, like, trust, understand, 'get' and share commonality with the people (personally and professionally) in your life. Understanding and appreciating innovation will help you make changes for the better in yourself, as you re-invent you and your approach to business.

In the penultimate volume, I look at the final element of the ROAR model. The 'other really cool stuff' which I believe will assist you in becoming an extraordinary rainmaker lawyer, such as, commercial savvy, business nous, effective and efficient time management and the seduction of persuasion. I also suggest that you may wish to consider enlisting the help of a business coach, confidence coach, stress management coach, life coach or happiness coach, if you feel the need.

The final volume brings everything together. It's a wrap-up volume. If you're up for becoming a Tomorrow's Lawyer, today, by making the transition from traditional lawyering to entrepreneurial lawyering of the truly naked kind, then Volume 12 is an information rich volume where I present you with a summary of the key takeaways and quick fix tips from Volumes 1-11, to achieve exactly that. We look back over the entire ROAR model and I share with you the ROAR model diagram. We then look forwards and I discuss the kind of future mankind is likely to experience and proffer some ideas as to the enlarged options you might consider due to your now expanded portfolio of skills.

Given this outlook, I even have the audacity to suggest that we should make our future XXX rated; sexily serendipitous, salubriously serene and socially savvy.

I dare you to get off your butt, fulfil your dreams and make it count. Read on...

about the author

HI! WELCOME to *the naked lawyer*. I'm Chrissie Lightfoot, an entrepreneur turned solicitor (non-practising) turned entrepreneur and CEO of EntrepreneurLawyer Limited.

I am absolutely delighted to be your host and to have this opportunity to entertain you whilst sharing with you a new approach to 'how to get more clients, sales, referrals, income, value, growth and success'.

Whether you are a lawyer or not, if you have had dealings with the legal profession, or if you simply wish to try some refreshingly new ways of marketing, branding and selling yourself with a view to achieving more choice, change and control in your career and life, then *the naked lawyer* is an absolute must read for YOU!

The lady doth protest too much, methinks?

bit of background

I'm a lawyer (2009 newly qualified solicitor) and an entrepreneur. I'm also:

- Designated blogger for the Law Society Gazette 'In Business' blog (regular contributor to the Law Society Gazette's management section – UK);
- Mentor for The Prince's Trust 'Million Makers Corporate Challenge' (UK Yorkshire region);
- Women's enterprise ambassador (UK);
- Past vice-chairman of the Federation of Small Businesses (Teesside Branch – UK);
- A national award and prize winning researcher (UK);
- A company prize winner;
- Contributor to the book *Big Rocks: Balancing Life & Work*;
- An innovator, rainmaker and sales legal coach; and
- A woman on a mission dedicated to innovation in legal services provision and advising to benefit both lawyers and entrepreneurs.

Feel free to check out my track-record and profile by Googling me or checking out my profile on LinkedIn; I'd welcome the opportunity to connect with you: http://linkedin.com/in/chrissielightfoot. More information here: http://entrepreneurlawyer.co.uk/about/chrissie-who.

author's note

the naked lawyer has been greatly enhanced by both the business and life experiences of my fellow lawyers, entrepreneurs, mentors and friends in both the legal world and business world, to whom I am extremely grateful.

To each of you: thank you. Now raise your half-full champagne glass and join me in a toast to celebrate the wonder of this extraordinary world and amazing gift of life!

Where appropriate some (or all) of the names, gender and/or context have been changed in the stories that could be construed as negative towards an individual and/or a company.

Nevertheless, all stories are based on true accounts.

Volume 1 was first published in June 2010. This revised Volume 1 contains a few amendments and additions because, as I suspected, the world has moved on and so have I since writing the original version.

Accordingly, as I was scribbling feverishly away compiling the complete box set of 12 volumes herein, which comprise *the naked lawyer* in its entirety, I figured it was befitting to update Volume 1 so that I could share with you the progressive thoughts which popped into my legal beagle mind.

I trust you will find the additions progressive, enlightening and entertaining... as a career, business and life should be perhaps?

If you'd like to get in touch at anytime as you are working your way through *the naked lawyer*'s various volumes then I'd be delighted to hear from you.

Warmest regards

Chrissie Lightfoot

The Entrepreneur Lawyer (of the naked kind)

dedicated to YOU

... and the wonderful life YOU choose to create and truly live in this extraordinary world...

legal notices and disclaimer

I'D LOVE to believe that every reader of *the naked lawyer* will follow the advice within and become wonderfully successful as a result. The truth is that I can't promise that will happen for you and/or your company.

As the information in *the naked lawyer* is of a general nature I simply can't guarantee that it will suit every individual and/or business and/or every situation. One size does not fit all –truly!

Plus, I won't actually know for sure whether you will actually read *the naked lawyer* in its entirety and follow my suggestions. Believe me, I wish I could, but I can't.

So, here's the legal gubbins...

copyright notice

copyright acknowledgements

Grateful acknowledgement is made to each of Bob Burg, Tom Peters, Stephen Roulac, Gary Russell, and Cole Silver for granting me permission to reprint their respective (substantial) excerpts from each of their copyrighted works, which I believe have contributed powerfully and significantly to the messages that I have conveyed throughout *the naked lawyer*:

- Burg, Bob, *Endless Referrals: Network Your Everyday Contacts Into Sales* (3rd ed., New York: McGraw-Hill Books, 2006)
- Burg, Bob and Mann, John D., *Go-Givers Sell More* (London: Penguin Books, 2010)
- Peters, Tom & Barletta, Martha, *Trends: recognize, analyze, capitalize* (New York: DK Publishing, Inc., 2005)
- Peters, Tom, *The Brand You 50: Fifty ways to transform yourself from an "employee" into a brand that shouts distinction, commitment, and passion!* (New York: Alfred A. Knopf, Inc., 1999)
- Roulac, Stephen, 'Learning How To Break Away To Get Alpha Results', *Global CEO* (2008)
- Russell, Gary, *Big Rocks: Balancing Life & Work* (Sausalito, Calif.: Lifestyle Press, 2005)
- Silver, Cole, *How To Create Wealth and Freedom in Your Law Practice: 101 powerful client development and retention strategies for attorneys* (New York: The Silver Group Ltd., 2009)

legal disclaimer

foreword

By Peter Groves

LATE ONE evening, still at my desk, I had a phone call. A recruitment consultant, or headhunter, or £outstanding as a colleague used to call them, with an American accent, told me she was seeking someone in my area of law for a leading firm. A salary that Croesus would hardly have dreamt of. Did I know anyone who'd fit the bill? Perhaps I would? Only one condition: a fully transportable following of at least a million. Sterling. Per year. Would that be a problem?

Merely knowing the law is not enough. I naïvely thought it would be, and perhaps 30 years ago I was right, but anyone trying to make a career in the law now needs other skills. Either knowing the law is a given, or it doesn't matter, because often all that's needed is a way to lay off risk. But your chances of success will depend on who will buy into your knowledge of the law, or lay off their risk onto you. We all have to be – or try to be – rainmakers. Like it or not (and I certainly don't), we are all in business, and success in business doesn't come from knowing more about your product than anyone else, or even from having a better product than anyone else: it comes from turning contacts and prospects into clients, and keeping them.

We all have to sell ourselves – and if that has unsavoury undertones to you, I share your discomfort. Whether our profession is the second oldest, or comes in somewhere after spying, medicine and engineering, it's impossible to ignore similarities with the oldest one. Fortunately, the similarities don't run too far, but lawyers who wish to avoid the equivalent of walking the streets around King's Cross need a reliable collection of clients whose idiosyncrasies they understand, plenty of referrals and a flow of new prospects. It is the rainmakers who will flourish in the modern legal profession.

I can talk the talk, but walking the walk is another matter. Of course, the world is full of people who tell you they can teach you how to do that – but in my experience that's never going to work. Transforming oneself from a technically competent (or even brilliant) lawyer into a successful practitioner requires not just a few teachable skills, it needs a fundamental change in your outlook. I can be given all the knowledge in the world about pole-vaulting, but I'm never going to be able to put it all together and sail over the bar. I'll be forever stuck in the zone where the pole stops me clearing what I could do as a high jump. I'm in a place so far removed from Sergei Bubka that I'll never get close.

Of course, we can train our bodies, acquire the muscles we need to launch ourselves into the air, build up our speed on the runway, plant the pole accurately. In my case, perhaps with effort I could work out how to arrive at the take-off point on the correct foot. We can splash out on expensive equipment. But our minds wouldn't automatically shift to the right place too. That might need a different sort of coaching.

Sales and marketing skills are not inherent in a lawyer's make up. Perhaps we actually became lawyers because we lacked what it might take to be a salesperson, a politician or an investment banker. If we are going to get into the right mental place to make rain, we'll need to leave our comfort zones. And the perfect inspiration to get us out of our comfort zones is Chrissie Lightfoot. She's already been a solicitor but found that she wasn't content to settle for the comfortable life. She wanted more from being a solicitor than just law: she was one of the few natural rainmakers to find their way into the profession.

So, how to get out of your comfort zone? A bit like pole-vaulting, there's no gradual way to do it. You're either vaulting, or you're not. Jump in, throw caution to the winds, and perhaps like the ancient Greek athletes, get naked.

No, I don't mean literally. The world is not ready for lawyers publicly disrobing in large numbers. It probably never will be, not without some radical changes in the physical condition of the average lawyer. But Chrissie takes the nakedness metaphor, calling her 12-volume set of books *the naked lawyer*, and squeezes every last drop of value from it. This is on-the-edge stuff, not for the faint-hearted: even for the liberally-minded it might sometimes be over the top. But do you know what? It got me reading (nothing like the promise of something vaguely sexy to do that), got me out of that traditional lawyerly comfort zone and, having engaged my attention, kept it.

I'm not going to talk about the lessons you will learn from reading this book, the changes they are likely to make to your outlook, even to your life. I'm not going to reveal what Chrissie wrote that caused that lightbulb moment, bringing home what was wrong with me all along. No, definitely not. You'll have to read it for yourself, and see whether the lightbulb comes on for you too somewhere.

I'm just going to say that the author of a book about sales and marketing, which compels you to read it as strongly as *the naked lawyer* does, clearly knows a thing or two about rainmaking.

Peter Groves, IP Lawyer (30 years experience), author of A Dictionary of Intellectual Property, *London, UK*

introduction

I'D ALWAYS had a desire to be a lawyer from a very early age. It wasn't the Perry Mason, Ally McBeal, Boston Legal or Lord Digby Jones (see http://www.digbylordjones.com) portrayal of the profession that attracted me. It was pure challenge, strategy and frustration...

After all, the reality is that the perception of a lawyer and the legal profession remains as someone or something that we need usually in a stressful, difficult situation/ time and that (as a buyer of legal advice/ services) you're going to get whacked with an expensive bill for a piece of work that you don't understand for the privilege of not being communicated with very often throughout the process.

So, why would I want to be tarnished with the same brush? Simple: I saw opportunity. I saw change, innovation and the digital age on the horizon.

early 20s treadmill

The thought of being a lawyer in my early 20s made me cringe mainly because I wasn't ready to jump on that treadmill at that particular time. No offence intended, I hasten to add, if you are a budding lawyer, that is, a trainee solicitor, trainee lawyer or trainee attorney. That was a different era and decade, remember (1990s)?

I actually believe that if you are about to enter the profession right now, it is a wonderfully exciting time as the way in which legal advice and services can be delivered has a great deal of scope, variety and opportunity for you.

But I always felt that I would acquit myself better once I'd experienced 'business'. Hence, I went off and did a load of other interesting stuff instead first.

I knew that one day I would be a lawyer. I am now, having come to the legal profession in later years, albeit I am not practising at the moment, of my own choosing. I might again in the future, who knows?

law matters in business

The fact of the matter is I always had to deal with legal matters in my business affairs. I was particularly interested in how the law could be used to benefit one's business and personal goals.

For example, if you've got great intellectual property how do you make it work for you, such as, exploit it (Bill Gates was/is a master at this) and protect it? Or, how do you structure a company from day one if you know you'll want to exit with minimal taxation implications, as well as motivating and rewarding employees tax efficiently along the way?

not a pretty picture

Bottom line, my dealings with lawyers throughout my portfolio career and in my businesses before entering the legal profession did not paint a pretty picture. I felt, and knew, from personal experience and those of my entrepreneurial colleagues, that there was a lot of room for improvement in the delivery of legal services (on many fronts and in many ways).

For example, there was/is a major gap between the lawyers' picture and the entrepreneurs' picture of what great client service was... and is.

going naked native

And therein was my calling. I felt that 'going native' would help me understand 'why' lawyers behaved the way they did so that I could serve the entrepreneurial client in a better way.

Having gone native, I do now understand.

Throughout the legal profession per se there is a lot of history, tradition, conservatism, outmoded models, structures, regulation, Luddite[1] mentality, fear, ignorance, arrogance and egos rattling around which can make the job of a 'digital age lawyer' very pressured, stressful and frustrating, invariably affecting the level, quality and type of legal service provision.

It is difficult for the lawyers who 'get it' practising within the legal profession, to help bring the profession kicking and screaming into the 21st century to deliver top notch client service when their colleagues are still stuck in their Dickensian ways.

Don't get me wrong, there are bastions of entrepreneurial legal service and advice to be found and there are indeed some awesome entrepreneurial lawyers in the field who 'get it' and are committed to delivering service excellence.

These are the kind of lawyers who aren't afraid to be naked. That is, even though they may feel vulnerable stepping out of their comfort zone, they recognise that they need to leave their ego at the door. They manage to strip away the usual bravado and can identify and empathise with the person standing in front of them in a way which makes the client feel comfortable and truly cared for.

With the Naked Lawyer, what you see is what you get. Clients like that.

This is what makes one proud to be a lawyer in this respected profession. But it's the exception rather than the norm. Unfortunately outstanding client service is still a rare occurrence in the legal profession. Am I right?

a greater calling

I entered the legal profession with an open mind as experience up until that point had taught me that theory and practice do not always meet.

I also felt that entering the profession in later years meant that I could put the transferable 'soft skills', namely, all that 'fluffy stuff' such as client care, customer service, emotional intelligence, researching, marketing, networking, selling, persuading, negotiating, wooing, relating, branding, communicating, innovating, commercial savvy, management and leadership acumen into practice for the benefit of the client and those whom I served in the firm.

If I enjoyed the day-to-day work, then maybe I'd stay. At the very least, whether I did or not, if I felt I needed a new challenge (more likely), I also knew that the training – knowledge, skills and experience – would help me be a better businesswoman so I could benefit others.

Being 'legally qualified' was another skill to add to my entrepreneurial professional skills handbag.

I was privileged with the opportunity to 'legally serve' entrepreneurs for a while alongside one or two lawyers who did 'get it'... until a greater calling beckoned whereby I could utilise my true talent for the benefit of many, rather than a few...

entrepreneurlawyer

And so it came to be. EntrepreneurLawyer Limited was founded recently in a bid to help lawyers and entrepreneurs come together in a positive way.

totally naked

the naked lawyer book comprising all 12 volumes, which contain the full ROAR model (ROAR – Reach Out And Relate), is the sum total of my life's knowledge, experience, skills and talent that I wish to share unreservedly with those of you who want to take control of your career, business and life in a positive way.

I hope you find it enlightening and that it brings you many hours and years of both professional and personal development, success and fun...

Enjoy!

Reference

1. The Luddites were a social movement of British textile workers who resisted and protested to the changes produced by the Industrial Revolution.

Volume 1: RIP – announcing the ROAR model

what's the problem?

entrepreneurs are from Venus and lawyers are from Mars

Practical experience, in both the business world and the legal world, has led me to conclude that 'Entrepreneurs are from Venus and lawyers are from Mars'.

A gross, general and sweeping statement you may think but, having had a foot in both camps – as a lawyer for the past six years and entrepreneur legal advice buyer for 20 years – I reckon I'm entitled to say it.

And the following...

In general (with some exceptions), I feel that we lawyers are absolutely useless at looking after clients' real needs and expectations.

When all that the client wants is to be made to feel special, to be understood, to be charged a fair price, to be treated like any other customer would be treated in any other industry and yell, 'I'm a name, not a number', law firms and their lawyers (partners) have arguably exploited their privileged positions for many years.

Go and ask any buyer of legal services. Am I right?

I cringe at the thought that lawyers see clients as 'fees' and that the lawyers within the firms are called 'fee-earners'. Shameful. I also cringe at the mindset within the higher echelons of the legal profession which, by and large, still treats its lawyers in a similar fashion to its clients.

Believe me, we 'junior' lawyers also wish to cry out, 'I'm a name, not a number'... I remember my 'code' for the time-recording system where I worked as a lawyer was AB1. What's all that about? Old hat, insensitive, inappropriate, that's what. For the client and us – the grinder's monkeys. AB1 made me feel like a robot. Star Wars' C3PO would have been proud, no doubt!

changing landscape

I've already said that the perception of a lawyer and the legal profession remains as someone or something that we need usually in a stressful, difficult situation/time and that, as a buyer of legal advice/services, you're going to get whacked with an expensive bill for a piece of work that you don't understand for the privilege of not being communicated with very often throughout the process.

Until now... perhaps...

The 2008-10 global recession, combined with the Legal Services Act 2007 (LSA) or Tesco Law[1] as it is sometimes known, and alternative business structures mean that increased competition from client-centric major players, 'DIY free legal documents providers' via the internet and virtual law firms will all challenge the legal profession's established engagement model, increase client confidence and levels of expectation and set high new standards in customer service.

Throw the enlightened consumer, digital era and technological advances over the past few years into the mix and what have we got? The lawyer's traditional way of life and 'the firm' under threat; 800 years of history is due to come to an end when the reforms of the LSA take full effect in England (October 2011).

Recently Alastair Moyes of Marketlaw stated that, "law firms need to work hard in the face of commoditised legal providers". In April 2010 he bravely stuck his neck out and suggested that we, today's lawyers, need to embrace radical change and reinvent customer service to avoid our industry "becoming the nearly dead dinosaur that the US car industry became."[2]

I reckon Alastair made two very poignant points.

Let's face it, we lawyers can no longer afford to be Luddites because the transformation of how the world of legal business operates is already underway.

If we consider Professor Richard Susskind's predictions in relation to the role of lawyers and law firms in the new world of consumer legal services (detailed in his provocative 2008 book, *The End Of Lawyers?*[3]), there is further change on the horizon.

The predictions detailed in Susskind's 1996 book, *The Future of Law*[4], have already come to fruition. Perhaps we should heed his recent prediction that the market is not going to tolerate costly lawyers for jobs that can equally or better be undertaken by less-expensive workers or through smart systems and processes.

Enter 'de-lawyering' (passing work to paralegals), 'disruptive' technologies (computerised systemising, packaging or commoditising), entrepreneurial alternative providers and streamlined law firms.

It's now 2010. What Susskind wrote about in 2008 we are currently witnessing.

To quote *Neuromancer* author William Gibson, whether we like it or not, "the future is here... it's just not evenly distributed yet."[5]

It begs the question, will traditional lawyers be needed? The answer, you're no doubt pleased to hear (lawyers, although moot for entrepreneurs), is that it's not all doom and gloom.

Susskind believes that some tasks, for example those requiring deep expertise or interpersonal communication, will still require the traditional lawyer. Furthermore, as to whether law firms can survive, he believes that entrepreneurial law firms will not see threats in all of these developments and some will actually find opportunity.

I would add that entrepreneurial lawyers recognise this and have already begun to act. You will identify these lawyers as beacons of light blazing a trail in customer service excellence and innovation while doing battle with colleagues who are stuck in their Dickensian ways.

Inertia and resistance to change always remind me of Einstein's view that "great spirits have always encountered violent opposition from mediocre minds."

I passionately believe that traditional lawyers, entrepreneurial lawyers and the next generation have a wonderful opportunity in this enlightened, consumer-led digital era to become 'super lawyers'.

rise of the super lawyer

What do I mean by 'super lawyer'?

Let's propose that the most expensive piece of real estate is what lies between our ears – 'deep expertise', Susskind calls it, while I call it 'lawyerly intellectual capital' (LIC) – and that there is LIC too complex to be commoditised (which there undoubtedly is), requiring both interpersonal communication and intrapersonal communication.

Accordingly, LIC is where the true value lies. Arguably, what we need to ensure is that we can effectively communicate that LIC is what the consumer needs, wants and desires of us. Enter 'soft-skilling' to improve our powers of persuasion, communication, relationship building, conversation strategy, marketing, cross-selling, up-selling and selling per se.

If technology can take away as much grunt work as possible and leave the real LIC of value to the super lawyer, then that should be something we welcome, right?

To survive and thrive in the years to come I propose that a paradigm shift is required in the mindset (thinking), behaviour, actions, focus and expectations of both the law firm (partners/owners/directors) and the existing practising lawyers and next generation of lawyers.

As both a lawyer and an entrepreneur (legal purchaser), I believe that the lawyer's role is not just about being technically proficient in the use of words (drafting and advising) – it's much more than that.

Actually being able to truly *relate* and care about the client and his/her business and/or predicament is fundamental to what true lawyering and LIC is all about.

Extraordinary relationships and customer service will be the holy grail at the heart of the successful super lawyer. Building an enduring value relationship with the consumer, utilising 'fluffy soft-skills stuff' combined with a total consumer-centric focus, is where the real value will be for the lawyer, law firm and consumer of today and the future.

All of the above may actually just give the legal profession a raison d'être in the digital world.

I wholeheartedly believe and advocate that the legal profession needs to welcome innovation, embrace radical change, reinvent customer service and work hard and smart in light of the inevitable commoditisation and evolution of legal provision.

However, I seriously question whether established law firms and 'traditional lawyers' are geared up, positioned and truly prepared for the competitive challenges ahead.

Are we confident that we already possess the skills required to become super lawyers? If not, the godsend is that with ever-increasing availability and acceptance of the delivery of soft-skill coaching to the profession there is help at hand.

wakey wakey

I don't for one moment think that we lawyers will become extinct. Not all legal advice, services and provision will be commoditised. It's not possible, probable or even desirable.

But I do agree with one anonymous contributor to a Law Society Gazette blog post recently who aptly stated, "It's not the End of Lawyers, it's the End of Law Firms as we know them. They just don't know that yet."

The tide has turned. The legal profession is now experiencing the dawn of a real buyer's market and the dawn of a much needed 'soft skills' age.

In this new era where supply is outstripping demand, clients (customers/consumers) are now setting the agenda and becoming much more discerning about their choice of supplier at many levels.

No longer is it merely about 'what' you do as a lawyer; but to the customer 'how' you engage with them... 'how' you communicate with them... and 'how' you add value to their relationship with you.

It's because of the present and future trend in the ways in which the buyers of legal advice, services and provision can choose who, where, how, why, what and when they wish to purchase legal products, that we lawyers need to arm ourselves with 'soft skills' in order to prepare and position ourselves for the evolution, and arguably, revolution of an outdated profession. I shall return to and address this comment in further detail in Volume 12: XXX rated – tomorrow's lawyer.

Hopefully, as *both* legal service buyers and lawyers increase their understanding and improve 'the relationship' between them, both parties will be happy with the outcome – improved cost effective, time effective and time efficient legal provision which creates value for both the buyer and the lawyer.

The gap between the legal world and the business world needs to be bridged and this is the decade of opportunity in which to do the very same before our white-collar jobs become so disembowelled that we find ourselves surplus to requirements.[6]

There are lawyers and entrepreneurs in abundance... but there are few entrepreneur lawyers and entrepreneurial lawyers at present to serve the growing numbers of entrepreneurs (legal advice buyers).

Reinventing customer service will require every lawyer (every traditional lawyer, entrepreneurial lawyer and next generation lawyer) to embrace and action a consumer-centric mindset and behaviour – a paradigm shift in most instances. Scary as this might seem, failure to do the same may well mean that 'the end of lawyers' could actually come to pass – for some traditional lawyers.

Nils Montan, a practising IP lawyer in the US for over 30 years, believes:

"the traditional paradigm of law practice really needs to change to face the challenges of our times. Actually, it needed to change a long time ago and most of us knew it when we started to practice, but many of us had our spirits crushed by the 'system.' I say 'viva the revolution.'"[7]

Contrast Nils's view with the one allegedly doing the rounds here in the UK, where a 'mature' long serving partner (of Nils's age) on the subject of all this 'upheaval' was heard to say something along the lines of, "I'm glad I'm old and won't have to deal with all this change. I'll be out in a year or two, thank goodness."

Sad. What a shame. At a time when the next generation of lawyers and consumers could actually benefit from the knowledge and wisdom of the 'traditional lawyer' this particular individual has had his lot. He no doubt enjoyed the spoils and riches of his past 40 years in practice – wandering through the blessed wilderness in the good times. But when the going gets tough, he ducked out.

It's little wonder the legal profession is perceived as it is.

Hey-ho, good riddance I reckon, with an attitude like that. Make way for Generation Z where a fighting, bold, positive, ambitious, energetic and progressive attitude will see the legal profession onto bigger and better things for the benefit of the consumer.

By the way, Nils is 60 years old.

Lawyers who 'get it' are not fazed by life stage, new challenges or new technologies. They embrace it.

we're all tombed

Perhaps the most famous epitaph in the world is the one alleged to be on the tombstone of W.C. Fields. As an everlasting reflection of the love-hate relationship with his 'beloved' hometown Philadelphia, his epitaph reads, "All things considered, I'd rather be in Philadelphia".

Wearing my lawyer hat, as I contemplate the threat of our possible extinction – RIP – all things considered, I think I'd rather be a super lawyer. Wouldn't you?

why am I writing the naked lawyer?

If you've read the previous section you've probably figured out why I'm writing *the naked lawyer*.

It's timely, it's needed and it's bang on the nose to help ambitious professionals and business people like you fast-track your way through a decade of uncertainty, challenge and opportunity.

who am I to tell you how to market, brand and sell YOU?

Truly, who am I to share with you how to market, brand and sell yourself in a bid to get more clients, sales, referrals, income, value, growth and success whilst assisting you with choice, change and control in both your career and life?

Furthermore, why listen to what I have to say...?

For a bit of background, feel free to check out 'about the author', the introduction, my track-record and profile to give you some comfort as to who I am. This information will give you a feel for my professional experience, knowledge, skills and talent which just might be of benefit to you. That's for you to decide.

Of note, I may actually be the first entrepreneurial trainee solicitor in the UK to successfully create a personal brand together with devising a refreshingly unique relationship building, relationship sales and relationship marketing approach which achieved impressive marketing and sales results.

This was achieved using soft-skills which appealed to prospective clients and referrers. It involved mixing traditional and conventional marketing and sales methods, techniques and systems with new, unconventional and innovative techniques – the ROAR model – revealed and documented herein.

Throughout my final year as a trainee solicitor and since founding EntrepreneurLawyer (a period of a little over a year during the 2009 recession), I generated and referred £562,000 of new client legal work enquiries.

You're probably thinking I'm bragging or maybe you're even grumbling, 'so what?', 'big deal!'

Please permit me to continue and hear me out... I am *not* sharing the above to impress you, rather to impress upon you that there are opportunities to significantly enhance YOUR career prospects and options, add value and income to the company you serve and possibly even increase your own income (whatever stage you are at in your career), sense of achievement and personal fulfilment, by following the proven blueprint sales development ROAR model contained here in *the naked lawyer.*

If you need, want or desire to get more clients, sales, referrals, income, value, growth and success (any or all of these) as an individual or as an entity, then *the naked lawyer* will help you. Simply put: if I did it, then why can't you?

I came to the legal profession in later life – working in a mid-tier established law practice in Leeds, England (2006-09) – with prior marketing, sales, business development and innovation experience and responsibility, having worked in the management consulting, new media and leisure industries.

Achieving the above had absolutely nothing to do with my age or experience, but everything to do with my skills, mindset and attitude – 'soft skills' – the subject of *the naked lawyer*.

The great news – soft skills can be learned. If YOU can learn to do what I did (and do) whatever level or stage in your career you are at, and you amplify the same by each and every individual in the firm then what have you got? Hmmmm... just imagine the company wide group dynamic potential...

I'd love you to benefit greatly from *the naked lawyer*!

Before entering the legal profession I knew that to survive and thrive, simply being a technically excellent lawyer was not going to be good enough (at any stage of my legal career) to deliver extraordinary client service and be successful in the digital age.

When the global recession hit in Q3 2008, it was patently obvious to me that technical expertise alone was not going to guarantee that I would distinguish myself and those in the firm whom I served from our peers in the legal world, be able to bring in new clients, achieve sales and even perhaps secure my and/or our future; I was a trainee solicitor at the time.

I knew deep down that I needed to be *present* and *available* for our potential clients (and existing clients) where they were then and would be in the future... and that meant venturing into social media, social networking and the 'trending' platforms.

I use the word 'trend' though there is some disagreement in both the business world and the legal world as to whether social media and some of the platforms are fads or trends.

'Fad' or 'trend'? Who cares?! If it works, does it matter? Why not just 'give the tools a go' which are obviously causing a buzz in the present?

I've always found that trying new stuff can bring things whizzing out of left field that I just didn't see coming. And usually when you're one of the pioneers, leaders, front runners and, dare I say it, 'risk takers', you steal a march on your competition.

Oh, and by the way, the new stuff usually works and you get to ride the wave on the up – where it counts most. When the next wave comes along you're already positioned to jump onto it whilst your competitors remain frothing around and drowning in the previous one.

I wouldn't say that I was an early adopter of social media (by business world standards) but I wasn't late either. However, I was probably one of the earlier adopters in the legal world.

I joined LinkedIn in October 2008 as I could see the marketing and sales potential, particularly in relation to building relationships and networking with local, national and international professionals and potential clients; you never know where an opportunity may come from for you and how you can benefit your clients and referrers.

I also observed that the platform could be useful to:

- Garner market knowledge and awareness;
- Raise the brand profile of the company and those for whom I worked at that time ('Brand,Firm''); and also my own personal brand ('Brand,Me') – more about this in *the naked lawyer* Volume 4: getting under your skin;
- Identify new referrers of mutual benefit;
- Target my market;
- Find suppliers/experts to assist our clients and the company; and
- Potentially meet new affiliates, associates, referrers and ultimately clients.

I started tweeting and facebooking in 2009 and I would say that I am now a self-confessed, fully fledged social media and social networking junkie; check out *the naked lawyer* Volume 6: social savvy junkie.

status quo doesn't rock anymore

I've always been rubbish at standing still, would and will not accept 'that'll do', taking orders, doing as I'm told, etc.

Not because I'm insubordinate, disrespectful or a rebel – at least I don't think so. Simply put, I have an attitude; an attitude which SUUUCKS – more about this in Volume 2.

It's the kind of nefarious attitude emanating from an enquiring, curious and analytical mind that's always probing, 'why are we doing it this way?', 'why don't we do it this way instead to save money and/or time?', 'how can this be improved?', 'why not try this?' and 'what's next?'

Status quo is not the ticket to evolution, in my book (figuratively speaking). It's certainly no longer viable, feasible or sustainable for the legal profession in a digital, fast-moving consumer-led world.

Continuous improvement and innovation is where it's at. Inevitably this means 'change'. I reckon if it was good enough for Socrates, Charles Darwin, Armand Hammer, Leonardo da Vinci, Albert Einstein, Tim Berners-Lee, Steve Jobs and Bill Gates, etc. (beacons of inspiration for independent thinkers) it's certainly good enough for me and ought to be for the legal profession.

Possessing 'vision' comes naturally to me. Some of you (lawyers) may think it's a curse, as vision may be misconstrued, wrongly, as 'risk'. I actually believe it's a blessing – albeit that I've always been at least five to ten years ahead of my time and it's not always been a good thing! But let's not go there – at least not in this book.

I also believe that if we have a gift and/or a natural talent (such as vision combined with knowledge, experience, skills and talent), then we should share it... and make it count. What the recipient does with the knowledge imparted is up to them.

We are, after all, each blessed with the greatest gift of all... choice.

'Choice', 'change' and 'control' are why I'm writing this book.

just sit there and do as you're told

In my role as a trainee solicitor in 2008-09 I had a choice.

For me, stepping into the legal profession after experiencing the leisure industry, new media industry and management consulting industry in my capacity as an employee, entrepreneur (business owner) and consultant – with their new world cultures, innovative business approaches and models, and in some cases, horizontal structures – was like stepping back to the land that time forgot.

I arrived into a new world. But it was an old world. An alien world at least ten years behind the world from which I came. Again, I will share more about this in Volume 2. Yet it was (and is) a world ripe for innovation. And that is why I was there... and am here now.

But I wasn't prepared for just how 'old world' it really was... and is. If any of you remember *The Pickwick Papers*[8], I liken it to the very same. And that was just the physical appearance.

Dealing with the mindset of the lawyers (colleagues and superiors) was a whole new ball game for me. I'd never experienced such parochialism and resistance to change before.

I suffered from shell shock for the first six months. Wilfred Owen[9] would have had a field day.

Someone said to me once that law firms like their candidates (trainees) to come 'oven-ready'. Meaning ready to be moulded into 'the firm' way; the kind of mentality which is 'this is the way we do things around here', without even considering that there could be a better way that the new intakes could bring into the fold.

The whole experience reminded me of the Jack Nicholson movie *As Good As It Gets*. Those inculcated into the legal profession having not experienced any other environment were undoubtedly accepting that 'this is good as it gets' – totally oblivious to the fact that there are much better ways to do things.

I remember vividly a discussion with a colleague in which she said, "I hear the same complaint about you Chrissie. You're so focused on marketing and sales. Why can't you just sit there and do as you're told like the other trainees, Mary-Ellen, John-Boy and Jim-Bob?", meaning sit there and do the legal work; which I was doing in addition to the marketing and sales 'fluffy stuff' above and beyond the call of daily duty.

We were at the start of the global recession. Go figure. You don't have to be an Einstein to work out why I saw the need to use some marketing and sales initiative. And these people are supposed to be the 'intelligentsia elite'?

Duh!

But some traditional lawyers just don't 'get it' because if truth be told they don't know any different. How could they? If they've never worked in any other industry save the legal profession how could they possibly know how good it could get?

Entrepreneurs, business people – I'll let you answer that one.

Horrified, I was questioning 'is this as good as it gets?'

I could either 'put up and shut up' – be another trainee clone in the old way and learn the old outdated 20th century ways of the forefathers – *not* – since they were already five to ten years behind the rest of the business world – or I could do something positive and innovative; cut a new way with a 21st century approach and add some value wherever possible. I chose the latter.

The colleagues who 'got it' were grateful. Who wouldn't be in the middle of a recession if a trainee took the initiative to help bring in more work?

I couldn't just sit there. Could you? If your future and your colleagues' futures were at stake and a gaping opportunity to serve new clients was apparent? I made the right choice... in spite of resistance and 'cold shouldering' from the old guard.

The majority of fellow trainees, qualified lawyers and partners couldn't understand where I was coming from. But clients did. As a result, today I am able to share with you the power of *the naked lawyer.*

eat my dictaphone

I had a similar 'difference of opinion' with another colleague on the ways of how to improve existing marketing and sales approaches and activities within a law firm.

This will happen to you too no doubt at some point in your career, as it's just not possible to work in a law firm (or any company for that matter) and for everyone to agree.

Utopia does not exist – unfortunately.

In a bid to help the firm generate more work from new clients and extend the referral network, for a while I took the initiative in getting up at 'daft o'clock' to attend a business breakfast meeting each week, before the daily technical law grinder's monkey fee-earning work kicked in. Like most business clubs you have to 'suck it and see' and stick with it for a period of time to build equity with fellow referrers by giving, giving and then giving some more. Having done this in previous businesses and roles prior to entering the legal profession I was confident that it would deliver results.

One of my colleagues who had 'dabbled' in this very same marketing and sales approach was less than convinced. He was rather cynical if truth be told. That's fine, I thought. No problem. He said to me one day, "if you get any sales from that I'll eat my dictaphone."

A month later I sent him an e-mail stating, "I'm popping out for lunch. Do you have any particular preference for the flavour or colour of the cherry to go with your dictaphone?"

The lesson? Just because a particular method or approach may be pooh-poohed shouldn't stop you from doing what you believe in. It just might work. In this instance, it did... it does... and I'll show you how. Keep reading...

naked straight from my mind

I'll be honest with you. *the naked lawyer* is proving a hard thing to write as lawyers2B, those already in the legal profession, legal education providers, suppliers and referrers to the legal profession, buyers of legal services and entrepreneurs (and by this I mean business people) have shared their personal views with me in relation to the present and future state of legal provision, customer service experience and desires, and relationship building trials and tribulations.

I am attempting to be the mouthpiece for entrepreneurs and other buyers of legal services who would really like to tell us lawyers that we're a bunch of arrogant, egotistical shysters and we really need to get our act together.

I'm also trying to convey the thoughts of lawyers (and partners) at different stages of their careers – some/most of whom are pretty hacked off right now for one reason or another – and marketing/business development/customer service managers within law firms – some of whom are also frustrated for one reason or another but can't say it because it would be like pressing the professional suicide button.

And I'm burdened with the frustrations of the suppliers to the legal profession who appear similarly hacked off because lawyers take so darn long to make a decision – if ever; the majority of firms are still run like a committee rather than a business. Lucky if the suppliers get any bloomin' decision at all because the partners are either reluctant to get off the freakin' fence or can't convince their co-partners to.

So, I see it as my role to say it for you all since I am in the fortunate position of not having to answer or kowtow to anyone. I don't need to worry about 'speaking out of turn' with the possibility of being thrown out of the legal nest for daring to challenge the status quo.

I have absolutely nothing to lose but everything to gain in helping to provide you with the solution to some of the problems noted in the opening section.

The ROAR model is a marketing, sales and relationship building model that will actually work for each and every one of you. It could be the solution.

You can shoot the messenger. That's OK. But I know that lots of people think about a lot of really good stuff but never have the guts to say what they're really thinking. Lots of people want to see change happen but don't have the nerve to stand by the courage of their conviction and do something about it. And lots of people have wonderful, revolutionary, brilliant ideas but never act on them.

So, I'm going to attempt to cover the whole spectrum of readers and your possible/probable circumstances – albeit probably impossible to achieve the same – that is, age, gender, race, traditionalist, revolutionist, couldn't give a monkey's, glass is half empty, glass is half full, glass is overflowing and glass is darn right shattered. Holy grail or paper cup syndrome, stuck in a rut, rat in a cage, waiting for the right time to jump sideways, upwards or onto another ship or path.

To each of you I say that if you believe and feel that you're stuck and life sucks right now because you can't change your job, then it's time to change your mindset. If you can't move, improve.

By improving you'll be better positioned for when the time comes – whenever YOU choose that to be.

generation Z

Generation Y and traditional lawyers watch out. I believe Generation Z are already here.

They are the best and brightest legal professionals and business leaders of the day who are poised to revolutionise and trail-blaze in the legal world and business world.

You will recognise these individuals, who are extraordinarily hungry for success and desire a truly fulfilling life (in every respect) as they feel the change, see the opportunity, grasp the nettle to continually learn 'soft skills' and are happy to look and ask for help. Fear, ignorance and/or arrogance have no place on their road to success.

They will be the industry leaders of tomorrow.

No matter what stage they are at in their legal or business career, they will grant the next generation of professionals the same degree of respect, understanding and opportunity to grow and develop in the exciting industry which they will create.

do you need to read *the naked lawyer*?

'No' – if you're not willing to listen and truly hear of a way that just might help you improve your situation, then don't bother.

'Yes, absolutely' – if you're curious, intrigued and want a better way (whatever you perceive that to be). For I know the ROAR model works because it worked (and continues to work) for me and I am therefore unwaveringly confident that it could work for you too.

naked straight from my heart

Most writers are reserved in their writing style, tone and approach for fear of causing offence, being rebuffed, receiving negative feedback and being vilified.

Sorry, not me.

If you don't like what I'm saying or don't want to hear what I'm saying, then that's OK. Ignore me. Confine me to the bucket labelled, 'that bird is talking a load of hyperbolic tosh', bang the lid on tight and don't ever let me out. No worries. I won't be taking it personally. It's your choice. If you do 'can' me, it's not going to faze me.

I'll tell you why. Because I know that there is a groundswell of legal and business people who already think, feel and act as I do because they recognise that change is here and more needs to come.

It's no coincidence that I have been contacted to assist a wide spectrum of people and institutions, ranging from fledgling ambitious young legal professionals to established and esteemed top-level barristers in helping to develop their practice, educational establishments and consultancy companies (in devising 'soft skills' programmes and 'partnerships').

If I can help even just a handful of you, then the vilification will be worth it... and most of all, I'd be honoured.

Why? Because I've stood in your shoes as a law student, trainee solicitor, newly qualified/junior/assistant/associate solicitor equivalent (in a previous business role) and am standing in your shoes as a business owner, supplier, referrer and buyer of legal services (past and present). I know how it feels and I understand when...

As a law student you're studying like crazy, tired, stressed, pressured, in debt up to the eye-balls, uncertain of your future, with no guarantee of achieving a training contract or what the landscape is going to be like once you 'make it' into 'the firm'.

As a trainee you still have all the same concerns you had when you were a student, plus you're unsure as to whether you're going to be 'kept on'. The salary, progression, opportunities and development you thought were likely may have altered due to the past couple of years i.e. the knock-on effect of the recession bashing the legal world.

As a newly qualified solicitor you may share similar concerns as the trainees and students (still got a load of debt perhaps and it's likely going to take much longer to pay it all off), plus you may have had to settle for practising in an area that your heart isn't really in but 'it'll do' because what alternative is there right now?

As a junior/assistant/associate solicitor, you may well have the same thoughts as all those who came before you:

- Eager to progress but perhaps limited opportunity;
- Tired of standing still, being overlooked, passed over or having the carrot dangled in front of you with the promise of partnership which seems elusive in the present;
- You may not even be sure you want partnership anymore because it potentially offers more liability than benefit at present;
- Perhaps you're even thinking, 'there's got to be a better way?' as the LSA kicks in big time; and
- You may even be thinking that you could fly solo right now, perhaps even join one of the entrepreneurial virtual law firms and potentially double your income. If you're at least three years post qualification[10] and confident in your technical ability, practise in a field which lends itself to niche solo activity with a minimal amount of collaboration required with other areas of law, for example, commercial/IP law or employment law, have a support network of more experienced lawyers to help with the more complicated legal stuff (that is, consider sub-contracting where necessary) and, arguably, most importantly have the ability to get clients (and keep them), then becoming self employed may begin to look attractive.

As a partner/owner/director, you may be worried about just everything right now. Fearful about 'holding things together' because you've invested your whole life (and money) into 'the firm' so far, possibly have a bank guarantee in place to secure a massive overdraft (either joint or several), a lease obligation like a millstone round your neck, co-partners stressed and sniping at each other because you can't agree on the best way forward and hacked off with suppliers that keep pestering you (who promise the earth to help turn things around but actually deliver squat) whilst you're trying to manage and juggle the day to day stuff – like doing some law, managing people, networking and buoying up the sales pipeline.

As a sole practitioner/barrister (in chambers) you may no doubt share some or all of the above.

As a buyer of legal services you despair at the lack of customer service, end up chasing the lawyer for one reason or another, get passed from pillar to post, end up building a relationship with the lawyer's voice-mail, are always wary of 'the bill' and 'what other costs are going to come out of the woodwork?', and most of all end up with black and white law rather than a commercially savvy legal solution befitting your particular circumstances.

Harrumph.

Question: Is this as good as it gets? Answer: It doesn't have to be. You have a choice. You can seek change and take control. You can do something. You can improve yourself.

You can get naked – *the naked lawyer* soft skills education programme is here to help you through the transition.

But it's not easy when you're out of your comfort zone and in alien territory. I know. You feel vulnerable – naked. But that's OK. Because it's OK to be open, honest, transparent, grounded and with personality shining... *human*.

Clients like that. Being human builds equity.

it's a box of frogs

A colleague once said to me "Chrissie, you're as mad as a box of frogs". I took that as a compliment.

She got me thinking. Her comment reminded me of Pierce Brosnan in the movie *Dante's Peak* in which he plays a volcanologist who is desperate to convince his colleagues that a town is in danger from a volcano about to erupt. He and his colleagues have been stationed there and tracking activity.

What Brosnan says is:

"If you put a frog in boiling water it will jump right out [frog 1]. But if you place a frog in a pan of cold water and heat the water gently over time, it will just sit there until it eventually boils to death [frog 2]."

His message is simply this: if we'd arrived here today we'd know we were in trouble.

I liken this to the transition occurring right now in the legal world. If you've been in the legal profession for some time and are more of a 'traditionalist', you're probably like frog 2. But for an outsider looking in, that is, a non-lawyer, or if you're an entrepreneurial lawyer, you're like frog 1.

Either way, the legal profession is pretty much like a box of frogs at this very moment... It's a mix of frog 1 and frog 2, hopping around and not quite sure which way to jump in what one might describe as a 'Luddite v Evangelist' face-off.

Interesting times...

what you're about to experience

WARNING: Whilst I will be dealing with serious matters by providing serious messages, solutions, material and ideas throughout *the naked lawyer*, you will no doubt have realised already that I have chosen to deliver the very same in a fun and informal kind of way.

new, informative, fun and sexy!

In the volumes which follow you will note that I continue in this approach together with an 'adult' element and theme throughout. Kind of. Don't get me wrong, it's all done in, 'the best possible taste'; I believe the late Kenny Everett[11] would agree.

Why have I chosen this approach? Well... We read a lot of stuff, but more often than not cannot remember most of what we've just read. Key messages can be lost within a very short time frame. Yet, we tend to be able to recall the things we read which tickle us...

It's as simple as that really, plus... The approach is new, it's daring, it's risqué, it's fresh, it's innovative, it has a new way of looking at things, and in its own unique way it's kind of ground-breaking – certainly for the legal profession; a profession desperately needing to embrace new ways. As it is, generally speaking, at best it pays lip-service (on its surface), and at worst is stultifying in welcoming innovation and change.

Ironically, the approach which I speak of above, the approach of and within *the naked lawyer*, is all of the things we arguably need in this digital age, topsy-turvy era and transitional legal world right now. I passionately believe we need to embrace change (because it's happening all around us whether we like it or not), try new stuff, take some risks, be bold, break into new territory, and strike a balance between the seriousness and fun in both our professional and personal lives...

So, *the naked lawyer* is going to be a delightful mix of serious information combined with fun and sexiness... I have every confidence that when you work through *the naked lawyer*, you will understand and appreciate precisely why *the naked lawyer* is an apt title for this book, on both a serious note and a fun note...

'Never judge a book by its cover', eh? Pah! It's not called *the naked lawyer* for nothing.Truly, this is one book cover where you can rely on your sound judgement. So, if you don't wish to have a laugh, either at me or yourself, then *the naked lawyer* is probably not your cup of tea. Go and work through a hum-drum professional or academic personal development/self-help/marketing/brand/sales book or educational programme or workshop instead, perhaps. It's your choice.

Only those of you with a real passion for a new and refreshing way of learning, with a sense of humour and with an appreciation for sex will truly enjoy it. I am confident that we are many... The world's population is knocking on for seven billion.[12] Enough said.

naked straight from my gut

In case you hadn't got the picture by now, I'm not going to beat around the bush. I'm just going to say it as it is. No nonsense. No sugar-coating. Pure gut-wrenching feeling. I will reveal all... well, almost all... in a practical way.

This book is *not* going to be like the usual boring, dry-rot, scholastic, academic, management and marketing clap trap tomes. There's a place for that – it's called the law school and law firm library.

We're going to have some fun, because when we have fun, we learn best. But you haven't got time to kick-back and leisurely read fluffy stuff. I understand. And yet you want to progress... but you haven't got time for all that flowery, touchy feely, waffle mumbo jumbo because you're too busy; the clock is ticking, the billable hour is pressing. Tick-tock. Tick-tock.

You just want to get right down to the, 'give me the hard, fast juicy stuff, thank you, so that I can get on with putting this sales stuff into action'. So this is what you're going to get. Lots of hard-hitting, practical quality goodies. *the naked lawyer* goes beyond the popular 'How to...' kind of educational book gubbins.

You will find the volumes are information rich with timely tools to effectively solve an age old problem with a modern day solution; namely, how to market, brand and sell YOU when perhaps you're not a natural salesperson aka rainmaker.

AND, so that the read is both entertaining and informative, it will be peppered throughout to delight you with secrets and tales spun by an actual 'Naked Lawyer' prancing around in little law law land...

I'm going to share with you 'my story' whilst providing practical activities for you to undertake along the journey ahead as you read and 'work' through *the naked lawyer*.

Occasionally it will be supported with a little authority, theoretical waffle and example gurus on the appropriate subject where necessary – just for good measure, further substance and comfort, I hasten to add.

12 volumes

the naked lawyer is a quasi story, sales blueprint, life manual and workbook. In essence it's a workshop, but in a book, where you are free to attend and complete the activities totally at your convenience, leisure and pleasure; but at a fraction of the cost you would expect to pay if you were to attend a workshop programme of this nature over three to five days!

Throughout the 12 volumes herein I'm going to map out exactly what I did, why and how in the approach to, *'how to get more clients, sales, referrals, income, value, growth and success'*.

It will be a blueprint that you can follow, and hopefully improve upon as you work through it and do extremely well for yourself and those for whom you work.

ROAR – three musketeer models

The ROAR model is absolutely unique. And timeless. You will not find it anywhere else except in *the naked lawyer*. I will tell you why. It was devised recently by me as a result of my experience and knowledge from different industries.

The ROAR model embraces three proven successful motivational, sales, and behavioural and communication approaches from the sport and leisure industries topped off with bits and bobs from my own innovations.

The motivational approach which ROAR embraces and celebrates is that of renowned motivational guru Jack Black, whom I came across in 2000.

The sales approach and model that ROAR utilises, in part, is that embraced by one of the most successful health club providers at the turn of the century, the leader in academy sales and professional development training and development – Cannons Health & Fitness Limited.

The behavioural and communication approach, model and modules which ROAR fixates on is that created and used by Gary Russell and Sir Clive Woodward of Winning Profile, successfully adopted and applied by Gary Russell for the past three decades in various industries.

I applied these combined approaches and models from outside the legal profession, within the legal profession, and sprinkled a few innovations within and throughout.

Hey, they worked. They are a winning combination and formula. I shall reveal the details in relation to the combination and work through them with you in the following volumes.

getting the most out of the naked lawyer

the umbrella for the rainy days

You can't deny that we've had a rough ride in the last 24 months. Business and life have been pants... for most of us... lawyers and business people alike. It's been tough... and it's probably going to be tough for the foreseeable future.

But let's not despair and let's be positive... As stated previously, I honestly believe that *the naked lawyer* could help you.

who will this book help the most?

Whether you're eager to get into the legal profession (either for the first time or to reclaim your rowing place on the good ship legal enterprise) or desperate to get out; or maybe you fall somewhere in the middle and are just keen and determined to progress; perhaps you need to have dealings with a lawyer and desperately do or don't want to; or maybe you're a non-lawyer who's keen to succeed in your career, business and/or life... (that covers just about everyone I reckon); then *the naked lawyer* is definitely for you.

In a nutshell, it's for you if you desire a truly fulfilling life; if you're looking to get 'unstuck' or you wish to prevent yourself from getting stuck at some point in your career(s) and life; if you're ambitious and wish to progress; if you're looking for a better way and are curious as to why and how; if you are 'open-minded' and open to wanting more choice, change and control in your career(s) and life; if you have the ability to laugh at yourself and if you enjoy learning in an informal, fun and entertaining way.

It's certainly *not* for the Luddite, faint hearted, slacker or prudish.

For entrepreneurs and business owners, this book will be a fascinating read and insight into the present day legal profession as well as a unique and refreshing transparent sales blueprint that may well be relevant for you, your company, your industry and/or your sector too.

But, for sure, I reckon *the naked lawyer* will help lawyers (and 'the professions') the most, particularly, as the legal profession has experienced an unprecedented downturn and is undergoing a transition of a scale never before anticipated or experienced.

For the first time in legal history, a crash cut so deep that it affected almost everyone in the profession, even those who are about to enter it. The pain is real... for all of us... financially and emotionally for the most part.

Many firms throughout 2008 to the present day have reduced hours, frozen salaries, reduced bonus pools, cut headcount, frozen recruitment, deferred entry for trainees, as well as drastically reduced training, marketing and business development spend – all in a bid to slash costs. Some of you may even have re-trained to work in another area of law as a stop-gap with a hope to return to your chosen field.

Even though the industry battened down the hatches and is only beginning to open them up again, you may be reading this thinking, 'this isn't what I signed up for'. I know. I've been there. I've sat in your seat and had your thoughts, concerns and worries. I mulled over the choices, contemplated change and ultimately took control. So, what are you going to do about where you are now and where you'd like to get to, and how?

This book is for you. I want to get you thinking and then get you going. It may provide some of the answers to questions you have or should be asking.

get real – perception and reality

The perception may be that we have come through the worst of the recession, but the reality is that the decade ahead is going to present new economic challenges and significant changes to political, social and technological trends.

The profession is *not* going to return to the halcyon days when clients simply walked through the door, where value work and margins were plentiful, ensuring salaries and bonuses were continually plump.

Get real – the digital age and the 'enlightened consumer' are here to stay. Like it or not. As lawyers we need to adapt, innovate and embrace the opportunity to alter the buyers' perception of what being a lawyer really is. It's our opportunity to change the negative perception of the old profession and sculpt the new positive perception of a consumer-centric tomorrow's lawyer.

be a lawyer of tomorrow, today

If you want a successful legal career, you will need to get out of your comfort zone and dare to be different. You will be vulnerable – naked – but the transition into the new way could possibly be what saves you and/or provides you with the fulfilling career and life that you dream of.

As a profession we need to cull old, outmoded, restrictive structures, practices and ideas and embrace innovative thinking and action. You need to become a lawyer of tomorrow, today. You will need to be entrepreneurial, innovative, relationship-focused, client-focused, proactive, of a positive mindset and 'soft skilled up' to attract the clients of the past, present and future. Listen to what your clients, referrers, suppliers and enlightened partners who 'get it' want and expect.

Never before has the need been so great for lawyers and law firms to be armed with 'soft skills' in the pursuit of generating more new client leads and converting to sales, whilst leveraging more sales and referrals from existing clients and referrers, and building enduring professional relationships with new and existing clients.

The 'soft skills' that give you the ability to generate work, build and leverage solid relationships, market and 'soft sell', will stand you in good stead whatever the future holds and wherever you decide to take your career and life.

No matter what stage you are at in your legal career the dawning of this new decade will inevitably bring unprecedented challenges, the likes of which your professional services career has not previously witnessed, let alone equipped you to manage...

the naked lawyer can help.

the blueprint

the naked lawyer is literally a totally transparent blueprint of everything that I did to achieve £562,000 of new client legal sales generation enquiries and referrals – being careful NOT to reveal any confidential information and confidences, I hasten to add; as a lawyer you would expect me to toe the line.

It is jam packed with examples, case studies and 'to do's' ('just do something!' and ROAR steps) focusing on ten key elements – with hundreds of proven successful steps, tips, hints and secrets – in how to market, brand and sell YOU in a bid to get more sales, referrals, clients, income, value, growth and success.

During *the naked lawyer* I also share with you one or two examples of what I am doing right now to achieve sales success utilising the ROAR model in my own business.

education programme

As *the naked lawyer* is about 'choice', 'change' and 'control' it's actually an education programme – a workbook workshop – where you are in charge of the pace of your professional growth, in relation to your investment in time and cost.

If you choose to dip in and out of the volumes herein – and if you do not implement the suggestions within them, that is, work through the 'just do something!' practical activities, examples and case studies – then you will not have the full picture. The ROAR model will be incomplete and you will not receive the complete benefit of the model. You will only have completed a part of the jigsaw.

To get the most out of the programme 'workshop' you will need to complete all 12 volumes at some stage – and that means reading and carrying out the 'just do something!' practical activities. You will then experience the full power of the ROAR model education programme.

To benefit the most, I recommend you work through the volumes consecutively as it is a natural progression of the development and building process – but it is not essential that you do so. The choice is yours – you may wish to 'dot around'. That said, I strongly recommend that you read and implement Volumes 1-4 to begin the programme as these are the foundations upon which you will build your temple.

Not all of you will wish to put the full effort in. That's OK. You'll still gain something and find *the naked lawyer* useful and positive. For one thing, you'll have some fun and a few laughs at my gaffes.

But if you do give it the full 100 per cent, then I am confident that you will experience a deep, fulfilling learning curve of value in your professional, and possibly personal, development and growth that goes way beyond anything you'll find in any other book of this nature.

The choice is yours!

sneak preview Volumes 2-12 'How to...'

To give you a feel as to the kind of practical activity and sales results-orientated advice I aim to share with you in the following volumes, I'd like to give you a gift – a simple case study.

It's a solid example of how I achieved potentially very lucrative sales, collaborative partnership deals, and passed a couple of sales referrals (prospects requiring legal advice/services) using social media and social networking. You may wish to 'give it a go' yourself...

... because it works.

the activity

Step 1

- Create a group on LinkedIn, assuming you've joined LinkedIn already – if not, DO!
- Tip – make sure your brand is in the title. For example 'The Entrepreneur Lawyer' is my personal brand...
- Sunday 2 May 2010 I decided to launch 'The Entrepreneur Lawyer Relationship Sales Network' (LinkedIn Group).

Step 2

- Kick-start the group with at least one discussion, if not two.
- Tip – two initial discussions provide choice for the member. Choose an intriguing, interesting and/or potentially controversial subject matter with a strong headline.
- In order to kick-start conversations (achieve involvement and engagement), I placed two discussion topics on the group board; 'Penny A Brick... Why I became a Lawyer'[13] (a curious headline to create intrigue) and 'Where does "sales" begin?' (a nice broad open question).

Step 3

- Place the same discussion (if appropriate) on your blog (if you have one. If you don't, create one!).
- Tip – give it the same title.
- I had placed the 'Penny A Brick' story as a post on my blog a week earlier.

Step 4

- Call to action – send a message to all of your LinkedIn connections inviting them to join the group.
- Tip – give a teasing heads up such as, 'you may benefit from....'
- I sent a message to *all* of my LinkedIn connections making them aware of the discussions and invited them to join The Entrepreneur Lawyer Relationship Sales Group. At the same time I placed the discussions in relevant/appropriate groups that I participate in on LinkedIn.

Step 5

- Place the same discussion in other LinkedIn groups that you frequent.
- Tip – tweak the description so that it is bespoke to the actual group.

Step 6

- Use Twitter, Facebook and your LinkedIn status to amplify the call to action message.
- I tweeted, facebooked and placed the message on my LinkedIn status bar.
- If you wish to see an example of the wording used, then trace me back on Twitter, Facebook, in the LinkedIn discussions and on the EntrepreneurLawyer blog.

Step 7

- Facilitate the discussions.
- Tip – foster conversations. Ask more 'open' questions. Be proactive. Be present.

Step 8

- Ask the new members to connect with you. This helps build your network – fast.
- Tip – start building rapport.

the outcome

Within 36 hours (Wednesday 5 May) there were 260 group members and a very large number of:

- New direct LinkedIn connections added to my LinkedIn network connections;
- Visitors to the entrepreneurlawyer.co.uk blog and comments on the post;
- New sign-ups on EntrepreneurLawyer's e-mail list to receive the E-ntrepreneur Bullet newsletter and *the naked lawyer* free Vol 1 eBook (potential customers); and
- bit.ly clicks exceeding 1,000.

I noted that my tweets had been re-tweeted, LinkedIn group facilitators had shared the 'Penny A Brick' discussion with their group members (I guess the humorous side with regard to the story was touching!) and group members had shared the 'Where does "sales" begin?' discussion with other people whom they thought would be interested – I know this because these people contacted me direct (via LinkedIn and e-mail) informing me of the same.

The outcome of the activity was such that:

- It woke up existing contacts/potential clients who got back in touch, which led to Skype calls and face-to-face meetings to discuss potential sales (workshops and in-house training);
- It ignited new contacts and potential clients (on LinkedIn and on EntrepreneurLawyer's website/blog);
- It initiated affiliate interest and contact including a well-connected and experienced professional in Silicon Valley at the ready to assist with US development and growth;
- It led to a mentoring role;
- It created interest from media – an actual podcast opportunity is now in the pipeline and helped toward the Law Society Gazette request that I be a designated blogger for its 'In Business' blog; and (the holy grail)
- I received an e-mail from the 'top dog' of an establishment which led to a telephone conversation which then led to a face-to-face meeting (all within a three-week period) and a proposition in relation to a potentially lucrative high-level deal which had actual mass sales potential.

Not only did I gain new clients, and actual sales – potentially very lucrative – within a very short period of time, but I also received enquiries from entrepreneurs, business owners and lawyers (UK and international) with either business/sales queries or legal problems/issues initiated from the LinkedIn discussion groups which led to Skype calls, all within a time frame of two to three days.

I was therefore able to refer/introduce the new contact to a practising solicitor and/ or attorney to help them with their legal advice requirement. This in turn helped build the referral relationship between myself and potential buyers of my service in the future. I guess this is evidence of the power of social media and social networking in the flowering of a business relationship...

You can grab the attention of a potential client from a tweet, who then gets involved in a group discussion on LinkedIn, who then wishes to engage in a telephone conversation with you and then meet face to face (either 'in the flesh' if geographically achievable/appropriate or via Skype video call if you're geographically challenged!) which leads to direct sales, referrals, affiliate relationships and the start of many professional relationships with real potential; all within a few days.

Not bad, I reckon, for a day's preparation (writing a blog post and a couple of discussion topics) and a couple of days' marketing and facilitating. All for free, save for the time element, of course.

titillating tip

Sales begins by 'buying' the salesperson – YOU. You may not think you are, but you are.

If you interact with customers/consumers/ clients, then you are a salesperson – a rainmaker. And if you're not, then you're going to have to be. I will explain why in Volume 2. But, for now, allow me to make this concept a little more appealing to you...

Rainmaking is like sex! If you like sex, and desire to be an extraordinary lover, then you're sure to like rainmaking and may well become an extraordinary rainmaker because why and how you approach the two activities are pretty much the same. Again, I shall explain more about this concept in Volume 2: wakey wakey rise and shine.

Nevertheless, it is my belief that to survive and thrive in the digital era you're going to have to learn how to market, brand and sell yourself – offline and very much online.

How else are your potential clients going to know that YOU are the right choice for them if they don't even know you exist amongst the hundreds of thousands of alternative providers who do what you do?

What makes you special? How are you going to differentiate you? What is 'Brand,You'? These are just a few of the questions you should be asking yourself right now.

I've already suggested a new way of looking at things, for example, rainmaking being like sex... You will find when you read the following volumes that I reveal one of the secrets to my success as a rainmaker in law law land was down to viewing and treating legal clients and mavens (referral key-influencers and activists) akin to gym members and club-land head honchos respectively.

If you want to take control of your future and take it in the direction you would like – maybe get 'unstuck' by improving yourself – then you need to be open to the idea of starting to look at things differently, and then begin to add more strings to your bow; the kind of strategic strings, soft skill strings, activity strings and answers to the questions above which you will learn if you read and action all of *the naked lawyer* Volumes 1-12.

grow your fuzz to get more buzz!

OK, I'm teasing you. I admit. What do I mean by 'grow your fuzz to get more buzz'? I'll let you know... if you keep reading...

Before the next volume, I'd like to leave you with something to reflect on.

the Desiderata poem

I came across the Desiderata poem when I was nine years old. It struck a chord even at a young age. I believe this helped me (and continues to do so) with my approach to life and view of the world. It may help you too...

It also alerted me to 'the lawyer', 'lawyering' and copyright law; lawyers whom I thought were rather smart and a subject matter that I became somewhat curious about.

Together with my 'Penny a Brick' experience, I began to have an interest in 'the law', business and human nature.

The common myth is that the Desiderata poem is of unknown origin, centuries old and was originally found in a Baltimore church in 1692. It was copyrighted, in 1927, by lawyer Max Ehrmann (1872-1945) based in Terre Haute, Indiana. Typical lawyer – didn't miss a trick.

Whatever the truth of the matter, here it is (Max Ehrmann © 1927):

"Go placidly amid the noise and haste, and remember what peace there may be in silence.

As far as possible, without surrender, be on good terms with all persons. Speak your truth quietly and clearly; and listen to others, even to the dull and the ignorant, they too have their story. Avoid loud and aggressive persons, they are vexations to the spirit.

If you compare yourself with others, you may become vain and bitter; for always there will be greater and lesser persons than yourself. Enjoy your achievements as well as your plans. Keep interested in your own career, however humble; it is a real possession in the changing fortunes of time.

Exercise caution in your business affairs, for the world is full of trickery. But let this not blind you to what virtue there is; many persons strive for high ideals, and everywhere life is full of heroism. Be yourself. Especially, do not feign affection. Neither be cynical about love, for in the face of all aridity and disenchantment it is perennial as the grass.

Take kindly to the counsel of the years, gracefully surrendering the things of youth. Nurture strength of spirit to shield you in sudden misfortune. But do not distress yourself with imaginings. Many fears are born of fatigue and loneliness.

Beyond a wholesome discipline, be gentle with yourself. You are a child of the universe, no less than the trees and the stars; you have a right to be here. And whether or not it is clear to you, no doubt the universe is unfolding as it should.

Therefore be at peace with God, whatever you conceive Him to be, and whatever your labors and aspirations, in the noisy confusion of life, keep peace in your soul.

With all its sham, drudgery and broken dreams, it is still a beautiful world.

Be cheerful. Strive to be happy."

References

1. The LSA reforms the way legal services in England and Wales are regulated. In essence the reforms place the consumer interest, 'at the heart of the regulatory framework'.
2. http://www.lawgazette.co.uk/blogs/in-business/time-solicitors-reinvent-their-customer-services
3. Susskind, Richard, *The End Of Lawyers? Rethinking The Nature of Legal Services* (Oxford: OUP, 2008)
4. Susskind, Richard, *The Future of Law: Facing the Challenges of Information Technology* (Oxford: Clarendon Press, 1996)
5. William Ford Gibson (born 1948) is an American-Canadian writer who has been called the "noir prophet" of the cyberpunk subgenre of science fiction. He coined the term "cyberspace" and popularized the concept in his debut novel, *Neuromancer* (1984). In envisaging cyberspace, Gibson created an iconography for the information age before the ubiquity of the Internet in

the 1990s. http://en.wikipedia.org/wiki/William_Gibson

6. A reference to *The Naked Lawyer*, Volume 2: wakey wakey rise and shine, in which I refer to Tom Peters' heart-stopping prediction that 90 percent of white-collar jobs as we know them will be disembowelled by 2020; Tom Peters & Martha Barletta, *Trends: recognize, analyze, capitalize* (New York: D.K. Publishing Inc.,2005)
7. A quote by Nils Montan: http://entrepreneurlawyer.co.uk/products-services/ebook
8. *The Pickwick Papers* is the first novel by Charles Dickens.
9. Wilfred Edward Salter Owen (1893-1918) was a soldier in the first world war. He was one of the leading British poets whose realistic war poetry focused on the shocking horrors of the trenches and its effects.
10. It is a requirement in England and Wales under The Law Society and Solicitors Regulation Authority that a solicitor must actively practise for three years post qualification and satisfy leadership and management competencies before they can become self-employed.
11. Kenny Everett (1944-1995), born Maurice James Christopher Cole, was an English comedian, radio DJ and television entertainer.
12. World population currently estimated to be 6,870,900,000 by the United States Census Bureau.
13. http://entrepreneurlawyer.co.uk/penny-a-brick-why-i-became-a-lawyer

Volume 2: wakey wakey rise and shine

RIP – announcing the ROAR model

Hi again! I say 'again' because hopefully by now you will have read Volume 1 prior to beginning this Volume 2. If not, you must. You will need to have read Volume 1 because:

- It provides you with background information in preparation for this Volume 2; and
- If you intend to do the quiz questionnaire at the end of this volume then you will need to read Volume 1 together with this Volume 2 in order to answer some of the questions.

To reap the benefit of the ROAR model you will need to read and action all 12 volumes as ten key elements comprise the complete ROAR model (which I write about in Volumes 2-11). It's only when you string them all together that the powerful beneficial effect takes place.

However, it's entirely up to you. This is, after all, your personal journey. You are in control. You are manager of your own time, pennies and cents. You alone are master of your own mutiny.

The ROAR model will have you thinking, feeling and acting differently about the way you market, brand and sell yourself, which is the way you develop and manage your career, business and life.

Whilst reading the book, if you get the feeling that I'm teaching you how to suck eggs, then please forgive me. That is not my intention. I'm simply presuming that some of you may be starting from scratch with the ideas and substance, whilst others may already be somewhere along the enlightened path (and no doubt rather sophisticated in your thinking – yes?). I believe though, I must cater for all stages and levels along the 'how to market, brand and sell yourself' spectrum, so please do bear with me if you're a little more advanced.

No doubt some of you will learn a lot, others a little. But this much I know... Each of you will take away at least one thing from reading *the naked lawyer*... even if it's simply a laugh, a smile or a really good feeling!

I sincerely hope (and believe) that whether you are a newbie to the legal profession, a seasoned professional or a seasoned partner, after reading (and acting upon) this book you will experience a 'eureka' thought, feeling or action.

If you're truly blessed and pixie dust falls from the stars and lands upon you whilst you're sat reading *the naked lawyer*, you may even experience all three.

OK now. Enough build-up. Let's begin...

get a grip

a few home truths

Home truth 1: In these challenging and difficult times every lawyer, non-lawyer, law firm and company needs to be pro-active in becoming self-reliant. Period. The global recession and its aftermath have taught us this harsh but obvious lesson.

Home truth 2: In order to survive and succeed in your career and life in the decades ahead you're going to have to learn how to promote yourself, aka, market, brand and sell yourself. Being technically good in your role will *not* be sufficient.

Home truth 3: You must 'know yourself' before you can possibly be able to understand and 'know your client'. Ignorance is no longer bliss – it never was by the way. You have to *know*.

Home truth 4: You must be absolutely honest with yourself before, during and after your journey. Totally unwaveringly honest with yourself. You might be tempted to put on a face to the outside world and attempt to fool them as to who you are, why you do what you do and what you want out of your career and life... but *don't* do it. You must be transparent – naked – in your thinking, feeling, doing and being. Don't be a fool to yourself, or attempt to fool others.

Home truth 5: Empathy will be one of the fundamental skills you must acquire. You will need the ability to step into the shoes of your referrers, suppliers, prospective clients and existing clients in order to truly understand how you can best serve them.

I know all this because these home truths are what I told myself before starting out on my journey. They turned out to be the foundation of my success, and, my continued success, just as much!

So, "let's start at the very beginning" because in the words of Julie Andrews in *The Sound Of Music*, "it's a very good place to start."[1]

Let's take a stab at 'empathy'... From here on in, when reading *the naked lawyer*, try and imagine that you are me. I'd like you to feel that this is your journey. So, step into my shoes. They are now yours. When I speak of 'me', 'my' or 'I' throughout this book, it's as if you are me. (Guys, there is absolutely no need to sling on the heels, flowery frock and make-up. Restrain from the urge. Please!)

You will of course need to substitute the circumstances to mirror your reality and choices. For example, you may not be a solicitor, attorney or lawyer, so substitute those words with whatever you regard yourself to be.

Here's the bad news... This is probably the most trying and testing volume of the 12 to work through because it will force you to think, feel and act deeply – possibly very differently from what you are used to. You will be challenged to dig deep into your soul, your very being, your core, and you will be asking yourself many questions. Ultimately, you will be expected to come up with the answers that are only true to you.

But here's the good news... Applying your heart, mind and energy now will give you the solid foundation for the building blocks yet to come and make Volumes 3 through to 12 much easier to perform.

simply the best

I'd like to take this opportunity to guide you as to how you can get the best out of Volume 2.

For the next two hours, as this is approximately how long it will take you to read the whole volume non-stop, I will be sharing with you my story and point of view together with personal thoughts, feelings and actions. You may not agree with, or approve of, them. That's OK. They are here, nonetheless! You can do with them what you choose.

You will find that at the end of the majority of sections I make practical suggestions for you to *do something*. For example, make a note or a list, pause, reflect, go fetch (research) or think about something deeply. Heads up... this is not just a book. It's a workbook. Not simply a jolly! For YOU...

The practical activities you will find collated in a structured way towards the end of the volume in the 'after dark activity, ROAR steps'.

As I am sharing my story with you, ideally, I would like you to sit back and relax, put your feet up, grab a drink (whether of the non-alcoholic or alcoholic kind is your choice – a wee tipple if it's the right time of day might make the read even more fun!) and enjoy the read the volume from beginning to end, non-stop.

I'd love you to experience the story, empathise, and let the words flow, resonate and touch you. Maybe underline stuff that grabs your attention as you read... but nothing more. Once you have read the entire volume, you will see that I guide you back to the relevant sections so you can carry out the 'after dark activity' in a studious fashion. This is, after all, a serious activity requiring thorough application and soberness! *This is your life* we're dealing with here. So *MAKE IT COUNT*. For some of you, the activity you engage in could actually be life and career changing.

You may wish to stop-start and do the activities immediately when prompted during the read, or you may wish to go at it cover to cover and do the activities in one fell swoop at the very end. It is completely up to you. You are in control. You must do what suits you best.

It is entirely up to you how you prefer to work through the volume. I hope I have succeeded in catering for all needs and learning styles. Feel free to let me know if you feel I haven't by getting in touch and suggesting an alternative way that I can take on board for future publications. I'd be delighted to hear from you.

One last point... Whilst this is my story, the focus is all on YOU... and about YOU. My mission is to help YOU. My modus operandi is by being your private dancer prancing around in law law land. Use me. Abuse me. Dance with me.

My raison d'être? To assist YOU in being simply the best!

guru wisdom

My professional and life journey started many years ago... as a wee girl when I began reading books and wisdom written and shared by gurus. I was hungry to 'know'.

At a very early age I realised that throughout my professional life, I was going to be working for and with business people, so I figured I'd better get to grips with understanding trends, understanding organisations, understanding the people in them and the people I will be serving. But first and foremost I realised that I'd better understand myself most of all if I had any chance of ever making anyone happy (let alone me).

Naturally, I gravitated towards reading stuff which would teach me how to 'find' myself, understand 'me', make the right choices to create an optimal lifestyle and to identify my life's true priorities.

I was helped by the wisdom of Lao Tzu and Pearl Bailey respectively: "Knowing others is wisdom, knowing yourself is enlightenment", and "you never find yourself until you face the truth."

During my junior and teenage years of the 1980s, I began to read about understanding organisations (business) and trends from the works of Tom Peters, *Thriving On Chaos*; Charles Handy, *Understanding Organisations, The Elephant and The Flea, The Empty Raincoat*; Moss Kanter, *The Change Masters*; James Collins & Jerry Porras, *Built To Last, Good To Great*; John Harvey Jones, *Making It Happen, Troubleshooter*; and Thomas Peters & Robert Waterman, *In Search Of Excellence*.

In my 20s, which spanned the 1990s-2000, I focused on understanding more about people, including myself, and read more hard-core stuff, in particular psychology, spiritual, business and trends texts, by authors such as: Mihaly Csikszentmihalyi, *Flow: The Psychology of Happiness*; Maslow, *Hierarchy Of Needs*; Carl Jung, *Nostradamus*; James Redfield, *Celestine Prophecy*; Deepak Chopra, *Ageless Body, Timeless Mind*; Maltz, *Psycho Cybernetics*; Jack Black, *MindStore* and Bill Gates, *Business @ The Speed Of Thought*.

I was particularly enamoured by the technological revolution unfolding and the founding father entrepreneurs of the very same who helped create what we are doing right now, that is, web based communication and interaction – the likes of Tim Berners-Lee (inventor of the World Wide Web), Vint Cerf (father of the internet) and Jakob Nielson (authority on how people use the internet).

In my 30s, from 2001-10, I began reading the new kids on the block, in particular subjects covering marketing, sales, innovation, change, customer service, communication, talent, futurology, law and ethics.

For example: Seth Godin, *Meatball Sundae, Permission Marketing*; Malcolm Gladwell, *The Tipping Point*; Robert Scoble & Shel Israel, *Naked Conversations*; Gary Hamel, *Leading The Revolution*; Chip Conley, *The Rebel Rules*; Jack Welch, *Straight From The Gut*; Bruce Abramson, *Digital Phoenix*; Marcus Buckingham & Donald Clifton, *Now, Discover Your Strengths*; Tom Rath, *StrengthsFinder*; Tom Rath & Donald Clifton, *How Full Is Your Bucket?*; Gary Russell, *Big Rocks: Balancing Life & Work*; Philip Kotler, *Marketing Moves*; Locke, *Gonzo Marketing*; Ken Blanchard, *Whale Done!, Gung Ho!*; Spencer Johnson, *Who Moved My Cheese*; Stephen Lundin, *Fish*; Chris Anderson, *The Long Tail*; Andy Bounds, *How To Make Your Communications Stick*; Regis McKenna, *Total Access: Giving Customers What They Want*; Ming Zeng & Peter Williamson, *Dragons At Your Door*; Clayton Christensen, *The Innovator's Dilemma, The Innovator's Solution*; Richard Susskind, *The Future Of Law, Transforming The Law, The End of Lawyers?*; Ray Kurzweil, *The Singularity Is Near*; Roger Steare, *Ethicability*; Chris Brogan, *Social Media 101*; and Bob Burg, *Go-Givers Sell More, Endless Referrals*.

You see I figured knowledge wasn't/isn't just power. Having knowledge in the 21st century was/is going to be about survival as we move toward singularity. More about that concept in Volume 12: XXX rated – tomorrow's lawyer.

I therefore view continual learning as a life-long quest... not only out of pleasure, but necessity. Maybe that's something you should think about too. Why? Because your present and future may well depend on it.

Here are some highly relevant quotes by Tom Peters from the introduction to his book, *Trends*:[2]

"We're in a ... Brawl with No Rules

"Business, politics, and, indeed, the essential nature of human interchange have come unglued. We have to make things up as we go along...

"Job shrinkage is inevitable. Whether because of outsourcing or automation... you can't count on any job being 'there for you'. What you can do is find ways to move yourself and your company up the value chain... and into the heart and soul of the New Economy."

Actually, if you work for someone else, you could never (and can never) count on any job being 'there for you'. Fact. There's always the sword of Damocles hovering above your head ready to chop, chop, chop.

Watch out for the double dip and inevitable next recession. Over to Tom again:

"Success = SAV = 'Screw Around Vigorously'

"Yesterday's strictures and structures leave us laughably – and tragically – unprepared for this Brawl with No Rules."

In other words, be prepared to try new stuff. You may recall in Volume 1 I said that status quo doesn't rock anymore; it never did by the way. American writer Rebel Brown concurs and boldly suggests we should 'Defy Gravity'[3] Hear! Hear! I commend it to the house!

"Dizzy, Disruptive Age

"'Leadership' from on high... is obsolete. New Leadership draws on a new skill set – the hallmarks of which are improvisation and inspiration."

We are all leaders. Leaders of our own lives and careers. It's definitely time to improvise and be both inspired and inspiring.

Of note, great leaders always put their people first, whether running a household, company or a nation. I reckon if we are to be great leaders of 'Me, Inc.' (see below) then it calls for putting whoever is the receiver of our Me, Inc. stuff first.

Tom Peters goes on to suggest that:

"Ninety per cent of white-collar jobs as we know them (and, ultimately, 90 percent of all jobs as we know them) will be disembowelled in the next 15 years. Done. Gone. Kaput. Between the microprocessor, 60/60/24/7 connectivity, and outsourcing to developing countries, the developed nations' white-collar jobs are... doomed. Time frame? Zero to 15 or 20 years."

Gosh... Seems like we've got a decade to get our [bleep] together!

"It's a Brand You World

"'Winners' (survivors!) will become de facto bosses of ME Inc. Self reliance will, of necessity, replace corporate cosseting. Old-style corporate security is evaporating. Upshot: Free the cubicle slaves! The only defense is a good offense! Hackneyed? Sure. But no less true for being so. A scary... but also immensely exciting...New Age of Self reliance is being birthed before our eyes."

I first came across the term 'Me,Inc.' in 2000. It was in a series of personal development, strengths and talent workshops at Cannons Health & Fitness Limited (where I was working at that time) presented by Gary Russell (my mentor and friend to this day) who was no doubt influenced back in the 1990s by Tom Peters' mantra "What do I want to be famous for?"

This was five years prior to Tom Peters writing about it in *Trends* in 2005 (but only a year after Tom Peters writing about 'Brand,You' in his book *The Brand You 50*[4] in 1999) and a further five years prior to my reading both *Trends and The Brand You 50* whilst in the process of writing *the naked lawyer* in the summer of 2010.

So, in actual fact, I had been exposed to the concept and power of 'Me,Inc.' a decade earlier whilst working in the leisure industry, new media industry and management consulting industry.

The initial introduction to 'Brand,Me' inspired me to delve into the concept further. I also read an article by Alan Webber, editor of *Fast Company* magazine and a member of *USA TODAY*'s board of contributors, back in 2000 entitled: 'Put a "brand" on your work'. In it, Webber zoned in on how important it was going to be for individuals to be thinking about branding themselves as it was going to be essential to differentiate one's talents in the present and future. Smart!

In 2005 Tom Peters wrote:

"New Value-Added derives less and less from 'product' or 'service' quality, and more and more from... Something More. ... Something called 'Branding'."

He goes on...

"This is a story about Talent. It's a Brand You World. 'Lifetime Employment' at a corporation (aka 'cubicle slavery') is out. Lifetime self-reinvention is in. The only fool proof source of job security is... your talent. And your talent will express itself by building a scintillating portfolio of WOW Projects and by Thinking Weird."

We'll look at 'Brand,Me' in Volume 4: getting under your skin.

what a Charlie

I confess, I'm a lifeaholic and portfolio skills junky. Author and guru Charles Handy influenced my teenage years and adult direction in life; he helped me understand organisations, business and people. I guess you could say he helped me sculpt the compilation lifestyle and portfolio careers that I have chosen to pursue.

Back in1994 he wrote about the future of work in *The Empty Raincoat*[5] and in particular about the portfolio worker, coining the phrase 'portfolio career'. Nowadays we speak of 'compilation career' and 'compilation lifestyle'. It resonated with me, big time. I could empathise. And I could see the future on the horizon. I could see the trends...

We will look again at the concept of 'portfolio career' in Volume 12: XXX rated – tomorrow's lawyer. For now, let's focus on acquiring a portfolio of skills...

portfolio skills handbag

I didn't, and still don't, want a 'job for life'. I knew from an early age that I was interested in lots of stuff personally and professionally, both in my leisure pursuits and types of career.

I also realised that a 'job for life' was probably going to become obsolete for my generation. It was a thing born out of the industrial revolution that suited the working methods of the 19th and 20th centuries, but an unlikely reality for the 21st century and a world where technology was influencing change at an alarming rate.

I yearned to truly experience life and I wanted to experience many leisure interests and careers throughout it. Realising that a lifetime might not be enough to fit it all in (and I wouldn't be able do everything all in one go), I figured I could do some of it at the same time. I could have two or three trains going at one stage and maybe change tracks every now and then and keep the other one or two going as well.

So, in my teens, I made the decision to secure my future. I decided to get myself a handbag full of skills so that I could make the world my oyster rather than my clam. And, I figured that I could do more than one thing at once, hence, the compilation lifestyle and portfolio career approach. I also figured that the more skills I could learn, the more prepared I would be for the choices before me at whatever stage. Ultimately, by taking this approach to life I would have more control over the direction I wished to take it... where, when and how I chose.

My personal professional handbag of skills – as a result of education and/or experience to date – comprise:

- Sales;
- Marketing;
- Operations;
- Human resources;
- IT; and
- Legal.

Oh, and finance... by default. I believe they are the fundamentals for business nous and life savvy.

Even though I never trained to be an accountant, I had a good teacher: my father was a chartered accountant and my tender years were spent observing him and my mum building a very successful UK-wide business from the kitchen table.

Then I picked up a few other bits and bobs skills along the way, having taken every opportunity to attend training and coaching courses to satisfy my thirst for knowledge and personal and professional growth, such as an understanding and appreciation of:

- Brand – 'Brand,Me' and 'Brand,Firm';
- Promotions;
- Public relations;
- New media;
- Social media;
- Social networking;
- New marketing;
- Relationship marketing;
- Relationship sales;
- Customer relationship management;
- Innovation;
- Business strategy and planning;
- Business development;
- Negotiating;
- Persuading;
- Management;
- Leadership; and
- Emotional intelligence.

Having owned my own businesses, been around the block a few times, worked in a range of forward thinking enterprises in different industries with polar cultures along with being blessed during the journey with talented mentors, protégés, friends and colleagues, it's surprising what I learned and how I grew in a short period of time – emotionally, mentally, spiritually. Not physically though. I'm still 5ft 2 and ¾ inches; never grew a millimetre more since the age of 14. Rats!

You might think I'm a Jill of all trades. That's OK.

But I'm not. Actually I'm a great advocate of, and work tirelessly at, nicheing, specialising and becoming an expert. But I apply a multi-disciplinary approach, utilising all of the skills listed above, as I find it brings a whole new dimension to the outcome of my work and how I serve others.

A friend of mine, Stephen Roulac – Founder & CEO of Roulac Global Places (a very successful global company) and marathon runner (contender for the USA Olympic squad 1968) – is someone who I believe epitomises the words 'achiever' and 'fulfilment'. On the subject of 'success' he said, "I learned that one needed to master many disciplines to be effective."[6]

I reckon this applies to lawyering too. So, may I respectfully suggest the following... Get reading!

Not just law. Get reading about understanding business (strategy, planning, marketing, sales, operations, HR, IT, finance), understanding people, understanding trends and ultimately understanding the future, whether you plan to be a partner/director/leader or not during your working life. You will need the knowledge to help market, brand and sell YOU. And, to help you take control of your career(s) and life.

just do something!
Make a note of the kind of books and magazines you need to start reading. Have a look at those I have already mentioned – authors and subject areas in particular. Identify contemporary publications – search Google perhaps. Now go fetch... and start reading more!

phwoar them: sales begins with me

I hate to break it to you but, whether you like it or not, sales begins with you. It begins in YOUR mind, YOUR heart and YOUR gut. Sales does not begin with a product at 'the law firm' nor does it begin with 'the firm', or 'the marketing lady', or 'the business development guy', or 'the outsourced agency' and certainly not solely with 'the partners'.

How do I know this? I'll let you into a secret... When I went about my sales activities – in other words 'rainmaking' – as a trainee solicitor, I wasn't trying just to *woo* and *wow* the receiver, whether they be referrer, maven (key influencer), supplier, knowledge worker, prospective client or existing client. No, nowadays, they already expect to be *wooed* and *wowed*.

I was trying to *phwoar* them.

One thing's for sure. Rainmaking will positively suck, *big time*, if you approach it from the tried and tested 'old way' of selling, that is by focusing on 'Me, Me, Me' and 'the firm'.

Approaching rainmaking in the new way – believing and knowing it's all about THEM (referrer, maven, supplier, knowledge worker, prospective client or existing client) and focusing wholeheartedly on THEM by helping, educating, informing, serving and giving, giving and then giving some more – you will very soon become the only lawyer that pops into their heads when they need YOU, or someone like you, who's equipped with your skills, knowledge, experience and talent.

By putting the clients' interests above everything else, and taking lots of time to figure out what they really need, want and desire, rather than what you at first think they do, and then providing exactly that, you will become an invaluable resource.

Now, as you're going to have to get to grips with rainmaking at some point in your life, whether personally or professionally, when you're marketing, branding and selling YOU, I'd like to at least make it a little appealing to you...

It is my personal belief, bold opinion and suspicion, that rainmaker lawyers have better sex! I reckon you can tell by the way they go about their daily work. They're so confident, bouncy and jolly. Their heads and hearts seem aligned; they smile, crack jokes, obviously love what they do and they positively shine. If you stand close enough to them you can probably even feel and hear them crackle. You know the type. The ones swanning around in their swanky ties, polished brogues, tailor-made designer suits and shades who take three hours over lunch, spend a small fortune enjoying themselves 'entertaining' clients, live the champagne lifestyle in spite of the recession and still appear to have more wine, (wo)men, song, money and fun compared to you.

You either love 'em or loathe 'em.

If the former, you simply have visions of being like them and constantly pray 'please God, unshackle me from these chains at my desk otherwise I'm going to chew my arm off.'

If the latter, you really want to punch their lights out because you're sat working your butt off 16 hours a day (at least), trying to salvage the latest gold-dust deal going to rats whilst they appear to be off on a jolly half the time.

What's their secret? I'll tell you. It's all in the mind... Rainmaking is purely about confidence... seduction... performance... delivery...and follow on.

Whether you're a poor rainmaker or an extraordinary rainmaker will depend on your thoughts, feelings and actions. It goes something like this:

- Poor rainmaking activity is like unfulfilling sex – at least for one of the parties involved. Don't really care what the other person thinks. Couldn't give a monkey's how the other person feels. Haven't got a clue what you're doing. No real effort or interest. The whole experience is over in a jiffy. And it's all about me, me, me. In other words – all take. Pure self-interest.
- Good rainmaking activity is pretty much like good sex. It's not the tools that matter, it's what you do with them that counts. Kind of like you can tell a good bottle of champagne not by the size of the bottle, but by the size of the cork. That is: focus, quality and application.
- Great rainmaking activity is very much like great sex. Spending lots of time exploring, researching and thinking about what you could do next to delight. And by being attentive whilst adventuring and pleasuring and doing lots of giving, giving and giving some more.
- Extraordinary rainmaking activity is definitely like extraordinary sex! Yowza!! Continual mind focus. Continual nurturing. Continual stimulation. Continual discovery. Continual delivery. Continual follow on. Continual improvement. Continual innovation. Continual research and development.

Now, I don't know about you but I'd like to believe that I'm an extraordinary rainmaker (moot, but possible) because I'd like to believe I'm an extraordinary lover (moot, but possible).

I believe this because when I experience extraordinary sex it tends to happen when my mind is totally focused on the other person. I'm continually wanting to please, I'm continually being very personal and although I'm receiving a lot of attention, I'm actually truly focused on giving even more in return.

The outcome inevitably is that both parties are more than satisfied. Truly.

Can you honestly say you experience that? Do you want to? Then change your mindset. Focus on THEM. Not YOU.

Quoting Cole Silver (an esteemed lawyer and marketer in NYC, US) on rainmaking: "it is not about me. It's about the benefits and value I provide to my prospects and clients."[7]

I reckon if you strive to be an extraordinary lover then you have it in you to be an extraordinary rainmaker. And vice versa. So, as you approach 'sales begins with me' from here on in simply imagine you're going to achieve extraordinary sex and action accordingly...

And remember. It's not just a *woo* or a *wow* exercise... It has to be a *phwoar* event! That way, you're guaranteed success.

Big Rocks

First and foremost I must stress that the concept of Big Rocks[8] was born out of Dr Gary Russell's behavioural model and The Focus Lifestyle approach. More about this in detail in Volume 8: talking dirty to a saint when I'm a pure little devil.

One of my earliest studies when I did my first degree was on the subject of 'Women Entrepreneurs in the 1990s: Relative Work, Relative Leisure'[9]. In general, for most of us, but not all, life consists of some form of work, leisure and family. Most of us have a mix of the above in our lives but if not, we will have different and possibly more Big Rocks. The idea is simply to work out what are your Big Rocks in your life, make them a priority before all else and ensure you create the time and space to enjoy them.

So, I sat down and asked myself 'what are my Big Rocks?' Answer: work, family, leisure and personal momentous tomorrows. You will need to devise your own Big Rocks, even label them perhaps, such as Lawyer, Husband, Children, Surfing, etc. We'll look at this again at the end of the section.

whizzy work

I have always been, and probably always will be, a workaholic.

Btw, if you're aiming to work (or are already working) in the legal profession then by default you are probably a workaholic (kind of). Or your family may think you are, as you will to tend to spend endless hours at the office.

Why am I a workaholic? Partly because I always choose to pursue a career and role doing something I love, so why wouldn't I want to spend hours working on stuff I enjoy, especially if I'm learning, growing, developing, being of value and making a difference?

And partly, I suspect, because I'm just nuts.

It's probably my biggest rock, as when I'm truly *'in the flow'*, as Csikszentmihalyi[10] calls it, I feel fulfilled.

fizzy family

I tend to spend time with my 'significant other', friends and family either out of desire or duty. And that's being brutally honest. Enough said on that topic. Whichever it is, lovers, friends and family make me laugh... and cry. They create joy... and pain. It's all part of my life's rich tapestry. And a Big Rock.

lolly leisure

Ah 'leisure'. Woo-hoo. Play time. It doesn't matter what stage in life we are at, I reckon leisure is the alpha to the omega, the day to the night (or night to the day), the antidote to the poison and the one tonne weight that balances the scales.

I need it, in whatever form, whether I choose to make it active or passive and experience it shared or alone. I spent three years studying the meaning of leisure, understanding how the sector can best serve the customer/client and five years helping people enjoy it (I guess I should re-phrase that!).

Gazillions of spondulicks are spent on it every year. That's testament to the value we place on it.

I believe in, and practise, a blend of active and passive leisure, as most of us probably do. But when I do active leisure I make it count. A wonderful friend of mine always encourages me to train (exercise) hard. A while ago he said to me, "you have to make the miles count. There's no point in training if you're going to produce 'junk miles'." His words echo every time I put on my 'leisure' shoes, step outside the door and hit the road, whether on foot or cycle. No junk miles. This way I improve. That's the theory anyway.

Doing active pursuits helps blow away the cobwebs, clear the mind, gets the blood boiling, heart pounding, adrenalin pumping and spirit rocking.

I truly feel alive! And refreshed ready for work (in most instances). Whether I enjoy active leisure to compete or for fun, to spend time with family, friends, work colleagues or alone it has many physical, psychological, emotional and spiritual benefits:

- Active leisure tones the parts that passive leisure cannot reach; and
- Passive leisure provides the necessary rest and recuperation for more active stuff.

It's a mega Big Rock.

pmt

Abraham Lincoln famously said, "It's not the years in your life that count, it's the life in your years."

What a wonderful quote. I buy into it totally. For me, life is an adventure. I want to make each day count. I believe every day is a blank page just waiting to be scribbled on. Every day I wake up excited thinking, 'what am I going to learn today?'

Accordingly, I look to create Personal Momentous Tomorrows (PMTs). That is, I'm the kind of Naked Lawyer who is always searching and asking – what's next?, what's the challenge?, what's new?, what can I learn now?, where/what/who else is there to experience during this wonderful gift of life and extraordinary world? and how can I help more?

I want to constantly live life to the full by striving for personal momentous tomorrows. Do you?

A major Big Rock.

just do something!

Take a little time now to reflect on what you consider to be your Big Rocks. Write them down. Cherish them. And start prioritising them in your life (more than you've ever done before). Get rid of all the 'noise', the 'interference', the unnecessary 'clutter' and start making time, or more time, for your Big Rocks.

emotionally intelligent or emotionally defunct?

what is emotional intelligence (EI)?

EI is all about understanding and interacting with people, both yourself and others. You either learn the attributes and skills or invariably experience them through time.

It's the opposite of intelligence quotient (IQ). IQ is all about one's academic ability. Apparently we reach our IQ peak at the age of 19-20. We reach our EI peak age 40-50. Ah-ha, good news. I haven't peaked yet!

But, it's actually our EI which differentiates us where top level results are concerned.

Author Daniel Coleman, defines emotional intelligence as: "the ability to manage our own feelings so that they don't run us."[11] It's a critical characteristic in sales people (which you and I are). You have to be in control of your own emotions. Guru Bob Burg in *Go-Givers*[12] defines EI as: "the ability to keep your focus on others' feelings as you acknowledge and honor your own."

I define it as one word: *maturity*. Let me expand a little...

It's about using 'thinking about feeling' to guide our actions (behaviour). It's about the 'why' we do what we do: the motivational factors, values, beliefs, attitude, awareness (of self and others), self-control/regulation, self confidence and how they are externalised in our 'soft skills': communication, management, leadership, persuasion, empathy, body-language skills, etc.

You may think that some of us reach it before or after others and/or some of us may never reach it at all, no matter what age we reach.

I recall at least one incident in the past few years when a colleague bellowed so loudly and disparagingly at another colleague in front of the whole floor (comprising five departments), that it stopped me in my tracks and made my stomach churn. Do you know that feeling? The one where you swallow hard but your stomach flips over and over as you swallow again. You don't quite know where to look and what to do. Whatever had caused the outburst was obviously a serious matter... In law law land they usually are.

However, I questioned whether it was an emotionally intelligent way to deal with the issue, irrespective of the scale of the issue/mistake. I'll leave you to answer that one yourself.

I do not subscribe to the maxim 'you have to earn respect'. I actually believe we should freely give respect... but we can also take it away. Similarly, we should freely receive respect to begin with but we can lose it because of our behaviour. Needless to say, I lost my respect for my bellowing emotionally defunct colleague that day. And my respect for the emotionally-intelligent disparaged one in how she reacted, grew exponentially.

Invariably, there have been circumstances and people that have led me to feel frustrated, exasperated, not valued and ultimately very angry. Yup, I've been shouted at and down to in front of an audience during my career, usually as a result of the aggressor feeling – needlessly – that their power base was threatened in some way. But what we say and do is up to us. We choose how best to respond/re-act and behave in a given situation. I reckon maturity is determined by the choice we make in how we react and behave.

What I will share with you is that I have noticed that as I have matured (moot), that when I act with emotional maturity, in other words call on my emotional intelligence, it tends to raise the bar in the communications that I engage in and the progress made by all.

This quote neatly sums it up for me. I'll share it with you: "Feel with your mind, think with your heart."

Thinking with my heart helps me make emotionally intelligent decisions. I'll let you ponder on this for a moment...

who am I?

As I've already said, my personal journey started many years ago... I knew and felt that in order to structure my career I'd better get to know myself, be comfortable in my own skin, be happy with the real me and ultimately love myself and what I'm doing in and with my life... By the age of 14 I became master of my own mutiny; co-incidentally at the same time I stopped growing – in height! Whether this was due to immaturity, impressionability or maturity (moot) or perhaps instinct even, who knows? However, I continued to learn and grow – emotionally, mentally and spiritually – in the ways of the guru masters.

Year 2000 was my epiphany. I was 29 and 'in my prime' as Emily Brontë would have it... I was exposed to Jack Black's MindStore System For Life, the Concept Belief Action (CBA) and the Sender Receiver Outcome (SRO) behavioural model from The Focus Lifestyle approach as devised by Gary Russell, and the Cannons Train professional development and sales mantra. An awesome threesome.

Then in year 2004, I experienced another epiphany, when I applied all of the above in my approach to why I wanted to become a lawyer at that stage in my life and how I set about doing what I did.

By the summer of 2008 I was spending a lot of time soul searching (working through what I'm sharing with you in this Volume 2) and then researching and cutting a niche (Volume 3: slowly slowly catch a nichey), with a view to developing a personal brand (Volume 4: getting under your skin) so that I could find the right way of marketing and selling myself (Volumes 5-12) for the benefit of 'Brand,Me' *and* 'Brand,Firm'.

I must admit though, at least to myself if not you – even though I am – that during the period 2004-08, the 'significant other', whether it was 'the husband', 'the boss' or 'the firm' had in some way affected me.

In spite of how desperately I fought to be myself, those particular years and months throughout that period took their toll. I wasn't the person I once was. I'd compromised, adapted, changed, aligned, 'softened'... whatever... to mould into these significant others' view of what they wanted me to be... or expected me to be.

However, in summer 2008 I had reached the point in my career and life when I sat back and asked myself the following: Who am I? Who am I really doing this for? Why am I doing this? What do I really want? And, ultimately, what happened to 'me'?

It was Robin Sharma's wisdom that resonated with me – big time. I can't recall where exactly I heard it but he said something along the lines of: "There's no victory in becoming the best version of someone that you're not." I was forced to conclude: "I'm not 'Chrissie' anymore. And I don't feel comfortable not being the real me and I certainly don't like how I've changed or what I've become."

Bruce Springsteen's lyrics in his song, *Better Days*, hit the mark: "It's a sad man my friend whose livin' in his own skin and can't stand the company."[13]

Crack of thunder, bolt of lightning, here goes (again)... self realisation eureka/ epiphany moment about to strike. "This is false. This is rubbish. Who the [bleep] am I? I'm not the person I once was or the person I want to be. What the [bleep] am I going to do about it? How the [bleep] am I going to change things?"... So, not sure who I was any more, I remembered who I 'naturally' used to be. I then asked myself who I'd like to become. That helped me gain a realistic fix on my then current position.

You may be at a point where you feel you need to re-invent yourself and find again what interests you. If you are, let me help you. You're someone who is on the way from where you were to where you're going. And if you're smart, which of course you are, you will no doubt ask yourself the same questions and may be coming to a similar conclusion.

So, you must be in the 'right place'... for the time being at least. And people who are in 'the right place' find that the right things happen naturally around them.

You're reading *the naked lawyer* aren't you?

just do something!

Take a while now to reflect, think deeply and ask yourself 'Who am I?' Perhaps ask yourself some of the questions I did. Write the questions down. And then answer them. Honestly. Privately.

Take your time... Keep your jottings safe. Remind yourself of your answers every day.

what will make me feel happy and fulfilled?

So, I then asked myself, 'what will make me feel truly happy and fulfilled?' Ultimately I found it easy to realise the answer. I simply inverted what I knew I didn't want. So that's what I did. And continue to do.

When I entered the legal profession I knew I didn't want to be a cubicle slave, wage slave or a grinder's monkey in an established law firm for the rest of my life, churning out technical black and white law and waiting for the, elusive, time when I'd be made partner.

I wanted to be in control of my own mutiny... and I knew that the above would simply be a waste of my natural talents, strengths, skills, knowledge and experience if they weren't going to be allowed to blossom.

I'd had plenty of business and life experience prior to working in the legal profession, and enough nous to realise that the profession and industry was heading for a major shake up at some point in the future due to technological, consumer and world trends. Although I didn't know exactly when and didn't foresee the global recession.

For that reason, I knew there would be opportunities and options available to use my talents, strengths, knowledge, skills and experience for the benefit of the client, my colleagues and the firm... if I was in the right place, that is 'in the right seat and on the right bus' as Collins & Porras phrase it.[14]

I knew that I'd have to keep my head down, serve my time, do my porridge... blah, blah, blah, to get to where I needed to get to.

However, by the time I'd waded through trough loads of treacle (and porridge), throughout my three years as a trainee solicitor, I'd had enough of 'just sit there and do as you're told' and 'don't worry, it's our job to bring in the clients' from the partners, even though I admired and respected them greatly for their technical lawyering skills.

I was frustrated because the crucial change that I could see needed to happen throughout the entire organisation (and profession as a whole), in particular in relation to the culture and the mindset of the partners within it, and how it needed to be done, was just not going to happen, largely because of the traditional structures, policies and politics, as well as the ingrained self-interest which prevailed. Change was not going to happen in 'the firm' in my lifetime. Hell would freeze over first.

Offering me a newly qualified solicitor's position and dumping me in a chair labelled 'get your traditional corporate lawyer here' was like putting Santa Claus in the old folks home and having them sit on his knee, rather than his usual audience of kiddies at Toys 'R' Us. Give me a sign emblazoned 'Frustrated Lawyers 'R' Us' and then I'll be happy. Enough said. (It was a nice chair by the way.)

I knew that both they (the partners/ decision-makers/change-masters (not!)) and the profession had a long way to go to catch up with the rest of the business world in 'New World Thinking, Behaviour and Action', for the benefit of their employees, their clients and ultimately themselves in this challenging new age.

The gurus were right. I'd experienced 'The Good Way' in previous companies and careers. I'd practised their ways... successfully... in previous industries and they were spot on. I just wasn't able to operate in 'The Good Way' in an 'Old Way' set up. I wanted freedom to pursue... to grow and develop.

Whilst I had every respect for my colleagues' intellectual grade, I questioned their EI levels where soft skills came into play because I'd been blessed to work with people in other industries, who were much further along the EI development path, simply because they'd been exposed to the new thinking and behaviour sooner. Indeed, at least a decade before.

In the few months preceding my moving on from the law firm where I did my training, the partners and I were debating my future role in the firm on qualification, going forward with a view to a dual lawyering and 'business development' role.

I say 'business development' because we lawyers simply accept this term unquestioningly as, by and large, we still use it as a kind of umbrella term. Sadly, we have a problem really understanding the difference and nuances between marketing, sales, innovation and business development. Bless.

Lawyers (in particular), listen up... *they are not the same*. They are discrete disciplines requiring deep expertise which actually drill down further. For example, marketing comprises PR, promotions, advertising, networking, social media and social networking amongst other things which are discrete specialisms within the field of marketing. Oh, and by the way, looking after existing clients is *not* marketing. That's CRM – customer relationship management.

Whilst we're on the subject I believe that social media (SM) and social networking (SN) cut across all four disciplines (marketing, sales, innovation and business development) because SM&SN are really all about building and nurturing relationships. More of that in Volume 6: social savvy junkie.

As a comparison, it's kind of like being a corporate lawyer – you're a specialist in that area but you probably know Scooby-Doo about personal injury lawyering.

So, when the partners were discussing with me the idea of a dual role, what they really meant was a sales and innovation role combined with a lawyering role, as the firm already had in place a full-time 'business development' person... who was actually a marketeer. Hmmm.

However, I fervently believe, and have proven, that if you truly desire to be a successful lawyer in this digital age, you need to understand, and possibly even master depending on the goals, mission and vision you create for yourself, all of the four major disciplines – marketing, sales, innovation and business development. In fact, I'm confident that most successful rainmaker lawyers would testify to this statement.

When the partners and I were trying to figure out how best to use my talents for the benefit and fulfilment of everyone in this 'dual role', I have no doubt they had the best of intentions when they told me that they understood my skills and how I added value to the firm, but in their own words they raised the 'concern'...

"Chrissie, we're just not quite sure you want to be a lawyer."

They were right. I had stated on a number of occasions to the partners throughout my three years at the firm that "I don't want to be a lawyer". Kaboom! Professional suicide button pressed firmly, you're thinking. Chrissie's out of the legal nest faster than a Tiger Woods, Ashley Cole or (potentially) Wayne Rooney marriage.

Actually, the rest of the sentence reads as follows... "I don't want to be a lawyer, not the traditional kind of lawyer that is. Clients want the 'New World Lawyer. The Entrepreneurial Lawyer.' I know, because I was a frustrated and dissatisfied business client prior to entering the profession."

So, yes, quite right Mr Boss Lawyer. I didn't want to be a traditional lawyer. What I omitted to say further on that occasion, was what I was really thinking and feeling which was... "Clients want their lawyers to be highly commercial and to get off the freakin' fence and give them real commercial solutions, not hog-wash black and white legal gubbins. It's a given clients expect technical legal advice to be top notch. But what they also want is a big dollop of real value (green notes), customer service excellence, care, empathy, understanding and gratitude for giving you the business thrown in for good measure. Plus, introducing the client to people who would benefit their business would be warmly welcome... if you can manage that too... thank you."

After putting in an inordinate amount of personal time and effort largely outside working hours to develop a couple of niches for the firm, and having run into numerous brick walls, I had reached the point where I could see no through road. I actually thought: "I can't stay here because my brain, along with my patience, is going into flat-line and my frustrations are at warp factor 10!" Like Monica in the hugely successful American sitcom *Friends*, I'd "simply lost the will to scold".

I knew I wanted to be an entrepreneurial lawyer – the new world lawyer type; the kind of lawyer the client wanted. The Naked Lawyer type, in fact. I had imagined it. I was living it; sub-consciously and consciously.

I wanted to help entrepreneurs, by which I mean business people. I wanted to touch their lives in a way that they wanted and expected, not in the way the 'traditional lawyer' and/or 'the firm' thought they should.

Being of a positive mindset and solutions orientated disposition, I actually reached the point during the 'discussions' when I saw the light as to how my knowledge, experience, skills and talents could best be utilised, capitalised on, and how I personally would feel happy and fulfilled.

It meant 'moving on' from the firm, turning my back on the opportunity of being a full-time practising corporate solicitor in law law land and venturing Full On into the business world of law law land.

By this I mean I realised I could help many entrepreneurs and many lawyers, rather than a select few. Not by practising as a lawyer, but by sharing my knowledge and experience in how each and every individual can market and sell 'Brand,You', for the benefit of YOU and your employer. I'd recognised and identified a 'need', an even greater opportunity... A gaping niche which was crying out to be filled.

And so it came to pass. Here I am now. And here you are too... Let's move on.

I am guessing that if you're reading *the naked lawyer*, you're already a star and/or certainly have the makings of one. You are a seeker.

Thus, duly note this. If you try to squash a star into a square hole, all you achieve is a star with its edges crumpled. If you're feeling a little squished around the edges at the moment then ask yourself the following...

why am I doing what I'm doing?

I do what I do every day because I love what I do. I'm passionate about it. And I am simply myself when I go about my 'job' and daily life, in every way.

The present 'in' term for this is 'being your authentic self'.

In August 2010, Donna Seyle (non-practising lawyer), wrote a telling blog post. In it she states:

"there is another theme emerging ... somewhat understated but, I think, very telling in the evolution of practicing law as we know it ...The theme is a two-fold concept: practice law by aligning our professional selves with our authentic selves, and by authentically connecting with and caring about our clients. Not exactly consistent with what we learned in law school." [15]

Bottom line – if you are being true to yourself, your authentic self, you do what you say and say what you do. Your confidence shines. Clients like that.

Having confidence in yourself and therefore your own knowledge, experience, skills and talent, your prospective client is likely to pick up on that. Furthermore, if you have your unique flair and style and you exude confidence with it, this inevitably gives your client confidence in you.

Putting it in context (using myself as an example): I have a purpose, a belief, a cause. I want to help entrepreneurs. I want to do business with people who believe *why* I do *what* I do for THEM. This equates to my having a genuine passion for extraordinary service levels and to truly having their best interests at heart. I am thinking, feeling and acting from my very core, my guts, my heart, my mind to provide a solution bespoke and befitting solely to THEM... every time. I am able to do this because at my very core, I am a woman entrepreneur. Empathy.

Of course, we tend to think of the stereotypical entrepreneur as those we hear about in the media, such as the Dragons Den gurus and the high profile mega successful entrepreneurs, such as Bill Gates and Richard Branson.

But the vast majority of entrepreneurs have a much lower profile, the 'not so many zeros after the name' and 'not so revolutionary' kinds of entrepreneurs ... the likes of you and me – Mr & Mrs Smith (without the Brad Pitt and Angelina Jolie looks). Women entrepreneurs, young entrepreneurs and serial entrepreneurs that quietly make a living and small differences, so creating a footprint in time.

Personally, I've always been intrigued by the 'Del Boy' type. Survivors, no matter what. Always looking for a better way. And if anything, they tend to make you laugh! Crazy ideas, crazy products, crazy services, crazy people. In spite of the world laughing, the world moves on and progress is made because of these crazy entrepreneurs. Ironic... Wonderful.

An entrepreneur is probably the most stereotypical portfolio skilled character, portfolio career advocate and worker. In most cases entrepreneurs tend to have a few things on the go all at the same time. It's the nature of the beast.

Someone once said to me, "there are many things in life that will catch your eye, but only a few will catch your heart... pursue those." No doubt they were quoting someone famous. So that's what I did and do. My working as a lawyer, an entrepreneurial lawyer, was a natural extension of myself. And what I do now? Ditto.

just do something!

Take a little time now, and ask yourself the following two questions:

1. What will make me feel happy and fulfilled?, and
2. Why am I doing what I'm doing?

Write the questions down. When you've figured out the answers, again, write them down and keep referring back to them as a reference point to remind you *why* you do what you do. Simply put: if you're doing something you're not happy about, why are you doing it?

Pick me up again when you're ready...

what gets my Big Rocks off?

In case you hadn't figured it out by now, in my working life I'm interested in entrepreneurship; all kinds of entrepreneurs, innovation, new media, futurology and behavioural systems.

In my leisure life, I'm into cycling, big time. I'm also a bit of a wine buff – I do appreciate a fine wine.

What gets my Big Rocks off is doing the stuff that feeds me. That is when I'm connecting, interacting and getting involved with people who share the same interests as me. So, naturally, in order to have a happy and fulfilling working life, I set about cultivating my service proposition to find and attract the kind of people who share the same interests, both in my working life and leisure life, and with whom I can identify, and they with me. The goal: mutual empathy.

As Stephen Roulac said, "If an activity engages my interest, I seek to excel, not merely to participate." I concur.

Perhaps the secret and answer to the cry from frustrated partners/bosses of 'how do I motivate my employees so I can get more productivity out of them?' lies here? For this is the interesting thing. I'm not really doing it for me; well, I am, sort of, as I am a great believer in the law of returns, and have witnessed that when I *give* it comes back when I least expect it... and in multiples. But I don't actually expect it to. Let me explain...

Because I share the same interests as the people I wish to attract, I can be of more value to THEM due to the value and quality of my network and knowledge, which will inevitably have synergy with THEM. My network has more value because I am able to *give* more potential synergistic introductions, in other words: potential business to my synergistic new potential client because I have a 'new business pool pipeline' to dip into for THEM.[16]

And, if I can be of more value and give, give and give to THEM more than the average Tom, Dick or Harry lawyer because of that interest network, then the likelihood is that I am going to build a strong relationship with THEM ... quickly or certainly much more quickly than usual. Inevitably, the receiver of my giving naturally reciprocates my giving at some point in the future. If they don't, it doesn't matter, for...

"The manner of giving is worth more than the gift," Pierre Corneille.[17] This is why taking the time to reflect on your interests and acting on them matters. If you're constantly dealing with things which feed you, then self-motivation for lawyering, rainmaking and delivering extraordinary customer service inevitably grows ten-fold.

So, tell me... what gets your Big Rocks off?

just do something!

Take your time now to work through the answer to the above question. There may be many. Write them down. Reflect some more. We're going to return to your answers when we work through Volume 3.

self reliance reality check

Let's pause for a moment. Where are we so far? I know who I am, I know what I want, I know why I'm going to do what I'm going to do and I know what interests me. But hold on a minute ... have I got what it takes?

Reality check, Chrissie.

Time to conduct a 360 degree personal talent, strengths, skills, knowledge, experience, confidence and guts reality check. Accordingly, what are my strengths, weaknesses, opportunities and threats? Aka, a SWOT Analysis.

You probably don't want to know or hear how this relates to me. You don't care. So, I won't waste your time or mine chattering on about it. What you need to do is the exercise for yourself in the 'ROAR steps!' within the 'after dark activity', or at the end of this section. That is: list your strengths, weaknesses, opportunities and threats.

To begin this exercise I asked my friends, family, colleagues, mentors and clients what they thought were my strengths, weaknesses, opportunities and threats. I broke it down in the following way. I did this because how I see myself and how others see me may come as quite a shock, so I needed to understand it, take it on board and act on it.

I asked them, and then myself, a series of questions:

- What are my strengths?
- What are my natural talents?
- What are my skills?
- What knowledge do I possess?
- What experience do I have/can I draw upon?
- Where am I most likely to add value?
- How do I add value?
- What am I interested in?

- What are my characteristics?
- What are my areas for improvement (aka, weaknesses; I do not like this word as it is 'negative')?
- What am I uniquely good at?
- What can I become known for/famous for/an expert in?
- Who could I help the most?
- Why should I help them?
- How can I help them?
- What target market should I focus on?
- Why should I focus on a particular target market?
- How do I focus on that target market?
- How could I win business using my strengths, talents, skills, knowledge and experience?
- How could I attract and retain the kind of clients who share my interests?
- Who do I know?
- Who do I need to get to know?
- How am I going to get to know them?

I realised it would be the combination of my knowledge, experience, talent, strengths and skills that would bring about my future run of success. As well as my brutal objectiveness and thoroughness in being able to answer all of the above questions.

So, I also carried out a number of paper-based and computer-based tests at the same time:

- StrengthsFinder – to identify my core strengths, my natural talents;
- Self Perception Inventory;
- Learning Style Inventory;
- Learning Style Type;
- Personal Profile Analysis;
- Leadership Style; and
- Motivation To Work.

I'll pick up on these in depth in Volume 8: talking dirty to a saint when I'm a pure little devil, when we look at communication and behaviour.

If you are a 'doubting Thomas' about personality tests and psychometric tests, etc., then here is a quick snapshot of the outcome of one of the tests I did: "Quality senior management of this very focused young candidate will pay large corporate dividends. The reverse will invite a mutiny on the bounty." Really? Yes. It came to pass... Anyone who knows me would no doubt confirm this to be true.

I then took all of the responses and test outcomes and conducted a complete SWOT analysis which in turn I used to form the basis to identifying a niche, see Volume 3: slowly slowly catch a nichey and developing a personal brand, see Volume 4: getting under your skin.

As I said previously, the key was to be incredibly objective about myself. And brutally honest.

I decided to focus on the strengths, forget about the 'areas for improvement' (weaknesses), and switch the positive energy to squash the threats to enable me to concentrate on the opportunities.

just do something!

Create four electronic documents – separate pages – or get four sheets of paper. Give each of them a SWOT title – 'Strengths', 'Areas For Improvement', 'Opportunities' and 'Threats'.

Ask yourself, friends, family, colleagues, mentors, clients, teachers, anyone who you think can help you in answering the questions I asked myself in this section.

Think deeply. Dig deeply...then fill in each document as comprehensively as possible.

We'll return to your findings when we work through Volumes 3 and 4.

how do I get to fourth base?

I took a big risk at the age of 32, by upping sticks to enter the legal profession, with no guarantee of attaining a training contract or securing a position on qualification. Then again at age 37, I turned my back on the offer of a full-time corporate solicitor role in favour of starting my own company; at the height of the world's worst ever global recession. I bet you think I'd totally lost the plot, eh?

I could have just ticked along at the law firm and been comfortable rocking back and forth on my nice chair, the 'get your traditional corporate lawyer here' one... remember. But I knew in my heart it was right to move on. I knew it was time because I woke one morning and thought and felt: I don't want to go into work today. The message: I had lost my passion and vision. And I knew in my mind it was right... because I'd imagined my achievement and success in a new way forward. I had seen the light...

Just as I know that deep in my very soul I have to do what comes naturally to me. In Del Boy's trademark words: "you know it makes sense." So, when the time comes and I just 'know', I simply take a deep breath, a leap of faith and jump... *Guts*.

Why? In the words of the famous film star Bette Davis: 'No guts, no glory.' I make a choice. I face fear head on and smack it in the face. I get over the fear of criticism, being different, potential poverty, failure and even success. Sometimes you get the distinct impression that people don't like you being successful when you're going about doing what you're doing, pretty much like if you were a geek star at school and mates mocked you and called you a swot.

I think it was Eleanor Roosevelt who said, "you gain strength, courage and confidence by every experience in which you stop to look fear in the face." How true. Fear is quite simply a lack of faith.

I didn't allow fear to interfere!

just do something!

Just sit for a while now and ponder these questions: 'what scares me?' and 'what am I truly fearful of?'

Think deeply. List your thoughts. Face them. Can YOU overcome them?

You must revert to these jottings and constantly challenge yourself and battle with your 'fears' until you succeed in overpowering and overcoming them.

master of my own mutiny

Jack Welch influenced me greatly in my youth. Something he wrote has stuck with me all my life. He said: "Control your destiny or someone else will."

I read that Margaret II, Queen of Denmark pronounced: "I have always had a dread of becoming a passenger in life." Touché.

Two decades on, I had the great honour and delight of listening to Ruby Wax earlier this year at a 'Forward Ladies' women only event in Leeds, UK. What Ruby said (in the kind of style which resonated with me) actually captured in a nutshell my very own personal mantra (ad verbatim):

"If I can't drive this mother-ship, nobody else is."

Co-incidentally, guru Bob Burg, in a more philosophical tone, states: "What you have most to offer others, you have to offer least of all through what you say, in greater part through what you do, but in greatest through who you are."[18]

Who am I? I've already addressed this. Accordingly... I am the captain of my mother-ship and I am happy where it's sailing.

I have a question for you. Well, two actually:

1. Who's driving your mother-ship? and
2. Who's the daddy of your ambition?

just do something!

Take a moment to reflect on the above questions and then answer, honestly.

Until you reach the answer '*I am*', aka, 'YOU', you will not be able to take control of your life and/or career nor take it in the direction that YOU truly want.

So, get working on it...

delayed gratification

Like my good friend Stephen Roulac (in his sporting and business ambition and achievements), the concept of delayed gratification, that is, having to wait some time before the desired reward is realised, was something I was familiar with, from prior careers, experiences and ambitions.

I was prepared for the substantial delayed gratification that characterised lawyering. When I started out I was told that I had to toe the line for at least seven years after qualification before I would get to a point where I could expect any kind of reasonable results – the holy grail of partnership and with it a potential stake in the business. Because 'that's the way we do things around here' in law law land came the cry.

This reminded me of the seven year itch mantra. The likely scenario being that after seven years had passed, I probably wouldn't want the holy grail because I'd be onto the next cycle and challenge! Fine. I would only be 44 years old by then. Still a puppy. I buy into the Deepak Chopra philosophy of 'Ageless Body, Timeless Mind'.[19] No worries I thought.

However, I wasn't prepared for how frustrated I became in relation to the lack of innovation, forward movement in the profession and job content satisfaction.

When I began my journey my emphasis was not on one single, short term period, but on an extended period of time with a view to developing relationships with new clients and to grow alongside them.

Unfortunately, I knew and understood that the ultimate measure of the degree of technical learning in the legal realm is performance over an extended period of time, and the profession (or at least the firm I was working at) didn't really know how to handle a rainmaker come mature trainee and balance, capitalise or position these mature soft skills alongside the technical learning hard-core skills. This resulted in an obvious imbalance. Nevertheless, delayed gratification was to be expected... and I accepted that. That was until I could accept it no longer.

With the global recession and the turmoil in the legal profession, the legal industry and the 'business of law' at present, if your journey is to become a 'Tomorrow's Lawyer', I suspect the concept of delayed gratification may be even more true and prevalent, particularly if you find yourself aboard the wrong ship and in the wrong rowing position.

My advice, throwing in my two pennies/cents worth as a result of learning from my mistakes and experience – but you can of course ignore me... be prepared for the delay, curb your expectations in relation to the dream of a champagne lifestyle, try to be realistic, focus sooner rather than later in creating the truly fulfilling lifestyle you want, and ensure you become a rainmaker lawyer. The Naked Lawyer rainmaker kind of course. So, learn how to market, brand and sell YOU...

Keep reading...

making the dream a lifestyle reality

The great Martin Luther King said, "I have a dream..." A timeless statement... and probably one of the most famous. He was speaking for all of us. I don't mean the subject of his particular dream, I mean that he voiced what I believe lies within each of us – the 'I have a dream' desire.

Dreams come in all shapes and sizes. We have them at varying ages and different stages in our life. Some can be achieved in a short period of time and some take a very long time to come to fruition (if ever). Reaching for them and achieving them can often be as simple as making a decision and taking that first step.

For example, if your dream is to have your ideal job/career/business/partner, and you're in a job/career/relationship with something/someone who isn't with you on this ideal, the practical choice is to change the situation. That is end the current job/career/relationship. But, procrastination, anxiety, fear, financial squeeze, lack of confidence are some of the things that can keep us from taking action.

I don't know about you but I have lots of dreams – 'little goal' dreams and 'big whopper' dreams. It's what sustains, energises and drives me onward and upward. It's what makes me tick and helps me make sense of the world when all around me appears to be crumbling away.

My big whopper dream is to be financially free. By that I mean sufficiently financially secure (not necessarily 'bling') to pursue a nomadic lifestyle travelling and exploring the world – if I so choose as and when I achieve it. Albeit I've experienced a lot of travelling so far, it's kind of always been a bit part in my film noire!

I figured qualifying as a solicitor might help me toward that dream. Then the global recession hit. Law law land was shaken to its very core and creaking in its booties. Rats!

I realised I needed to reassess my situation. Ultimately the timeline and route to achieve the dream lifestyle I had envisaged had not only run aground but had hit the rocks. BIG TIME. I was marooned on an island where the natives were not too understanding. Harrumph...

So, I set a new course, having spotted a wonderful opportunity to turn what looked like a potentially depressing drowning failure of a dream into an exciting blue water adventure...

One thing's for sure. It's up to me to make my dreams come true. And I'm working on it... I started by jotting my dreams down and sharing them with 'significant others' to help get the ball rolling.

As for my ambition of becoming a solicitor – an entrepreneurial solicitor at that – when I graduated from law school and entered 'the firm', nobody guided me as to what would be the key to my overall professional success and fulfilment. The whole focus was simply on learning to be a good lawyer – the technical stuff.

Nobody taught me about marketing or sales, nobody showed me how to promote the firm or myself or *actively* encouraged me to do the same. In fact, the truth be told, it was I who took the initiative and asked a couple of entrepreneurial partners if I could get on and develop stuff. Incredulously, I was positively discouraged by some partners and made to feel somewhat an outsider because of my tendency to focus on sales, marketing, innovation, business development and customer excellence.

Strange. But true. In the telling words spoken in the movie *Full Monty*, "there's nowt as queer as folk."

Fortunately, I had the gumption and savvy to take care of that myself. Bottom line, I realised very soon that without the ability to develop a portfolio of business, I'd just be another grunt grinder's monkey. I didn't want that as it wasn't going to get me the lifestyle, job satisfaction and financial freedom I craved. So I set about creating my legal career by design and not by default.

The secret to creating the lifestyle, job satisfaction and financial rewards that I craved was to focus on building a portfolio of business. I did this by matching my portfolio of skills, my professional ethics, interests, strengths and talents with the needs, wants and desires of my (potential) clients.

It was about rainmaking and extraordinary client service. Period.

I figured that whether I turned out to be a technically average lawyer or a technically brilliant lawyer, the necessity to have a flow of existing and new clients, and to treat each of them as if they were the first or last Adam or Eve in this prancing Naked Lawyer's law law land, aka, planet, would be the key to my financial freedom and ultimate success. And my chances of sustained success would be dependent on this approach.

To quote Cole Silver:

"Whatever your position or role, eventually you'll realise that client development and rainmaking not only represent the key to your professional survival, but unlocks the door to your overall wealth, happiness and success as a lawyer... without a book of business ... you're just a fungible asset... an expense that is replaceable, subject to termination or reclassification when circumstances dictate."[20]

So, I wasn't going to wait for things to happen; I made things happen. I set about rainmaking. I set about making my dream come true. I couldn't, and didn't, rely on the firm's marketing department or partner's help when it came to my initiating my own rainmaking action. Bottom line, I had to take personal responsibility for my own future success.

Again, as Cole Silver neatly puts it:

"If you want independence and control over your life, as well as more money, friends, influence, freedom, and security... then the answer is clear. You have to become a rainmaker."

So, do you have a dream? If so, what dream do you have about your career and life? As Captain Sensible in the 1980s sang: "If you don't have a dream, then how you gonna make a dream come true?"[21] And with a name like that I just had to take him seriously of course.

Oh... and if you think you're too old to dream, think again. In the wisdom of C.S. Lewis and Goethe respectively: "You are never too old to set another goal or to dream a new dream", and "Whatever you can do or dream you can, begin it. Boldness has genius, power and magic in it. Begin it now."

In essence, my dreams are snapshots from the fairytale movie that my soul is producing about me. What are your dreams?

just do something!

It's time to ask yourself 'what are my dreams?' Think about small dreams and big whopper dreams. Jot them down. Share them with 'significant others'. You may be pleasantly surprised at their reaction and support.

Plus, you will find that by doing this exercise it will make you more determined in achieving all of your dreams!

a 'Formidable ME Strategy & Plan'

In order to make my dream a lifestyle reality, I approached my personal and professional development like a business strategy & plan – substituting business/company with ME.

In my 'Formidable ME Strategy & Plan' (FMSP), which covers the short, medium and long term, I had goals, a mission, a vision (ethos), research and development section, brand, product offering (lawyer), SWOT analysis, how to market and sell myself (sales and marketing strategy & plan), financials, operations, HR, location, systems & control procedures, risk & problems section/ contingency plans and tools diagnostic.

In essence, I had a game plan. Documented. Something I could lay my hands on to remind me of my journey and destination dream lifestyle. As it was documented I had an actual reference point that I could execute, and from that, follow on to ensure delivery.

I was going to be a player. A player with attitude. A player who would bring her individual qualities to the table for the benefit of entrepreneurial clients.

In the words of Stephen Roulac (reproduced with his blessing):[22]

"Delivering superior performance evolves from an explicit strategy, applied through specific tactics, implemented through conscious, conscientious and sustained application... While the popular perception is that success is the equivalent of winning the lottery – without buying a lottery ticket – truth told, success in any endeavour is the outcome of focus, preparation and sustained hard work. Certainly circumstances, natural talent, even luck may play a part. But even that trilogy is derived from initiative, strategic calculation and profound intentionality, for as Louis Pasteur notes, 'Chance favors the prepared mind.'"

I don't leave anything to 'chance'.

Briefly stated, I think what Stephen is saying is that predictable success doesn't just happen. You have to make predictable success happen by putting in the preparation required.

I had to take the initiative, grab myself by the scruff of my neck, get off my butt, and make it happen. Actually, boiling it all down, I believe my rainmaking performance throughout 2009 was actually directly linked with the FMSP I devised, combined with my positive thinking, self esteem and thick rhino skin.

Without the combination of all four elements I reckon I would have failed... catastrophically... and miserably. Essential to the FMSP was addressing risks and problems. Directly: what if x happened? What would be my contingency plan?

I had to do a 'what if' reality check:

- What if I don't qualify, by that I mean if I fail the Legal Practice Certificate (LPC) or Professional Skills Course (PSC)?
- What if I don't get offered a training contract?
- What if I get struck off before I even qualify due to daft behaviour?
- What if I achieve qualification but I don't get offered a position at the end of the training contract?
- What if there's a recession and no placement available at the end of the training contract?
- What if I don't get offered a position in the area of law I wish to practise?
- What if I'm offered a position but I don't want it. Hell, what if I'm not happy?
- What if I'm offered a position but career progression doesn't look good?
- What if I'm offered a position but the pay/deal is grim?
- What if I don't actually enjoy practising law?

Having carried out my 360 degree personal talent, strengths, skills, knowledge, experience, confidence and guts reality check, and an honest one at that, I figured I'd better have a plan B, C and D. Just in case.

I'd be a fool not to. After all, if plan A goes to rats, meaning if any of the above 'what ifs' become a reality, I could be cast adrift from the good ship legal enterprise, with no choice but to walk the plank and jump into a stormy sea. So, I'd better make sure I have all the bits 'n' bobs in the life raft to ensure my survival. Otherwise, I just might drown.

Do you have a plan B, C or D? I ask because I've always lived my life hoping for the best but being prepared for the worst. As the saying goes: "It pays to plan ahead. It wasn't raining when Noah built the ark."

Incidentally, what I am doing right now in my career and life is plan B. And I'm loving it. Because I'm driving this mother-ship and I'm the daddy of my ambition.

just do something!

OK now. Just settle back further into your chair. Look upward and focus on your 'what ifs'. Let your mind wander. Let it roam free. Be absurd. Think about worst case and best case scenarios. Jot them all down. What if what if what if what if...

Now, start thinking about what your plan B, C or D could be... just in case. It has to be equally compelling, if not more exciting than plan A. After all, it could become your reality! What would you consider doing with your career and life as an alternative to the path you're already on?

Write them all down. Keep your jottings in a safe place. You may need to return to them some day...

BHAGs in a row

I read something many years ago. I can't remember where but the guru was talking about BHAGS – Big Hairy Audacious Goals. I can remember thinking at the time 'I like the sound of that'.

My understanding from previous careers and ventures was that goals are simply one sentence mission statements. They can be personal and/or business orientated and help promote long-term vision.

So, I created some SMART (Specific, Measurable, Attainable, Realistic and Time-targeted) short term goals and some BHAGs to help devise my mission and vision, as knowing exactly what I wanted to achieve made it clear what I needed to concentrate and improve on during my journey.

For example, one of my goals was to pass the LPC without any re-sits (and the PSC). Another was to be offered a position at the end of my training contract. One of my BHAGs was to develop a niche entrepreneur offering and a place for it on the law firm's website (tick).

just do something!

Reflect now and jot down your short term goals and BHAGs. Be creative. Be bold. But make them SMART; this way you're more likely to achieve them and feel great about yourself! It will inspire and motivate you to stretch yourself further and to set yourself new goals each time you achieve the previous one.

mission possible

In a standard format, a mission statement should define the fundamental purpose of an enterprise, succinctly describing why it exists, what it does to achieve its vision and how it's going to get to the vision destination.

It ought to also tell you the fundamental purpose of the enterprise, define the customer and the critical processes and inform you of the desired level of performance.[23]

Accordingly, my mission statement was to be a statement which captured my values, priorities, interests and desires, to form a focus for my career and life development.

Having banged out a few short term goals and BHAGs I then drew up a mission statement... a blueprint for my life's work. In other words, what I wanted out of my professional life, what I believed was possible and how I was going to get there.

My mission: To bring lawyers and entrepreneurs together in a positive way; to help bridge the gap between the legal world and the business world; to aid understanding and build positive long term relationships between both parties; and to provide cost effective, time effective and time efficient legal advice which creates value for both myself and my client.

vision laughable

In a standard format, a vision ought to define the desired or intended future state of an organisation in terms of its fundamental objective and/or strategic direction. It ought to describe why it is important to achieve the mission and define the purpose or broader goal for being in existence.

Apparently, the difference between a mission statement and a vision statement is the vision must cover what you expect your professional life to look like in the immediate future (the short term end result; a snapshot of where and how you see yourself in the next five years), whereas a mission statement covers what you want out of your entire professional life.[24] In essence, the vision is about the destination. The *where* you are going.

Carl Jung said: "Your vision will become clear only when you look into your heart. Who looks outside, dreams. Who looks inside, awakens." Wide awake, I then set about creating a strategic vision for my future with a Yiddish expression foremost in my mind: "Man plans, and God laughs."

My vision: To help entrepreneurs succeed in business by providing extraordinary legal advice and business support by being an entrepreneurial lawyer. I wanted to be bold so I made my vision laughable. I also used my imagination, not a map.

I imagined being an entrepreneurial lawyer. And I became it.

just do something!

Take a moment to pause and reflect on what I have just shared with you. Then, have a go at writing your very own mission statement and vision.

Make your mission possible, but your vision laughable. It will spur you onward and upward!

ethicability unleashed

ethicability – what's all that about?

I would like to turn now to the subject of ethicability, as my goals, mission and vision were (and are) influenced and governed by my values, beliefs and principles – ethics.

Roger Steare in his flagship book, *Ethicability*,[25] defines 'ethics' as "moral principles that guide our behaviour, together with legal rights and duties that are acceptable in a particular society."

Roger focuses on the subject of re-moralising de-moralised corporations. I reckon it's particularly befitting and timely in relation to law firms, n'est ce pas? I actually believe that if you're going to set about achieving what Roger suggests, then this starts with re-moralising de-moralised individual lawyers/workers, such as you and me.

We are, after all, the heart of the corporation. Right?

Great leaders in great companies always put their people first. Right?

And if you are to become a great leader of your own mother-ship then you must put your clients first. Right?

conflicts of DIP

I loathe greed, fear and egotism. It's probably why I struggled in an established traditional law firm.

Roger Steare hits the nail on the head in his statement: "people think that greed, fear and ego are the drivers for adult behaviour. They are NOT." I agree. Wholeheartedly. My soul tells me so.

Roger also looks at ethics as a way of resolving personal 'conflicts of desire', organisational 'conflicts of interest' and 'conflicts of principle' when values collide. For example there may be a conflict between company values and your own personal values. I experienced this. I have no doubt you will (and possibly already do) too.

It is inevitable that we must also acknowledge that some conflicts are impossible to resolve therefore we must rely on emotional intelligence to inevitably kick in.

deciding what's right

When you get down to the nuts and bolts of Roger Steare's ethicability philosophy, it's all about 'how do we begin to make the right decision?' He suggests we ask ourselves:

- What are the Rules?
- Are we acting with Integrity?
- Who is this Good for?
- Who could we Harm?
- What's the Truth?

As I brought my personal values into my work place I had to try to align them to avoid conflict wherever possible and decide what was right in the circumstances.

just do something!

Take a moment now to pause and reflect on the potential and real conflicts you are experiencing, or may experience. Jot them down.

Then, consider what the 'right decision(s)' would be for YOU when conflict arises by addressing the five key questions above which Roger Steare asks us to consider. Again, jot them down for present and future reference.

the ME Code of Conduct

In essence, our values are learned and honed from our continual experiences and education, and then developed, reinforced and applied in our Big Rock roles and activities.

My values have certainly been shaped in this way and play a key part in how I perform and conduct myself (whatever I'm up to in work or leisure). They drive my personal belief-system and priorities and provide the framework in which I make decisions – little ones and even mega life changing ones.

My beliefs are those I share with those whom I interact with in my life. So, here you go. Let's start with what I don't believe...

I don't believe

- 'Just sit there and do as you're told' is the way to go if you're going to help bring about positive change, for yourself and/or others.
- I should stick within a paradigm or belief system that says there is only one way (or a few ways) to do things (btw, neither does Bob Burg – his comment duly noted, bought into by me and shared here with you).
- I should hold on to a belief or value if I have grown and experienced something which makes me change my mind.
- In judging people or people judging me. Ultimately 'we are who we are' and who really has the right to say 'this is right' and 'this is wrong'. Remember, different cultures and/or environments have different rules and laws, whether we're

talking about people cultures, company cultures or country cultures. Take monogamy and polygamy, for example. Enough said.
- I should force my morals, values, beliefs on others.
- I should stick my head in the sand when all around me is going to rats.
- In controlling or manipulating people (or that I should be controlled or manipulated).
- In comprise if it makes me unhappy; if I'm unhappy then I will make everyone else as miserable as hell and cause pain where none was intended. I'm a lover, not a misery-guts. Life *really really really* is too short.

I do believe
- In compromise when both parties are happy with the outcome.
- In adding value to people's lives whenever and wherever possible – whether emotionally, spiritually, mentally or physically.
- In adding value in my working life, be it for the firm/company for whom I work (as an entity).
- In innovation.
- In having an open mind.
- In change for the better.
- In my moral internal compass guiding me (albeit N & S do flip sometimes! I'm human).
- There is a 'right' and 'wrong' for each of us. For example, how we live our lives, who with, how we conduct ourselves at work and leisure (in private and public). You just know what feels right.
- In making soulful choices.
- In bringing a smile to someone's face at least once every day.
- In speaking and thinking from my heart and feeling with my mind.
- The right words spoken can be forever little drops of wisdom making rain shine.
- A positive mindset can overcome all challenges.
- Positivity breeds energy, motivation and passion.
- In focusing on giving joy rather than pain.
- In focusing on the positive, not the negative.
- In looking for better ways.
- Respect ought to be freely given, not earned.
- Loyalty ought to be freely given, not earned.
- In self reliance.
- In collaborative efforts.
- In conducting myself in a way that I can sleep peacefully at night.
- In paradigm shifts of necessity.
- In spontaneity.
- In sharing knowledge wholeheartedly and thoughtfully.
- In giving unreservedly (in whatever form).
- When I 'imagine' it can cause my 'then' and future reality.
- My soul guides my mind and my gut.
- In having an open and receptive mind, heart and spirit.
- Being controlling stifles progress, genius and spiritual growth.
- In being Light Of Foot (pardon the pun – Chrissie Lightfoot), meaning ready to meet new challenges, change direction, take risks.
- I will learn something new every day.
- I will experience something new every day.
- I will make each day count.
- I will wander along many paths in my lifetime (professionally and personally).
- I will come to many crossroads in my life.
- I have strength of mind and heart to deal with anything life throws at me.
- In aiming to be a solutions provider rather than problem creator.

- In being nice.
- In letting go (professionally and personally).
- I should spread my wings despite whatever opposition may come from it.
- In combining personal humility with intense resolve, thereby preserving core values to stimulate progress.
- In free will.
- In mankind.
- In myself.
- In living life Full On:
  - ☐ Study hard;
  - ☐ Work hard;
  - ☐ Play hard;
  - ☐ Train (exercise) hard;
  - ☐ Love hard; and
  - ☐ Rest hard.

  'Hard' = Full On. Giving it my all.

And... finally, but fundamentally... I am a woman first (a human being) and then I am an Entrepreneur Lawyer, of the Naked Lawyer kind.

For me, no matter what I do, it's either 'Full On' or 'Full Off'. There is no in-between. After all, what's the point of doing something half hearted, half mindful or half speed? It's never my best shot if I do... so why do it at all if I'm not prepared to put maximum effort into it to get the maximum benefit in return?

I reckon my mum has a lot to answer for with regard to my approach to life, because from an early age, usually in relation to scolding me when I made an absolute sow's ear out of a pocket money 'job', she used to say to me, "Chrissie, if you're going to do something, then do it well, or don't bother doing it at all."

She had a point. And kept 'my' pocket money. I learned fast.

Bottom line, I never really feel truly satisfied and fulfilled unless I know I've given something my all. Oh... and I've found that it's spunk and an enlivening personality that scores me big points throughout life, so I'm no longer afraid of sticking my neck out and letting my true self shine.

Does any of this resonate with you?

just do something!

Ask yourself the following:

- What are my values?
- What do I truly value?
- What do I truly believe?
- What's my belief system?

Now list all your answers. Keep them safe. Come back and check on these from time to time when you experience challenges in both your working and leisure life. You will certainly need to refer to them when you tackle Volumes 3 and 4.

c-c-c-courage

My life philosophy was born out of the *Wizard Of Oz* movie in the characters of the scare-crow, tin-man and lion. That is, in order to live life to the full I must live it with courage (lion), heart (tin man) and a brain (scare-crow).

Since my teens I can still hear the words that used to echo through the household – "stand by the courage of your conviction" – a favourite growl (and life lesson) by my father when challenging me – for which I am eternally grateful. As I have moved on in life no matter where I am in the world these are the words which seem to whisper to me when carried in the wind. They give me strength... and courage. I cling to them when I'm in the firing line dodging bullets from demons, imaginary ones and at times living breathing power monger control freak ones, that delight in making me question my own sanity, decisions, direction and 'knowing'.

I also believe that because I embrace courage, have heart and engage brain, that I am able to go about my life with confidence and to be an effective rainmaker. In the words of Zig Ziglar: "Confidence is going after Moby Dick in a rowing boat, and taking the tartare sauce with you!" Anyone got some tartare sauce?

To be an extraordinary rainmaker amongst a tribe of grinder's monkeys – "all serious daring starts from within"[26] – I had to have bold courage, stalwart belief, unwavering confidence and a finely tuned brain engaged in order to perform, deliver and follow on. Not unlike John Wayne, my take on it all was: "courage is being scared to death, but saddling up anyway."

I never doubted myself or the decisions I made in relation to where, what, when, why or how I went about rainmaking whilst a trainee solicitor in spite of the cold-shouldering from colleagues, for my attitude was simply "I'd rather be a lion for one day than a sheep for a thousand" (old proverb).

just do something!

Ask yourself: 'am I confident to stand by the courage of my conviction and take my life in the direction I truly desire?' Answer this honestly. If your answer is 'no' then you need to muster up some courage. Work on it! Take heart and engage brain!

Write your thoughts down. Return to these jottings with a view to striking out the barriers as we work through *the naked lawyer*.

If 'yes'... then what's stopping you from doing so right now?

rip – 'no regrets. I lived life full on!'

You may be questioning why 'RIP' in the titles and headings within the naked lawyer. Let me help you understand... In order to begin your journey I believe you must start with the end in mind. I did. And do.

Let me draw your attention again to the guru Tom Peters who in Trends wrote the following:[27]

"The moral of my story – the story of What's Essential about the present moment in business – comes in the form of a tombstone. It's a tombstone that bears the epitaph that I most hope to avoid.

"To wit: Thomas J. Peters, 1942-whenever, he would have done some really good stuff... but his boss wouldn't let him...

"Meanwhile, I know exactly how I do want my tombstone to read:

"... He was a player!"

His message is simply (not ad verbatim): 'don't sit on the sidelines, get off the sidelines and be a player, not because it's optional but because it's essential' in these challenging times.

I live my life, both professional and personal, 'Full On' with the end in mind so that come the day when I'm pushing up daisies, I won't have to come back and haunt my tomb scriber. I'd like to be content with what my epitaph shall read. What could your epitaph honestly read, now or perhaps in the future? Have you thought about your epitaph yet?

I have. Not only because of the Tom Peters tombstone story but also someone said to me a while ago, "what we fear is not suffering or even death. What we fear is that we have wasted life."

It resonated with me. Along with Jack London's mantras:[28] "The function of man is to live, not to exist" and "I would rather be ashes than dust! I would rather that my spark should burn out in a brilliant blaze than it should be stifled by dry rot."

I thought about my epitaph many years ago when I started along my journey and since taking on board the thoughts, teachings and wisdom of the gurus and geniuses past and present. My epitaph will read: "No Regrets. I Lived Life Full On!"

However, I am toying with an alternative inscription which is influenced by the actor Colin Firth's delightful line spoken in his role in the movie *Mamma Mia*: "Where's your spontaneity?"

We'll see...

just do something!

Think about what your epitaph is likely to read if your last day on this planet was today. Are you happy with it? If not, what would you rather it read?

Pause. Reflect. Search your soul. Now write the epitaph you would love to be associated with. From this day forward go and truly *live it*!

weird mindset, wicked attitude

positively mind-blowing

I came across Jack Black in 2000 when I was working in the leisure industry. I don't mean the now movie star Jack Black (so funny), I mean the then motivational guru and creator of *MindStore*.[29]

The Financial Times gave Jack's *MindStore System for Life* a really powerful write up at the time: "Tired? Stressed? Feeling negative about your job? Only capable of 'not bad' when asked about your health? What you need is a dose of Jack Black." I can remember thinking 'Bring it on. Give me some of that!'

When I attended Jack's conference, amongst lots of other really good stuff, he had this to say (from my recollection, not ad verbatim):

"You will be a great leader (akin to being a great leader of my own mother-ship) if you have:

1. Oomph – bags of energy
2. A Positive Attitude – passionate self-belief
3. A Futurist mindset – goal, mission and vision
4. L&R Brainpower – a magical way of utilising both the left and right side of the brain where L = logic, knowledge, teaching; R = imagination, expansion, creativity.

and the degree and application to initiate and embrace innovation and change."

We'll look at this in more detail in Volume 10: continual stimulation.

Having experienced something positively mind-blowing, from that day forward my whole way of thinking, feeling and doing ramped up ten notches. I came away from the conference a changed woman.

Why? Because I wanted a fulfilling life. How did I change? I switched my mindset. I now focus on the positive. Every time on everything... for the better. Every day I tell myself 'more energy', 'more giving', 'more fun', 'more belief', 'more goals', 'more mission', 'more vision', 'more imagination', 'more creativity', 'more choice', 'more change'.

Jack's MindStore System truly was (and is) a system for life which touched me to my core. I place a large part of my rainmaking success and achievements whilst working in the leisure industry at the time, and latterly when I applied it in the legal profession (and now) down to my MindStore epiphany.

Putting this in context I reckon that traditionally we lawyers and our law firms have been notorious in focusing on using the left side of the brain (logic, knowledge, teaching) as it's where we feel most comfortable and are no doubt naturally wired for our roles.

However, to be a successful 'Tomorrow's Lawyer' we're going to have to work on using the right side of our brains more, because success in marketing, branding and selling ourselves in a bid to be totally client-centric (our ability to attract and retain a client) will be determined by our ability to be imaginative, creative and expansive in the quality of our thinking and delivery of the same.

Ultimately, the secret as to what makes rainmakers so successful is the fact that they have a different mindset to the grinder's monkey. If you don't want to be (or remain) a grinder's monkey my point is simply that you can switch your mindset... if you want to. That is, *only* if you are in control of your mother-ship and you're the daddy of your ambition.

Cole Silver believes that the following are typical characteristics found in a person with a rainmaking mindset:

- They are enthusiastic and see opportunity everywhere;
- They know what they want and are committed to getting it;
- They believe it is possible to achieve what they want;
- They face their fears and move through them;
- They believe in their dreams and expect to get what they want;
- They learn from their mistakes and are abundant in their thinking;
- They are comfortable with letting the world know who they are;
- They feel that building a 'book' is the most important activity they're engaged in; and
- They focus on the client's needs and in building deep relationships.

People who know me would probably say that I have a rainmaking mindset (I tick the boxes in relation to all of the above characteristics).

Do you? If not, you can. It's within your control. It's within your mindset. Think extraordinary lover. Think extraordinary sex!

Putting this in context, when I go about my rainmaking activity I put myself in the shoes of my potential client. I wonder 'What are they thinking and feeling?' 'What do they need, want or desire?' 'How would I like to be treated?' 'What would I like to see happen?' I try to see the world as they see it. I try to see the problem as they see it and then go about resolving it in a way that gets the solution they were looking for, not what I thought they were looking for because I hadn't bothered to take the time to ask them and understand them fully.

That is, the trick is to stand in their shoes and *feel* their fear, their pain, their pockets (how short or deep) and to try and understand what *value* means to them. You have to take the focus totally off yourself and place it entirely on the receiver.

Genuinely, I want to help, educate, inform and give to them without expecting anything at all in return. *Genuinely*, I am *curious* about them and their business.

Curiosity is something we are naturally born with or perhaps something we must actively learn and practise if we wish to market, brand, sell and grow successfully because it's about being genuinely interested in our receivers.

I feel blessed that I was born with a curious and active mind. Even more blessed that I had understanding parents who were very patient and tolerant of my curious nature and positively encouraged and nurtured it. I was forever asking 'why', always searching, always exploring, always probing.

To this day my mother delights in reminding me of an episode when I was a little girl. Apparently, one day when I was curious as to the funny noises that were emanating from my parents bedroom, I threw their door wide open, strutted in, hands on hips, screwed up nose on face and exclaimed, "What are you two doing wobbling around like a big wobbly jelly!" Go figure what they were up to. "Out of the mouths of babes," Mum recants. Granted, I was only three years old. But, such was the hilarity of the event that a sibling was not conceived that day. It was a positively mind-blowing experience... for all concerned.

Oh... and have you ever heard the saying 'curiosity killed the cat'? If so, you may wish to question it. I do. I challenge it simply because I've also heard the saying that 'a cat has nine lives'. If I was a cat I reckon I probably would have had four by now.

I'll leave you to think on that for a wee while.

just do something!

I'd like you to look again at Cole Silver's list of typical characteristics found in a person with a rainmaking mindset. Is this you?

Honestly, 'yes' or 'no'?

If 'no', I'd like you to try and look at the positive in everything rather than the negative from now on. For example, the champagne bottle is half full rather than half empty kind of thing.

You need to work on switching your mindset. I can't do this for you. *Only you can do this.*

Pick me up again when you're ready...

my attitude SUUUCKS

Once I had both feet firmly in the legal profession, I quickly realised that to be a successful rainmaker in law law land I was going to have to have the right attitude.

Fortunately, as a result of my mind-blowing MindStore mindset epiphany a decade ago and subsequent application of a positive mindset thereafter my attitude was (and is) simply 'I am an entrepreneurial lawyer', not 'one day I will be an entrepreneurial lawyer'.

I would relax and imagine the future and I would see myself in my mind's eye being a successful entrepreneurial lawyer. My personal brand of Chrissie 'The Entrepreneur Lawyer' was a natural progression of my vision. We'll look at developing your personal brand in detail in Volume 4: getting under your skin.

In Jack Black's terms: I created a future history. I had envisaged my future in such detail that I had already created a history. I kind of tricked my sub-conscious into thinking I could achieve my dreams. In the genius wise words of Albert Einstein: "Imagination is more important than knowledge. Knowledge is limited. Imagination encircles the world." And I created my own attitude matrix...

My attitude positively SUUUCKS. It was and shall forever remain:

- Strategic – it is strategically positioned and directed;
- Unadulterated – passionate;
- Unconditional – in giving;
- Unwavering – in self-belief;
- Committed – to continual learning and curiosity;
- Kick-Ass – dynamic and pro-active; and
- Self-Assured – to achieve.

Why? Because I could (and can) see that if I waited (or wait) for things to happen in little law law land (and my life in general) I would simply get stuck. In Cole Silver's words:

> *"We wait for the right moment or the grand opportunity. We wait for the right job, partner position or the right case. In truth, waiting simply traps us and keeps us stuck."*[30]

I wasn't going to feel trapped or stuck. Ultimately I had learned to listen to my gut from an early age (reading Jack Welch, *Straight From The Gut*[31]) and due to 'experiencing' life by living it Full On. And my gut told me that to wait would be fatal for my future.

Inevitably, due to my attitude, people were (and are) either drawn to me or repelled because of how I made (and make) them feel. If I repel them, then that's OK. It's right. It's fitting. For them, and me. I have come to realise and accept that not everyone is going to like me... before I even open my mouth sometimes. I get over it. Move on.

Once I do open my mouth, and my attitude, values, beliefs, ME Code of Conduct, interests, emotional intelligence, etc. are 'out there', if they didn't hate me before then they may positively detest me from then on because I stand by the courage of my convictions. But that's OK. I get over it. No worries. Move on.

For I focus on those colleagues, referrers and clients who are drawn to me because they do 'get' me due to our shared 'best fit' synergies. And I can help them most. Because, in the words of actor Jack Nicholson in the movie *As Good As It Gets*, "they make me want to be a better man." Well, woman. You know what I mean. We'll look at referrers in Volume 5: raving referral lobsters rule.

If I repelled colleagues it tended to be because I had an attitude which smacked of irreverence at times due to the stultifying inertia of law law land; not, I hasten to add, an irreverence to my colleagues' technical legal nous and the practising of law in general, as I have every respect and deep admiration for them and the profession at large, for obvious reasons.

My attitude is my way of sorting out a natural 'best fit' so that I can serve the receiver better. My aim is to attract colleagues and clients who share similar interests, philosophies, behaviours, values, beliefs, attitudes, etc. That way we naturally gravitate towards each other and quickly build a relationship... and a more solid, mutually beneficial and giving one, at that.

It is true that there is someone for everyone. Whether in relation to a relationship with a colleague, client or lover. And that's why it's OK to be your authentic self as you will naturally attract those 'best fit' people into your life. The not so 'best fit' will be attracted to other people and they will be served by them instead. But that's OK because you can't win 'em all. You won't. Accept it. Move on.

Be comfortable in strategically positioning yourself by having a SUUUCKS attitude to win the ones who want to be won by you. Forget about the rest. Focus on the 'best fit' THEM.

just do something!

Just relax and let your mind wander. Try and imagine seeing yourself in your mind's eye as a successful 'whatever'. Write the image down. Describe it. Describe the feeling.

Then, look again at what SUUUCKS means. Can you honestly say that your attitude truly SUUUCKS? Now, apply your positive mindset, until it does!

Practise. Practise. Practise. And then practise some more...

motiv8tion

In general we are motivated to work by a combination of the following eight reasons:

- Financial;
- Recognition and praise;
- Responsibility;
- Relationship with manager;
- Promotion;

- Achievement on the job;
- Job content; and
- Co-operation with others.

Things that float your boat, by which I mean feed you, will include some or all of the above eight reasons. I believe 'job content' embraces the things which interest you element.

One of the tests I carried out on myself was to ask 'What motivates me?' Previously, I mentioned in the 'what gets my Big rocks off?' section that if you're constantly dealing with things which feed you, then self-motivation for lawyering, rainmaking and delivering extraordinary customer service inevitably takes care of itself.

A recurring theme in my personal and professional development throughout my life's journey is what Maslow's hierarchy of needs identifies as the 'pursuit of self-actualisation' i.e. personal growth, fulfilment, creativity, challenge, truth, meaning, justice and wisdom. I identified that what motivates me most is my striving for this higher need by pursuing my interests because as for most people in the western world physiological needs, safety, love and esteem have been pretty much taken care of.

just do something!

So, ask yourself: 'what motivates me?' Look again at the eight motivational elements. Which leap out at you? And, are you achieving them? Are you doing the things which feed you? If not, what are you going to do about it?

Answer: start the process to continually do and achieve the things that get your Big Rocks off!

a PEE Poor Work Ethic?

If you intend to be a lawyer (or already are a lawyer) then it's inevitable in this demanding profession and industry that you subscribe to some form of work ethic.

Where you are on the PEE Poor Work Ethic continuum (zero to ten, where zero is 'Don't bother getting out of bed on a morning' and ten is 'What work/leisure divide? Work rocks!') is determined by your own thinking, feeling and doing. Permit me to explain...

First off, let's define 'Work Ethic'. Wikipedia, my favourite online 'authoritative' (moot) resource devised by real people, has this to say:

"It's a set of values based on hard work and diligence. It is also the moral benefit of work and its ability to enhance character. Slacker and hippie cultures have challenged these values and criticised the work ethic concept characterising them as submissive to authority and convention and not valuable in and of themselves, but only if it brings a positive result. Others have said that it is more important to work smart than to work hard."[32]

And let's understand what I mean by PEE. PEE = Passionate, Enthusiastic, Energetic.

At the outset of my journey to become a lawyer, I knew that law would involve hard work. But it wasn't until I was integrally involved in the heart of the process that it dawned on me that I had no real appreciation for how hard the hard work really was. This is the difference between theory and practice. As with lots of things you can't know what it is like until you do it. It's like sex.

As a teenager I used to dream about having sex. Part of growing up and hormones ruling the brain I suspect. But this is normal stuff. Right? Had nothing to do with my experience and 'incident' at three years old. Right? But, if I'm honest, I couldn't experience the 'feeling of sex' in my dream state (theory) until I'd experienced sex for real for my first time in my physical awake state (practice). Do you get my point? You can't dream what actual sex is like until you've done it. Much like you won't know what it's like to be a lawyer until you are actually lawyering for the first time. Btw – I'm not talking about simulated sex here. But let's not go there!

I'll leave you to think on that for a moment. Pick me up again when you're ready...

Fortuitously, before getting involved in law, I came from a background of very hard work, both in working in the leisure industry and working in my own businesses (consulting and new media/internet). Indeed when I started in law I transferred the work ethic that had brought me successes to my legal involvements.

Law involves phenomenally hard work – make absolutely no mistake about it – not just in terms of education and training, but in terms of managing and organising one's life to do the training and all of the tasks associated with lawyering at a level of excellence that is expected and required. So, whether you're about to enter the law or are firmly entrenched in it, where do you see yourself on the PEE Poor Work Ethic continuum?

As an example, I would rate myself as having a PEE Poor Work Ethic factor nine. Unwavering. Why am I unwaveringly confident to say this? Because I:

1. Subscribe to (and practise) the Full On work ethic.
2. Am also a great believer in the AND rather than the OR so I believe in working hard AND smart. On average I work 14 hours a day six or seven days a week doing the things I love; there is no work/leisure divide – it's a lifestyle.
3. Was (and remain) driven by a cause... a purpose.
4. Have a dream, a mission and a vision.
5. Have the right mindset and attitude.
6. Know what motivates me.
7. Have genuine *passion, enthusiasm* and *energy* because I'm getting my Big Rocks off being my authentic self...

I wouldn't say that I'm a ten (that's a privilege for the likes of Bo Derek) because I also subscribe to the belief that there is always room for *more*, in the form of continual improvement, more passion, more enthusiasm and more energy, etc. Maybe when I attain my big whopper dream I'll be a slacker, or hippie. Who knows.

Btw, if your PEE Poor Work Ethic is *zero* you're probably a slacker (not my words, Wikipedia's – sue them). In which case you will not make it as a lawyer. Fact. Even if your PEE Poor Work Ethic is one to four, you probably won't make it as a lawyer, and definitely *not* as a rainmaker lawyer. Fact.

So, you have a choice. My recommendation, for what it's worth, if your PEE is zero to four then either go do something else, right now, before your epitaph reads 'Regrets. I had a few', or, change your mindset, and start putting some of this Naked Lawyer stuff into action.

If your PEE is four, I suspect you could go either way. Lawyer, non-lawyer. Toss a coin. Effectively you're Jo Average Lawyer, aka, monkey grinder lawyer at the bottom of the pickings (last in line for banana bounty).

Turning to the positive now and focusing on the main thrust of *the naked lawyer* in how to market, brand and sell YOU, if you're aiming to be a rainmaker lawyer then you've got to be at least a six on the PEE Poor Work Ethic continuum.

passion

You're probably thinking 'how the heck can this daft Naked Lawyer woman possibly be talking about being passionate about "law"? It's boring stuff.' Nuts, I know. But I am, passionate that is, not nuts – at least I don't think so.

Don't get me wrong, I'm *not* passionate about the deadwood, deadbeat hum-drum dusty tomes in law school and law firm libraries. You know, the printed word as sections, terms, conditions, articles, schedules, blah blah blah. I simply can't get excited about that. I have a life. A Full On life.

I am passionate about the application of it in how it is of real value and help to the client as a solution to their problem. And I am passionate about looking after my clients, getting more clients, namely, helping as many entrepreneurs as possible and delivering extraordinary customer service. That is, I am passionate about my dream, goals, mission and vision.

As Cole Silver says:

"If you're passionate about what you do, it will be easier to market yourself. You just can't fake that kind of passion. If you're not really excited about your practice, maybe you need to enter a new area of law or re-evaluate your legal career altogether."[33]

See, it's not just me who holds this view. Cole's been a very successful practising attorney and rainmaker lawyer for nigh on three decades.

There is no substitute for hard-work, dedication and wearing your heart on your sleeve, genuinely. Ask yourself: 'Am I passionate about what I'm doing?'

If the answer is 'no' then you must find your passion. If you had it, but lost it, then perhaps you may need to consider going and doing something else with your life. Go join the slackers perhaps. For in the words of Jack Black: "If you lose your passion and vision you lose everything."

I agree. It happened to me. It's why my plan A became plan B.

enthusiasm

Do you crackle? You're probably thinking 'now what's she on about?' Well, when you've got the right PEE Poor Work Ethic you will note people commenting 'Gosh. My dear, you're positively glowing!'... And that's without getting pregnant; lady lawyer reader I'm sure you'll 'get' this.

As I am excited about my dream, goals, mission and vision it is inevitable that I love what I do. I go about my work with zeal. I'm eager to get on. I am happy. And that breeds enthusiasm. Period. Quoting the esteemed Conrad Hilton: "Enthusiasm is a vital element toward the individual success of every man or woman."[34]

If you are enthusiastic you will positively crackle. If you crackle, you will spark your receiver. Why is enthusiasm important? In a nutshell, enthusiasm sells. Enthusiastic happy me = happy client = happy boss = happy firm. Everyone's happy.

Btw – don't rely on your boss or 'the firm' making you enthusiastic or happy. You have to create that from within yourself, at your core, by following the tips here in the naked lawyer even. And then you can externalise it on your client.

And remember, "Nothing great was ever achieved without enthusiasm" – Ralph Waldo Emerson.

energy

I tend to find that because I am motivated, happy, enthusiastic, have a dream, mission, vision and positive mindset, I actually have an abundant supply of energy to carry out my work and leisure life. My dreams and vision stir up latent energy and release all the required willpower and motivation to continually go forth, deliver and follow on.

The trick is to:

1. Cultivate your energy;
2. Manage your energy; and
3. Focus your energy on positive stuff.

As a lawyer it is inevitable that you will need a lot of energy; the working days are long and the pressures on the job intense.

Cultivating energy comes from your mind, heart and physical state. That is, your mindset and attitude (for example, thinking 'more energy', 'more creativity'), your passion (beliefs, values, interests, dreams, mission, vision) and eating, sleeping, exercising right (being healthy and fit so that you can operate at a high level). I hope I've helped you deal with cultivating energy at least a little due to the content in this Volume 2 as I've touched on most things save for how to eat, sleep and exercise right. I think I'll leave that for you to figure out; it's probably none of my business!

However, perhaps I could help by writing more Naked Lawyer books such as the *naked lawyer: Sleeping Patterns, the naked lawyer: Eat My Dictaphone* and *the naked lawyer: Fit For Purpose*. Just kidding ... or am I?

Managing energy is different. It's inevitable that as a lawyer you will be stressed. Stress saps energy as well as spurring it. You will both suffer and benefit from stress during your career. I know. I did. And everyone I worked with said they did and still do too.

The workload and pressure can be overwhelming at times as you're trying to juggle multiple tasks, people (clients and supervisors) and demands, which are usually time and money sensitive, at work, whilst attempting to balance your 'out of work' time intensive commitments (which can be both demanding as well as pleasurable) such as your other Big Rocks, for example continuing education, family, significant other, the day to day living kind of stuff, etc.

Too much stress is obviously not a good thing when you're trying to 'fit everything in' as it usually manifests itself in the form of headaches, over-tiredness, insomnia, broken relationships and mistakes (usually costly – for you, the client and ultimately the firm) which adds up to unhappy lawyer, unhappy client, unhappy firm. Prolonged periods of stress may result in total disengagement and lack of productivity by you and eventual departure from the firm and/or the profession; with or without the client.

I actually believe that stress can be good for you if managed and harnessed properly. If you're the kind of lawyer who thrives on stress to help keep you motivated in achieving the outcomes you desire, it can manifest itself as energy, enthusiasm and passion. Ironically, you're kind of happy because you're busy and 'on the go', progressing, developing, growing, solving problems, being helpful and of value (to both clients and supervisors).

Clients recognise your positive, happy aura and can see that you genuinely love what you do and become curious as to why. The relationship that you build with the client is therefore much stronger as the amount of 'touch' communication naturally increases. Accordingly the client is happy because when you communicate with them they can probably hear your smile down the phone; they are constantly 'in the know' and can see that you are genuinely interested in them and are working productively on their matter with a positive mindset.

When I was working at the law firm I used to go for a run during my lunch break to help manage the stress and my energy levels. It was a kind of 'second wind' and 'pick me up' to a) clear my head so that I could 'think straight' – I usually a) come up with great ideas and solutions whilst running, b) de-stress and c) get the oxygen flowing to ignite my brain and limbs again for the rest of the working day. Now, I'm not suggesting for one second that you do likewise. Donning Nike shoes, shorts and vest and trotting out like Roger Bannister over your lunch break may not be practical, or simply the thought of it may make you cringe. That's OK. But you will benefit from finding your 'something' which helps you de-stress and manage your energy during the day.

Focusing energy is different again. In case you hadn't realised by now I am a great believer in focusing on the positive in all things. By 'things' I mean 'things' and 'people'. Because of this belief and attitude I do not waste my time on negative things or negative people; tasks, colleagues or clients. I avoid them wherever and whenever possible. Why? And, how?

Why – because they take my wind. Those of you who watch(ed) the sitcom *Friends* will understand where I'm coming from here. They sap me of my positive energy and I feel drained when in their company. I'm sure you will have experienced this. Have you ever been in a conversation or a meeting when it's been such hard work with the other person that you've come away feeling like you've just gone ten rounds with Mike Tyson? Enough said. Would you choose to go back again? Enough said.

How – I focus on the positive people who will welcome more of my positive energy and reciprocate with more positive energy. Accordingly, we float each other's boat. We feed each other.

Simply put, focus on doing the stuff you love with the people you love. Those who 'get' you; colleagues, referrers and clients.

just do something!

So, again, where would you rate yourself on the PEE Poor Work Ethic continuum? Pause. Reflect. Take stock. Be honest. The number you come up with ought to determine what your next move should be. OK then. Let's crank up the gears.

If you haven't done the 'just do something!' practical suggestions where prompted so far, I reckon it's time for you to put some of this Naked Lawyer stuff into action for yourself.

Do you fancy a little 'after working hours' activity? If so, come and join me in some...

after dark activity
myths and predictions on lawyering

A little food for thought...

Which of the statements in Table 1 overleaf do you reckon are myths and which predictions? It's for you to decide. Of course you can substitute 'lawyering' with whatever your field is...

naked lawyer activity – a study worth casing

The Chrissie Lightfoot Naked Lawyer Activity – aged 39 going on 360...

During summer 2008 I worked through the ROAR steps. At this point in time I had completed two years of my training contract in a law firm working full-time – 18 months in the corporate law department and six months in the IP/Commercial law department – whilst doing my LPC part-time throughout that period. It was just before the recession hit in autumn 2008. Needless to say I was a very busy little Naked Lawyer in law law land.

Then	Now	Ahead
All lawyers are not equal	All lawyers are people therefore we are equal	Cyborg living
Champagne lifestyle	It's a living (moot)	Full On living
Traditional lawyering gravy train	Hit the buffers	Station closed
Partners get the work in	I get the work in	Collaborators get the work in
Ego massaging by and for partners	Skills massaging by and for all	Empathy massaging of client
Earn loads 'a' money	Only the Magic Circle lawyers do	Only Super Lawyers will
Elitist profession	Legal profession	Collaborative business essential
Lawyers know everything	Lawyers know law	Lawyers know people, business and law
Understand law	Understand law and regulation	Understand people, business, machines, law
Industrial Age	People Age and Digital Age	Singularity Age
Luddite	Change masters by default	Change masters by choice
The Firm	The Global Firm	The Universal Individual
Firm cosseting	Self reliance by all	Collaboration by all

Table 1: Then, now and ahead – Myths and predictions

2006-08 was an extremely busy period. It wasn't unusual for me to work 12-16 hours a day at the office and then do LPC study on an evening and every weekend. So, after I finished the LPC in July and August 2008 (I now had 'leisure' time due to the hole left from 'no more studying – woo-hoo') I set about working through what is now Volume 2 (ROAR steps!) of *the naked lawyer* and I started to create my FMSP together with what is now Volumes 3 and 4 of *the naked lawyer*. In September 2008 I began to put into action Volumes 1-4 through what is now Volumes 5-12 of *the naked lawyer*.

As to what I did, and for a real live case study, simply read *the naked lawyer* Volume 2 again. You can relive my activity by taking yourself through the same process.

Let me help you. Here's a condensed version of the key activities and exercises you may wish to carry out...

ROAR steps!

Take time out now to do the following steps. It may take you a few hours, a few days, a few weeks or a few months even. Btw – if you haven't done it within a year you need to get some help. Seriously. Because you will need all these little building blocks in place to move forward successfully.

The great news, I can help you. Or I will know someone who can.

- **Step 1:** Get reading – the gurus, on business, people, soft skills stuff and your interests.
- **Step 2:** Work out your EI and the priorities in your life now and going forward:
  - ☐ What are my Big Rocks?
  - ☐ Who am I?
  - ☐ What will make me feel happy and fulfilled?
  - ☐ Why am I doing what I'm doing?
  - ☐ What gets my Big Rocks off?

- ☐ Self reliance reality check – ask yourself the questions and your friends, family, colleagues, mentors, clients, teachers too.
- **Step 3:** Do a SWOT snalysis of YOU – and be honest! List your strengths, weaknesses, opportunities and threats.
- **Step 4:** Fourth base – Be gutsy. Face your fears and start dealing with them!
- **Step 5:** Create your dream and lifestyle.
- **Step 6:** Start devising your FMSP (Formidable ME Strategy & Plan):
  - ☐ 'What If?' – ask yourself the questions, create some additional/ different one's personal to you;
  - ☐ Goals – make them short and make some BHAGs;
  - ☐ Mission – listen to your intuition, focus on what you want out of your career; and
  - ☐ Vision – tip from Carl Jung: "Your vision will become clear only when you look into your heart. Who looks outside, dreams. Who looks inside, awakens."
- **Step 7:** Address your ethicability conundrum:
  - ☐ Conflicts of DIP;
  - ☐ Decide what's right;
  - ☐ Work out your Me Code of Conduct;
  - ☐ What don't you believe? Make your list; and
  - ☐ What do you believe? Make your list.
- **Step 8:** Work out your:
  - ☐ C-c-c-courage – do you have all three? Reflect; and
  - ☐ Epitaph – what is it? What do you want it to be? Write it out
- **Step 9:** Address your:
  - ☐ Rainmaking mindset – what are your characteristics now? Make a list. Where do you need to get to? Make a list;
  - ☐ Attitude – make sure it SUUUCKS;
  - ☐ Motivational factors – figure out what floats your boat? Write it down; and
  - ☐ PEE Poor Work Ethic – Rate yourself from zero to ten. Honestly! For *passion*, *enthusiasm* and *energy*.

Oh... btw... please feel free to check out the EntrepreneurLawyer website to see if CPD (and/or CLE or an alternative) accreditation is available in relation to carrying out the ROAR steps activities.

When you have completed all of the above, you will then be ready to go forth...

To help you further on your way, here are a few Naked Lawyer ROAR tips ...

ROAR tips

- Get a grip;
- Get personal;
- Get real;
- Speak up;
- Speak out;
- Find and be your true ME;
- Don't be afraid;
- Don't allow fear to interfere;
- Park ego firmly at the door;
- Give up waiting;
- Let go of resisting change;
- Be honest – with yourself and others;
- Be transparent;
- Just do something;
- It's time...;
- Respect everyone's uniqueness and individuality; and
- Do not tolerate people who are attempting to mould you into something you are not. If you do, you will fail in achieving fulfilment – of and for your clients, your boss/firm and most of all yourself and the dream, goals, mission and vision you set about to achieve.

be happy – be who you are

Until we meet again, I'd like to share with you some favourite quotes of mine that just might help keep you focused, motivated, inspired and confident during the journey you have just begun:

"A poor life this if, full of care, we have no time to stand and stare." (William Henry Davies – poet)

"Take the first step in faith. You don't have to see the whole staircase, just take the first step." (Dr Martin Luther King Jr.)

"One major thing that stands in between you and the fulfilment of your dream is the willingness to start, the courage to move ahead and the faith to finish." (Anon)

"If one advances confidently in the direction of his dreams, and endeavours to live the life he has imagined, he will meet with a success unexpected in common hours...If you have built castles in the air, your work need not be lost; that is where they should be. Now put the foundations under them." (Thoreau)

"Destiny is not a matter of chance, it is a matter of choice. It is not a thing to be waited for, it is a thing to be achieved." (William Jennings Bryan)

"Your time is limited so don't waste it living someone else's life." (Steve Jobs)

"Be who you are, and say what you feel, because those who mind don't matter and those who matter don't mind." (Anon)

"For what it's worth, it's never too late or too early to be whoever you want to be. There is no time limit, start whenever you want, you can change or stay the same, there are no rules to this thing." (From the film *The Case of Benjamin Button*)

"There are those that make things happen, there are those that watch things happen and there are those that wonder what happened." (Anon)

"A man who wants to lead the orchestra, must turn his back on the crowd." (James Crook)

"There is no passion to be found playing small – in settling for a life that is less than the one you are capable of living." (Nelson Mandela)

"A positive attitude may not solve all your problems, but it will annoy enough people to make it worth the effort." (Herm Albright)

And finally...

"If you shoot for the moon you'll at least land among the stars!" (Anon)

Perhaps you have some quotes and/or wisdom that touch you? If you do, keep them close, read them often, and allow them to inspire you.

ROAR quiz

A final challenge and this time, just for fun. There's a quiz questionnaire relating to this volume that you might want to have a go at. You will need to have read both Volumes 1 and 2 (tip – to the VERY end!) because the questions in the quiz relate to each of these. I challenge YOU!!!! I dare you to make one of your new goals here, whether you perceive it to be a short goal or a BHAG, and pit your wits against *the naked lawyer.*

You will find the quiz on the EntrepreneurLawyer website – http://entrepreneurlawyer.co.uk.

ROAR summation

Hopefully, after reading this volume and having carried out your 'after dark activity' your inner YOU will be well and truly awake and you are now eager to rise and shine.

Hopefully, the concept of marketing, branding and selling YOU (rainmaking) is looking a little more appealing to you. Think extraordinary lover. Think extraordinary sex!

Hopefully, if you've worked out your Big Rocks, done your EI analysis and SWOT analysis, started to devise your Formidable ME Strategy & Plan (goals, mission, vision), addressed your Ethicability conundrum, worked out your ME Code of Conduct and Epitaph, addressed your Rainmaker Mindset, Attitude, Motivation and PEE Poor Work Ethic, then you're probably chomping at the bit to know 'what's next?'

Well... it's time to cut yourself a niche. I'll show you how. Come and join me in Volume 3: slowly slowly catch a nichey.

References

1. *The Sound of Music* is a musical with music by Richard Rodgers, lyrics by Oscar Hammerstein II. http://en.wikipedia.org/wiki/The_sound_of_music
2. Peters, Tom & Barletta, Martha, *Trends: recognize, analyze, capitalize* (New York: DK Publishing, Inc., 2005). Reprinted with the permission of Tom Peters.
3. Brown, Rebel, *Defy Gravity: propel your business to high-velocity growth* (Austin, Texas: Greenleaf Book Group Press, 2010)
4. Peters, Tom, *The Brand You 50: Fifty ways to transform yourself from an "employee" into a brand that shouts distinction, commitment, and passion!* (New York: Alfred A. Knopf, Inc., 1999)
5. Handy, Charles, *The Empty Raincoat: Making Sense Of The Future* (London: Hutchinson, 1994)
6. Roulac, Stephen, 'Learning How To Break Away To Get Alpha Results', *Global CEO* (2008)
7. Cole Silver, *How to create wealth and freedom in your law practice: 101 powerful client development and retention strategies for attorneys* (New York: The Silver Group Ltd., 2009)
8. Russell, Gary, *Big Rocks: Balancing Life & Work*, (Sausalito, Calif.: Lifestyle Press, 2005)
9. Lightfoot, Chrissie, nee Burak, 'Relative Work, Relative Leisure: Women Entrepreneurs in the 1990s', BA (Hons) Leisure Studies Degree (Leeds Metropolitan University, 1996)
10. Csikszentmihalyi, Mihaly, Flow – *The Psychology of Happiness* (London: Rider, 1992)
11. Coleman, Daniel, *Emotional Intelligence: Why it can matter more than IQ* (1996)

12. Burg, Bob and Mann, John D., *Go-Givers Sell More* (London: Penguin Books, 2010)
13. *Better Days* is a song track by Bruce Springsteen from the album *Lucky Town*, released in 1992. http://en.wikipedia.org/wiki/Better_Days_(Bruce_Springsteen_song)
14. Collins, James and Porras, Jerry, *Built To Last: Successful Habits of Visionary Companies* (London: Random House Business Books, 2000); Collins, Jim, *Good To Great: why some companies make the leap... and others don't* (London: Random House Business Books, 2001)
15. Creating Law Practice: 'Love Your Clients, Love Yourself': http://lawpracticestrategy.com/2010/08
16. 'Synergy' meaning the interaction or cooperation of two or more agents to produce a new or enhanced effect compared to their separate effects.
17. Pierre Corneille, 1643, *Le Menteur* (The Liar) act 1, scene 1. Pierre Corneille was a French tragedian. He has been called 'the founder of French tragedy' and produced plays for forty years during the seventeenth century.
18. Burg, Bob, *Go Givers Sell More*, 2010.
19. Chopra, Deepak, author of 'Ageless Body, Timeless Mind' published in 1993; http://en.wikipedia.org/wiki/Deepak_Chopra
20. Cole Silver, *How to create wealth and freedom in your law practice*, 2009
21. Lyrics from *Happy Talk*, a song from the 1949 musical *South Pacific*, music by Richard Rodgers, lyrics by Oscar Hammerstein II. *South Pacific* is considered by some to be one of the greatest Broadway musicals. Several of its songs, including *Happy Talk* have become worldwide standards. http://en.wikipedia.org/wiki/South_Pacific_(musical)
22. Stephen Roulac, 'Learning How To Break Away' (2008)
23. http://en.wikipedia.org/wiki/Vision_statement#Mission_statements_and_vision_statements
24. *Ibid*
25. Steare, Roger, *Ethicability: how to decide what's right and find the courage to do it* (3rd ed., York: Roger Steare Consulting Ltd., 2009)
26. Eudora Welty, writer. In the final paragraph of her memoir, *One Writer's Beginnings*', 1984
27. Tom Peters, *Trends*, 2005
28. Jack London. American short story writer and novelist whose works deal romantically with elemental struggles for survival.
29. *MindStore System For Life* devised by Jack Black; I came across this system when I attended a two day business development conference in 2000 at the NEC in Birmingham, UK, courtesy of Cannons Health Club Limited; Jack Black was the keynote speaker.
30. Cole Silver, *How to create wealth and freedom in your law practice*, 2009
31. Welch, John F., *Jack: Straight From The Gut* (New York: Warner Books, Inc., 2001)
32. http://en.wikipedia.org/wiki/Work_ethic
33. Cole Silver, *How To Create Wealth*, 2009
34. A famous quote/statement by Conrad Hilton. American businessman, 1887-1979. Hotelier and founder of the Hilton Hotel Chain.

Volume 3: slowly slowly catch a nichey

wakey wakey rise and shine

Welcome! It is I. Your host. Your prancing, dancing, private little Naked Lawyer in law law land again. I trust you will have read Volumes 1 and 2 thoroughly prior to beginning this Volume 3. If not, you must.

Why? Because unless you do there is not a hope in hell of this volume achieving the whopper impact it is capable of for you. Volumes 1 and 2 provide you with important background information and practical activities which you will need to have done in preparation for this Volume 3.

Again, to get the best out of this volume, ideally, I would like you to grab a drink, sit back and chill out. I say again, chill out! Take a load off your feet and find yourself a nice comfy chair in a quiet area where you are unlikely to be disturbed for an hour or so. Switch off your mobile phone, your laptop, and anything else that's going to go 'beep beep' and distract you. If you can, turn the other half on mute for a wee while too!

Now, allow yourself to truly experience the story and let the words flow, resonate and touch you. Enjoy the read start to finish, non-stop.

It won't take you very long to get through if you read it straight through and leave the 'just do something!' at the end of some of the sections until you have completed the volume. Like Volume 2, you will find the 'just do something!' practical activities collated in a structured way towards the end in the 'after dark activity' – as ROAR steps. Here, I guide you back to the relevant sections so you can carry out the activities in a studious fashion.

And remember... Whilst this is my story, you are attempting to empathise by standing in my shoes. However, the focus is all on YOU... and about YOU. My mission is to help YOU. My modus operandi is by being your private dancer. Use me. Abuse me. Now dance with me.

Let's have YOU thinking, feeling and being – simply the best!

heads up

Let's recap. Having read Volumes 1 and 2 and carried out your 'after dark activity', your inner YOU ought to be truly awake. Hopefully, like me, you've now worked out your Big Rocks, done your EI analysis and SWOT analysis, started to devise your Formidable ME Strategy & Plan (goals, mission, vision), addressed your Ethicability conundrum, worked out your ME Code of Conduct and Epitaph, addressed your Rainmaker Mindset, Attitude, Motivation and PEE Poor Work Ethic.

You're probably chomping at the bit by now to cut yourself a niche. If not, you need to work some more on your *enthusiasm*. For those of you who are ready, let's get down to it!

In Volume 2 I proposed that in order to have a happy and fulfilling working life, we should set about cultivating our service proposition to find and attract the kind of people who share the same kind of interests, both in our working life and leisure life, and with whom we can identify and they with us.

For the goal, after all, wherever and whenever possible is: mutual empathy. Why? Because if you share the same interests as the people you wish to attract, you can be of more value to THEM and inevitably you will build a strong and enduring relationship with THEM ... quickly.

In Volume 2, 'what gets your Big Rocks off', 'just do something!', I asked you to consider the stuff that feeds you, remember? The connecting, interacting and getting involved with people who share the same interests as you. And to write down your answers. I also asked you to conduct a brutally honest and thorough SWOT analysis of yourself so that we could work on forming the basis to identifying a niche for you.

By now, you should have created four electronic documents – separate pages – or four sheets of paper with a title – 'Strengths', 'Areas For Improvement', 'Opportunities' and 'Threats'. Each of which should be filled by now as comprehensively as possible, with lots of strengths and opportunities identified no doubt?!

just do something!

Keep all of these documents and notes at the ready as we move through this volume.

nesting... the time of my life

I trust you will agree, we're one of the lawyers who 'get it'. We're about to pursue our goals, mission and vision with reference to the Awakening, the Knowing. We're masters of our own mutiny. We're driving our mother-ships, we're the daddy of our ambition, and we're about to set sail on a course of our choosing.

That is, we're not one (or do not wish to be one) of the monkey grinder's naive sheep blindly following an outdated Dickensian system and mindset where 'the firm' is failing to positively encourage and enthuse us to arm ourselves with the 'new' soft skills essential for our legal beagle survival and success.

Right? Returning to my story, I realised that *now* is actually the time of my life. I decided that I was going to make each day count. But I recognised that to do so would require *courage* to stand apart from the legal maddening crowd, and not unlike the internet extending universal commercial suffrage, one woman one dream was about to become one little naked lawyer, one brave voice. I was going to *nest*.

What do I mean by 'nest'? Well, I was going to carve out my unique initials in the tree of legal life. I was going to find myself a niche. A gap in the market. Not simply to ensure my survival and that of my colleagues, but something essential to achieving an advantage over the 'competition', present and future.

Why? Let me share something with you from Chris Anderson's *Long Tail:*[1]

"Ben is growing up in a different world from the one I grew up in, a world far less dominated by any of the traditional media and entertainment industries... His reality is the leading edge of all of our futures. Most of Ben's free time is spent online, both randomly surfing and participating in user forums such as Halo and Star wars discussion sites. He's not interested in news ... but follows the latest tech and subculture chatter on sites such as Slashdot (geek news) and fark (weird news). He instant messages (IM) constantly all day with his ten closest friends... he plays video games with friends, mostly online... the main difference between Ben's adolescence and my own is simply choice."

The era of one size fits all is at an end. It has been replaced by a market of multitudes.

Increasingly, the mass market has turned into a mass of niches.

Chris Anderson embarked on a research product that was to take him to all the leaders in the emerging digital entertainment industry, from Amazon to iTunes. Everywhere he went the story was the same: "niches are emerging as the big new market".

Furthermore, we are in the human economy. The human individual reliance economy. And to survive and thrive in this economy we must not only understand and respect our individual talent and strengths, (and not just simply pay lip-service to it) but positively embrace it, 'work' it, encourage it and develop it...

For today's 'multitude digital market' is a *very* different place to the market of the 20th century and the Dickensian parallel. Everyone bangs on about *team*. *Team* this, *team* that. Yeah yeah yeah. We all get it. Of course we do. I do. Lived and breathed it for the past two decades in wonderful companies with awesome colleagues achieving great results. You simply can't beat great team dynamics and collaboration. However, despite the 'tut-tut' teeth rattle chatter, 'There's no 'I' in team', when the team members question the motives of an individual who goes off and gets results due to their individual innate talent and strengths, duly note this all ye smart lawyers (which of course you are) with a truly keen eye for detail... there is a 'Me, Ta' (ta being slang for thank you) in 'team'. Nice anagram.

Funny how extraordinary teams flourish when the leader accounts for every individual's unique talent and plays to each individual's strengths within the team... ultimately, their *niche*. The word 'niche' is from the Latin 'nidus', meaning 'nest'. Also meaning: 'a specialised but profitable corner of the market'.[2]

Carving out a niche is actually just spotting something – a useful area, an opportunity, a skill that no one else has spotted, or truly exploited – yet. It could be something simple like knowing something no one else does, a talent, strength, skill combo and/or bringing things together in a way that no one else has to date.

And so it came to pass... I set sail to build me a nest... find myself a nice bushy tree... on a fruit rich island in global law law land.

storm before the rain...maker brand

I needed to check some stuff out, do some grunt ground work and brainstorming before I could take things further. *Research.*

Doing the research in relation to niche identification was actually the pre-requisite and foundation to devising my personal brand – 'Brand,Me'. And I figured I needed to get myself one of those, having read all about it from the gurus and noted already that I didn't know of any lawyers, particularly trainee solicitors, at that time (in the UK and/or globally), who had their own personal brand. Remember what I said in Volume 1 about being the first to do something?

I believe that all rainmaker lawyers need a personal brand. Period. Well... if you desire to be an extraordinary rainmaker you do.

Why? Because it helps your target market, your prospective clients and existing clients – your 'interest groups' – find, identify, understand and relate to you, and you with them. More about this and how to create your personal brand in Volume 4: getting under your skin.

big rocks rolling

seek and ME shall find

Knowing what feeds me, that is, my interests, my Big Rocks, and having a feel for and understanding of my strengths and potential opportunities, I began to apply my innate *curiosity* to research, investigate and study those interests in a bid to identify an opportunity... a niche.

So, with the mantra, 'Seek and ye shall find', firmly at the forefront of my mind, I started my niche quest with the broad category of 'entrepreneurship' and a few ideas in mind. I'd been studying, living and breathing entrepreneurship for the past two decades so I figured it was a good place to start.

I used the following list to help focus my efforts and to cut a niche which would play to all of my strengths, natural talents, knowledge and experience to date and where I wished to develop the same:

- Big Rocks/interests;
- SWOT analysis;
- Type of law interested in practising – commercial/IP/corporate;
- Industry and/or sector experience (track-record), knowledge, interest – leisure/new media/business consulting;
- Reputation in industries;
- Credibility in industries;
- Practical experience and applied knowledge in industries;
- Who I know in the industries;
- Leisure interests – running, cycling, swimming, wine, travel;
- Achievements and accomplishments to date; and
- Trends – global to local, pest (more on this further into the volume).

I scrapped the list from my SWOT analysis with the title 'Areas For Improvement'. I decided to bin it. It was a useful exercise though, as it reminded me of the things I really ought not to be wasting my time on pursuing further, as being mediocre at something in this area just isn't going to cut it. There's just too much fantastic talent out there.

Besides other people in the team dynamic will have those strengths that are my 'Areas For Improvement' and common sense says we should use and keep developing the strengths of every individual.

Focusing on making my Strengths even stronger is what I needed to work on. That's what all the winners (and survivors) do...

Here's the thing... David Beckham is famous for his key strength, his core talent, his trademark 'right foot crossing of the ball' which he refined to perfection after practising crossing the ball with his right foot for eons. Beckham didn't spend hours on end practising his crossing with his left foot, did he? Nor would he be rolled out and expected to deliver the same quality of precision placement of the ball if he did. Enough said.

Similarly, I looked at the list of Threats and tried to figure out how I could actually turn those into opportunities. And then I binned the list of threats. Again, I wasn't going to allow fear to interfere, remember? I was well aware of them, but I wasn't going to allow them to paralyse me. Focusing on the Strengths and Opportunities and keeping all things positive was the way to devise the niche.

just do something!

OK now. Let's kick off your niche identification foundation and research. Devise a list using headings similar to the ones I used in this section which will be bespoke to YOU. Feel free to add to the list. Think deeply about each line/heading in turn and jot down your immediate thoughts.

Pay particular attention to your interests, your strengths and your opportunities. Look at your 'Areas For Improvement'... now bin it. Trust me. It's not what you should be troubling yourself with. It has negative vibes. You must focus on devising a niche which is going to celebrate, excite and extol your natural talent, strengths and interests.

Similarly, the Threats which you envisage; think hard how you can turn those on their head and make them into Opportunities. Now bin the Threats list. It's negative. Focus, focus, focus on the positive at all times. Feel better now for binning the negative? Again, focus on your strengths, your opportunities, your interests in devising your niche.

If you don't have any industry/sector knowledge or experience other than law then don't worry; look to your interests – there will be an industry, sector and/or interest group which matches that, for sure. And then think about your reputation, credibility, practical experience, knowledge and contacts in that context.

Let's move on...

niche niche niche

In marketing world, it used to be that 'location, location, location' was *the* blessed mantra and holy grail which businesses clamoured to focus on and extol in order to win business.

In this digital era, arguably it has evolved into 'findability, findability, findability' with reference to the business being found online.

In essence, they're the same thing. And remain fundamental strategies in the drive to acquire a flow of new and retained business. Namely, carving out a *space* where only YOU will be found, which only YOU can occupy and only YOU can truly 'own', whether as an individual or an entity.

So, I reckon in 2010, and for the foreseeable future, it's all about 'niche, niche, niche'. As I began to undertake the research I quickly realised that the only way to cut a real niche was to find a niche of a niche of a niche... of a niche... of a niche.

And actually, like spread betting and/or having a portfolio of investments in order to spread risk, I figured it was sensible to have a few niches within a niche because it's important to corner a niche that is going to be profitable; and sometimes factors outside of one's control come into play, such as an economic crisis, political transitions affecting policy, strictures and structures, funding resources and sources, a particular industry may go through a downturn, etc.

Here's the list of niches that I identified to research further based on the list in the previous section:

- Small/medium sized enterprises (SMEs);
- Start-up companies;
- New media;
- Leisure;
- Entrepreneurs:
  - ☐ Women;
  - ☐ Young;
  - ☐ Serial;
- Corporate/commercial law; and
- Employee share schemes.

For example, one of my niches would be serving women entrepreneurs (niche), from start-up (niche) and/or an existing SME, within the new media industry (niche) in providing corporate legal advice (niche) appertaining to employee share schemes (niche). Drilling down. Why? Because it's a natural extension of myself... it's easier to empathise with my potential client, existing client and mavens. I am a woman in business. I am a woman entrepreneur.

I genuinely care. I can identify with women entrepreneurs, and they in turn will be able to identify with me. Building a relationship... fast... and providing extraordinary customer service, would be a no-brainer. Why? Because like attracts like... people like people who are like them. Fact. And, they particularly like you if you meet them on their own turf. Fact.

Done deal. Period.

just do something!
Have a look at my list of niches and how I drilled down from micro to macro in this section. Take your list which you created from the previous section and try and identify the 'drill down' of niches befitting to you. That is, create your very own bespoke list of niches.

trendy turn on

I knew that I also needed to carve a niche that would dovetail with a long term present and future trend. No point in choosing a declining trend and/or a declining market for my niche proposition to be feasible, viable and sustainable. That would be suicidal. Might as well go jump off the crumbling, ivory tower roof right now. Jeronimoooooooooo!!!!!!!!!

I figured I also needed a trend that would truly float my boat; got to keep my interest up otherwise I'd get bored, lose enthusiasm and move on. I know myself well enough. I'd done the EI self-awareness gubbins remember. It's the nature of the prancing little Naked Lawyer beast.

I'd spotted the woman entrepreneur trend back in the 1980s during the yuppie[3], dinky[4] and emancipation Thatcher years. I was fascinated by women entrepreneurs. As far back as 1993 I wrote a national award winning thesis entitled: *Women Entrepreneurs in the 1990's: Relative Work Relative Leisure,*[5] carrying this penchant through into my careers, my business ventures, the leisure industry, new media industry and management consulting endeavours.

So, 'Why not in the legal world too?' I asked myself. A world that I could see actually hadn't truly catered for this niche terribly well to date. I know. I was one of the women entrepreneurs who was pretty hacked off at the shoddy male chauvinist legal service of the 20th century and its continuance of the same in the 21st.

In 2000, Jack Black at his MindStore event spoke about the 'Entrepreneurial Revolution', describing entrepreneurs as the sexy leaders of the world; apparently they change fast, and are sophisticated. Yeah, I'd like to serve these people, I thought. Heck, I'd like to think I am one of them! Moot.

Then in 2005, Tom Peters shared his wisdom about trends stating: "Go where the buyers are and where the money is – among women and among aging boomers."[6] I figured I was onto something here. I was on the right track. So I did some more digging. I'll share some of my research activity and results with you, if you're interested...

what's happenin'?

I carried out a lot of desk research; that is, I read extensively from a mix of authoritative and non-authoritative sources; texts (previously shared with you in Volume 2); quality newspapers such as *The Financial Times* (FT), *The Sunday Times*, *The Wall Street Journal*; various business magazines and legal magazines; websites; blogs. I am convinced my colleagues thought I'd totally lost the plot. Many a day they would find me at my desk during the lunch break tearing out strips of pinky-orange newspaper clippings.

In Mr T's trademark line from the *A Team* TV series: 'I pity the fool' who attempted to read the FT after I'd danced all over it!

The top trends we could expect affecting small business and small-business growth in the period 2006-2011 were:[7]

- Retirement businesses: Millions of baby boomers will soon retire. Most boomers are still too energetic and engaged to just golf or garden. Boomer retirees will start businesses in record numbers;
- Entrepreneurship education: Younger and better business owners in the years to come. Students are flocking to

entrepreneurship classes and programs at college, and teaching children how to run businesses starts as early as elementary school. Also, there's a new field of small-business management;

- Immigrant entrepreneurs: Immigrants have always been a tremendous force for creating new businesses in the United States, and their numbers will keep expanding (this applies to the UK also). These businesses will be in all industries and level of complexity – not just the corner store or the new computer company; and
- Reluctant entrepreneurs: As jobs in large corporations continue to be eliminated or sent offshore, many people who would rather have a job will be forced to start businesses just to survive.

With regard to women entrepreneurs and savvy rich ladies:

- "Figures from the Centre for Economics and Business Research suggest the number of millionaires in Britain will nearly double to 690,000 by 2010 and quadruple to 1.7m by 2020; presently 46 percent of Britain's 376,000 millionaires are women, 53 percent by 2020. The figures are based on 'marketable' wealth, i.e. the value of housing, less mortgages, plus investments, savings and pensions."[8]
- "Women millionaires are set to outnumber men by 2020, due to more succeeding in business, bigger divorce settlements and longer life expectancy. Over the past two or three years there has been around 20 percent growth in women in the entrepreneurial area in London and that has been echoed across the UK. We are also seeing more women coming through as part of a family business; 60 percent of family firms have females in a board position."[9]

Interestingly, Coutts bank set up an online magazine *Coutts Woman* back in 2006. A sign of the times... and responding to a trend methinks?

The desk research was supplemented with field research... that was fun! For me, I set up a stack of coffee meetings during my lunch break, after work hours and during the weekends with a variety and number of entrepreneurs (business people), asking them what they needed, wanted and desired from a lawyer. Wearing my woman entrepreneur's hat, I knew what I expected but I'm not representative of all entrepreneurs of course; entrepreneurs are heterogeneous by their very nature, *not* homogenous.

Most importantly, I asked them, 'What's missing?', 'What's not been catered for?', 'If I catered for what you want, would you hire me?' I asked target market entrepreneur clients, prospective clients, and my lobsters – mavens; more about these in Volume 5: raving referral lobsters rule! I made a point to approach the best known, high profile, influential and most successful entrepreneurs in the region as well as the everyday kind of entrepreneur.

I also asked my 'competitors'. I say 'competitors' in inverted commas because I didn't (and still don't) actually view them as competition. We're going to be different you see, not direct competitors at all... just marginal competitors.

The outcome of it all? What did this signify for me? Opportunity. A definite niche waiting to be tapped and served... extraordinarily well.

keeping abreast

Researching, identifying, acting upon and nailing a niche is NOT rocket science. It's pretty much just common sense.

However, we lawyers may be very bright and knowledgeable but common sense and street savvy do not always sit easily with us intellectual boffins. I know, my mother frequently reminds me how dumb I was (and still can be) where street smarts and 'common' come into play.

Still learning... still some EI to work through...

But I did have enough smarts, I reckon, to spot that which Tom Peters highlights; that is, one needs to "'recognize' 'analyze' and 'capitalize'" on trends, and that "marketing to women is 'the biggest trend in the world'."[10]

I 'get' it. And I also appreciated that how I prepared and responded to these emerging trends, and positioned myself accordingly in order to exploit the potential would be the key to my survival and success. Furthermore, keeping abreast of these developing trends would actually give me a competitive advantage... some unique selling points (USP) and points of difference (POD); more about these in a moment.

Here are a few trends I'm aware of at present that may help you with your thinking and understanding about the kind of trends that you may wish to research and take note of as you work on cutting your own niche:

Area of law, 2010 trends:[11]

- Uplift in demand for compliance and audit lawyers in the pharmaceuticals sector due to the changes due to the anti-bribery act;
- The structured product investment market is picking up. Law firms are engaging in multiple hires, often for new roles (rather than replacement), particularly within derivatives, capital markets and mergers & acquisitions;
- With the insurance sector performing well demand for insurance, re-insurance and professional indemnity litigation has gathered pace. Big city firms are hiring high volumes of junior litigators as they're increasingly taking on more of this type of work;
- Rise in demand for private client lawyers due to increased economic confidence – the recent but short-lived boost to the property market appears to have helped finance the divorce market with family law particularly busy in private practice.

Whoppa future trends (perhaps?)...
Just a handful of ideas from myself and fellow members of the 'Future Trends' LinkedIn group:[12]

- Social enterprise.
- Ethical entrepreneurship.
- Singularity; more about this in Volume 12: XXX rated – tomorrow's lawyer.
- The portfolio worker – people creating multiple revenue streams in order to keep pace with the economy.
- Adjacent market convergence – a phenomenon more than a trend to watch.[13]
- Continued emergence, convergence and bundling of new technologies from wireless electronic computing, communication and entertainment to medical and green technologies; this will change the culture and the human race in ways that we may not be able to comprehend – the way boomers could not comprehend how the space race was destined to take them from typewriters and black & white television to the iPhone and YouTube.
- 'Green' technologies. Companies will all be affected, either directly or indirectly, by the emergence and adoption of 'green' technologies and services; carbon banks and credits; increased solar and wind power use; new bio-fuels

and the need for more sustainable and/or renewable resources.

- Battery technology. Regardless of what type of energy charges or recharges them, batteries are going to continue to evolve, becoming smaller, lighter, more powerful, and more environmentally friendly.
- Demographic forces will start to impact society, politically, socially and economically:
  1. Expect an end to cheap Chinese labour. China, through its one child policy, will not have sufficient labour for all its grand plans;
  2. The reverse pyramid of aging populations in Europe will cause major breakages of the social net and pensions; and
  3. Regionally based political upheaval will become the norm.
- Progressive innovation in online service delivery being citizen-centric through the semantic and integration webs through Web 2.0, Web 3.0 and Web 4.0.
- Open Collaborative Global Economy and crowd sourcing (which has grown exponentially over the past five years) using social networks, internet technology and global connectivity tools, aka applications for collaboration, knowledge management and brainstorming. Open collaboration, crowd sourcing, open innovation paradigms are already being adopted by leading companies and early adapter entrepreneurs.

com...prrr...tition?

I knew that the basic rule of thumb when checking out the competition is to look at who, what, where, when, why and how? Wwwwwh.

So, I applied this in relation to cutting my niche – who is doing what I'm thinking about, what are they doing, where, when, why and how, exactly? I checked it out. Local > Regional > UK > English Law Locations > Global

Of course there are lawyers who cater for entrepreneurs. There are lawyers who cater for women entrepreneurs, young entrepreneurs and serial entrepreneurs. There are lawyers who niche in the leisure industry and the new media industry.

But, when I dug deep, there were no *trainee solicitors* (or practising solicitors in the UK for that matter) doing what I was *exactly* proposing to do, that is, go at the markets in their introductory or growth stages, from my exact positioning, differentiation, USP, POD standpoint. Zip. Nada. Zero.

Of course, there is always competition... there always will be. But if you eliminate as many contenders as possible so that you're sat in a particular sweet spot, where you're not being compared to an apple because you are in fact a pineapple, then the reality is that you ought to steal a march on your competition and have an increased chance of success at wooing, enticing and delighting your target market client.

Did you know that there are only 35 Amur leopards left in the world?[14] Prrrrrrr... What does this mean? What's the significance of me sharing this with you?

going down and pushing up

Prrrrrrr... Well, it suggests that the Amur leopard is therefore rare. And if they're rare, then they're special, for one thing. And in demand, for another. And potentially valuable, for another.

Have you noticed also that when a member of the cat family is hunting its prey it goes down on its front legs and paws, crawling, slowly, slowly, before it pushes up in with an explosion of energy and force from the very same to pounce on its prey?

Well, I liken this activity to my preparation, research, positioning and differentiation in readiness for attracting and then surprising and delighting my target clients. Slowly, slowly, catch a nichey...

Ultimately, in readiness and anticipation for my desiring to ROAR with them – Reach Out And Relate, remember? I figure that whether I'm unique or rare, I should be able to capitalise on this trend and niche!

Consequently, because I have cut a niche, I do not view my 'competitors' as such. They're NOT really my competition, my enemy. They are really my collaborators because we each have something unique. I love my 'competitors' because they keep me on my toes (or should I say paws) and make me constantly work at nicheing, positioning and differentiating, which is what makes me special, desirable, useful and 'fit for purpose'.

We are, after all, all unique. Every single one of us. So, we should celebrate it and make the most of it. Make it count by defining and owning our own *space*. It's what I did, and what you must do! This way you will *not* be fearful of the 'alleged' competition, nor should you ever be.

The saying, 'Keep your friends close but your enemies even closer', will therefore pale into insignificance and you can simply focus on giving, giving and giving some more... and then receiving in return. And if you continue to fear and believe that your 'competitors' are truly competitors in the traditional meaning of the word, then I'd like to share something with you that my father once said to me: "Chrissie, you don't have to be the best, you just have to be better than the rest"... the phrase no doubt nicked from another bean counter.[15] Smarts!

When all is said and done, I'd prefer to prrrrrrr rather than worry about wwwwwh. Much more fun. Wouldn't you?

just do something!

OK. It's time to start your research. Grab your lists from the last two exercises. Begin with some desk research. Use Google search and Google's keyword tool[16] to find websites and blogs appertaining to the niche list you've devised. Similarly, check out interest groups on the same.

Search for trends too, within these niches and externally; that is, with the big picture in mind. Namely, global trends to local trends (political, economic, social and technical). Recognise a trend, analyse it and get ready to capitalise on it.

Create categories for each of your niches and the research results so that you have a point of reference to return to.

Check out your 'competition': wwwwwh – who, what, where, when, why, how – local to global.

Once you're well under way with your desk research begin your field research. Identify those individuals you ought to speak and/or meet with in order to make your research qualitative and not just quantitative.

Focus in on leaders, mavens, high profile, movers and shakers in the industry and/or sector (local; regional; national; global) – you will spot these individuals as they will be the ones who are 'on the scene' both offline and online – as well as the 'everyday' kind of person in your desired target market/interest group.

Ask the kinds of questions I did in the 'what's happenin'' section. Expand on them and make them bespoke. Once again, record and keep the results of your research in a safe place as you will wish to return to your findings in order to hone your niche(s).

Start building a relationship with these individuals; I'll talk about this more in Volumes 5, 6 and 7.

karma sutra professional specialty positioning that rocks

Just as there are lots of sexual positions to be found in the Karma Sutra, I realised that there are lots of sexy niches and sexy positions to consider in relation to how I was to differentiate my legal service offering and create value for my entrepreneur clients. Ultimately, it's about carving out a unique space in the competitive environment and focusing on delivering on that strategy.

I realised that the core value my service would provide, unwaveringly, was real gut wrenching, heart stopping, mind blowing entrepreneurial empathy, for, in the words of Jane Austen in the opening line of her famous novel *Pride and Prejudice*, "It is a truth universally acknowledged" that not many other lady lawyers (or male lawyers for that matter) have been, or are, true to form entrepreneurs prior to entering the profession.

Heck, it's pretty darn rare to find a lawyer who has had any commercial experience outside of the legal profession, let alone started their own business, spanning a period of 15 years *before* entering the legal profession (in general), albeit many have gone on to become business owners on leaving the profession... Quite rightly. Would have been a waste of such talent, knowledge and experience if not!

I've actually been involved in founding and running companies, start-ups and SMEs myself, in the new media industry and management consulting industry; I know and understand what it's all about. I understand, feel and know the entrepreneur's pain and joy, their challenges, their woes, their trials and tribulations, their expectations, their dreams... because it was and is my pain and joy too. I 'get' what makes them tick.

Ah... there's the rub. To truly 'know' one's client.

I knew that the legal messages I could send out would hit a nerve point; such as, how to attract, motivate and retain key talent in order to drive up morale, productivity and ultimately turnover and thereby minimise attrition, recruitment costs and losses, etc. as a by-product.

I also knew that I could provide a legal solution to that desire and problem – benefits – as a possible remedy to that pain, through delivering bespoke commercial/corporate legal advice, and in particular employee share scheme knowledge and experience, both in practice, when I considered the schemes in my previous ventures, and in theory, now proffering legal advice.

Not only that, I knew this group would need my services and would therefore be receptive to my propositions. I know what turns them on, what they want... and I can give it to them.

I've actually practised, aka experienced, a great deal of what I'll be preaching. As a lady lawyer with real life commercial savvy, business nous and experience, spanning two decades, having actively been engaged in the commercial hot seat prior to entering the profession. Not the usual commercial virgin lawyerly desk jockey providing 'ring fenced' legal advice of the kind clients are usually faced with.

These are USPs and major PODs, I reckoned.

I was actually setting about to position myself so that I was creating my own unique space. Invariably placing myself in the mind of the potential and existing client as the first person they would naturally think of to contact, as someone who would immediately jump on their wavelength, their bandwagon and truly identify and 'get' them.

differentiation that rolls

The learning, development and success that I had experienced in my roles prior to entering the profession had stood me in good stead when I turned my attention to becoming a lawyer.

I quickly recognised that to achieve the fulfilment which I desperately desired, I needed to use this prior learning and experience to my advantage wherever possible. Ultimately, the winning formula would be to differentiate myself absolutely and unabashedly from the plethora of 'traditional lawyer' clones. I could see that differentiation would be a much more rewarding path to achieve my dream, rather than just doing what everyone else was doing. To be quite frank, that sucks!

And to play to my competitive advantage would be a far more fulfilling and rewarding strategy than simply doing things the way everyone else did. Ugh... perish that thought too!

Shades of conveyer belt, 'soylent green'[17], here I come. No thank you!

I favoured tactics and strategies that played to my particular strengths... and uniqueness. In essence, from the positioning I had decided upon, I was attempting to create differentiation with a barrier to entry into my 'personal brand space' based on my unique experiences and background, so that any lawyer who might attempt to pit against me and those in the firm whom I served, would soon be dissuaded.

My mindset and FMSP battle cry was kind of like... 'go cut your own niche, buster! This is self-reliance field and we only welcome white flags here!'

I created my own space, my own domain, my specialism, my expertise; derived from prior learning, experience, education, strengths, skills, knowledge, talent and most of all through interests and genuine passion.

In my trainee solicitor role I therefore consciously sought to offer services that other lawyers did not, or could not, offer and/or match like for like. For example, part of my positioning and differentiation embraced pioneering a totally client-centric extraordinary relationship approach, when others – colleagues and 'competitor lawyers', that is, all those lawyers who were not working at the firm where I was – were concentrating primarily on the billable hour technical law humdrum.

Also, I set about emphasising my value adds such as being pro-active in finding new clients, connections, opportunities and innovating; that is, giving referrals, contacts, sharing industry knowledge, etc. to help the entrepreneurial client develop and grow their business, when others were mainly concerned with just getting the 'legal' job in and out.

I also focused heavily on providing a high-level of empathy and attention, when others were more reserved and primitive in their approach.

Fundamentally, by prioritising a strategic, systemised, task orientated long term approach, namely, building and nurturing relationships, when others were evidently primarily ad hoc, immediate term and time orientated in their approach, I meaningfully differentiated my offer from competitors. For me, it's an absolute no brainer that in today's highly competitive environment, smartly differentiating my services would be the key to my survival and success. Truly understanding the client's values, needs, and motivations was at the heart of my differentiation strategy. Applying the approach, strategies and tactics that I did, certainly delivered far greater results than any traditional marketing possibly could.

The positioning simply rocked, the differentiation quality rolled, and the good time entrepreneur niche lay ahead...

markets that hit the g-spot

My life was about to go from good to great to golden, so I was darn determined to make sure I identified markets that had sexy legs. Geographic segmentation, demographic segmentation, psychographic segmentation and business segmentation. I looked at them all.

But when it came down to it, what really turned me on was where the niches were in the market lifecycle; introductory stage > growth stage > maturity stage > decline stage. Ideally, I wanted to align my interest and passion with markets that were in their introductory stage and/or growth stage; lots of lean sexy legs...

Grrrrrrowth.

Gooooood.

Grrrrrrrrreat.

Goooolden.

Markets that are growing from good to great... usually aligning with golden trends... The g-spot.

Maturity stage means it's OK but decline stage may happen sooner rather than later so that doesn't turn me on too much.

So, women entrepreneurs, young entrepreneurs, serial entrepreneurs, new media (all forms), leisure (all forms), employee share schemes definitely turn me on... because they definitely have legs, are growing and dovetailing with global and market trends. Oh... and of course... They hit the g-spot! Woo-pah!! They're one of the new kids on the block – present and future – for sure. My research had identified the same.

Anything that didn't and doesn't hit the g-spot was, and is, in this Naked Lawyer's law law land, simply discarded... Not interested... Shop closed here thank you.

just do something!

It's time to find your niche positioning that will positively rock and your differentiation that will positively roll. Consider these questions carefully and write down your thoughts:

- What's the core value you could provide?
- What makes you unique?
- Would you be able to 'get' your target client?
- Would the legal messages you're going to send out hit a nerve point and then solve their pain?
- Do you truly understand your niche client's values, needs and motivations?
- Do they need you?
- How can your prior roles, experiences and learning be used to differentiate you?
- What unique experiences and background do you have?
- What are your USPs and PODs?
- What about geographic, demographic, psychographic and business segmentation?
- Does your target market client have sexy legs – the introductory and/or growth stage?
- Does your target market client hit the g-spot?
- Does your target market client dovetail with a golden trend?
- Can you create your own space, your own domain, your specialism, your niche now?

Take your time, be thorough, and enjoy positioning and differentiating yourself to rock and roll into the golden times.

Once you've completed the exercise, I'd like you to look back at your 'competition' research and analysis. If you've done a cracking job at your positioning and differentiation then perhaps you can now consider prrrrrrrring with them rather than worrying about wwwwwh?

It will be important when we look at lobsters and building relationships in Volumes 5, 6 and 7.

initiative rules! OK?

kneeling on the job

Inevitably, as a trainee solicitor, aka, very junior lawyer, the professional relationship with my superiors was very much the master-servant leadership and management style, where my boss was the master and I was the servant, just in case you had any doubt.

This is how it works in a law firm you see (in general, not exclusively of course)... The partner, aka the master, goes out and forages for the work. (S)he returns and passes the work to the trainee or junior lawyer, aka the servant; some of the work the master does for her/him self, of course. The master will choose which work is to be passed to whom, subject to how busy the master is in relation to his or her own technical law workload and the department workload in general; and the technical ability, learning curve, and availability of the servant (for the servant is usually servant to many masters at the same time depending on the size of the department and/or firm) who would then carry out the work under the supervision of the master.

Putting this in context and returning to my story, this meant on many occasions I was grovelling to my master for more interesting and juicy legal work... A la Oliver Twist, I was literally kneeling and begging, 'Please sir, can I have some more?' I was a hungry beast. I needed feeding. After a while I got tired of 'slim pickin's'... and waiting to be fed tasty stuff.

So, I decided to feed myself. I took control, used my initiative, and put my hunger, passion and niche research and identification into use.

carpe diem!

I am a great believer in carpe diem![18]

Accepting slim pickin's, kneeling, begging and praying for more interesting work and waiting for things to happen just wasn't my style; it didn't sit at all well with the FMSP.

Hanging around the water cooler and waiting for Boss Lawyer to say, 'Hey, Chrissie, here's an idea. How about finding a nice niche for yourself so that you can help us get fatter?' wasn't likely to occur either... Pigs would fly Santa's sleigh before that would happen!

So, I used my initiative. I approached my boss about my niche ideas... once I'd done the research... once I'd got the facts... once I'd got my prrrrrrrrr ideas together and could highlight a golden niche opportunity; supported with the wwwwwh for the bosses of course – they would understand the wwwwwh, but not the prrrrrrr. I wasn't even going to go there at that point in time as that would be jumping too many innovative steps ahead all in one go!

Tick-tock. Tick-tock – can have another more powerful significant meaning than the milestone around your neck in relation to making every six minutes count... The grains of sand of niche opportunity are pouring through the sand-timer at an alarming rate nowadays. If you're not careful, all the best grains may already have passed through... I'll explain this more in Volume 4.

dino dung

I'm sure you may recall, however long ago it was, when you were sifting through law firm applications, either as an applicant or recipient, or browsing through the firm's website whilst twiddling your thumbs because you thought you had nothing better to do than wait for the next job to rock in, handed to you in a banana leaf no doubt. Then you came across the 'we like our lawyers to use initiative' corporate mantra – the all too common box which needed to be ticked.

I remember. What a load of dino dung! Albeit nice in theory, from what I have witnessed and experienced, seldom is using one's initiative to 'cut a niche' applied in practice; with reference to the protégé using initiative and suggesting a niche or the master truly wanting the protégé to actually suggest it, use it and really do something about it... Likely random thoughts and behaviour of the boss: 'the trainee solicitor, the grinder's monkey, the audacity, tch,tch.'

NEWSFLASH: It doesn't sit well with the 'oven-ready', 'just sit there and do as you're told' partner with a closed mind and blinkered vision.

Here's the thing. Here's the challenge...

Duly note all ye ambitious lawyers and Dickensian practising lawyers:

"being a visible ambassador which connects the internal with external means drawing attention to yourself—a role which has traditionally been limited to a select few, such as a CEO, or formal spokesperson. In either of these roles, visibility is expected and it's part of the job... Today's corporate ambassadors can be anyone and the really good ones build bridges to multiple kinds of valued stakeholders (just like traditional ambassadors). But, despite becoming a more common role, corporate ambassadors face huge challenges. Colleagues will justifiably question the motives and contributions of ambassadors ... often times the perception of self promotion can be difficult to manage."[19]

I believe that I was quite fortunate actually... to a degree. My immediate line bosses welcomed the initiatives and niches I presented them with. Albeit, I found managing corporate ambassadorship in the established law firm I was at very challenging; and that's an understatement – unusual for me. For the majority of the partners did not buy into the blessing. They didn't understand. In fact, I'm absolutely convinced that even if they did understand, their traditional mindset would have still prevented them from seeing the light.

I nicknamed this 'majority bunch' of laggards – 'The Resistance'. Apt.

EI and the conflicts of DIP came to the forefront in this scenario of course. They will for you too no doubt.

Fundamentally, The Resistance didn't 'get' that if I was to align myself with the firm and establish a reputation in a niche, then I was not representing just myself, I was actually representing myself AND the firm I worked for. In essence, I was an 'ambassador' for both. A brand ambassador of 'Brand,Firm' and 'Brand,Me' perfectly dovetailed, aka, aligned, for one common purpose... the firm's success.

Some of you may be blessed with direct line bosses who actually mean what they say; that is, encourage you to use your initiative and approach them about a specialism and niche you're interested in developing, like I was.

I am extremely grateful to the two partners – you know who you are – who welcomed and made it possible for me to develop and get involved in a couple of niches for the firm. It was actually the highlight of my role and why I loved (and love) being a lawyer. It made my work more exciting, the daily technical law grind bearable and most of all, the relationships with our entrepreneurial clients highly enjoyable, solid and enduring.

Sans niche development and exploitation, I would have been a very unhappy bunny. The prance in my dance as a naked lawyer would have been quashed.

I wish to take this opportunity to thank each of you two entrepreneurial lawyer partners for your understanding, kindness and mentoring. At the very least, it is thanks to you that I am still on this planet and can share this tome of sales erotica!

So... My tip for all you budding, extraordinary, rainmaker naked lawyers... Be prepared for The Resistance. Have *courage*. And make sure your attitude SUUUCKS.

Good luck... catch this pixie dust to help you on your way...

just do something!

So, ask yourself the following:

- Am I getting 'slim pickin's'?
- Do I want more tasty stuff?
- Is hanging around and waiting for my boss to ask me to find a niche going happen?
- What am I to do with all this niche research, analysis and potential I've discovered?
- Do I have the courage to stand firm against The Resistance?

Pull your research, analysis and findings together into a proposal ready to present to your boss/line partner/mentor.

Don't be afraid that (s)he will nick your idea and all that hard work you've done. If you've done your positioning, differentiation, USPs and PODs correctly there's not a cat in hell's chance they can do this without you. Remember, it ought to be unique to you; it's your *unique space* that will benefit you and your firm.

Keep your proposal at the ready. We need to add to it before you present it.

why fourplay matters

I looked upon doing the research and cutting myself a niche as foreplay to becoming an extraordinary rainmaker. I was thinking, extraordinary sex...

Having a niche, a specialism, an expertise, an interest gave me an opening gambit, albeit I was a very junior solicitor. I'll show you how...

First of all, I identified those professional services firms who shared a similar niche focus, particularly in relation to sector and/or industry focus. For obvious reasons, namely, a synergistic referral client base – complementary product/service offerings, not conflicting.

Second, I identified and then approached the right partner asking him to meet with me.

Third, I prepared for the meeting by concentrating on how I would be able to refer work to him based on my employee share scheme niche focus.

Fourth, we met and engaged in fourplay. Namely, there was synergy between our umbrella niche focus, he on the accountancy side, and me on the legal side. The two make an awesome referral combo:

1) Media > 2) Entrepreneurs >
3) Corporate > 4) Employee Share Schemes

1) Niche > 2) Niche > 3) Niche > 4) Niche

Fourplay.

The meeting was a success and we've passed numerous referrals to each other from that day forward.

I was able to arouse the partner's curiosity because I sent him a message which would grab his attention. When we met I shared information with him which would be of interest to him, which in turn meant he would desire to work with me (and ultimately the firm) based on my credibility. I was able to convince him of this due to my positioning and differentiation attributes, together with obvious knowledge of the niche and markets we were discussing (employee share schemes; media; business per se talking EBITDA, ROI, etc.) which meant we were both keen to develop our professional referral relationship as a result.

Fourplay matters because knowledge is power.

Allow me to share with you now fourplay in action within the legal, accountancy and finance verticals respectively, using professionals with whom I'm working alongside at present, as further examples:[20]

Paul Verrico: 1) Accidents at work 2) Corporate criminal defence 3) Regulation and compliance 4) Health & safety

Nick Davies: 1) Medical 2) Medium/large corporate 3) Employment taxation 4) Tax efficient structuring of employee reward

Andrew Neligan: 1) Financial planning 2) Legal profession 3) Retirement planning 4) Pension and investment advice

Specialising in a niche means that it can be used to open doors and be the thing that clinches a deal, because it gives you the ability to talk proper shop at the highest level with a senior professional even if you are a very junior lawyer.

Once the door had been opened, as for actually doing the legal work appertaining to the employee share scheme referrals thereafter, it meant my boss would supervise me and he would develop the relationship between himself and the two firms further. I will go into this in more detail in Volume 5: raving referral lobsters rule!

No more slim pickin's. Just a thought.

law of attraction of law

I'd like to share with you two secrets...

You may be wondering why I particularly honed in on focusing on women entrepreneurs as a niche. Apart from the obvious: that I have a natural empathy, an interest, a passion; the trend is for ever increasing numbers of women entrepreneurs (globally) and wealthier commercially savvy ladies. Meaning women entrepreneurs are likely to have the wherewithal, either their own or the backing of their partners, ergo the woman entrepreneur niche has the potential to be a profitable little nest.

Secret #1

We women are extraordinary lobsters! Fact.

In the American sitcom *Friends*, Phoebe explains that lobsters mate for life. Once they've found their mate, they're friends forever. With reference to the on-off relationship between Ross and Rachel, when they get back together she exclaims, "Aw... he's her lobster!"

The lesson is quite simply that they are friends for life. And friends care. Friends like to help. Their friendship is special. I look upon lobsters like mavens (key-influencers), aka top quality referrers. More about this in Volume 5: raving referral lobsters rule!

I'm a lobster. And proud of it. You need to become one too if you're going to become an extraordinary rainmaker.

In the business world and the women entrepreneur world, we understand that it IS different being in business as a woman compared to being in business as a man. Similarly, in law law land. It is different for us lady lawyers.

It still *is*. Fact. Period. But that's OK. Because we make those differences count and use them to our advantage. For one thing, we naturally want to help each other more to survive and thrive, whether in the business world or legal world.

This is the thing... We're fabulous communicators. We love to talk, we're natural at 'giving' and 'mothering', and gifted at 'gathering'... from birth. It's in our genes. We like to 'nest'. You're probably thinking 'yeah, yeah, I know that Chrissie, heard all that before. Tell me something new. Tell me something I don't already know!'

Well, as ever, the ultimate savvy guru Tom Peters 'gets' it; and he's a bloke... but of the undoubtedly very switched on wise owl kind. Tom neatly sums it up: "women reward women-friendly marketing."[21] In essence, women are brand champions because when a woman is happy with a sale she refers twice as much as a man, *and* women buzz market well because women thrive on people power...

Simply put: We've got more rabbit than Sainsbury's.[22]

Do you now 'get' why I figured women entrepreneurs are a fabulous niche, irrespective of industry and/or sector specialism? They help a *lot* with fuzz; more about this in Volume 7: nurturing fuzz to get more buzz.

Secret #2

Men follow women! Fact. It's in their genes. Genes not jeans! Stay with me now...

I noted when working in the leisure industry, and in particular the country club and health club sectors that they were all driven by sex... Guys go to the health club to check out the gym bunnies. Fact. Attract lots of women to the gym, the guys will follow. Attract women lobsters to the club and even more women and men follow. Attract attractive (confident) women and/or women lobsters and... YOWZA!

It was my role to attract and retain club members to either the health club or country club so I quickly realised that schmoozing (attractive, as in confident) women lobsters was a sure fire way of achieving that goal! It was part of the marketing, promotional, sales and customer relationship management drive, together with attracting the mavens (key-influencers), head honchos, gang leaders, whatever, male or female, because it was they who decided where to go and who to 'rub shoulders' with. That is, the lobster decided what the 'in' place was to be. The tribe followed.

The lesson: It's all driven by sex... and gender.

So, prior learning and experience got me to thinking along the lines of Annie singing, "betch ya bottom dollar that tomorrow" this is likely to be the case in law law land too... Attract the women and the men will follow... especially when the lady is a raving lobster... and attractive because of her confidence... bonus!

For example, 'it is a truth universally acknowledged' that we women entrepreneurs rabbit on a lot, whether at dinner parties, cafes or wine bars. We're sure to natter at some point along the lines of:

"What a busy day I've had today. Got the shopping in early for the office party, sorted out that big deal I mentioned to you last time we spoke, and I even managed to meet with my lawyer to tie up a few loose ends on a couple of contracts. She was fabulous. Had it all prepared and sorted in a jiffy. Saved me a bundle of time. Managed to get in and out of there in time to go and pick Jimmy up from school. Great value too. Thought it was going to cost me an arm and a leg. Oh, and she gave me a great lead too; potential buyer for a line of the stockings and push-up bras."

To which the listener (male or female) responds, "Oh, really, who's your lawyer?" Enough said.

Of course. I figured it was all going to be relative. I'd suck it and see in law law land. After all, the saying, 'You have to speculate to accumulate' still rings true. As Einstein so wisely put it: "When you are courting a nice girl an hour seems like a second. When you sit on a red-hot cinder a second seems like an hour. That's relativity."

what's next pussy-cat?

All this talk of Amur leopards, the mention of roar, the virtual sound of prrrrrrrrrrrrrrrrrrrrring, and all this prancing and dancing going on has got me thinking of the lyrics by Tom Jones:[23] "what's new pussy-cat?" Well... prrrrrrrrrrrr

After we've indulged in some 'after dark activity' we're going to create 'Brand,You'!

after dark activity

rawhide to roarhide

OK now. Let's keep those Big Rocks rolling rolling rolling... rolling rolling rolling... rawhide style! Or should I say roarhide style?

Cutting yourself a niche in the interest area that you desire and playing to all of your strengths and natural talents will make ROARing, reaching out and relating, much more fun. Trust me... I'm a lawyer...

So, let's get rolling...

naked lawyer activity – a study worth casing

During summer 2008 I set about working through what is now Volume 3 as a pre-requisite in devising a personal brand which I look at in Volume 4: getting under your skin. As to what I did, and for a real live case study, in how to cut yourself a niche, simply read the story again in this Volume 3. You can relive my activity by taking yourself through the same process.

Let me help you. Here's a condensed version of the key activities and exercises you may wish to carry out...

just do something!

Take time out now to do the following exercise in the step sequence provided. It may take you a few days, a few weeks or a few months. Slowly, slowly, catch a nichey.

Try not to take too long though as the world is moving along at a frightening pace and arguably the legal profession is too, albeit dragging its hob-nob creaking booties, and you don't want to miss your chance to be the first to capture a really cool niche space.

Do you?

- **Step 1:** Kick off your niche identification foundation and research by devising a list using headings similar to the ones I used in the 'seek and ME shall find' section which will be bespoke to YOU.
- **Step 2:** Have a look at my list of niches and how I drilled down from macro to micro in the 'niche niche niche' section. Take your list which you created from the previous section and try and identify the 'drill down' of niches befitting to you. That is, create your very own bespoke list of niches.
- **Step 3:** Begin your desk research and field research. Recognise a trend, analyse it and get ready to capitalise on it. Check out your 'competition': wwwwwh.
- **Step 4:** Work out your positioning and differentiation. Work through and answer the questions I ask you at the end of the section 'markets that hit the g-spot'. Take your time and be thorough. Make a note of your positioning and differentiation so that it is clear to you. Once you've completed the exercise, look back at your 'competition' research and analysis. Perhaps you can now consider prrrrrrrring with them rather than worrying about wwwwwh? It's a mindset

thing. Refer back to your work in Volume 2 if necessary.

- **Step 5:** Ask yourself the questions detailed at the end of the 'dino dung' section. Be comfortable that you want to move ahead. Pull your research, analysis and findings together into a proposal ready to present to your boss/line partner/mentor. Keep your proposal at the ready. We will need to add to it before you present it; we need to work through Volume 4 to complete your proposal.

ROAR tips

- Be confident;
- Don't be afraid to stand alone;
- Celebrate your uniqueness;
- Be thorough – research deeply, slowly, methodically, systematically;
- Brainstorm! Think lots!
- Be creative;
- Be commercial;
- Be innovative;
- Be courageous;
- Don't wait;
- Don't stand still;
- Be sexy in your positioning;
- Be sexier in your differentiation;
- Be particular in pursuit of the g-spot;
- Say 'NO' to kneeling on the job;
- Use your initiative; and
- Engage in fourplay.

ROAR summation

niche one my friend

You should by now have laid down the foundations to help you to become an extraordinary rainmaker. You should have worked out your niche, or niches, drilled down through a niche of a niche of a niche of a niche of a niche, sorted your positioning, differentiation, USPs, PODs and target market(s), and be in prime form and at the ready for a little fourplay.

I just loved the movie *Dirty Dancing*, appreciating Patrick Swayze's talent as he gyrated around so sexily in his Milk Tray outfit. He really turned me on with his macho bravado in the final scene when he pronounced, "Nobody puts Baby in the corner."

Don't allow your firm or your boss to put you in the corner, scrabbling around for slim pickin's. It isn't going to get you where you want to get to in relation to your dream and your FMSP. The only corner you want to find yourself in is the nest you have so painstakingly carved out in topsy turvy law law land where your interest target market clients want to shack up with you.

This really is the time of your life and you owe it to yourself to make your dream come true.

References

1. Anderson, Chris, *The Long Tail: How endless choice is creating unlimited demand* (London: Random House, 2006), 3
2. Thompson, Della, *The Concise Oxford Dictionary* (9th ed., Oxford: OUP, 1995)
3. Short for 'young urban professional' or 'young upwardly-mobile professional'. A term that refers to a member of the upper middle class in their twenties or thirties http://en.wikipedia.org/wiki/Yuppie
4. Short for 'dual (or double) income, no kids yuppie'. An acronym to describe a high-earning couple who choose not to have children and are therefore able to afford a more expensive consumer lifestyle than those with families. The term was coined during the 1980s, at the height of yuppie culture http://en.wikipedia.org/wiki/DINKY
5. Lightfoot, 'Relative Work, Relative Leisure'
6. Peters & Barletta, *Trends*
7. 'Turn trends into business advantages', *TimesUnion.com*, 08/08/06 http://timesunion.com/AspStories/story.asp?storyID=506509&category=BUSINESS&newsdate=8/8/2006

8. 'Grey, female and loaded...', *Sunday Times*, 13/08/06
9. 'Coutts seeks suitably rich females for LTR', *Daily Mail*, 28/08/06, 51. LTR means long term relationship.
10. Peters & Barletta, *Trends*
11. Badenoch & Clark, 'Professional Talent Spotlight – August 2010: Recruitment market commentary', 08/10, 7.
12. Source: ideas from the 'Future Trends' members of the LinkedIn group http://www.linkedin.com/groupItem?view=&srchtype=discussedNews&gid=145854&item=24909662&type=member&trk=EML_anet_qa_ttle-cnhOon0JumNFJt7dBpSBA
13. http://www.informaworld.com/smpp/content~db=all~content=a713767054
14. The Amur leopard, also known as the Manchurian leopard, is a wild feline predator and one of the rarest felids in the world with an estimated 30 to 35 individuals remaining in the wild. Critically endangered, it is considered to be facing an extremely high risk of extinction in the wild http://en.wikipedia.org/wiki/Amur_Leopard
15. The term 'bean counter' is often used negatively to describe an overly zealous or fastidious accountant. http://www.wisegeek.com/what-is-a-bean-counter.htm
16. https://adwords.google.com/o/Targeting/Explorer?__u=1000000000&__c=1000000000&IdeaRequestType=KEYWORD_IDEAS#search.none
17. *Soylent Green* is a 1973 American science fiction film. It depicts a dystopian future suffering from pollution, overpopulation, depleted resources, poverty, dying oceans and a hot climate due to the greenhouse effect. Much of the population survives on processed food rations, including 'soylent green'. http://en.wikipedia.org/wiki/Soylent_Green
18. Popularly translated as 'seize the day'. *Carpe* literally means 'to pick, pluck, pluck off, cull, crop, gather'. 'Carpe diem' is a phrase from a Latin poem by Horace. http://en.wikipedia.org/wiki/Carpe_diem
19. *How To Be An Effective Corporate Ambassador* http://darmano.typepad.com/logic_emotion/2010/09/how-be-an-effective-corporate-ambassador.html
20. Paul Verrico is a solicitor-advocate based in Leeds, England: http://uk.linkedin.com/in/paulverrico; Nick Davies is a senior tax consultant based in Leeds, England: http://uk.linkedin.com/pub/nick-davies/6/538/23b; http://www.garbutt-elliott.co.uk/taxteam.htm; Andrew Neligan is a Certified Financial Planner. His approach to Financial Planning earned him an award at the 2009 FT New Breed Adviser awards. http://www.icl-ifa.co.uk
21. Peters & Barletta, *Trends*
22. Original quote: 'You've got more rabbit than Sainsbury's', Chas and Dave (singers from the UK) – meaning 'you talk a lot'; Sainsbury's is a UK supermarket chain.
23. *What's New Pussycat?* is a song made famous by numerous singers, including Tom Jones, written by Burt Bacharach and Hal David. http://en.wikipedia.org/wiki/What percent27s_New_Pussycat percent3F_(song)

Volume 4: getting under your skin

slowly, slowly, catch a nichey

Welcome back! Catch this big hug from your private Naked Lawyer dancer in law law land. Well done so far! Hopefully you've enjoyed reading Volumes 1, 2 and 3 and you've been enthusiastic in engaging in all of the after dark activities prior to beginning this Volume 4. If not, please do so.

Why? Because if you haven't then you've been missing out on some really cool stuff! Volumes 1-3, together with this Volume 4, are the golden nuggets which lay the foundation and are the keys to unlocking the latent potential within YOU to enable you to get more clients, sales, referrals, income, value, growth and success.

In Volumes 5 through to 12, I show you how you to strut your stuff using all the dazzling rocks from Volumes 1 through to 4 to truly come alive as a naked rainmaker lawyer!

Simply put: you need the content within them, the important background information and practical activities which you should have done, in preparation for this Volume 4. Without it, this Volume isn't going to make a great deal of sense, unfortunately. Some, maybe, but surely you want to get the most from it?

phwoar!

As I have said in previous volumes, to reap the full benefit of the ROAR model you will need to string all 12 volumes together to experience the powerful beneficial effect.

'Yes', you will get something out of Volume 4 as a stand-alone read. But, I kid you not, the outcome in relation to the brand you create for yourself may well not be as *phwoar* as it should be!

As always, duly note... Albeit this is my story, you ought to be trying to empathise with me. Nevertheless, as ever, the focus is all on YOU... and about YOU. My mission is to help YOU. My modus operandi is by being your private dancer. Use me. Abuse me. Dance with me. Come with me while I share with you how to achieve a 'Brand,You' way of life.

rock 'n' rolling from bland to brand

By now you should have laid down the foundations to help you become an extraordinary rainmaker... better still, an extraordinary lover!

You should have worked out your Big Rocks, done your EI analysis and SWOT analysis, started to devise your Formidable ME Strategy & Plan (goals, mission, vision), addressed your Ethicability conundrum, worked out your ME Code of Conduct and Epitaph, addressed your Rainmaker Mindset, Attitude, Motivation and PEE Poor Work Ethic, researched and identified an ideal niche and niches within the same (drilling down through a niche of a niche of a niche of a niche of a niche), sorted your positioning, differentiation, USPs, PODs, and target market(s) and be in prime form, at the ready, for a little fourplay.

Having read and done the practical activities in Volumes 1, 2 and 3 you ought to be 'nichely' sat, well and truly perky, to get to work now on your personal brand. If we get your 'Brand,Me' right, many clients, lobsters and suppliers will be drawn to you because of what it extols. By positioning, differentiating and branding yourself well, you will naturally provide extraordinary service and be able to market and sell yourself in a whole new different way.

Let's steer away from broader, impersonal marketing methods and focus on your rainmaking and professional business development based on relationship-building and ROARing through your personal brand. It's time to strive to build your very own cohesive business identity and show both law law land and the business world that you can be modern, entrepreneurial, innovative and truly accommodating... Let's show 'em what you're really made of!

just do something!

Keep all of your notes and documents from Volumes 2 and 3 at the ready as we move through this Volume 4.

what's in a name?

from sweet rose to crapbag

One of the most famous lines and significant meanings in English literature is that shared between Juliet and Romeo in William Shakespeare's play *Romeo and Juliet* (II, ii, 1-2):

"What's in a name? That which we call a rose By any other name would smell as sweet."

Juliet means that a name is an artificial and meaningless convention, for she loves Romeo but not the Montague name. I would disagree that a name is meaningless, particularly in this digital age. If you asked me, 'What's in a name?' I would say *everything!*

Our name provides us with a strong identity. Get it right, and it can be a hugely effective marketing tool, such as, 'Chrissie Lightfoot'. Get it wrong, and it can be of detriment, such as 'Crapbag'. For example, should I call myself 'Chrissie Lightfoot' or 'Chrissie Crapbag?'

I use 'Crapbag' as an extreme example of a name that would probably cause embarrassment. This was certainly the case in my favourite American sitcom *Friends* when Mike, Phoebe's boyfriend retaliated to Phoebe changing her name to something ludicrous. To prove a point, he did likewise. He became Mike Crapbag; to Phoebe's *huge* embarrassment.

It's not the kind of name you would wish to work up into a personal brand as the connotation is *not* pretty! And it certainly is *not* a great marketing tool!

Conversely, if I said to you Bill Gates, Michael Jordon, Ivana Trump, David Beckham, Abraham Lincoln, I am confident that you would agree that each of these names convey a very strong identity. And, as you read these names you would have felt some kind of emotion, whether in the negative or the positive. The emotion would have been triggered simply by your mind conjuring up a memory and perception perhaps of each of their individual personality, image, appearance, values, behaviours and attitudes, aka their brand.

I have previously mentioned that we should consider 'Me,Inc.', aka, 'Brand,Me' despite the fact that we are 'betrothed' to 'the firm'. Inevitably, working so darn hard to become a part of 'the firm' we invariably allow our role, such as 'lawyer', or 'trainee solicitor', etc. to define us – a 'general' identity shared by many.

Which is wrong. It simply is not good enough for YOU!

I battled against such defining, simply because saying 'I'm a lawyer' is generic (whatever level or stage of career I would be at) and severely restricted my ability to distinguish myself, not only from my colleagues but also from the 'competition'. After all, every second person you bump into these days happens to be a lawyer! A little exaggeration here, perhaps? Needless to say, I reckon it's absolutely imperative to carve out a unique identity, a personal brand of extraordinary quality and distinction.

Even with our christened names we can choose how we wish to be known in order to 'work' it to our advantage...

get you digging me!

2006: I began my corporate life in law law land as 'Christine Lightfoot'. However, when devising my personal brand I began with the end in mind. That is, if I was going to expend a great deal of time, effort and money into devising my personal brand, with the long term in mind, I wanted to make sure that when potential clients, referrers, suppliers and colleagues, etc. went looking for me that they would find the right 'Christine Lightfoot', with personal brand 'whatever'.

2008: I began by surfing the web to research if there were any other 'Christine Lightfoots' occupying a space in cyberspace already. Sure enough, there was. There was a lady barrister in the USA with an established track-record and presence already visible on carrying out a quick Google search.

Accordingly, I figured I needed to differentiate myself from this existing lady in order to avoid confusion. She had her space. Respect. Now, I was going to own mine.

Accordingly, I decided to start using the name 'Chrissie Lightfoot' rather than 'Christine Lightfoot' on all my correspondence and online handles as I could see the value in that going forward; I was able to secure the domain names chrissielightfoot.com, chrissielightfoot.co.uk and chrissielightfoot.eu for one thing!

And, actually, I much preferred 'Chrissie' to 'Christine'. 'Chrissie' is the real me. It's the name I was known as and jumped to as a wee girl throughout my junior years, teenage years and young adult life. I was only ever called 'Christine' when I was in trouble. Big trouble!

'Chrissie' is informal, approachable, more friendly and less 'stuffy'. It's my authentic self actually, the true 'Brand,Me' as a starter for ten in my brand stable for consideration.

From that simple exercise I realised that it was important to begin building my personal brand, in whatever format it took, with my name as 'Chrissie Lightfoot' from that day forward, because there was very little 'competition' in that space on the web.

You're probably wondering, 'Why was this so significant?' Well, at the forefront of my cunning plan in devising my personal brand was the thought, 'How do I win business on the strength of my personal brand?'

The secret? With an understanding of the power of search engine optimisation, keyword search and the growth of real-time search in social networks, ergo, social search optimisation, it was a no brainer that people would search on obvious keywords and associated words within social network platforms. It turned out that snaffling prime keywords and placing them in my brand would result in potential clients finding me via a social search when they go digging purely on the strength and relativity of my brand name.

It worked for me, it ought to work for you too!

So, let me now share with you how I created my brand, so that you can follow and create yours too...

just do something!
Check out your name (whatever combination you desire, that is, you may want Christian name and surname, or you may wish to include your middle name too perhaps?) by doing a Google search to see if someone already occupies 'your space'. If so, get creative! Consider alternative names. When you've settled on an appropriate and 'not so competitive name' already permeating cyberspace make sure you register your correlating domain name(s), if available.

Ideally, you need to find a name that *does* have an available domain name as you may wish to develop a blog or mini website using your name at some point in the future. Ideally snaffle the .com, .co.uk and .eu suffixes – all worthy domain name suffixes of value.

personal brand creation

Honestly, there's little mystery in how I built my personal brand. I did it simply by doing what you did in your preparatory work in Volumes 2 and 3 and then completed the process with the final steps. And by no means am I an expert. However, I'm happy to share with you how I approached it simply because it worked for me, so it could work for you too!

Simply put: my personal brand, my 'Brand,Me', is derived from who I am, who I want to be and who people perceive me to be. A personal brand is something that each of us can relate to because it is what other people see as a reflection of our individual identity and values. Arguably, each and every one of us has a personal brand, whether we like it or not.

If you're smart (which you are of course), you'll create the one you want, massage it, manage it, take control of it... and exploit it.

what's in a brand?

I thought of my brand in my own personal terms. That is, my authentic self; my personality, character, self-image, values, strengths, talents, skills, experience, etc. I thought about how my character and self image affected the relationships in my life; personal and professional. And then I asked myself how I am likely to be seen and how I would like to be seen by others.

Why? Because I knew that my brand is a perception that would have strong meaning and significance in the minds of my potential and existing clients, referrers, suppliers and colleagues. I realised that my 'brand' ought to portray how other people perceive me and how they feel about me. And, fundamentally, why they would choose to hire me rather than one of my 'competitors'.

Taking the niche positioning, differentiation, USPs, PODs and 'competition' research that I had undertaken, my personal brand positioning, differentiation and niche was a natural extension and outcome of the same. Namely, it came naturally to me in how to define the unique qualities I could offer potential and existing clients, what unique services I could offer and what it was that would make me special because I could answer the following questions:

- What is my particular niche expertise?
- What makes me truly different?
- What level of brand equity could I have with my target market clients?
- What do I do better than any other lawyer?
- What could I do better than any other lawyer?
- What makes me stand out?
- How do I add value?
- Am I well known already?
- Could I be?

- Why should a potential client instruct me to do business with them rather than any other lawyer?

What flowed next was figuring out my brand positioning, aka brand values. I reflected back on my mission statement which described my purpose; the driving force for my raison d'être.

My mission: To bring lawyers and entrepreneurs together in a positive way; to help bridge the gap between the legal world and the business world; to aid understanding and build positive long term relationships between both parties; and to provide cost effective, time effective and time efficient legal advice which creates value for both myself and my client.

I then created my brand values with the understanding that they should dovetail with my mission statement. In essence, my brand values describe how I desire to be regarded by others, that is, my reputation with potential clients, referrers and suppliers, etc.

My brand values:

- Entrepreneurism;
- Innovation;
- Dynamism;
- Pro-activity;
- Engagement;
- Value Added;
- Transparency; and
- Ethical.

just do something!

Look again at your notes and documents from Volume 2 in relation to 'who am I?'; who do you want to be and how do people perceive you. Look again at your strengths, skills, talent, experiences, values, attitude, personality, characteristics, self awareness and self image. Ask yourself, 'How am I likely to be seen and how would I like to be seen by others?' Write your thoughts down.

Then ask yourself the above questions (as I did) in the 'what's in a brand?' section. You may wish to refer back to your notes from Volume 3. Think deeply, reflect and again, write your answers down.

Now go back to your mission statement and notes from Volume 2 in order to work out your brand positioning, aka brand values. Take your time. Put some clear thinking into this exercise. And enjoy! Once you have decide on your brand values, list them, as I did.

let's get emotional

The Secret Millionaire, Carl Hopkins – marketing expert and successful entrepreneur, whose expertise lies in brand creation and development – amongst other things, says the formula to a successful brand is as follows:[1]

"If a brand were a formula it would be the product of two things: A prediction of what to expect, multiplied by the emotional power of that expectation. If you encounter a brand and don't know what it means or does, it has zero power... If, however, you know what to expect of a brand and it delivers on that expectation, then it is a powerful brand."

I know from experience that extraordinary rainmaking comes down to focusing on the benefits we consistently bring to potential clients and our ability to truly focus and deliver on that at all times.

I also know that clients buy on emotion and justify/reason with logic. So, naturally, I asked myself, 'What are the most powerful emotional benefits I can deliver to my potential and existing clients?' Accordingly...

in essence I promise you ROAR value

I reckoned the most powerful emotional benefits must focus on my PODs and have at least the following three qualities:

- Be extraordinarily important to the target client;
- That I must be uniquely suited to delivering it; and
- My competitors are not currently addressing it – nor will it be easy for them to address it in the future.[2]

It's a no brainer that strong brands deliver substantial benefits:[3]

- Increased revenues and market share;
- Increased customer loyalty;
- Increased profitability;
- Increased clarity of vision; and
- Decreased price sensitivity.

Leading organisations have discovered that brands are their most valuable asset (along with their people) for a number of reasons, the above to name a few. I reckoned, therefore, that if a firm could cultivate multiple personal brands within it then the likelihood was that the 'substantial benefits' noted above would be even more enhanced.

brand essence

I therefore needed to address my brand essence – the word or phrase I wanted to become ultimately renowned for. It needed to capture the very core of me, the soul of my brand, have clarity and simplicity, and be aspirational, enduring and timeless. It had to deliver the 'big Chrissie Lightfoot idea' through words and appropriate images that I could drive forward and take me into the practice areas I had identified as being of most interest and optimum benefit to me and the firm...

ROAR, Reach Out And Relate, says it all really.

brand promise

Hard-upon came the creation of the brand promise; the most important part of the 'Brand,Me' design. I knew that my brand must promise a relevant, compelling and differentiated benefit to my target market client.

Accordingly, I asked myself this question: 'What is the promise made by me to the legal world and the client groups I desire to serve?' Answer: My brand promise... Only The Entrepreneur Lawyer delivers extraordinary ROAR experiences to entrepreneurs.

just do something!

Work out your brand essence and brand promise by reading the 'in essence I promise you ROAR value' section again and referring to your practical activities in Volume 3.

my 'Brand,Me' secret exposed

I'd like to share with you a secret... I actually didn't come up with my personal brand name all on my own. My Boss Lawyer helped... significantly. Allow me to share with you the story.

It was autumn 2008. Boss Lawyer together with the then managing partner (now senior partner) and I were engaging in a business development brainstorming session. I was sharing with them my ideas surrounding the creation of an 'entrepreneur team' within the firm, the development of the entrepreneur niche, the entrepreneur product and service 'bundle' proposition, and how we might consider taking it forward to attract serial, women and young entrepreneur clients in target market industries and sectors.

Taking into consideration the research I'd done in relation to positioning, differentiation, USPs, PODs, client and referrer understanding, awareness and perception of myself (having asked them during my research) and sharing the very same with my co-entrepreneurial lawyers who 'got it', I said to Boss Lawyer something along the lines of:

"Being known and/or identified as a trainee solicitor just doesn't cut it out in the business world. It's too generic as I am engaging in conversations with top level executives, decision makers, with a view to capturing their attention. It's too bland. First impressions count. Big time. It doesn't express who I am, how I can help them, how I and/or the firm can be of benefit and/or value to them, whilst I'm prostrating myself as an ambassador of the firm and a potential solution to their needs and expectations. They need to be able to relate to me and identify with me within ten seconds.

"At the moment, if I am asked, 'what do you do?' I say, 'I am a business woman with legal intelligence'. Why do I say this? Because it grabs their attention. It's intriguing. It's different. It allows me to expand when their curiosity gets the better of them and they follow up with another statement and question, namely, 'that's interesting, what do you mean?' Ideally, I need a name, a title, a brand or something that truly reflects who and what I am."

To which Boss Lawyer immediately proffered... "you're an entrepreneur lawyer." SMART COOKIE! His instinctive response and natural perception of me aligned with my research. Enough said. It seemed obvious. And I guess that's the point...

Also, I reckon it's worth noting that it helps if you share your ideas with other people as it may actually be them who come up with the obvious personal brand for you.

This is a classic case and example of where perception really is reality.

And so, from that day forward, I decided that my personal brand would be: Chrissie Lightfoot, 'The Entrepreneur Lawyer'.

It's very simple, straightforward, distinct, obvious *and*... bonus... it tells a story, which is why it makes it easy to relate and understand. I intend to keep it that way. Long term. So should you... when you devise yours.

It actually lends itself to a story. The brand is the story. And Tom Peters, business guru, unabashedly believes that the story is actually more powerful than the brand and that we should think story first, brand second. So, I'm happy with the outcome of the 'Brand,Me' exercise.

Being the first to use a personal brand, such as Chrissie Lightfoot 'The Entrepreneur Lawyer', matters a great deal in cutting a special unique place, a space, particularly in cyberspace! You will no doubt come to this conclusion yourself when you devise your very own personal brand.

Take a moment now to reflect on the 'Brand,Me' process diagram in Figure 1 on the following page.

just do something!

Share your ideas in relation to your 'Brand,Me' with other 'trusted' people; it just might help stimulate you further! If at all possible, create a personal brand which is simple, straightforward, distinct, obvious and tells a story!

brand unstable?

OK. It's autumn 2008. I've now got myself a personal brand. What's a little Naked Lawyer in law law land to do now? Brand stable domination of course!

Mega flurry of activity ensues to secure 'The Entrepreneur Lawyer', and variations of the same, particularly in cyberspace.

the 'Brand,Me' process

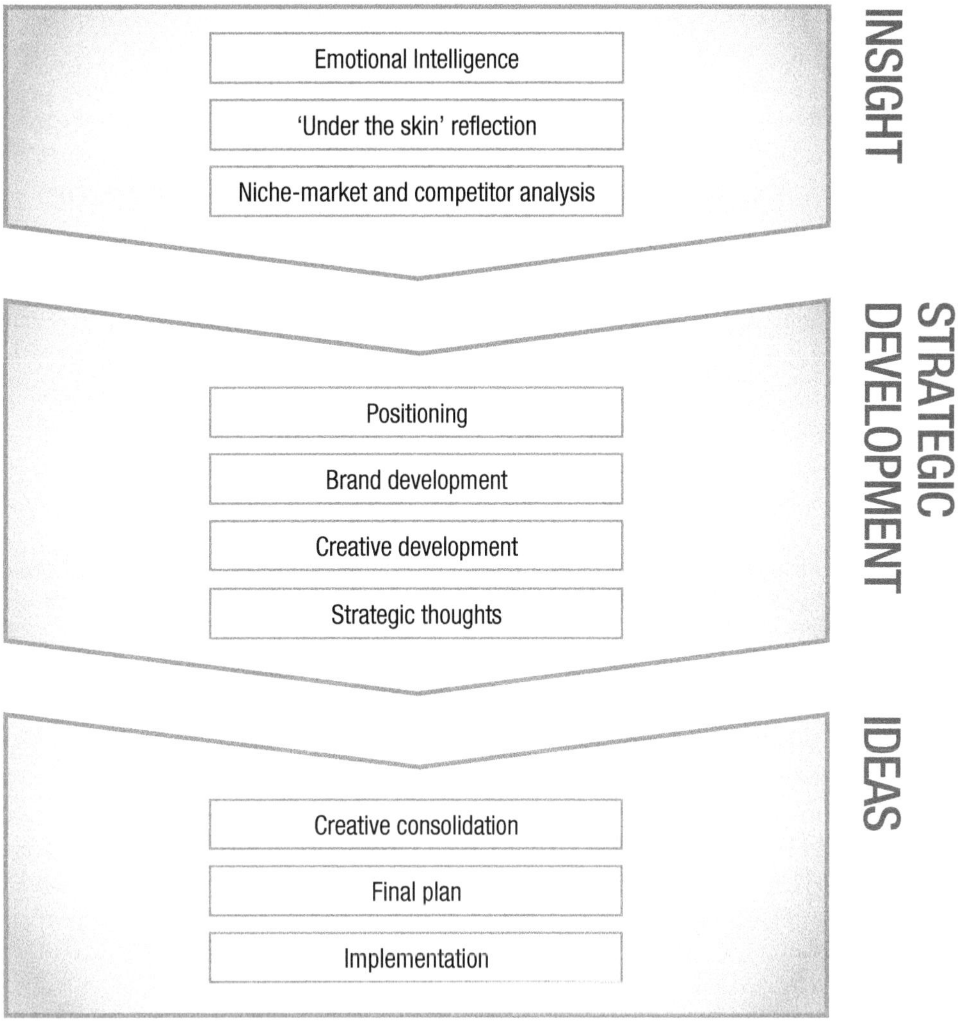

Figure 1: The 'Brand,Me' Process diagram, © David Clarkson and Chrissie Lightfoot

Why? Because bucking the internet and web trend in relation to social media and social networking, the development of Web 2.0, 3.0 and 4.0 on the cyber horizon together with the semantic web, I figured I'd better secure the relevant domain names and handles on key social media and social networking platforms – the likes of LinkedIn, Twitter, Facebook and YouTube, to name a few.

To complete my brand stable I knew sufficient about company law, commercial law and IP law to understand the value in securing domain names, trademarks and company names in a bid to protect, and also exploit, the IP associated with my personal brand.

Btw: my attitude positively SUUUCKS at this point of course. And my thought process included, 'NUTS to the whole darn thing!'...

think nuts! just grab 'em

Now – just do it, go fetch!
Unconventional – it was and is in law law land.
Timing – think about now and the future.
Social – on every platform possible offline and online.

Nab 'em. *Fast*!

I have approximately 100 domain names registered that are significant to my personal brand and identity. The .com domain suffix is still the most prestigious and 'valued' of course, but .co.uk suffix is pretty important for UK companies and users; the new .co suffix has recently been released, but for a premium fee.[4]

Domain name hi-jacking, cyber-squatting, trademark infringement, identity theft are just a few of the legal nasties I hoped (and hope) to avoid... I've always favoured prevention rather than cure in all aspects and respects.

I also appreciate that brand consistency rules! Feel free to Google me; 'chrissie lightfoot', 'the entrepreneur lawyer', 'entrepreneur lawyer', 'entrepreneurlaw'. You will note that the brand, the message, the theme are consistent. If not, please do get in touch and let me know as I will have screwed up and welcome your heads up to help rectify my clanger(s)!

For example, my brand stable is as shown in the box out.

just do something!

Secure your relevant personal brand handles on all social media and/or social networking platforms and secure your key domain names that are directly relevant to your brand.

Personal brand:	'The Entrepreneur Lawyer' ChrissieLightfoot.com ChrissieLightfoot.co.uk ChrissieLightfoot.eu
Company name:	EntrepreneurLawyer Limited
Trademark (US):	Entrepreneur Lawyer
Trademark (UK):	Entrepreneur Lawyer
Domain names:	EntrepreneurLawyer.co.uk EntrepreneurLawyers.co.uk TheEntrepreneurLawyer.co.uk
LinkedIn:	Chrissie Lightfoot The Entrepreneur Lawyer
Twitter:	EntrepreneurLaw
Facebook:	Entrepreneur Lawyer
YouTube:	Entrepreneur Lawyer

Duly note twitter only allows 15 characters as a handle.

Consider registering the trademark and securing the company name, even at this stage to allow for flexibility in your career; you never know how the future might just pan out.[5]

'Brand,Me' and 'Brand,Firm'

Often, particularly corporate branding ('Brand,Firm') is planned to be 'championed' through 'personal' branding ('Brand,Me'). We all recognize the use of spokespersons in 'the firm' who are selected because of their 'personal' branding's affinity with 'Brand,Firm'. But, arguably, this same concept is in play at the lowest common denominator with rainmaker lawyers aka salespersons at whatever level they reside.

For private clients and commercial clients alike, as I have previously stated, sales begins by 'buying' the salesperson/spokesperson which may be 'personal branding'. Regardless of how the legal profession feels about the internet and its impact on the profession present and future, it happens that the internet allows equal footing for all to host their brand (resume).

Invariably, this implies that personal branding has and always will be a major part of everyone's marketing plans. It would be helpful for us all to keep that in mind. One advantage of having personal branding in your law firm is that it creates that truly personal element in your marketing and sales campaigns.

Since 'Brand,Me' typically goes to work for 'Brand,Firm' I fail to see why some lawyers believe they are, by definition, competing, or of lesser value than 'Brand,Firm', or subservient to 'Brand,Firm'.

If anything I believe corporate branding provides a useful framework. As legal professionals we would do well to think about the short, medium and long-term impact of every career move.

You may recall my mentioning The Resistance in Volume 3, and that I found managing corporate ambassadorship in the established law firm I was at very challenging. Albeit I did proffer the argument that actually I am an 'ambassador' for both. A brand ambassador of 'Brand,Firm' and 'Brand,Me' perfectly dovetailed, aka aligned, together for one common purpose... Firm success.

effective rainmaker tips

In my bid to be an effective rainmaker and corporate ambassador, I was diligent in conveying the message that I was proud to represent 'the firm' and align it with my own identity, both internally and externally. If you'd have chopped my arm off it would have bled pantone 'xyz' – or whatever the correct pantone reference is for the firm's marketing collateral.

Being a corporate ambassador had an interesting burden... albeit joy. I had to work my butt off; and that's an understatement. I had to prove I was willing to put in hard graft, just like everyone else, in relation to the daily grind. Invariably, I had to be sure to get the basics of my daily grinder's monkey technical law duties accomplished and then pursue ambassador duties after the priority technical legal work business was taken care of.

I carried out the majority of my ambassador activity 'in my own time', i.e. before work, lunchtimes, evenings and weekends.

When engaging in public at both online and offline venues, I was careful to balance corporate responsibility with individual personality. Albeit I was my authentic self, I was always cognisant that I was representative of the firm and those whom I served.

I was also keen to leverage my networks to the benefit of the firm. Prior to entering the legal profession I was quite well connected, networked and plugged into a number of communities which would be valuable to the firm. I was pro-active in expanding these networks exponentially with a view to creating a wealth of connections; sharing that wealth created value for all.

I didn't live in the ivory tower. I was keen to escape into the business world to connect, engage and get involved with prospective entrepreneurial clients in ways that would be mutually beneficial, whenever possible!

In time, I am confident that personal branding and corporate ambassadorship is something that will become the norm rather than exception in law firms, *at every level*, starting with paralegals and trainee solicitors.

My view and approach are both shared by David Armano, Senior Vice President at Edelman Digital, when he speaks of co-branding, sharing, working hard, representing and engaging being the hallmarks of a good corporate ambassador.[6]

just do something!

Duly note the tips in relation to being an effective rainmaker through harmonising 'Brand,Me' and 'Brand,Firm'.

brand un...convention...ally

Albeit a junior lawyer devising a personal brand defies convention, it didn't prevent me from pursuing such a thing. I had the best interests of the client and the firm at heart, as well as securing my own career and future. This is self-reliance era, after all. I also had the blessing of two key partners, which helped immensely.

I intimated in Volume 1 that I would share with you a few tips of how ROAR works in practice using my present company, EntrepreneurLawyer Limited, as an example.

Well, when it's your own game plan you can make up your own rules. Hell, you can even break all of 'em if you wish, not unlike Chip Conley![7] So, that is precisely what I've done.

As I've said previously, I'm not a brand expert. However, when you are master of your own mutiny you can create whatever products and services you want. You also have a licence to innovate where it pleases you.

With regard to *the naked lawyer* book I decided to create 'Brand, Product', that is, I created a brand for a product. *the naked lawyer* book is, and of itself, a brand – 'The Naked Lawyer'.

As Tom Peters so coolly puts it:[8]

"one woman/man global powerhouse is not an oxymoron in the new millennium... Brand You: The Whole World really is Your Oyster. (If you've got a SERIOUSLY COOL PRODUCT to sell... and a "brand structure" to support it...and Imagination...and Determination...and the Web.)"

In essence I have established the following:

- 'Brand,Me' – Chrissie Lightfoot 'The Entrepreneur Lawyer'
- 'Brand,Product' – *the naked lawyer* (books, e-books, articles, etc); I do hope it's seriously cool!
- 'Brand,Firm' – EntrepreneurLawyer

I have, of course, applied the same brand stable thoroughness of IP protection and exploitation to *the naked lawyer* 'Brand, Product' as I applied to 'The Entrepreneur Lawyer' brand stable.

just do something!

Perhaps you may wish the consider devising a 'Brand,Product', bespoke of course, in relation to your personal brand, your product offering and keeping in mind the brand of the firm, that is the entity, that you serve?

'Brand,Me'... everywhere!

making 'Brand,Me' count

Having put all the ground work into creating my personal brand I was going to make darn sure that I got 'The Entrepreneur Lawyer' brand name everywhere. I was (and continue) to make 'Brand,Me' count.

Whenever I sign off *anywhere* it is always, 'Chrissie Lightfoot – The Entrepreneur Lawyer'.

Whilst at 'the firm' I placed 'Chrissie Lightfoot – The Entrepreneur Lawyer' on my e-signature strip, business cards (albeit written in the blank area as I refused to have trainee solicitor on the card), blog post entry sign-offs (in the body of the text along with relevant urls so that it got picked up by the reader easily and indexed by Google), LinkedIn groups, LinkedIn endorsements and *all* social network sites I frequented. I realised that it's all about reinforcing my brand at every opportunity in order to make it believable, and also managing the perception and delivery of it so that I was (and am) in control of the messaging the market receives.

Someone once said to me that "Branding is NOT everything... but everything IS branding." It resonated. It stuck with me.

In relation to my personal brand life cycle I figured it needs a lot of attention at the inception (formation) stage but then needs careful handling, aka, management, through a lot of focus going forward. For I believe I have created a brand which will last forever. Products and services may come and go. However, personal brands should be consistent throughout and last a lifetime, I reckon.

I believe I have succeeded in creating an image and am living up to it. I practice what I preach. I make every effort to ensure my 'brand values' are delivered consistently in my thoughts, feelings and actions – behaviour – in my bid to build a consistent and positive reputation as 'The Entrepreneur Lawyer'. Since there will always be a logical need to cultivate my 'reputation' there will always be a need for my 'Brand,Me' and I will need to invest time and effort in the long-term process of building my reputation.

Inevitably, building a successful brand will take time, but I am confident I have made the positive first steps and it will be something I am continually prepared to invest time, effort and money in to improve the reputation and continually deliver on the brand promise.

I have unwavering *faith* in my brand.

just do something!

Once you have decided on your personal brand, begin to sign-off everywhere with it! Read again the examples as to where in your efforts to reinforce and manage your brand.

Now, truly, live up to your brand... And believe in it!

trump crumbling ivory towers

To be a successful rainmaker lawyer with a strong personal brand, I believe if we take the message from personal brand guru Dan Schawbel appertaining to all people whatever their role; his advice is simple but effective:[9]

- Put your name on everything;
- Work your tail off;
- Dress for success;
- Be the best at what you do; and
- Authenticity rules.

Schawbel suggests Donald Trump as a perfect example of how a personal brand ought to be 'worked':

"Trump puts his name everywhere, and therefore more people know about him, his family, and his connection with luxury products. You need to make sure your name gets out there in the same regard. Whether it's your Twitter profile, your Facebook page, your business cards, your resume, or a presentation you're working on at work, your name should be everywhere. This creates a consistency that will remind people of who you are, and what value you can contribute."

Still, I reckon his ex wife, the infamous Ivana, trumps even Donald with her wonderfully memorable quote: "Don't get mad. Get everything!"

If you reckon you're sat in a crumbling ivory tower law firm, perhaps you could heed Ivana's words of wisdom, in particular by applying them to securing your personal brand and brand stable... I did. You can too!

after dark activity
think 'sexy legs' brand

OK then. It's time for you to get jiggy with creating your very own personal brand. As you do, I'd like you to think extraordinary rainmaker, extraordinary lover and extraordinary sexy legs. Look to making your personal brand 'sexy' by ensuring that in the very least it has longevity (legs) and at best, has a killer story!

naked lawyer activity – a study worth casing

During summer 2008 I set about working through what is now Volume 4 (ROAR steps) of *the naked lawyer* in devising my personal brand.As to what I did, and for a real live case study, in how to create your very own 'Brand,Me', simply read the story again in this Volume 4. You can relive my activity by taking yourself through the same process.

Let me help you. Here's a condensed version of the key activities and exercises you may wish to carry out...

ROAR steps

It's now time to do the following exercise in the step sequence provided. As I've said before, it may take you a few days, a few weeks or a few months. But don't take too long or else a 'competitor' may snaffle your ideal brand!

- **Step 1:** Check out your name by doing a Google search to see if someone already occupies 'your space'. Make sure you register your correlating domain name(s) if available. Ideally you need to find a name that does have an available domain name. Ideally snaffle the .com, .co.uk and .eu suffixes; all worthy domain name suffixes of value.
- **Step 2:** Look again at your notes and documents from Volume 2 in relation to 'who am I?'; who do you want to be and how do people perceive you? Look again at your strengths, skills, talent, experiences, values, attitude, personality, characteristics, self awareness and self image. Ask yourself 'how am I likely to be seen and how would I like to be seen by others?' Write your thoughts down. Then ask yourself the questions in the 'what's in a brand?' section. You may wish to refer back to your notes from Volume 3. Think deeply, reflect and again, write your answers down. Now go back to your mission statement – notes from Volume 2 in order to work out your brand positioning aka brand values. Take your time. Put some clear thinking into this exercise. And enjoy! Once you have decided on your brand values, list them, as I did.
- **Step 3:** Work out your brand essence and brand promise by reading the 'in essence I promise you ROAR value' section again and referring to your practical activities in Volume 3.
- **Step 4:** Share your ideas in relation to your 'Brand,Me' with other 'trusted' people; it just might help stimulate your grey cells further! If at all possible, create a personal brand which is simple, straightforward, distinct, obvious and tells a story!
- **Step 5:** Secure your relevant personal brand handles on all social media and/or social networking platforms and secure your key domain names that are directly relevant to your brand. Consider registering the trademark and securing the company name, even at this stage to allow for flexibility in your career; you never know how the future might just pan out.
- **Step 6:** Duly note the tips in relation to being an effective rainmaker

through harmonising 'Brand,Me' and 'Brand,Firm'.

- **Step 7:** Perhaps you may wish to consider devising a 'Brand,Product', bespoke of course, in relation to your personal brand, your product offering whilst keeping in mind the brand of the firm, the entity, that you serve?
- **Step 8:** Add the research, target market, niche and brand sections to your FMSP. Pull the niche and brand sections together into a separate proposal ready to present to your boss / line partner/ mentor. Keep your proposal at the ready for the right opportunity to meet with your boss.
- **Step 9:** Once you have decided on your personal brand, and met with your boss if/when required (most likely if you are servant to a master in a law firm), begin to sign-off everywhere with it! Read again the examples as to where in your efforts to reinforce and manage your brand. Now, truly, live up to your brand... And believe in it!

ROAR tips

- Get everything – brand stable;
- Be accommodating;
- Be creative;
- Don't allow your role to define YOU;
- Get digging;
- Get surfing;
- Be authentic;
- Harmonise 'Brand,Me' and 'Brand,Firm';
- Be NUTS;
- Think domination!
- Share your brand ideas;
- Think emotional benefits;
- Think big personality;
- Think search engine optimisation;
- Think social search optimisation;
- Think brand reputation; and
- Make 'Brand,Me' count!

ROAR summation

a new 'Brand,Me' in law law land

Woopah! You will no doubt be pleased to know that I reckon that's the really hard stuff done now. Everything you have read and worked through in Volumes 1 through to 4 has you sitting pretty as a potentially brand new 'Brand,You' in law law land.

You can now look forward with the greatest anticipation of what is yet to come. In Volumes 5 through to 12 we're going to put all this wonderful stuff into extraordinary practical use.

References

1. http://www.kloog.co.uk/index.php/home/marketing-expert/marketing-tips
2. *Ibid.*
3. *Ibid.*
4. I use http://www.easily.co.uk to register my domain names but there are many other providers to choose from. I highlight this one simply to get you started, if you're interested. There's also http://www.godaddy.com
5. TM & IP lawyers whom I work alongside at present include: Peter Groves – IP & TM specialist, UK Lawyer: http://www.petergroves.co.uk; http://uk.linkedin.com/in/petergroves81; and Anthony Verna – TM & copyright specialist, US Attorney; http://www.linkedin.com/in/anthonyverna;
6. David Armano, SVP at Edelman Digital. http://darmano.typepad.com/logic_emotion/2010/09/how-be-an-effective-corporate-ambassador.html
7. Chip Conley , *The Rebel Rules: Daring To Be Yourself In Business* (New York: Simon & Schuster, 2001)
8. Tom Peters, *The Brand You 50: Fifty ways to transform yourself from an "employee" into a brand that shouts distinction, commitment, and passion!* (New York: Alfred A. Knopf, Inc.,1999), 190
9. http://www.personalbrandingblog.com

Volume 5: raving referral lobsters rule!

getting under your skin

Welcome back, again! Here's a big hug from your private Naked Lawyer dancer in law law land.

skinny dipping?

Now that we've laid the foundations to unlocking the latent potential within YOU to enable you to get more clients, sales, referrals, income, value, growth and success, it's time for you to really strut your stuff using all the dazzling rocks from the previous volumes to truly come alive as a naked rainmaker lawyer!

If you haven't read and done the preparatory work in the previous volumes then you may wish to go back and do so.

Why? Because you will need the content within them, the important background information and practical activities in order to get the best out of this volume. Fundamentally, the ROAR – Reach Out And Relate – may not be as effective without the foundations you should have laid in Volumes 1 through to 4.

Again, I say, ideally, to reap the full benefit of the ROAR model you will need to string all 12 volumes together to experience the powerful beneficial effect. You need to get totally naked.

Skinny dipping is OK, that is, if you wish to dip in and out of the individual Volumes, but it positively rocks Full On if you go all the way, take everything off, and take the full, deep plunge. Go on...

Go grab a drink, settle into a comfy chair in the 'only disturb me at your peril' designated area and hang chilly. I say again, be *cool. Chill out.* Just *chill out*!

Now, allow yourself to truly experience the story and let the words ebb, flow and wash over you.

As always, please note... Albeit this is my story, you ought to be trying to empathise with me. Nevertheless, as ever, the focus is all on YOU... and about YOU. My mission is to help YOU. My modus operandi is by being your private dancer. Use me. Abuse me. Dance with me.

Swim with me now while I share with you how to lobster trot and positively click your way into being a highly successful and happily naked rainmaker lawyer!

plunging in where lawyers fear to tread

Let's just have a really quick recap shall we, for the sake of good order? Oh, and so that we can hit the sea bed swimmingly in this volume and those which follow of course.

Returning to my prancing Naked Lawyer in law law land story... It's Summer/Autumn 2008. I've:

- Worked out my Big Rocks;
- Done my EI analysis;
- Done my SWOT analysis;
- Addressed my Ethicability conundrum;
- Worked out my ME Code of Conduct;
- Got myself an Epitaph;
- Addressed my Rainmaker Mindset, Attitude and Motivation;

- Realised my PEE Poor Work Ethic;
- Researched and identified an ideal niche and niches within the same;
- Sorted my positioning, differentiation, USPs, PODs, and g-spots (target market(s));
- Found myself sitting pretty as a potentially brand new 'Brand,Me' in law law land; and
- Started the process of devising and continually updating my Formidable ME Strategy & Plan (FMSP); goals, mission, vision, target market identification, niches, personal brand.

Now, I thought, it's... Time to put all this stuff into positive action. Time to take the plunge and go where most lawyers fear to tread. Time to exit 'The Comfort Zone', 'The Ivory Tower' and 'Law Law Land'. Time to free the cubicle grinder's monkey slave. Time to venture into raving 'Referral Lobster Net-Kingdom' and 'Client Territory'. Time to be build some bridges to multiple kinds of valued referrers and potential clients.

Oh-oh. Naked!

Why? Because it's about survival in the self-reliance human economy and legal world and thriving in the topsy-turvy digital era.

I totally 'get' where Cole Silver is coming from in his belief that:

"Unfortunately, the majority of attorneys assume that all they need in order to be successful in their practice is a high degree of expertise in their chosen area. This is no longer true. The only factor that will ensure your continued success is having more knowledge about marketing... the ironic thing about marketing is that it could be the very activity that brings many attorneys back to the enjoyment of practicing the law. The development of deep and rewarding client relationships, which are in alignment with your interests and values, offers a solution for a less stressful, freedom-driven, and purposeful career as a lawyer."[1]

Rewarding client relationships; aligned with my interests and values; purpose; less stress; freedom. This resonates *big time* with me. I fancy some of that.

Someone once said to me, 'It's OK to have a little of what you fancy every now and again'. What's wrong with a *lot* of what I fancy then eh?! Plus, I'm in my prime, I thought. NOW, really is, the time of my life. My attitude simply SUUUCKS, that's cool. And, I'm ready for some extraordinary fourplay. Do you remember me sharing that with you in Volume 3? If not, go back for a quickie revision.

Here's a summary:

1) Media > 2) Entrepreneurs >
3) Corporate > 4) Employee Share Schemes

1) Niche > 2) Niche > 3) Niche > 4) Niche

Fourplay. Specialising in a niche opens doors, windows and digital devices like there's no tomorrow!

And so, the next step... I figured it's time to build myself a network of value, both offline and online, utilising *everything* I've devised so far. And, I reckoned the best way to do this, was to work *smart* and extraordinarily *hard*! I reckoned that getting an army of like minded and like interested soldiers – raving referral lobsters – on the case would speed up the process and I'd have a *lot* of fun along the way too! I'd start with building an extraordinary raving referral lobster network. My very own Referral Lobster Net-Kingdom...

what's a raving referral lobster?

You may recall in Volume 3 I shared with you the, "Aw... he's her lobster" scene in the American sitcom *Friends* where Phoebe explains that lobsters mate for life. Once they've found their mate they're friends forever. The lesson is quite simply that lobsters are friends for life. Their friendship is special. Friends are always there for each other. They can be counted on. And friends care. Friends like to help.

I look upon lobsters like mavens; key-influencers; head honchos; gang leaders; tippers, aka, top quality referrers. How do you recognise a maven? They:

- Genuinely and naturally want to help and give;
- Have an uncanny genius of being at the centre of events;
- Get groups to 'tip', that is, groups of members with social power;[2]
- Engage in 'people collection' as a business strategy;
- Are people we rely on to connect us with other people and information; and
- Are information specialists.

A raving referral lobster is all of the above. I'd like to think that I am one. Moot. But possible. Or, at the very least, I am constantly striving to be one. And proud of it.

You need to become a raving referral lobster too if you're going to become an extraordinary rainmaker.

referral lobster net-kingdom hard-core FMSP

So, I figured I must devise a formidable referral strategy and plan, as an adjunct to the overall big picture relationship marketing and relationship sales strategy and plan, within my FMSP, as to how I go about building my referral network, and therefore prospective and actual client pool.

I believe the traditional marketing and sales strategy and plan has evolved somewhat in the past few years, particular since social media and social networking hit the scene; more about this in Volume 6: social savvy junkie.

I went about devising and updating my FMSP with a view to building a raving Referral Lobster Net-Kingdom by taking a tactical rifle gun approach; that is, unwavering *focus* with strategic precision, tactical execution and pain-staking follow-on.

Using a shot-gun approach simply isn't good enough these days. *No argument.* Don't even think about taking that approach. You'll be wasting your time, energy and money. As internet based technology, social search, Web 2.0, 3.0 and 4.0 (and no doubt 5.0, 6.0, 7.0, etc. in years to come) advance, then bespoke, discrete, nicheing will become even more prevalent – niche interests; niche groups; niche targeting; niche searching; niche rifle approach.

My focus: to identify and build an enduring professional relationship with those raving referral lobsters who are:

- Synergistic – niche, interests, commonality;
- Benefits orientated;
- G-spot focused;
- Connectors;
- Curious;
- Giving;
- Authentic;
- Genuinely interested;
- Information specialists;
- Pro-active;
- Dynamic;
- Entrepreneurial;
- Ethical; and
- Caring.

That is, everything which mirrors my niche and personal brand. So, more research, more preparation, more curiosity, and more updating of the FMSP with my findings.

Let's face it. We get out what we put into something. Right? I wouldn't dare go into a client meeting (existing or prospect), or attend a dinner/networking event, without researching and preparing in advance the 'who', 'what', 'where', 'when', 'why' and 'how' elements surrounding the individual and circumstance in which I will find myself in. So, why would I approach something as important as my survival and professional future (as well as that of my colleagues) with any less method and/or rigour?

As the saying goes, 'It's not what you know, it's who you know'. And then, 'It's not who you know, it's what you know about who you know'.

Right?

Big Rocks, wwwwwh and prrrrrrr revision

Think back to Volumes 2 and 3 where we looked at identifying our core interests and cutting a niche by researching the 'competition'; specifically looking at who, what, where, when, why and how. And then how prrrrrrring may be a preferred focus in contrast to being concerned about the 'competition'. That is, being unique, special and rare, thereby obliterating 'fear' of the competition and embracing collaboration perhaps?

Well, I figured I needed to carry out a similar process in relation to identifying raving referral lobsters... When I researched my niche (Volume 3) I made a note of some of the 'industry VIPs' and potential mavens. I dug a bit deeper now as my purpose was to actually meet these people and to start to develop an enduring relationship with them, both offline and online. I will look at the online stuff with you in Volume 6: social savvy junkie.

just do something!

Time to do some more digging. Research. Take a look at the list in the 'hard-core FMSP' section again. Think about the kind of referrer lobster you need to identify who will mirror your niche and personal brand. To help in this process, go back to the Volumes 3 and 4 'after dark activity' outcomes. Now, ask yourself, 'who do I know' and 'what do I know about who I know?' to get the ball rolling.

Consult your findings in relation to Volume 3, that is, your niche wwwwwh research and outcomes. Did you spot industry VIPs at that time? If not, go back, dig a little further, and find them. Consider, are these the kind of lobsters you would like to click with?

Write down all of your thoughts and your findings. Now devise your unique, bespoke list, of your ideal kind of referrer.

why focus on building a raving referral network?

You may be wondering, 'Why the primary focus on building a referral network, Chrissie?'

I'd like to share with you a secret... Laser focused, calculating, tactical and strategic referral/third party engagement, interaction and involvement is *the* most effective and efficient way of growing a client pool. *Period.*

In a nutshell: it's all about being present, available, visible and giving, giving and then giving some more to the raving referral lobsters in g-spot niches, offline and online.

I know this, from previous experience and successes in industries outside the legal profession. Accordingly, I believed law law land would be *exactly* the same. The more lobsters and ideal clients in my lobster net-kingdom I can net, the more powerful the dynamic, reach and positive outcomes for us all. I was confident that it would remain *the* secret to truly building my network and area of influence, expertise and specialism... fast!

Why? Friendly mutual referrals and building a raving referral lobster network will beat traditional forms of marketing and networking hands down because referral relationships are truly deep and granular.

Networking per se can be inefficient, unfocused and ineffective at times. But referral networking and referral 'working' is a completely different kettle of fish (pardon the pun). With a dedicated, focused and educated raving Referral Lobster Net-Kingdom of value it means I can be confident in casting my 'prospective client pool' net far and wide.

The secret lies in the depth of the relationship and real understanding between the referrer and I in our genuine and authentic desire to help each other. *Fact.*

who could I rave with?

It's brain-storm and brain-dump time, I reckon... Having done my research, again, I asked myself the following: *'who would be* my ideal raving referrers?'

Answer:

- Friends;
- Family;
- Colleagues past and present;
- Synergistic professionals;
- Synergistic support professionals, organisations, associations to the legal profession;
- Synergistic clients;
- Synergistic suppliers;
- 'Competitors'/collaborators;
- Shared interests/commonality individuals and groups;
- Synergistic niche 'industry VIPs'; and
- High profile people and key influencers.

Namely, people who are likely to know, like and trust me.[3] *And,* furthermore, understand, 'get' and share an interest/commonality with me. More about this in a moment.

You may recall my saying the following in Volumes 2 and 3:

"if you share the same interests as the people you wish to attract, you can be of more value to THEM due to the value and quality of your network, knowledge, attitude, enthusiasm and work ethic, which will inevitably have synergy with THEM. Your network will have more value because you will be able to GIVE more potential synergistic introductions, in other words: potential business to your synergistic new client because you will have a 'new business pool pipeline' to dip into for THEM."

Exchange the word 'client' with 'referrer' in the above... Fundamentally, my ideal raving referrers are those people that I can *give* the most to.

To give you an example of 'who' I identified and struck up referral relationships with, here you go:

- Synergistic professionals – lawyers, accountants, independent financial advisers (IFAs) and bankers.
- Synergistic support professionals, organisations, associations to the legal profession – local to global – business consultants; business angels; those in the public, private and voluntary sector organisations in a 'placement'/'awareness'/'influence'/ 'facilitating' position in relation to supplying their members/clients/with regard to funding knowledge (grants/ loans/equity investment) and/or sector/ industry knowledge and/or legal knowledge. For example, government quangos/agencies; the Employee Ownership Association.
- Synergistic clients – those who hit the g-spot, same niches, mirror my personal brand, mainly entrepreneurs.
- Synergistic suppliers – 'techie' people, marketers, media people.

- 'Competitors'/Collaborators – other solicitors/lawyers/barristers/attorneys in different firms locally, regionally, nationally and internationally.
- Shared interests/commonality individuals and groups – leisure and business, for example, runners, cyclists, wine enthusiasts, entrepreneurs (women; young; serial), domain name traders.
- Synergistic niche 'industry VIPs' – media entrepreneurs, leisure entrepreneurs, employee share scheme advocates.
- High profile people and key influencers – key note speakers at events; for example, Deirdre Bounds the high profile and successful woman entrepreneur who founded, built and sold out i-to-i travel for a seven figure sum a few years ago.

On the subject of raving with other fellow lawyers I found the following: referrals to and from lawyers can be mutually beneficial, particularly if you develop a relationship with other lawyers who have niche practices and specialisms that are outside your own field of expertise and the firm you represent. Oh, and other jurisdictions of course, I hasten to add. It's great if you can refer a potential client in their direction, whether due to the fact that you may be conflicted or do not have the specialism within the firm which is required for the client, as the likelihood is that they will return the favour... given time.

However... as we're all perfectly aware, the financial world has gone totally tits up which means the 'big deals' are no longer as prevalent as they used to be pre autumn 2008. 'Slim pickins' for everyone is firmly the order of the day – apart from the blessed Magic Circle firms, no doubt where Zebedee may well be still smiling on his magic roundabout.

So, duly note the following from my experience, observations and discussions with senior people in law law land 2008 to the present day...

Say, you're a lawyer in a mid-tier firm or lower tier firm (full service kind of company) and had a fabulous referral relationship with other lawyers in firms scaling the heights of the good ship legal enterprise mast prior to the global economic fall-out in autumn 2008. Perhaps these have been top-tier firms? Or, any firm the next level up from your firm's legal industry placing. Then you may have passed up prospective client work to them because your firm wasn't geared up for the mega big deal and/or specialist task required.

Conversely, they usually passed you the lower value client work they didn't want because it wasn't 'meaty' enough for them or their hungry bosses to bloat the corporate giant sails. Well, there's not so much of that two way osmosis going around post winter 2008 because wherever possible, we're all holding on to every scrap of client work and gold dust deal we can possibly get our grubby little beagle paws on.

So, when drowning our sorrows at the realisation that the champagne lifestyle has *indefinitely* flown out of the window along with Peter Pan's coat tails, along with the reality that we're still expected to work long hard hours for the same amount of money (if we're lucky) although progression may not be as rapid as it used to be (particularly corporate lawyers here), we may well find many similarly unhappy lawyers on the referral and networking scene who are regularly pill-popping and/or glugging copious amounts of alcoholic beverages and/or manic depressive.

To top it all off, we may well struggle to hold down a relationship, personally and professionally. Due either to any or all of the three things I've mentioned above, or the 'depression' pervading the legal profession since autumn 2008 through to the present day. The latter being as a result of the increased stress and burden on those lawyers who survived The Big Gull Cull of 2008 and 2009 but now find themselves working at 100-125 percent capacity every day (including weekends in some cases).

We're either so drugged up, one way or another, or so darn exhausted from working so hard that our sex life has simply gone for a swan song! Depressing.

One of my Boss Lawyers said to me in 2008 something along the lines of, 'why aren't you out networking with other lawyers, Chrissie? That's where you should be to develop your legal career.'

Yeah. Right... I'd have rather eaten my own feet.

Knowing and witnessing the above, ask me whether I would rather have focused on *referring* and *networking* (schmoozing) with my fellow (negative mindset in destructive mode) lawyers or with dynamic, positive minded, real g-spot potential referrers (of the non-lawyer kind) and clients who hold The Nod, real influence and purse-strings to 'the next job' placement?

Sorry Mr Boss Lawyer et al. Tell you what, you go convene and chin-wag with your comfort zone buddies. Go get some back-patting consolation from your mates who will no doubt say, 'there there... everything's going to be alright. We'll just keep doing what we've always done and we'll always get what we've always got.' Hmmm. Get real, *wake up* soon-to-be extinct traditional lawyer, I thought...

Not my scene. Not cool. Not best use of my time and certainly not the best way for me to bring in more clients to the firm, and keep YOU in the lifestyle you can only dream of again... even if it hasn't dawned on you yet!

I think I'll carry on doing what I'm doing if you don't mind, thank you very much.

That is... Give me referral and networking *face time* with the synergistic clients, industry VIPs, professionals (sans lawyers), support professionals, suppliers, collaborators and key-influencer high profile business people any day! Going straight to the heart of the most likely mutual referral probability makes much more sense, n'est ce pas?!

Remember, the lobster decides what the 'in' place, thing and person was and is to be. And the tribe will follow – Volume 3 revision. Much more fun swimming with entrepreneurial raving referral lobster women and men, I reckon... Besides, it's a much bigger pool to splash around in...

just do something!

Take a look at the two lists above again. Ask yourself, 'who would be my ideal raving referrers?' with the thought in mind, 'who are the people who are likely to know, like, trust, understand, 'get' and share an interest/commonality with me?'

Think deeply. Take your time. There's no rush. But in time, you need to make your own 'hit list'. Think rifle shot approach. Feel free to use the lists above as a starter for ten. You may wish to add to the list, expand on the detail, and obviously make it bespoke to your circumstances, aka, role, niche and personal brand.

what can I rave about?

And so it was, off I went, dancing into Referral Lobster Net-Kingdom and Client Territory. *What* did I have to rave about with those who I communed with?

Well, having done my research on THEM, both personally and THEIR business, I selected THEM based on our shared interests, commonality, niches, aka our synergy. Albeit I raved primarily about THEM; that is, with a view to suggesting how I may be able to help them get more business, it was inevitable that as a result of the conversation and professional relationship developing, I actually got the opportunity to rave about the following. In this order:

1. THEM – personally;
2. Clients – theirs, mine, my firm's;
3. Colleagues – theirs, mine;
4. Firms – theirs, mine; and
5. Me – how I personally will be of benefit to THEM in relation to my niche specialism, knowledge and referral network, etc.

I repeat. In that order! Remember, it's all about what I/YOU can do for THEM. Remember also, I/YOU are an ambassador of 'Brand,Me' *and* 'Brand,Firm'.

just do something!

OK now. Be a little more thorough in your research. Once you've identified your target lobsters, make sure you're armed with as much knowledge as possible about THEM, their colleagues, clients, firm, achievements, circumstances, ambition, etc; find little nuggets, gems and rocks which will dazzle them and prove your interest in them. Discern the same degree of knowledge about your own colleagues and firm.

You need to get to *know* your lobsters, even before you've met them, and you need to truly *know* your colleagues' strengths, specialisms and interests, so you can talk about them too. You *know* you of course. Now figure out *how* you're going to be of benefit to THEM, both you personally and your colleagues and firm, from *all* of the preparatory work you've already done.

Make a list of those benefits and *be prepared* to share them with your lobsters. This is the hook to get the really big lobsters to bite and *want* to engage in mutual referral activity.

when should I rave and build?

As to *when* should I go raving? Morning, noon, night and weekends; daily, weekly, monthly, bi-monthly, quarterly, annually.

Well, as previously stated, the daily technical law grinder's monkey work took priority. Understandably so... Client legal work needs, wants and desires come first, last, always. Accordingly, the majority of my referral network building, activity and schmoozing, took place in the morning (before I came to the office), noon (during my lunch break), night (after work) and weekends (in my own 'leisure' time). Essentially, outside of the 'normal' working day and 'in my own time'. More importantly – above and beyond the normal trainee solicitor required duties.

However, I did take the opportunity whenever there were any gaps in the normal daily grind, usually when there was a lull in client work and support to be done – when 'slim pickin's' were on the daily menu – and used my initiative to work up some referral, marketing, sales, business development and innovation activity.

just do something!

Begin a schedule of *sales* activity. Plot in times in your Microsoft Outlook calendar and identify designated times which you will dedicate to referral activity; consider before work, lunch-times, evenings and weekends. Don't forget, at this stage you're *building* your referral network, ergo you can expect to put some 'out of work' hours into this activity for a good few months (I reckon about six months).

Don't forget your Big Rocks. Be realistic with your time and commitments. Make sure you factor in 'flexibility' and 'interruption'.

But stick to it! Commitment to doing this is essential otherwise you will not be able to build your referral network fast. Relationships take time to build so you *must* do the ground work now, and continually. We'll come back to this in Volume 7.

where do I rave and build?

As to *where* did I rave and build my Referral Lobster Net-Kingdom? Precisely where my g-spot niche target market interest group clients and referrers would hang out, of course.

Both offline and online. I will share with you my online referral build and client build activity in Volume 6, as I feel it requires a special focus and designated volume to explain and help you to understand what I did (the power and effect of social media and social networking), and how and why I was successful in achieving referrals, enquiries and sales, online to offline and online again.

For example. With regard to my offline referral and networking activity, I ensured that I was present at the following:

- Entrepreneur, innovation and bespoke industry/sector (new media; leisure; 'the professions') networking events, seminars, lectures, dinners, awards, trade shows, competitions (in a capacity as a business judge and/or mentor and/ or role model), workshops, educational courses appertaining to my niches and specialism:
  - ☐ Institute of Directors – monthly gathering and ad hoc events;
  - ☐ Chamber of Commerce – ad hoc;
  - ☐ Business Network International breakfast meeting (06.30-08.30) – weekly;
  - ☐ Employee Ownership Association – annual, ad hoc;
  - ☐ Women's Enterprise Ambassador Network – ad hoc;
  - ☐ Forward Ladies – ad hoc;
  - ☐ Business Link Yorkshire – ad hoc;
  - ☐ Yorkshire Forward – ad hoc;
  - ☐ Business Enterprise Fund (Bradford) – ad hoc;
  - ☐ Various 'informal' business network groups locally – weekly; and
  - ☐ Various regional educational establishments; universities, colleges and entrepreneur associated hubs – ad hoc.
- Leisure clubs: running, cycling, swimming, health club – daily/weekly.

In general I was (and remain) actively referring and networking with raving referral lobsters *everywhere* and *whenever* I get the chance! Whether it be sat on a train, in a wine bar, at a dinner party, in a coffee shop. There's always an opportune place for a naked rainmaker lawyer to give and receive...

just do something!

Take the time now to research and identify the kinds of places you need to frequent to meet your lobsters. Use the list above to give you some ideas. Now create your own list bespoke to your circumstance, niche, brand, etc.

how will I build my lobster net-kingdom to last... fast?

I figured that due to the mega downturn in the economy, global to local, and with the legal profession in particular being hit really badly and prospects for the future looking rather grim, I needed to build a raving Referral Lobster Net-Kingdom *fast* in order to get more clients, sales and income into the firm and for those whom I served. With my previous reading of *Built To Last* at the forefront of my mind I also knew, instinctively, and from experience, that I needed to build the referral network to *last*.

So, as to how to build my Referral Lobster Net-Kingdom, and build it to last, and fast, I put my personal brand into action... I made it 'work' for me, and my firm... I was pro-active *everywhere* and got my name *everywhere*! Offline and online. 'Brand,Me' *and* 'Brand,Firm'. *Every day*.

In addition to the networking events, seminars, lectures, dinners, awards, competitions, workshops, trade shows, educational courses appertaining to my niches and specialism, I set up bespoke meetings with the lobsters for coffee, lunch, drinks after work, coffee house on a weekend etc, where I focused on learning all about THEM, their needs, wants and desires and how I could be of benefit to THEM.

My whole approach consisted of my thinking 'extraordinary sex', 'extraordinary lover', 'extraordinary rainmaker', my attitude SUUUCKS, I need to engage in fourplay... I have already shared with you the fourplay process in Volume 3; you may recall the referral activity I engaged in with a synergistic accountant? And, in Volume 4, I shared with you that Donald Trump is a perfect example of how a personal brand ought to be 'worked':

"Trump puts his name everywhere, and therefore more people know about him... You need to make sure your name gets out there in the same regard. ...your name should be everywhere. This creates a consistency that will remind people of who you are, and what value you can contribute."

So, I simply swung all of this into full on action.

Spring 2009: a lawyer colleague came back from a networking event one day and exclaimed "Lightfoot, your name's everywhere". Mission accomplished.

My colleague and I were obviously doing something right. The very fact that we were 'out and about' in the right business places, same places and similar places, meant ambassadors were out in force and 'Brand,Firm' was firmly on the agenda in Referral Lobster Net-Kingdom and 'Client Territory'.

I'll share with you a secret. To be successful in getting your message 'out there', aka your 'Brand,Me', you've got to be absolutely committed. You've got to be driven and passionate about it. It's about *quantity* and *quality* of strategic activity. In essence, you've got to put *lots* of time and major effort into it.

I'll let you into another secret... To truly build a referral relationship fast, and build it to last, is to truly *engage*. The hook to truly engage is: *commonality + curiosity*. Having a shared interest and/or passion is one thing. But if you're curious about your receiver, it's the ultimate flattery.

You have to use this, get in and build a solid, enduring relationship. And we women really know how to do this stuff.

As mentioned previously, I will share with you how I built my online referral network and potential client pool in Volume 6. And, as to the truly nitty gritty detail of how I built my referral and client relationships both offline and online, I will share this with you in Volume 7: nurturing fuzz to get more buzz. Namely, the nuances of relationship marketing and relationship sales; how to build on, sustain and leverage relationships – rapport, conversation strategy, behaviour, commonality and curiosity, collaborating with competitors and follow on, to name a few.

just do something!

It's time to swing into action. You've identified who your target lobsters are, where to find them, when you need to 'go fetch' and what you can rave about. So, get pro-active *everywhere*. Get your name *everywhere*! 'Brand,Me' *and* 'Brand,Firm'. Every day.

In addition to the 'formal' networking events etc. you've identified, set up bespoke meetings with the potential lobsters for coffee, lunch, drinks after work, coffee house on a weekend etc, where you focus on learning all about THEM, their needs, wants and desires and how you will be of benefit to THEM. Think 'extraordinary sex', 'extraordinary lover', 'extraordinary rainmaker', my attitude SUUUCKS, I need to engage in fourplay...

gimme those two drugs!

So, how do I manage to do all this referral and networking stuff as well as my daily technical grind? Where do I get the energy from? Answer: two drugs. Not the pill popping, alcohol induced or manic depressive kind I hasten to add.

1. Love – passion; and
2. Adrenalin – endorphins.

Love is the drug, together with adrenalin kicking in, as I get my Big Rocks off being my authentic self, indulging my weird mindset, wicked SUUUCKS attitude and PEE Poor Work Ethic so having genuine *passion, enthusiasm* and *energy* in everything I do. Remember Volume 2? It's a mindset thing...

Two drugs. Free and natural. Love and adrenalin. Drive pushes me – adrenalin. But it's passion which pulls me – love!

just do something!

Get into the right mindset. Give yourself a real talking to. Remind yourself *why* you're doing what you do... Because you love it! You're interested in your dream, your niche, your brand.

80:20/G:R

I went about building my raving Referral Lobster Net-Kingdom with the famous Pareto principle, more commonly known as the '80:20 rule',[4] foremost in my mind too. By understanding and embracing this universal principle I applied it to my approach to extraordinary rainmaking activity...

I focused 80 percent of my marketing and sales activity, relationship marketing and relationship sales, aka, relationship building, time and effort in *giving* to referrers and clients (THEM promotion; *push* promotion), and only 20 percent on actively promoting the 'me, me, me', that is, 'what I want' and 'what the firm wants' (*self* promotion; *pull* promotion)...

80 percent *giving*. 20 percent *receiving*. 80:20/G:R.

To be more specific, I spent 80 percent of my time trying to find connections and more new business for my referrers and clients, and 20 percent of my time and effort on direct client target market new business activity for me, aka, my firm and those whom I served. Invariably, I was confident that 80 percent of my new client sales would could from the 20 percent of the raving referral lobsters and clients whom I helped generate new business.

I placed this faith and belief on experience, my SUUUCKS attitude and the fourth law – The Law of Influence – devised by Burg and Mann which states, "Your influence is determined by how abundantly you place other people's interests first."

just do something!

Return to your Outlook calendar and be more specific about how you're dividing your time. Ensure 80 percent is all about finding referrals, connections and more business for your lobsters (and clients), aka, push promotion; THEM promotion.

clicking with peeps I know, like, trust and...?

Undoubtedly, it's a no brainer that people will do business with people they know, like and trust. A referrer or client ought to trust me as a lawyer. Trust ought to be a given, in part, due to the solicitor/lawyer/attorney-client code of conduct and ethics, attorney-client privilege yarda, yarda, yarda.

And yet, by no means is it truly a given. It is my responsibility to be able to convey to the person I am interacting with that (s)he ought to feel and know that (s)he can trust me and that I will act with the utmost integrity, respect and caring in their best interests – whether (s) he be a referrer and/or client. Because we share similar interests, have commonality, I can empathise with and genuinely care about them and their circumstances so the likelihood is that the trust and bond will develop much more quickly than the usual referrer and/or client relationship.

It's the getting to know them/me and like them/me part that I reckon requires the real focus. And, I think it's actually more than know, like and trust... I reckon, people will do *more* and *better value* business with people they know, like, trust, understand, 'get' and share a common interest with...

understand, 'get', share a common interest

From previous experience, I know that one of the most effective ways of getting my message 'out there' is to enlist the help of raving referral lobsters to do it for me. Fact. Reality. It works.

The secret to achieving this lies in being educated by them, and in my listening and really hearing THEM, so that I can be of real benefit to them. That is, I need to truly understand them! I will then 'get' them and therefore understand how I can be of most value to THEM. The educating, learning, listening and hearing process I used was my very own creation of a 'Get,Them' system of understanding devised to tease out the information I would need to be of real value to them; duly note, again, my focus is on THEM:

- Get THEM as to who they are;
- Get THEIR colleagues;
- Get THEIR product/service (in detail!);
- Get THEIR g-spot (markets in detail!);
- Get THEIR niche (PODs and USPs, in detail!);
- Get THEIR brand – 'Brand,Me' and 'Brand,Firm';
- Get THEIR ideal prospective key client;
- Get what really benefits THEM;
- Get THEIR firm;
- Get what gets THEIR Big Rocks off; and
- Get THEM to feel extraordinarily valued.

In other words, my entire focus is to help THEM get *more* business – from existing clients and new clients! When I connect them with a potential client it proves I am interested in helping them be successful and that I am the kind of person who genuinely wants to help them.

Outcome? I become *the lawyer* who immediately pops into their heads. And in return? I expect nothing.

But in reality, it is *reciprocity*. They wish to be educated about me; they run through the above list in the same way. It's kind of like our earthling ritual of courtship and our ethics of dating, which goes something like this... Getting to know, like, trust, understand, 'get' and share a common interest with your potential lobster is like getting to know , like, trust, understand, 'get' and find a common interest your potential new lover. You have to *woo* them. Actually, you're aiming to *phwoar* them, remember? Think back to previous volumes. Think extraordinary sex:

- Your whole focus is on THEM; well, if it isn't, it should be!

- You express your interest in them.
- You're curious about them.
- You want to get to know them so you ask them lots of questions.
- You find out their values, interests, etc.
- You listen and hear intently.
- You're working out if you like them.
- You want to understand them.
- You're figuring out if you have things in common.
- You're looking to click – you're looking to 'get' them.
- You want to impress them and go out of your way to be nice – you want to be liked back.
- You want to make them feel special and valued.
- Ultimately, you want to know, like, trust, understand and 'get' them before you go jumping into bed with them – figuratively speaking of course...

Now, how many people can you say have made you feel truly extraordinarily special and valued? And vice versa? Would you like to?

just do something!

It's time to really educate yourself, truly learn, listen and hear all about your lobster. You can't expect to be able to be of benefit to THEM and refer value clients and value work in their direction unless you truly know, like, trust, understand, 'get' and have commonality with them.

Take a look again at the 'Get,Them' list above. These are the kinds of things you need to learn and understand about your lobsters. Now, create your own 'Get,Them' system. Have this ingrained in your mind when you meet your lobster so that you can ask the kind of questions necessary to glean that information. Use the list as a starter for ten. Feel free to add to it and make it bespoke to your needs.

dirty dancing with Big Rock lobsters

the devil's in the 'Me,Tale'

Remember 'positioning that rocks' in Volume 3? Well, I figured if I'm going to go fishing to catch a big raving referral lobster then I need to go fishing where the right people aka Big Rock lobsters are! And I need to position myself in front of them. And I need to introduce myself as somebody who will be of benefit to them.

And, remember Volume 4 and my sharing with you that a story is actually more powerful than a brand? Well, if your brand begins to tell the tale then that's hot stuff! Having the right brand invariably attracts the attention and interest of the right kind of lobster and inevitably helps with the initial introduction and conversation which naturally flows.

'The devil's in the detail', as they say. Actually, it's in the 'Me,Tale'. If you want to click in the raving Referral Lobster Net-Kingdom with the real Big Rock lobsters then it helps, big time, if you have YOUR story at the ready to share with your audience... when asked, of course.

For example: 'The Entrepreneur Lawyer'. Walk into a meeting with an entrepreneur lobster or entrepreneur event of any kind with the brand 'The Entrepreneur Lawyer' on marketing collateral and it's an instant talking point. It's intriguing. It's curious. It has commonality. It invites comments such as, 'I've never heard of an entrepreneur lawyer before. Tell me about you.' And so the story unfolds as I instantly switch the focus on THEM. More about this in Volumes 6 and 7.

So, I went dirty dancing and sharing my 'Me,Tale' in the Big Rock pool of raving referral lobsters.

just do something!

You need to prepare your story. The explanation in relation to your personal brand; the killer words that will tweak their interest, quell their curiosity and to help them realise you share the same interests, aka, have commonality. The eureka moment. The *why* you are the right choice to be of benefit to them – whether potential lobster or client.

So, put some deep thought into this. Now write down what you feel will be the best things to say so that having met you they will know, like, trust, understand, get and be willing to share with you.

the ROAR benefits system

As I mentioned previously, I went about building a raving Referral Lobster Net-Kingdom by taking a tactical ROAR rifle gun approach; that is, unwavering *focus* with strategic precision, tactical execution and pain-staking follow-on. I actually devised my own system in relation to my personal referral and client development activity in order to track the following:

- My giving and receiving of referrals;
- Conversion from estimated sales to actual sales;
- Detail in relation to follow on activity; and
- Targets.

It was also what could be regarded as the bones of a mini CRM system when combined with the detail in my Microsoft Outlook folders and calendar, that is, referral, prospect client, and client contact records. It was a simple Excel spreadsheet which I am happy to share as a template with you. It's basic and I am sure that your firm may have a far superior referral, client development, CRM system in place. But if not, you're welcome to take a peek at mine. It proved extremely useful to me in identifying how pro-active I was for referrers and clients and in return how effective they were for me too.

After all, extraordinary rainmaking comes down to continuous improvement. And, how can you improve your outcomes if you don't have a SMART system in place to at least begin the benchmarking through analysis of data integrity?

To give you an idea of the power and benefit to be had in building, leveraging and sustaining a referral network of value, when I analysed sales enquiries, sales estimates and sales actual for the period September 2008 to December 2009, 30 percent of sales enquiries came from referral lobsters but 80 percent of the total £sales estimates and £sales actual came from that 30 percent. I guess the Pareto rule of thumb kind of works after all.

You will find the template on the EntrepreneurLawyer website.

just do something!

Look again at the component parts of the ROAR benefits system. Feel free to check out the template on the EntrepreneurLawyer website.

Now, devise your own personal referral and client development activity system. Your call. You may have a sophisticated system at the firm where you work so check that out and how you can use it to best effect.

fish-nets!

super lawyer fish-nets

In the words of Bob Burg:

"The superstar, mega successful, high-dollar-earning networker is the greatest and most active giver you know. He is constantly referring business to others. She is always on the lookout for a piece of information that will interest someone in her network of friends and prospects – regardless of whether or not it's business related...Genuine networkers give. They give actively and without

expectation. They are always thinking about what they can give, how they can give, and to whom they can give...They are who I term superstar networkers... They are always asking themselves who they can set up with each other. They know that everyone they know or meet might be a valuable contact to someone else in their network. The fun part is introducing them and setting up the relationship."[5]

Bob believes that 'superstar networkers' share two powerful traits:

1. They are givers; and
2. They are connectors.

I would add two more traits...

3. They are listeners; and
4. They are empathetic.

They have the ability to take the focus and onus *totally* off themselves and their firm and project the need, want and desire for the success of their recipient for the benefit of THEM. I reckoned that in order to be an extraordinary rainmaker lawyer not only did I need to net the big fish superstar networkers *and* superstar referrers (because there is a distinction between the two, I believe), but I myself needed to be a superstar networker and superstar referrer too! To be accomplished at the four traits was a BHAG to add to my FMSP.

just do something!
Strive to be accomplished in the four traits. You may wish to make it one of your goals and amend your FMSP accordingly.

i'm having a stocking malfunction!

With the next volume soon to be upon us, Volume 6: social savvy junkie, I'd like to share a quick story with you as an aperitif.

I was at a business networking bash one Christmas evening. Towards the end of the meal each of the members/attendees was asked to stand up and share their thoughts with the entire gathering in the room in relation to the question, 'How would you help your fellow members if you won the lottery?'

When it came to the turn of one of the lady entrepreneurs she exclaimed from her seat, "I can't get up. I'm having a stocking malfunction!" At which the room filled with raucous laughter and we all raised our glasses of full bodied red wine and took a large swig of the very same in a toast to her good humour, honesty and obvious embarrassment.

My point is simply this... The fabulous thing about networking and referring using social media and social networking platforms online means that you can do it in the comfort of your own home... without embarrassment if you lack the usual bravado, confidence or even suitable attire! You don't have to be 'out and about' offline or 'on the scene' offline to be effective and helpful. When online, nobody gets to see the ladder in your tights or bigger than usual holes in your fish net stockings!

One of my favourite mantras is, 'Shy birds get nowt!' With online networking and referring this is where this mantra really does come to life and where you really can come into your own... I'm excited about sharing with you my online escapades in due course!

after dark activity

extraordinary lobsters make extraordinary rainmakers

Without a shadow of doubt, building a raving Referral Lobster Net-Kingdom of value... fast... and to last, will stand you in really good stead for becoming an extraordinary naked rainmaker lawyer.

Period. It worked, and works, for me. It could work for you too!

Extraordinary raving lobsters make for extraordinary rainmakers. Extraordinary rainmakers make extraordinary raving lobsters. So, in order to identify, meet and click with these Big Rock raving referrer lobsters, and to become one yourself, it's now time for you to get jiggy with building your very own raving Referral Lobster Net-Kingdom.

As ever, I'd like you to think extraordinary rainmaker, extraordinary lover, extraordinary sex and now... extraordinary lobster!

naked lawyer activity – a study worth casing

During autumn 2008 I set about working through what is now this Volume 5 (ROAR steps) of *the naked lawyer* in reference to building a value referral network both offline and online. As to what I did and for a real live case study in 'How to build your very own referral network of value', simply read the story again in this Volume 5. You can relive my activity by taking yourself through the same process.

Let me help you. Here's a condensed version of the key activities and exercises you may wish to carry out...

ROAR steps

It's now time to do the following exercise in the step sequence provided. As I've said before, it may take you a few days, a few weeks or a few months.

- **Step 1:** RESEARCH. Take a look at the referrer description list in the 'hard-core FMSP' section. Ask yourself 'who do I know' and 'what do I know about who I know?' to get the cogs turning. Identify industry VIPs. Consider, 'are these the kind of lobsters I would like to click with?' Write down your findings and thoughts. Now devise your unique, bespoke list, of your ideal kind of referrer.
- **Step 2:** Take a look at the two lists in the 'who could I rave with' section. Ask yourself:
  - ☐ 'who would be my ideal raving referrers?', with the thought in mind –
  - ☐ 'who are the people who are likely to know, like, trust, understand, 'get' and share an interest/commonality with me?'

  Think deeply. Make your own 'hit list'. Make it bespoke to your circumstances – role, niche and personal brand.
- **Step 3:** RESEARCH again. Arm yourself with as much knowledge as possible about your lobsters, their colleagues, clients, firm, achievements, circumstance, ambitions etc. Discern the same degree of knowledge about your own colleagues and firm. You know you of course. Now figure out how you're going to be of benefit to THEM, you personally and your colleagues and firm, with all of the preparatory work you've already done. Make a list of those benefits.
- **Step 4:** Begin a schedule of sales activity. Plot in times in your Microsoft Outlook calendar and identify designated times when you will dedicate to referral activity – consider before work, lunch-times, evenings and weekends.
- **Step 5:** Research and identify the kinds of places you need to frequent to meet your lobsters. Use the list in the 'where do I rave and build' section to give you some ideas. Now create your own list bespoke to your circumstance, niche, brand, etc.
- **Step 6:** Get pro-active everywhere. Get your name everywhere! 'Brand,Me' and 'Brand,Firm'. Every day. In addition to the 'formal' networking events etc., set

up bespoke meetings with the potential lobsters for coffee, lunch, drinks after work, coffee house on a weekend etc, where you focus on learning all about THEM, their needs, wants and desires and how you will be of benefit to THEM. Think 'extraordinary sex', 'extraordinary lover', 'extraordinary rainmaker', my attitude SUUUCKS, I need to engage in fourplay...

- **Step 7:** Get into the right mindset. Give yourself a real talking to. Remind yourself why you're doing what you do... because you love it! You're interested in your dream, your niche, your brand.
- **Step 8:** Return to your Outlook calendar. Ensure 80 percent of your allocated referral activity is all about finding referrals, connections and more business for your lobsters (and clients), aka, push promotion; THEM promotion.
- **Step 9:** Look again at the 'Get,Them' list in the 'understand, 'get', share a common interest' section. Create your own 'Get,Them' system. Have this ingrained in your mind when you meet your lobster so that you can ask the kind of questions necessary to glean that information. Use the list as a starter for ten. Feel free to add to it and make it bespoke to your needs.
- **Step 10:** Prepare your story. Put some deep thought into this. Then, write down what you feel will be the best things to say so that the lobster, having met you, will know, like, trust, understand, get and be willing to share with you.
- **Step 11:** Look again at the component parts of 'the ROAR benefits system' in that section. Feel free to check out the template on the EntrepreneurLawyer website. Now, devise your own personal referral and client development activity system. You may have a sophisticated system at the firm where you work, in which case, check that out and see how you can use it to best effect.
- **Step 12:** Strive to be accomplished in the four traits. Consider making it one of your goals; if so, don't forget to add the same to your FMSP.

ROAR tips

- Take the plunge;
- Exit 'The Comfort Zone';
- Exit 'The Ivory Tower';
- Build multiple bridges;
- Strive to be accomplished in the four traits:
  - ☐ *Be giving;*
  - ☐ *Be a connector;*
  - ☐ *Be a listener;*
  - ☐ *Be empathetic;*
- Live your brand;
- Get your name *everywhere;*
- Rave about THEM;
- Be 80:20/G:R; and
- Work your 'Me,Tale' off!

ROAR summation

raving lobsters simply click 'n' mix

Building a raving referral lobster net-kingdom is one of the first real *doing* elements in applying the 'how to market, brand and sell you' preparatory *thinking* foundations in relation to your hard work from Volumes 1 through 4. This is where your EI, niche and personal brand begin to come into play and be of real value in your path to becoming an extraordinary rainmaker lawyer.

Hopefully you've enjoyed the click-start and you've started mixing up with some raving lobsters. Keep thinking extraordinary sex, extraordinary lover, extraordinary rainmaker and now extraordinary lobster!

References

1. Silver, Cole, *How to create wealth*, 2009

2. Gladwell, Malcolm, *The tipping Point: How Little things Can Make A Big Difference* (New York: Little, Brown and Co., 2000)
3. Burg, Bob, *Endless Referrals*
4. It is a common rule of thumb in business; e.g.,'80 percent of your sales come from 20 percent of your clients.' The Pareto principle was named after Vilfredo Pareto, a 19th century economist. http://en.wikipedia.org/wiki/Pareto_principle
5. Burg, *Endless Referrals*

Volume 6: social savvy junkie

raving referral lobsters rule!

Welcome back, again! Here's another big hug from your private Naked Lawyer dancer in law law land.

Unlike the previous volumes, the 'social savvy junkie' is going to take a slightly different format. It's going to be fast paced and more punchy in style; the nature of the information and the practical activities which naturally flow lends itself to lists and bullet point format rather than lots of prose. I figure this is the best way to convey a lot of information in a short space to be truly useful to you. Hope you don't mind?! If you do, well, hey-ho. Too late. You're here now. And I'm sure you won't be disappointed in me serenading you for a wee while...

With this volume you will note that I have *not* provided you with 'just do something' activities as you read and work your way through the volume. I have placed all of the activities in the 'after dark activity, ROAR steps' section at the end of the book as I feel that this is definitely the best way to tackle this element of the ROAR model.

It's best if you allow yourself to enjoy the read start to end, non-stop, and truly experience the story, then trot off and apply everything you've read all in one go at the very end. You will realise why when you've read the volume.

Now, switch off totally from the daily grind. Chill out! Allow yourself some private time. This is YOU and ME 'alone' private dancing time. Get rid of any 'nuisance'. Go grab a drink, settle into what I hope by now is OUR special comfy chair in the 'only disturb us at your peril' designated area and simply relax. Time to calm down and take a chill pill.

Dance again with me now as we line dance, hip hop, flamenco, jazz and swing together as I share with you how to use social media and social networking to positively waltz your way into being a highly successful and happily naked, rainmaker lawyer!

promises to reap

Building a raving Referral Lobster Net-Kingdom, is one of the first real *doing* elements in applying the 'how to market, brand and sell you' preparatory *thinking* foundations in relation to your hard work from Volumes 1 through to 4. Volumes 5 through to 12 of *the naked lawyer are* where your EI, niche and personal brand begins to come into play and be of real value on your path to becoming an extraordinary rainmaker lawyer. Hopefully you've enjoyed the click-start and you've started mixing it up with some raving lobsters.

Keep thinking extraordinary sex, extraordinary lover, extraordinary rainmaker and extraordinary lobster!

I promised you in the previous volume that I would share with you how to build, leverage and sustain a raving Referral Lobster Net-Kingdom. So, as I believe in 'promises to keep', I'm going to share exactly this with you; as well as how to build a prospective client pool, using social media (SM) and social networking (SN), so that my 'promises to keep' actually becomes 'promises to reap', where YOU reap the benefit of my secrets.

After all, YOU might as well save yourself some time and piggy-back on my quick wins. That's what you're paying for, n'est ce pas? I'm going to share with you what's worked (and continues to work) for me.

If you're already dabbling in building and leveraging a referral network, using SM and SN in particular, then your experience and what's working for you will of course vary from mine, depending on how much resource (time, money, human support) you are investing and your particular role and circumstances, both offline and online. But I'm confident that I may reveal at least one or two things that you may not have come across as yet, particularly using the full on ROAR model and approach.

If you know everything and are doing everything which I am about to share with you, then PLEASE do get in touch with me. I'd love to hear and learn from you so that I can satisfy my hunger for knowing more and developing further both personally and professionally for the benefit of others. By sharing, you will no doubt help me achieve my dream that much more quickly!

Now, let's swing on shall we?

Quick recap... Returning to my prancing Naked Lawyer in law law land story... Empathise now. It's summer/autumn 2008. I've:

- Worked out my Big Rocks;
- Done my EI analysis;
- Done my SWOT analysis;
- Addressed my Ethicability conundrum;
- Worked out my ME Code of Conduct;
- Got myself an Epitaph;
- Addressed my Rainmaker Mindset, Attitude and Motivation;
- Realised my PEE Poor Work Ethic;
- Researched and identified an ideal niche and niches within the same;
- Sorted my positioning, differentiation, USPs, PODs, and g-spots (target market(s));
- Found myself sitting pretty as a potentially brand new 'Brand,Me' in law law land;
- Made sure the raving Referral Lobster Net-Kingdom offline has swung into action; and
- Started the process of devising and continually updating my Formidable ME Strategy & Plan (FMSP); goals, mission, vision, target market identification, niches, personal brand, referral network building.

Time to swing online and devise a raving Referral Lobster Net-Kingdom along with a potential client pool there too, I reckoned.

negativity fries

Right, let's get one thing straight, dance partner... I am *not*, repeat *not*, going to waste any time in this volume waffling on about the following: social guidance, that is, social media policy; strategy; risks; snags; compliance policies; privacy in social networking services; security issues; protection of (fair use of) intellectual property; regulatory requirements on the use of SM.

Why? Because you'll find plenty of information on all that negative stuff (albeit important and serious matters for consideration, implementation and action) in cyber-world without me sticking my nose in. For one thing, this is the kind of stuff which prevents YOU from getting on and using SM and SN. We lawyers being 'conservative by nature' is a real understatement where SM and SN come into play. For another, it's not directly relevant and/or it conflicts with *the naked lawyer* and/or the ROAR model when

I am advocating that you should actually be using SM and engaging in SN. Of course there's risk. There's risk in most things we do.

But listen up... Other lawyers are doing it! Your clients are doing it! And it's here to stay. So get with the programme!

If your firm already has a SM guidance thingy in place then of course you will be duty bound to follow it; as you should, for the sake of good order. By straying from it, you will no doubt experience a hissy fit from your Boss Lawyer and probably find yourself cast adrift from the good ship legal enterprise.

This may well be a positive thing, the SM guidance thingy that is (or being cast adrift; I guess it depends what you want!), because it means you *can* get on and *do* something with SM and SN to your advantage, your referrers and clients advantage, and for those whom you serve, with their blessing, subject to the 'guidance'.

If your firm has not laid down the law with regard to social guidance then hey, you're lucky. All you need is a big dollop of common sense and some handy tips from those of us who have been prancing in SM and SN for a while now to help negate any risk.

Right? Unless of course you deliberately wish to press the professional suicide button and say and do something daft on a public forum. That's your judgement call. You alone are responsible and accountable for your actions. We all are. Period.

positivity jives

So, I'm going to focus on the positive impact, benefits and rewards to be had using SM and SN; more sales, more referrers, more clients, more income, more value, more growth, more success. For that's the Naked Lawyer mantra... focus on the positive. Positive mindset, strengths and opportunities, remember?

why why why delilah?

I am going to share with you how (as a trainee solicitor in 2008 and 2009) I used (and continue to use in a new capacity now as CEO of EntrepreneurLawyer since September 2009) SM and SN to build relationships, generate referrals, sales leads and instructions, all with a view to getting more clients, referrals, sales, income, value, growth and success. It could work for you too!

SM & SN... yeah baby

So, what is SM?

"Social media is a new set of communication and collaboration tools that enable many types of interactions that were previously not available to the common person."[1]

Hey, that means me, and you. It's synonymous with Web 2.0. Example SM tools are: blogging, podcasting, video and social networks (including business networks) such as LinkedIn, Twitter, Facebook, YouTube, etc. They're all fab for raving referral lobster and client development activity – forming, building, leveraging and sustaining enduring relationships of value, whether professional or personal.

I found early on in my online fumbling, that SN is awesome for having conversations, useful for creating brand awareness, niche identification and exploitation and promulgating involvement, interaction and engagement, particularly with 'new' people outside of my usual haunt. SM and SN did *not* replace my overall big picture marketing and sales strategy and plan. I factored in SM and SN to pervade my marketing, sales, business development and innovation activity as part of my overall FMSP.

It was (and remains) obvious to me that there has been a paradigm shift in marketing and sales from offline to online. In essence, what was occurring back then and even more so now, is relationship marketing and relationship sales which have come about largely because of the advent of SM and SN. Accordingly, I actually saw (and still see) SM and SN as a wonderfully refreshing way in which to market and sell 'Brand,Me' and 'Brand,Firm'.

"Nobody puts Baby in the corner", remember? Self reliance human economy, remember?

the resistance

Most of the lawyers I knew were taking a conservative approach to SM and SN back in 2008 and 2009. No surprises there eh? We lawyers are not renowned for throwing caution to the wind and welcoming new, open and *free* kinds of technology. In spite of the fact that SM and SN had experienced (and continues to experience) explosive growth over the past few years, the legal profession has generally been traditionally conservative in embracing this opportunity.

Whilst my colleagues were, at worst, uninterested, and at best, sat on the fence squabbling over the social guidance stuff, in other words, looking for reasons *not* to do something (as ever), I reckoned I would just get on and do it anyway. OK, so I was bit of a rebel – a maverick perhaps – in the law firm where I was learning 'my trade' during 2008 and 2009, by embracing SM and SN... Guilty as charged m'lud... throw me in the ivory tower dungeon for daring to challenge the status quo... woopah! I like bread and water... staple necessities, nothing fanciful. Keep it basic is usually a good way to go these days, whether out of choice or necessity!

Yeah, a risk. But heck, hang the laggards! 'So what if my attitude SUUUCKS?', I thought. I didn't want to become a dead dinosaur. I would prove to The Resistance that this SM and SN stuff actually had some valuable sexy legs...

In 2008, not unlike Adrian Dayton, Andrew Sharpe, Nils Montan, Jorge Colon, Donna Seyle and Julian Summerhayes (to name a few) – all fellow lawyers, innovators and early adopters of SM and SN – I could see that this new media thingy was really good stuff in winning new business for us lawyers... if used correctly!

Fast forward to 2010. Let's have a quick look at a few interesting statistics in relation to the legal profession and SM use shall we?

- Ten percent of lawyers brought in business last year from social media.[2]
- Businesses are generating real customers with social media and blogs – the most rapidly expanding category in the overall marketing budget.[3]
- Inbound marketing channels continue to deliver dramatically lower cost per lead than outbound channels do.[4]
- There are 80 million professional peeps on LinkedIn in over 200 countries.
- 500 million+ users on Facebook (one billion projected by the end of 2011). That's approximately 1/14 of the world's population, soon to be 1/7.

why? just suck it and see

As I mentioned in Volume 1, I knew that I needed to be present and available for our potential clients (and existing clients) and referrers where they were then and would be in the future... which is in and on the 'trending' SM and SN platforms. Albeit there is some disagreement as to whether SM and SN was, and is, a 'fad' or 'trend', I reckoned I'd just suck it and see. I couldn't care less if it was/is a 'fad' or 'trend'. SM and SN were obviously causing a buzz back then and I figured it would be likely to be hanging around for the foreseeable future. So, I figured I'd just give the tools a go.

SM and SN are a real phenomenon actually. It's little wonder the Facebook story has hit the big screen as *The Social Network* movie.

What I realised very early on, was that the real beauty of the advent of SM and SN was it truly does create a level playing field for us all. It was (and is) great for freeing up the cubicle slave and for helping with my self reliance survival and thriving cunning strategy and plan – the FMSP. Pre the world wide web and the SM and SN revolution, what may have taken oodles of years to establish, such as building a referral network of value and showcasing one's credibility, expertise and influence, can now be entrenched in a matter of months.

I did it. You could too!

It was my experience and observation that one of the most frustrating aspects of being a junior lawyer (and a 'mature' trainee; I was 37 years old in 2008-09) was being seen as credible, of value (talents, strengths, knowledge and experience from previous roles), and as a viable expert in my niche specialism within a profession running amok with dinosaurs and laggards. Contrary to this, referrers and clients could see why and how I could benefit them.

SM and SN enabled me to rid my shackles of the cubicle slave grinder's monkey 'get your traditional corporate lawyer here' comfy chair, *and* the talons and negative Dickensian mindset of The Resistance. Quite rightly.

At least now with these tools, potential referrers, clients, suppliers, collaborators and industry VIPs would know I existed.
Even consider me to be a person of influence, a true giver and connector and therefore of real benefit to THEM (and 'the firm' even if those whom I served did not realise it or appreciate it at that time) in the making. Fat chance of that without these awesome tools eh?

Heck, I reckoned I'd actually have some FUN amongst this serious work stuff too. So, off I pranced and danced onto the trendy platforms. To this day, I'm having *lots* of fun and success. For example, one of the conversations I recently engaged in with another legal beagle, @Sendall, on Twitter had me ROTF LOL (rolling on the floor laughing out loud). He said to me @TheNakedLawyer: "I often tell clients if we lose I will sit in the middle of Fleet St naked and eat my wig!"

Now that's what I call true Naked Lawyering!

why SM matters

In a nutshell, this is why I figure SM and SN matters:

- Social media predictions for 2010:[5]
  - ☐ The future of 'Brand,Me' is social.
  - ☐ Employees (lawyers) and entrepreneurs alike will discover, on a widespread level, their SM presence and SN make or break their professional fates.
  - ☐ More than 80 percent of professional recruiters plan to use social media platforms to screen job applicants, and also source 'passive' candidates – people who would considera better offer from a different company.
  - ☐ SM education and accreditation will be a significant factor in 2010 hiring and outsourcing decisions.
  - ☐ With 92 percent of B2B buyers using the internet for their purchasing research (and that includes legal advice/services), and SM ever more critical to being found online, B2B adoption will accelerate.

- ☐ Because social activity and relevant content inform search engine results, social search optimisation (SSO) trumps search engine optimisation (SEO).
- ☐ It is essential to take action now in the social arena. There's simply too much to lose, and countless opportunities to gain.

- SM and SN are happening now and are here to stay. They are shifting from growth to maturity.
- Two thirds of the global population visit SN sites – ahead of personal e-mail.
- My 'competitors', referrers and potential clients are using it and doing it – I need to be and go where they are.
- Competition is intensifying – LSA 2007, alternative business structures, virtual lawyering are already here.
- Winning new clients and delivering legal advice is becoming global by nature and opportunity.
- There are 1.2 million qualified solicitors/lawyers/attorneys in the UK and US (not to mention the hundreds of thousands of lawyers globally) with greater numbers coming through law school and competing for training contracts or internships year on year – I need(ed) to be different.
- It will help me stand out from the maddening crowd, aka, The Resistance.
- SN on the web allows equal footing for me to host 'Brand,Me' and 'Brand,Firm' – for free.
- Sales begins by 'buying' the salesperson/spokesperson which may be 'personal branding' – 'Brand,Me' and 'Brand,You'.
- Having a strong online presence helps establish trust, credibility, expertise and influence.

I'm not hiding in my ivory tower! I don't want to become extinct! I want to live!

why I engage in SM... with honourable intentions

OK, I admit it. I'm a self-confessed, fully fledged, SM and SN junkie.

Why? SM and SN provide the *free* environments where I can do all of the marketing, sales, innovation, business development, advertising and PR I would normally do offline, online... at a fraction of the cost and from the comfort of my desk, living room or wherever else I happen to lay my hat... head... or prancing naked lawyer legs.

My intentions were, and remain, honourable... This is what I USE these tools for and what I give and get from them:

1. Sharing 'Brand,Me': I want peeps to think about my stuff as I showcase my expertise and experience in a compelling manner, in order to attract my niche comrades so that I can help THEM.
2. Growing and leveraging my referral, client, supplier, affiliate and interest group network: to build an enduring relationship with them by sharing relevant connections.
3. Sustaining and deepening individual relationships: this is where the pixie dust stuff happens! Nurturing the relationships so they become enduring and truly of value.

In more detail:

- Doing business.
- Getting found – I'm findable due to engaging in SM and SN activity – search engines rank me higher.
- Attracting new clients and sales – getting more clients; finding sales enquiries/leads and responding accordingly.

- Giving and getting referrals – giving referral opportunities to connections (and receiving the same) and my clients and/ or associates.
- Introducing professionals with synergy to help them be successful – linking and introducing; SN makes short work of the 'six degrees of separation' to connect people with common interests.
- Market knowledge and awareness – legal and business sector/subject/ niche areas, through use of LinkedIn groups; polls; events; status updates; questions and answers; posting articles; slideshows, etc.
- Garner sales and marketing material – ideas for new products/ services, articles, blogging, tweeting, etc.
- New marketing – BUZZ.
- Target marketing – identifying my lobsters and client's ideal client and my ideal lobsters and clients.
- Finding suppliers/experts to assist my clients and the firm.
- Meeting potential referrers, clients, affiliates and associates.
- Building relationships and networking with local, national and international professionals – I figure it's best to keep an open mind because experience has taught me that I just might never know where an opportunity may come from and how I can therefore benefit my clients and referrers.
- Chatting, conversing – I can tune in to billions of online conversations where I listen, learn, ask for help and give help, respond to new developments and keep abreast of trends.
- Brand awareness – profile raising; 'Brand,Me' and 'Brand,Firm'; planting the seeds of my PODs and USPs in the minds of seekers.
- Best practice collaboration – mainly through groups, sharing knowledge, hints, tips, secrets that help referrers and clients get more clients, sales, referrals, income, value, growth and success; such as what you and I are engaging in right now.
- My professional CV exposed to millions of people.
- Personal growth, satisfaction and fulfilment – it's rather humbling to see the quality, calibre and range of professionals and potential clients using SM and SN platforms. As the Desiderata states, "There will be greater and lesser persons than yourself". It feels good to give, to learn and to keep growing (professionally and personally) and perhaps help a few other professionals along the way too.

what a load of twaddle

'I haven't got time.' Pants!

As I've previously mentioned, we lawyers know that lawyering is darned hard work; it's stressful, demanding and time intensive. It's not unusual to work 12 hour days, six or seven days a week. And that's just handling the technical law stuff. Accordingly, one of the prime excuses for The Resistance not partaking in marketing and sales activity (whether offline and/or online), and in particular SM and SN activity was, and is, the cry of, 'I just don't have time'.

Really? What a load of tosh!

Duly note this... Entrepreneurial, tomorrow's lawyers, of the naked kind, who do 'get' it – *make* time. And then reap the rewards by bringing in new business. If you're curious, feel free to go check out the really cool guys in our 'uncool sector' who are using SM well (see Activity 4 later in this volume).

Perhaps instead of share dealing, like some of my colleagues were doing during 'work' time, the time could be spent doing some SM and SN activity in a bid to get more clients and income into the firm coffers?

Choice! Yes, actually you're going to have to make time! At least, if you don't want to become 'surplus to requirements' or extinct, you do. It's a mindset thing. And by now, you should be on top of that. Right?

easy like a Sunday morning

This is how I approached, operated and managed my SM and SN activity. The prancing Naked Lawyer in law law land:

- Went about it all with a positive mindset, SUUUCKS attitude, PEE Poor Work Ethic and formed a habit;
- Let the technology work. I integrated all of my SM and SN so that one message went across multiple platforms;
- Worked in designated time slots, that is, I allocated a specific time to carry out my SM and SN activity;
- Used Microsoft Outlook calendar, contacts and tasks, and the sales spreadsheet I had created to help with time slots, strategy and planning, focus, project management and analysis; and
- Created templates to assist with speed of replies to enquiries, connections and followers, etc. but then tweaked the template to make the reply bespoke to the sender.

This made my life easy... easy like a Sunday morning. By creating an organised 'bust a gut daily work out' schedule (see the later section), at least I could reclaim a little of my easy like a Sunday morning lie in.

building my network fast... to last

secret agent provocateur

So, how did I go about building my network fast, and to last?

2008-09: After prancing around as a Naked Lawyer in Client Territory using SM and SN to identify more raving referral lobsters, not unlike a Jenny Bond secret agent, I managed to find out (by trial and error – but having lots of fun along the way!) what really works in attracting raving lobsters, generating sales enquiries, meeting new clients and ultimately receiving new instructions.

I'll share my secret with you, shall I? It was this provocative combo:

- Having a strategy and plan – the FMSP;
- Having a personal brand – 'Brand,Me';
- Being:
  - ☐ Findable;
  - ☐ First;
  - ☐ Unique;
  - ☐ Different;
  - ☐ Interesting;
  - ☐ Curious;
  - ☐ Pro-active;
  - ☐ Dynamic;
  - ☐ Omnipresent;
  - ☐ Available;
  - ☐ Fearless;
  - ☐ Innovative;
  - ☐ Entrepreneurial;
  - ☐ Engaging – 'chatty'/conversationalist;
  - ☐ Entertaining;
  - ☐ Transparent;
  - ☐ Human – I took my 'lawyer hat' off and let my personality shine...; and
  - ☐ Authentic – with a GSOH (good sense of humour). After all, most of us like to laugh, smile and have fun!

think niche, brand, lobsters!

In essence, I applied *absolutley everything* that I have already shared with you in Volumes 1 through to 5 of *the naked lawyer*. The crux of it was this...

The application of the EI, niche and brand stuff bundled up in the 80:20/G:R ROAR approach. Namely, clicking with peeps I knew, liked, trusted, understood, 'got', and with whom I shared a common interest. I simply applied the wwwwwh and prrrrrrr:

- Why was I here – to be helpful, of benefit;
- Who was I going to rave with – my lobsters and niche peeps who I would identify online. I searched for and then connected with them;
- What was I going to rave about – them and their messages, their needs, their information requirements;
- Where was I going to rave with them – in groups, forums, events, blogs;
- When was I going to rave with them – every day, anytime, there's always someone awake; and
- How was I going to rave with them – use the tools and let the technology work for me.

esp

Here's another little nugget of information I'd like to share with you... You may recall I mentioned in Volume 4 that I had a respect for, and appreciation of, the power of SEO, keyword search and the growth or real-time search in social networks, ergo SSO. It was a no brainer that people would search on obvious keywords and associated words within social network platforms. Accordingly, I was confident that extraordinary search power (ESP) – the combination of SEO and SSO as a formula – would hold the key to my finding, and being found by, the kind of peeps I had my heart, mind, gut and brand, set on in my bird's nest dream sight.

The online early days consisted of Web 1.0 when the new industry of SEO emerged. Google became a billion-dollar business. The recommended way to be the 'Queen of Findability' was to consistently add 'information rich' and 'keyword relevant' content to a webpage.

Back to the future, it's now Web 2.0 (almost Web 3.0). The new industry of SSO has emerged; Twitter rocks and Facebook rules; the new kids on the block... and hey, wouldn't you know it, another billion-dollar business. Good on 'em!

My understanding is that SSO works in a fashion not unlike SEO inside SM platforms too, so it becomes even more important to be found inside LinkedIn, Twitter, Facebook, Plaxo, Ecademy, Biznik, Alias, Merchant Circle and FastPitch – the dominant and emerging SM sites for professional peeps and businesses. Because social activity and rich keyword content inform search engine results, it's probable that SSO will be a powerful contender in trumping SEO as the primary force to be reckoned with for real time search.

It's no co-incidence that Google has done a deal with Twitter. The real power is in the real time search (keyword search) of Twitter. Similarly, LinkedIn and Twitter are bed buddies. Tweeting and updating my LinkedIn status regularly with keywords results in my being found high up in the Google ranking. Accordingly, I reckon, keyword content in SM and SN platforms and within bespoke websites and blogs, will continue to be king of the online realm of findability, for now at least, until a new technology supersedes it.

2010: Silicon Valley is now on with Web 3.0. Ah, now there's the rub... If we lawyers haven't even got to grips with Web 1.0 properly, just think of the missed opportunity in relation to Web 2.0, let alone Web 3.0 and Web 4.0 now on the horizon.

2012: Scary eh?

2015: EEK!

I do *not* profess to be an expert on SEO or SSO, but I wasn't going to allow the 'experts' to bamboozle me with high tech SEO gobbledegook either. I simply applied common sense, a positive mindset and my understanding, knowledge and experience of online marketing research, marketing, new marketing, relationship marketing, relationship building, branding, sales and capitalising on new technologies and tools, in order to benefit from the power buzzing and surging from the very same.

Oh, and in true Marti Pellow of pop band Wet Wet Wet lyrics style, I managed to "Get by with a little from my friends."[6]

Smart niche positioning coupled with the use of related keywords, keyword rich optimised content, strategic keyword density and brand consistency (kind of tell them, tell them and tell them again) is a win win strategy.

SEO and SSO dovetailed and aligned in my FMSP helps 'Brand,Me' get found and to generate new client leads, enquiries, referrals and instructions. FACT. No argument! I have the evidence to prove it... read on...

go...ogle... permissively

You may recall I mentioned to you in a previous volume that we have to try and look at things differently. How about this...? Google = 'Go'...'Ogle'. It's about ogling peeps and peeps ogling you. It's OK to be a permissive 'Googler'.

That's the whole point of Googling. To find and be found, especially if we understand that Generation Y and Generation Z, the referrers and clients of the present and future, are of the mindset 'JFGI' (just f***ing Google it) when they wish to source something.

You just know it makes sense that you need to be found where the seekers are looking. D'ya think?

Here are a few tips for you.

1. Set your homepage to Google and make your Google dashboard bespoke to your interests by selecting widgets and gadgets which are pertinent to you. There's a LinkedIn widget where you can view Questions & Answers in your chosen field, for example, corporate law. When you power up each day you can see the 'shout outs' from LinkedIn users in relation to corporate law questions. You might be pleasantly surprised to find questions such as, 'Does anyone know a lawyer who can help me with a contract?'
2. Similarly on twitter. Have your hootsuite or tweetdeck open all day too; similar shout outs are happening and/or you can simply go search using keywords real-time.
3. Aim to dominate at least pages pages deep on Google with regard to your 'Brand,Me'; the more often your name comes up associated with your services and products, the higher you will rank on search engines when peeps who don't know you look for those services and/or products.

How do you find new clients and sales? Err, see above. It's a starter for ten. Findability, visibility and presence means future business! Period. If you don't get your AIG (ass in gear) and get a grip of SEO, SSO, SM and SN you'll be missing a trick. You need to be doing SEO *and* SSO right now otherwise you risk opportunity loss. And possible extinction.

I'll share with you an example of how this stuff works... In a bid to generate new clients in the employee share scheme niche that I was focusing on in 2008 and 2009, I researched keywords associated with the same. We (the firm, Boss Lawyer and I) developed an 'employee share scheme' specialism area on the firm's website for the bespoke service offering and correlating webpages. I then wrote rich keyword content which was SEO and SSO friendly, applied keyword density strategically and placed these keywords and content within the firm's webpages, on my personal blog posts, and within articles and my personal SM and SN messages.

My Boss Lawyer even recognised the potential merit in this exercise so he allowed the moths to fly forth from the corporate piggy bank, and we embarked on a Google Adwords employee share scheme campaign. We capped the adword spend as it seemed that approaching our virgin campaign judiciously would save money... *and face...* if it bombed. I didn't have a problem with the saving face element of course, as I was confident it would work. Because:

- I did a similar thing when I worked in the health club industry, that is, I tried a new way of doing something to attract more gym members using 'the new way marketing and sales technology stuff' at that time; and
- Having worked in new media prior to entering the profession, I also had an understanding of online search and buying behaviour (I also dabble in domain name trading).

I also couldn't give a rats what The Resistance thought – no point in trying to convince the doubting laggards. At least we were trying to *do something* positive by bringing in new clients and being prepared to try new ways. Nevertheless, I wasn't going to be the one explaining to co-partners if it did go tits up. So I could understand that Boss Lawyer was a little concerned in saving face and money.

Happily, the result of our campaign was the firm netted a five times return in investment (ROI); the outcome in relation to netting a couple of new clients and increasing brand and niche specialism awareness. The exercise of course raised the profile of 'Brand,Firm' as well as Boss Lawyer and 'Brand,Me' as lawyers and a law firm specialising in employee share schemes. Woopah! Result.

This SM and SN stuff actually brings in new business. I dare you. Go on. Just do something. Go, ogle!

high five junkie!

LinkedIn line dance

As my intent was to meet raving referral business professionals and potential clients, LinkedIn (LI) was, and is, (IMHO – in my humble opinion) the big whoppa business SN platform to get jiggy with.

Back in 2008 I kicked off my SM and SN activity with LI. It seemed the obvious choice judging by the number of peeps who were using the site already. Interesting facts:[7]

- A new member joins LinkedIn approximately every second, and about half of its members are outside the US;
- It is growing at a rate of one million peeps per day; and
- Executives from all Fortune 500 companies are LinkedIn members.

Quoting LinkedIn:

"Your professional network of trusted contacts gives you an advantage in your career, and is one of your most valuable assets. LinkedIn exists to help you make better use of your professional network and help the people you trust in return. Our mission is to connect the world's professionals to make them more productive

and successful. We believe that in a global connected economy, your success as a professional and your competitiveness as a company depends upon faster access to insight and resources you can trust."

So, I'm going to dedicate the majority of the 'high five junkie!' section to LI. However, what I say here about LI kind of applies to all the other SM and SN platforms; simply do the same. This is my personal way of going about all this SM and SN minefield stuff. It doesn't make it *the way*. I'm simply sharing with you what is working for me. This is what is getting me results. It may just get you results too.

what I'm doing on LinkedIn

1) Attention, Interest, Desire, Credibility, Action is the format I use; it's the 'why' and 'how' I present information. For example, with LI:
   a. Attention: I have an attention grabbling title/name – 'Chrissie Lightfoot The Entrepreneur Lawyer' (Brand, Me) with keywords in the title and headline/tagline too.
   b. Interest: full profile, 100 percent, a good mix, covering work history, educational history, interest groups, articles, Trip It app (which details your travels), blog posts, regular status updates.
   c. Desire: created by making the reader curious and my sharing updates regularly and getting involved in conversations in groups and asking and answering questions.
   d. Credibility: being recommended by peeps, and my recommending them.
   e. Action: I have a call to action (inviting peeps to do something now; contact me) in my 'contact settings' at the bottom of my profile homepage.
2) Start with the end in mind: 'who' I want to ROAR with.
3) Focus on my brand and niches: all the work I'd put into the USPs, PODs, etc. so that I attract the right kind of lobsters and clients – target market peeps – referrers, clients, suppliers, other professionals, affiliates, partners, etc.
4) Consistency of message, availability and involvement.
5) Get personal: personalise everything; I talk to 'YOU', in other words, directly to the reader.
6) SEO and SSO my profile and messages.
7) Nice photo: headshot supporting 'Brand,Me'. Warm, approachable, welcoming, professional.
8) Title/tagline: as said above; 'Chrissie Lightfoot The Entrepreneur Lawyer' (Brand, Me) with keywords in the title and tagline/headline too. I change the tagline from time to time. Sometimes I have one-off keywords and other times I use a description such as, 'Helping You Market, Brand and Sell YOU! For lawyers, by a lawyer'. My title lets people know 'who' and 'what' I am, the tagline tells you how I can help you. We discussed Answers above and this is another communication opportunity.
9) Make headlines: I try to give YOU an experience, something worth talking about by providing interesting status updates – information, quotes, news of interest, perhaps.
10) 100 percent profile: very detailed. This is my opportunity to tell YOU my story. I also populate my profile with keywords in my summary, job descriptions, specialties, interests, awards.
11) 'Current' job: I make sure I have the kind of descriptions that seekers will search for. For example, CEO (not MD), Founder.

12) Line dance: I look up people and companies – high value targets – and ask to be connected to them and their connections. I line dance! I use 'advanced' search (top right of the LI page) in order to find my exact target lobster and client. I am a premium member which means I can get really granular (see glossary) with this feature, particularly in relation to seniority level.

13) Be an expert, using Q&A and Groups features:

   a. Answering a question: this is where I share knowledge and provide value to others (moot). I simply find the questions pertinent to the legal industry, my niches and specialisms and share my knowledge, thoughts and opinions. The benefits?
      i. It demonstrates my expertise;
      ii. Builds karma – good will, with readers and the person who posed the question; and
      iii. If I am selected as providing a 'best answer', it goes on my profile; it can affect how readers perceive me and begin the process of 'know, like, trust, understand, get, share an interest.'

      I also sign off using my brand (Chrissie – The Entrepreneur Lawyer) and sometimes provide a link back to my website – depends on the kind of question and whether it's good netiquette – as I find that when I answer a question, traffic to my website and blog increases.

   b. Join groups. The benefits?
      i. Means my reach is amplified. Albeit I can reach 2,000 direct connections on LI (as that is the number of my connections at present), being a member of 50 groups (the maximum, as LI caps the number of groups we can be a member of at 50) means I can actually reach millions (all of the people within that group and THEIR networks).
      ii. Engage in conversations and cultivate new relationships – nurtures network.
      iii. Raises 'Brand,Me' awareness and 'Brand,Firm' awareness. My title – Chrissie Lightfoot The Entrepreneur Lawyer; 'Brand,Me' – is visible in a mini profile when I answer questions, post discussions, or add news articles – sharing 'Brand,Me'.
      iv. Starting a discussion: the discussion topic gets e-mailed out to all group members, and sometimes it goes in the subject line of the receivers e-mail inbox as 'from Chrissie Lightfoot TheEntrepreneurLawyer and other [x] group members on LinkedIn' – it gets my name, 'Brand,Me', in front of loads of interested people.
      v. People ask to connect with me – grows my network.
      vi. Opportunity to promote x,y,z; there is a designated 'promotions' tab.
      vii. I may identify and create a lead.
      viii. I may quickly move from online to offline and continue the sales process.
      ix. Market research.
      x. Expands my knowledge: in the know and up to date with what's happening in my field and my potential client's field. For example, trends, industry knowledge, present thinking.
      xi. Amplification: when peeps see a discussion and/or article of interest they post it on their LI status too. For example, when I posted the 'Frustrated Lawyers R Us' discussion and article link, other peeps picked it up and posted it/shared it on their

status bars (and tweeted it). Adding news articles enables me to share value through the content I provide. As I engage with group members over time they get to know me and I get to know them – 'know, like, trust, understand, 'get', share interests'. What tends to happen is if they like my content they begin to like me... they become curious and check out my profile and then ask to connect.

xii. Being present – a potential client will think of me first before another lawyer/attorney/solicitor if I'm there, being helpful, being personable, being responsive and available to listen.

Which group? I find as many groups as possible that are relevant to me and my company. I simply go to the groups directory and search for relevant groups, then look up the discussions which float my boat and get involved by joining the conversations:

- ☐ Niche target clients;
- ☐ Niche target referrers;
- ☐ Interest groups – business and leisure;
- ☐ Pro-active groups – people who use the group to discuss and actually do!
- ☐ Colleagues.

c. Create my own group. The benefits? I get to manage my group with all the perks:
   i. Sales process! It's a sales pipeline.
   ii. Engagement, conversation, build relationship.
   iii. Send announcements which plop into group members' e-mail inbox! Woopah.
   iv. Send invites to join the group.
   v. Control over discussions featured – can help members' discussions flourish (including my own).
   vi. Ease of request to connect which grows the network.
   vii. Be the facilitator – keeps the conversations going and flowing; nurturing relationships.

14) Get recommended: if you don't ask, you won't get. 'Shy birds get nowt', remember? I'm proactive about generating recommendations, as it enables YOU to see what other people have to say about me and make a judgment call as to whether you think I can help you and/or want to contact me. There's no point in me telling you 'I'm fab'. You wouldn't believe me. But if somebody else does (a third party; somebody standing in your shoes) then you are more likely to believe them. If I've been helpful and provided a service to be proud of, then I shouldn't be shy in asking for a recommendation. I'm also pro-active in giving recommendations too, as I know this is important in helping my connections be successful in attracting more referrers and clients.

15) Events: handy for checking out events of interest and sharing news of events with referrers, clients, contacts, etc.

16) Apps: there are lots to choose from. I use Slideshare (so I can display my articles), Trip It (so I can share with people where I'm visiting so that we can hook up perhaps) and WordPress (so peeps can get a feel for my latest blog posts); they're all related to sharing information of interest. As I create more video content I will no doubt drop one of the existing apps and

pop a video app on there instead, as it will make my profile three dimensional. The only problem with the Apps feature, I reckon, is LI limits the number of apps you can have on your profile. I have managed to get past three.

17) I aim to be present every day (subject to illness) just like I'm 'out and about' offline every day.

18) In relation to inbound marketing and outbound marketing per se, I'm a permissive inbounder, meaning I'm more than happy to connect with most peeps (even if I've never met them because I see that the whole point of LI and other SN platforms is to meet new people I wouldn't ever have come across). But I'm a targeted outbounder, meaning I am very 'rifle shot' in my approach, because my intent is to build bigger and stronger relationships with my target lobsters and clients.

19) LI Premium Account: it's a Social Customer Relationship Management (SCRM) system; very granular regarding search and behaviour of connections and interest seekers. Helps with my findability, marketing and sales efforts.

Twitter hip hop

What is Twitter? It's a free SN and microblogging website, a more viral form of blogging, that allows peeps to post and read messages (tweets) of up to 140 characters on an author's profile page. It's hip, it's hop, it's simple and it's effective.

I joined the twitterati in 2009. Once again, I could see the value in this tool as it had all of the great benefits similar to LI. However, what was, and is, neat about Twitter, is it's a feeder to my other SM and SN sites – LI, Facebook, YouTube, blog, website. Mind boggling Twitter statistics:[8]

- 106 million registered users;
- 300,000 new users per day;
- Three billion requests a day;
- Users are sending 55 million tweets per day; and
- Its search engine gets 600 million requests per day.

So, here's a whistle-stop tour in why and how I use Twitter.

- I have three Twitter accounts:
  1) EntrepreneurLaw ('Brand,Me', 'Brand,Firm' – the big picture);
  2) TheNakedLawyer ('Brand,Product' – purely about *the naked lawyer* e-book series); and
  3) FullOnLiving (the personal life of Chrissie Lightfoot – my leisure interests mainly).
- I secured my twitter handle(s) to correlate with my brand stable(s) (as above and duly noted in Volume 4).
- 80:20 rule: I mainly tweet information of benefit to my followers. The focus is on THEM. One in five of my messages is self-promotion.
- Retweet other peeps' stuff, and mention them: I help promote my followers.
- I twit to woo: to converse, ask questions, share legal and business news of interest, brag about and promote other peeps.
- I follow the followers of my 'competitors': continually identify key influencers/mavens (active SM types) – my target customers and affiliates and referrers
- If they follow me back, and I have a direct link with them, I use Twitter as a form of instant messaging.
- I have too much e-mail traffic, so I can be more selective and just follow certain people on Twitter.

- Clarity and focus of message. Being a woman I tend to be rather verbose (surely not, you're no doubt thinking!). However, because my message can only be a maximum of 140 characters, it forces me to be prompt and to the point.
- 'Brand,Me' is consistent with my other SN profiles.

Benefits:

- Helps me connect meaningfully with my target lobsters and clients.
- Helps me build my network fast; niche market.
- The 'search' – this is where the real power is because I'm finding peeps who are having conversations on a topic real time. I basically use twitter for real-time search. I simply search on keywords I know I will be helpful as a solutions provider to the tweeter.
- Tweeting my keywords gets me ranked higher in Google.
- Through regularly tweeting about my niche interest and/or expertise, I become known for it and peeps start to gravitate toward me and follow me. Over time I become a trusted expert and become relied upon to send my followers interesting and relevant stuff, including links.
- Sharing free information, being helpful and being memorable helps establish the 'know, like, trust, understand, 'get', share an interest/commonality'.
- Raises 'Brand,Me' and 'Brand,Firm' awareness, grows and leverages my network, nurtures relationships.
- Helps me reach gurus – thought leaders.

Tips:

- Create lists. Check out other peeps' lists (those who share the same interests; and your 'competitors' – peeps who do a similar role to you) and follow their followers. It will help you build your following fast and engage in conversations with the kind of peeps you aim to help. Most followers follow back if you're interesting and have commonality.
- Use hashtags – for example #lawyers or #entrepreneurs – finding other peeps who are taking about stuff that may be of interest to lawyers or entrepreneurs.
- Hashtag 'Brand,You' and 'Brand,Firm'. For example I hashtag #entrepreneurlaw, #thenakedlawyer – it generates buzz!
- Do *not* use Twitter like an advertising tool. It's bad karma, bad netiquette. You'll hack peeps off.
- Use:
  - Hootsuite – for managing your multiple social network platforms;
  - Tweetulater – for setting up an auto tweet;
  - Budurl.com – so that you can trace and track how effective/useful your message was; and
  - Hashable.com – for ease of connecting peeps.

Facebook flamenco

Facebook (FB) – not just a playground for kiddies. It's here to stay for the foreseeable future and, despite in the early days being used on the whole for personal social use, now many businesses, including law firms and much of the legal media, have their own pages. It's a hotbed for adult flamenco action of the Naked Lawyer kind!

I use FB in the same way as I use LI and Twitter as I reap the same benefits. Duly note:

- I am a relatively recent adopter;
- I've integrated my FB stuff with Twitter and LI – when I post on FB it

automatically posts into my LI status and EntrepreneurLaw Twitter feed;

- I have a 'Chrissie Lightfoot 'account; and then...
- A dedicated business page: Entrepreneur Lawyer.

I plan to get more jiggy with FB. Feel free to 'friend' me.

YouTube 'n' all that jazz

YouTube is the second most popular search engine; Google being the first. Oh, and it's owned by Google. I've already shared with you the importance of SEO, SSO and keywords – findability – *and* as a picture can paint a thousand words, the video inevitably brings a three dimensional element to content; so I reckon it's a no brainer to have a presence on YouTube. Albeit YouTube is renowned for its 'arty' flavour – music channels – it's got masses of business channels. Enough said. I'm a recent adopter, but a quick learner!

I have two channels:

- http://www.youtube.com/TheNakedLawyer; and
- http://www.youtube.com/EntrepreneurLawyer.

You're welcome to come and dance with me here.

blawg blawg swing

My blog is my *nest* for all my SM and SN stuff. I drive peeps to my blog. Why? Because if peeps come to my blog it helps me engage with them. Engaging means I will have the opportunity to build an enduring value relationship with them. It's a community of like interested peeps.

Through time, we get to 'know, like, trust, understand 'get' and share interests'. Inevitably, it means that potential clients come to me pre-qualified and pre-sold which means more clients, referrals, sales, income, value, growth, success. For example, I may have created buzz from Twitter, FB, YouTube and LI in relation to *the naked lawyer* book, but my blog is where I truly build, leverage and sustain the relationship with my new potential clients.

My website is in fact blog technology; it's SEO friendly. My blog *is* my website. So, it's only a hop skip and a jump for my potential clients to taste the goodies. *the naked lawyer* e-book is actually available to download from my website which is also where my blog resides. Albeit blogging is by no means a new technology, it still remains a cheap and effective way to reach my potential lobsters and clients.

Again, I use my blog in the same way as I use LI, Twitter, FB and YouTube as I reap the same benefits. Tip: use your blog content (posts) multiple times. For example, my posts can be found on other peeps' blogs, often with permission because they also welcome the same.

Back in 2008 whilst attending an offline networking event, someone said to me that in order for me to be successful online I needed to get a grip on blogging and SM. He was right. Perhaps I have managed to convince you of this too?

just fumbling around ROAR style

So, bringing it all together then, how does my SM and SN activity with regard to LI, Twitter, FB, YouTube and my blog click together, in helping me build my raving Referral Lobster Net-Kingdom and generate new business?

Let me share a couple of case studies with you and examples of how peeps find me and know about me.

case study 1: Article – 'Tomorrow's Lawyer'

- January 2010: I wrote an article of interest to a targeted audience (*Leeds & Yorkshire Lawyer* – The Leeds Law Society Official Journal – published 31 January 2010). One day to research and write.
- Placed the slideshow on LI profile.
- Placed on LI status, Twitter, FB.
- *Reach* – 9,000 readership in Yorkshire and Humber, plus my connections on LI and followers on Twitter and FB.
- *Out* – Over 120 new LI contacts as a result because peeps were interested and enquired to connect. Leads for the future. Picked up by the *Clapham Omnibus* (The Journal of the South London Law Society).
- March 2010 republished by the *Clapham Omnibus*.
- Another 5,000 readership, 40 new LI connections immediately. London/South leads for future.
- *And* – It was retweeted, bit.ly, and article viewed from my website/blog.
- *Relate* – Led to eight meetings (partners and business development managers of law firms and sole practitioners), got two potential clients for coaching/training worth (£xk) plus (£xk) potential sales of the e-book . That is, a sales pipeline established and actual sales achieved. Re-engaged/connected with older leads and contacts.
- Further action:
  - ☐ 5th May tweeted Alistair Moyes's article with my comment re customer service (see Law Society Gazette and on LI status too because it automatically drops in).
  - ☐ Relate example: Raymond McLennan RT @entrepreneurlaw. The tweet was: "'The End Of Lawyers', dead dinosaur, reinventing, radical change – a few choice words from an article & comments here..." (also on his LI status).
  - ☐ Placed 'Tomorrow's Lawyer' on news sections of the LI groups that I engage in.
- Further action required:
  - ☐ Place on JDSupra.
  - ☐ Create a post around the subject on my blog.

case study 2: 'Penny A Brick' post on my blog

- 25 April 2010 wrote a post 'Penny A Brick – Why I became A Lawyer'. Two hours to write.
- 25-26 April, placed on my website/blog, tweeted, LI status bar, The Entrepreneur Lawyer Relationship Sales Network Group discussion and placed on other appropriate LI Groups. Two hours to place in groups
- *Reach* – 1,300 on LI direct, group members.
- *Out* – peeps got back to me and made an enquiry/a connection/became leads as a result:
  - ☐ xxxx signups on Mailchimp (potential buyers – building customer list);
  - ☐ LI/Home/Who's viewed my profile. In the last day 62 peeps viewed my profile. 210 searches (three days running);
  - ☐ 568 page views on my blog post within three days;
  - ☐ 39 comments on post on my blog; and
  - ☐ 1,024 budurl clicks (800 within a matter of days).
- *And* – retweeted by others.
- *Relate* – Potential sales in the pipeline. Moved readers around from whichever group and led them to The Entrepreneur Lawyer Relationship Sales Network Group, the blog post and call to action

to join me on Twitter, Facebook and sign up for the e-ntrepreneur bullet (newsletter) to be informed of free e-book *the naked lawyer* Volume 1.

Wee reminder. Don't forget you can set up your Google homepage to have LI Q&A visible so you can see distress shout outs, for example:

"Does anyone know a good lawyer? I have a...

- Contract I need doing/advising on.
- Shareholder dispute to sort.
- Start-up situation.
- Business to sell.
- Trademark query and need representation."

example of how peeps find me

In relation to my request, 'May I respectfully ask how you came across me?' in my LI template message (which you will note I share with you in a following section), the following are *actual* responses. It will give you a feel as to how it all fits together:

- Hope you are having a nice weekend! I was talking about your work to some of my friends and family. They are really excited to hear more about it. Are your blogs and tweets the best way to go about it? Does your book Naked Lawyer have a hard copy edition? I would love to give it to my newest sister-in-law who is law school. I would love it if you could mentor her.
  Best Regards, [ ]
- Killer site and blog. We need to talk! [This was sent by the Orange County Trial Attorney – 2009 'Top Gun' Trial Lawyer of the Year...]
- Your Linked In page came up on my home page and I noticed you were a member of The Yorkshire mafia too...We are in quite a few similar groups, and also I have read your blogs on the Law Society Gazette website. I very much enjoy reading your updates.
- The Naked Lawyer got my attention, as well as your past and current activities. As an IT Lawyer developing my profile within Privacy and Networking legal approaches, I would love to follow you and add you to my LinkedIn network. Regards, [ ]
- Regarding the source of The Naked Lawyer reference, I reach your page thanks to this FB group: LawRD - Reports on Demand. They published this URL to your eBook:
  http://entrepreneurlawyer.co.uk/products-services/ebook/
  Hope this information works for you. I will take a look at the rest of the webs and blogs that you sent. I love being a lawyer and I laugh about my profession and myself a lot
- Hi Chrissie – one of our Partners came across your group and joined it yesterday and he forwarded it to me as well. I thought it looked interesting so I signed up! ([ ] Marketing Manager of a law firm).
- I came across you on Twitter. I'm Digital Marketing Director for a business publishing company. We run a Business law advice website called [ ] so I felt you would be a good contact.
- Re how I came across you, you were suggested to me by LinkedIn – maybe something to do with my legal background – however I also noticed you are also a member of the Yorkshire Mafia!
- I was searching for an Asset Manager and came across your profile. It was your legal work/experience that interested me

having completed a law degree myself, as well as expanding connections.

- Yes, I came across you through sharing the same group, Legal Blogging. I read your profile with great interest and thought we have got many good things in common. From your lovely response, I can see already that our connection could be the beginning of a very special relationship. Thanks very much for the Naked Lawyer eBook – I am looking forward to reading it tonight!
- [ ] needs a solicitor's opinion on a legal contract giving shares to employees... any recommendations?
  The above 'shout-out' message was sent out through twitter; somebody recommended me via twitter and then [x] viewed my LI profile and website/blog and then contacted me direct via e-mail and telephone; I referred [x] to one of my lobsters (a practising solicitor).
- Nice to meet you. I came across your network by way of one of the other attorneys in my network. I practice class action law in California and I believe your reference was on one of the other class action folk's profiles. Sounds like you have some interesting information.
- I found you while browsing for entrepreneurs. I am in the planning stages of forming my company with 3 other partners. We will concentrate on developing countries first and see where it will take us.
- Thank you for accepting my invite. I came across you when I did a search for lawyers in the UK on the group women 2 women business (a group we both share).
- Chrissie I have been inspired and intrigued by your profile. I fully appreciate how busy you may be but I would like to buy you a coffee or a glass of wine when you're in London next.
- [ ] asked me to let you know it was me who recommended he make contact with you. He has accepted the position of promoting our latest film and wants to expand his new Linkedin network.I came across your name in my business travels and had intended making contact first but [ ] beat me to the punch after I mentioned your name in a recent conversation. Sorry but I can't remember who it was but they will be a contact of mine somewhere on Linkedin who started the ball rolling........
  All the best, [ ]
- Well, I'm delighted you accepted my invitation. I read a couple of your posts and really liked them. That's basically how I came across you. I noticed your group when I was searching groups that might make sense for me to join. I am a marketing professional who has spent the past 8 years working in a law firm. I love lawyers and the business of law. It looks like you have a great group...
  Are you also on Twitter? You can find me @[ ]
- I found your profile by chance really. I thought you came across extremely positively and had an interesting profile, so just thought I'd try and connect.
- I hope you will forgive the presumption of my approach, but you were recommended to me by my husband, (who is in the legal profession). I admire your entrepreneurial style, and as a fledgling entrepreneur would like to add you to my network as I always think it is highly useful to share skills across professions.
  Best regards, [ ]
- You had contributed some excellent commentary to The Virtual Lawyer blog. I greatly appreciate your field observations and look forward to reviewing the

resources you note in your e-mail. That material promises to be very perceptive. It will be a pleasure to communicate with and learn from you.

Cordially, [ ]

bust a gut daily work out

blow your horn

Reflecting back on why SM matters, why use SM (from the earlier sections), the information and activities from previous Volumes, 3 and 4 in particular – cutting myself a niche and creating a personal brand – along with the information I have shared with you in social savvy junkie, I am sure you will agree with me when I say: it's *imperative* to use SM and SN to... *blow your horn*! Daily.

I set about placing my brand everywhere, everyday, mastering multiple platforms in concert to engage with everyone whom I identified as needing to hear my shout out: "Here I am peeps, this is who I am, this is what I can do for you, this is where, when, why and how I *can help you*. Get your tomorrow's lawyer, here, today!"

Being omnipresent had (and has) the effect of peeps getting the feeling that I am simply everywhere; I just might, therefore, actually be worth *knowing* as The Entrepreneur Lawyer who could actually be of benefit and value to THEM. It tells them, I'm available. I'm present. I'm visible. I'm contactable. You can ROAR with me. I'm here for YOU.

Let's get this straight too... I wasn't, and am not being, egotistical or narcissistic (and nor will YOU be) in what can only be viewed as unashamed and unabashed self promotion. Really? Yes! Remember, the underlying raison d'etre of 'Brand,Me' (and 'Brand,Firm') is to be totally client focused, by being distinctive in emphasising a promise of value delivered to a target audience to whom I can deliver some clear benefit and show my relevance to a specific brand community.

To be an extraordinary rainmaker and an extraordinary ambassador of 'Brand,Me' and 'Brand,Firm' requires confident and shameless self promotion. THEY need to KNOW I exist and I am their 'best fit' solution to mirror and match their need, want and desire. Fact.

This goes for you too and 'Brand,You'. If you're not comfortable with this then don't bother reading any further. Go and crawl under your desk, or a rock perhaps, one of your Big Rocks maybe and hide there until this digital era and law law land big lull passes over like the Black Death. Not!

All I can say is this, again: wakey wakey! Get a grip! C-c-c-courage! Dino dung! Nuts! Take the plunge! Carpe diem! Get your AIG and get out there and blow your horn!

Tally ho ... I'll see you there!

I must, I must, I must improve my lust

As I went about my daily SM and SN activity I was thinking extraordinary rainmaker = extraordinary sex... again. Remember Volume 2 where I shared with you the idea that rainmaking is like sex? Quick recap...

- Poor rainmaking activity is like unfulfilling sex – at least for one of the parties involved. Don't really care what the other person thinks. Couldn't give a monkey's how the other person feels. Haven't got a clue what you're doing. No real effort or interest. The whole experience is over in a jiffy. And it's all about 'me, me, me'. In other words – all take. Pure self-interest.
- Extraordinary rainmaking activity is definitely like extraordinary sex – continual mind focus; continual

nurturing; continual stimulation; continual discovery; continual delivery; continual follow on; continual improvement; continual innovation; continual research and development?

Well, let's replace 'rainmaking' with 'SM and SN' shall we? Poor SM and SN activity is like unfulfilling sex! So, don't bother with SM and SN if you're going to approach it like rubbish sex. Extraordinary SM and SN activity is like extraordinary sex. Truly.

Because extraordinary SM and SN activity is all about LUST. Continual:

- **L**inking;
- **U**nderstanding;
- **S**ocial savvy; and
- **T**ouching...

of THEM... Potential and existing lobsters. Potential and existing clients.

I simply prrrrrrr in linking with them, understanding them, being socially savvy with them, touching them constantly; figuratively speaking of course in my communications! We'll look at this in Volume 9 touch touch and touch me again. Through LUST, giving and connecting unconditionally, I continually delight in helping them get more business!

To give you an idea as to the kind of SM and SN activity I engage in, ergo, what you may wish to consider doing yourself, I'd like to share the following with you:

daily lust

Here is a glimpse of my daily SM and SN LUST activity (schedule). It's what I do every day; 80:20/G:R. I dedicate a minimum of two hours per day (up to six hours some days) to SM and SN activity in allocated time slots morning, noon and night, above and beyond my core role. I may reply instantly to a message I see as sometimes it's important to be quick off the mark, especially if it's a request for help and potential work!

My top five priorities each day are as follows, in this order:

1. Give introductions/connections/links;
2. Share fresh content;
3. Increase followers/connections;
4. Build relationships; increase engagement of contacts and converse; and
5. Increase 'Brand,Me' awareness.

In detail:

- Check: messages; mentions; retweets; direct messages:
  - ☐ Hootsuite – send at least one daily message across Twitter accounts, LinkedIn status and facebook; send a thank you for. 'mentions' and 'retweets'; I mention/retweet other peeps stuff of relevance i.e. law, entrepreneur, business, sales and marketing related stuff;
  - ☐ Twitter – as above;
  - ☐ Facebook – as above;
  - ☐ LinkedIn – messages – personal and The Entrepreneur Lawyer Relationship Sales Network group; connection requests and replies;
  - ☐ YouTube accounts – messages and growth;
  - ☐ Blog posts – administer and place comments; connection requests and replies;
  - ☐ Hashable – make introductions;
  - ☐ Budurl.com – statistics;
  - ☐ EntrepreneurLawyer website – statistics; and
  - ☐ Mailchimp – sign-ups/list (who).
- Send an autotweet message from both TheNakedLawyer (7pm UK time) and

EntrepreneurLawyer (4pm UK time) Twitter accounts.

- Facilitate and manage The Entrepreneur Lawyer Relationship Sales Network group, get involved in the discussion(s) of the same and other LI groups wherel have placed a question that correlates as above. Approve new members.
- All those peeps that sign up to The Entrepreneur Lawyer Relationship Sales Network group discussions, I send a message to them asking to connect on LI, follow on Twitter (x2) and become FB fan, sign up for free Volume 1 of *the naked lawyer*, the E-ntrepreneurLawyer newsletter and check out EntrepreneurLawyer blog.
- All those that comment in the groups on my discussions, as above.

weekly lust

- Send a #ff shout out about my key Twitter followers.
- Check out synergistic blogs and make a comment.

monthly lust

- E-ntrepreneurLawyer Bullet (newsletter).

The box out shows examples of my templates too, to give you an idea of how you can help reduce the time in managing your SM and SN enquiries and responsibilities.

after dark activity

stamina rules!

OK dance partner. You're going to need some stamina for what's coming next! You're

template response to LinkedIn requests

when a person has joined The Entrepreneur Lawyer Relationship Sales Network group

Hi [ ]

Just another thought, if I can help you in anyway please feel free to get in touch.

May I respectfully ask how you came across me? In the meantime check out the following as they may be of interest and benefit to you:

The Naked Lawyer eBook Vol1 (free) – http://budurl.com/TNL1

Frustrated Lawyers R Us – http://budurl.com/mutiny
Zen & The Art Of Legal Networking – http://budurl.com/SNzenLaw
Rise Of The Super Lawyer – http://bit.ly/9py6qM
Traditionalist v Modernists – http://budurl.com/ItsABoxOfFrogs

At the very least they may make you smile :-)

Warmest regards

Chrissie
The Entrepreneur Lawyer

when I am invited to connect to someone

Hi [ ]

Thanks for reaching out. Delighted to connect. If I can help you in any way please feel free to get in touch.

May I respectfully ask how you came across me?

Come and join me in my group here on LI too as it may be of interest and benefit to you –The Entrepreneur Lawyer Relationship Sales Network.

Also, check out the following – 'same same' benefits:

The Naked Lawyer eBook Vol.1 (free) – http://budurl.com/TNL1

Frustrated Lawyers R Us – http://budurl.com/mutiny
Rise Of The Super Lawyer blog post – http://bit.ly/9py6qM
Traditionalist v Modernists blog post – http://budurl.com/ItsABoxOfFrogs
Zen & The Art Of Legal Networking – http://budurl.com/SNzenLaw

At the very least they may make you smile :-)

Hope to see you soon in the group!

Warmest

Chrissie
The Entrepreneur Lawyer

when I am doing the inviting, off the back of a LinkedIn group participation

Hi [ ]

Thanks for taking the time to get involved and share your thoughts in the group. Very much appreciated. I'd be honoured and delighted to add you to my professional network here on LinkedIn.

Warmest regards

Chrissie
The Entrepreneur Lawyer

going to need to draw on your positive mindset, SUUUCKS attitude and PEE Poor Work Ethic, Full On! It's now time for you to line dance, hip hop, flamenco, jazz and swing your way into building, leveraging and sustaining your raving Referral Lobster Net-Kingdom and potential client pool...

naked lawyer activity – a study worth casing

During autumn 2008 I began working through what is now this Volume 6 of *the naked lawyer* with a view to using SM and SN to build a value referral network and potential client pool online.

As to what I did, and for a real live case study, read the story again, including the exercises, secrets and tips shared within this Volume 6. You can relive my activity by taking yourself through the same process.

However, here are a number of activities to help you on your way:

activity 1: LinkedIn profile and headline

- Get your brand up there:
  Example – 'Chrissie Lightfoot The Entrepreneur Lawyer'.
- Remember *findability* and *identify* with potential lobsters and clients...
- Stand in the shoes of your potential clients in order to start the keyword search process. What will your potential clients and referrers be searching for?
- Keywords matter – populate your profile with relevant keywords appertaining to your niche, specialism, particularly in the (blue area) headline, naming your three websites, summary, and specialties areas on your profile page.
- Three key websites – name them using keywords if at all possible and make sure they go to direct pages e.g. 1) your firm's homepage 2) your firm's department 3) your specialism and/or profile page if you have one and/or your personal blog.

activity 2: Building a network fast (LinkedIn connections)

- Look through your business card collection and rolodex. Populate your Microsoft Outlook with their contact details. Then, import all of your contacts from Outlook into your LinkedIn set up. Now, send them a message asking them to join you on LI.
- In relation to all those who accept your invitation to connect, check out who they are connected to that will be of value to you and ask for a connection – line dance.
- Everyone you meet at a networking event, in meetings, clubs, trade shows, seminars, lectures, courses, dinners, awards, wine bars, cafes, train journeys, etc. – ask for their business card and whether they are on LI. If not, send them an e-mail and invite them.
- Check out who's viewed your profile; you will find this on your LI homepage. This is the blurb which says that you have 'appeared in Search results [x] times in the last day' – to the seekers who you can identify correctly, send them a message saying, 'I note you viewed my profile recently and I'd be delighted if I can help you. Perhaps we could connect?'
- Groups ... be visible and active in them because people notice you and your knowledge/expertise, etc. and they usually *ask you* to connect. You can ask them to connect too as they are more likely to even without 'knowing you' as they are familiar with you. As a group manager, that is, if you have your own group you have access to every individual in your group – ask them to connect with you – they all say 'yes'

because they wouldn't have joined your group otherwise!

- Place comments on blogs that are relevant to your niche and industry.
- Write an article in your area of expertise and share it – everywhere. Upload it as a pdf in the slide-share app thereby placing it on your LI profile page.

Example pro-activity:

- I receive at least five-15 requests to connect per day.
- I request at least five-15 requests to connect per day from Groups and/or who's viewed me and/or my own searches to identify a target client or referrer.
- I spent one to three hours per day (seven days a week)on SM activity whilst I was a trainee solicitor (2008-09).
- I spend two to six hours per day (seven days a week) on SM activity now building my own business (2010).

activity 3: Find and join a group on LinkedIn

- Important to use social media as a platform to discuss issues because when you engage potential clients and lobsters on these platforms, there is a public forum showing how you think, how you behave and how you act.
- Remember that kindness attracts kindness.
- Give and give and give.
- Share free information (not legal advice – duh!!!!); for example niche sector/ industry news.
- Have an opinion.
- Be helpful.
- Make conversation.
- Be engaging.
- Be human.
- Be quick to respond.

For an example, see my group list on my LI profile page.

Want to create your own group? Look again at the activity in Volume 1 that I shared with you. Follow the steps. You will note that you can set up template messages for when people join your group which helps with time management and building your relationships early on. Example: "The Entrepreneur Lawyer Relationship Sales Group; feel free to come and join me and the members! We're a friendly, helpful kinda bunch."

case study: The Entrepreneur Lawyer Relationship Sales Network (LinkedIn Group)

- Formed group 18 March 2010 (the day the EntrepreneurLawyer.co.uk website went live).
- Sunday 2 May:
  - ☐ Placed 2 discussions on the group to kick-start conversations; 'Penny A Brick ... Why I became a Lawyer' and 'Where Does "Sales" begin'.
  - ☐ Began to market using SM – call to action to join The Entrepreneur Lawyer Relationship Sales Group.
- *Reach:* Sent LI message to 1,260 LI connections; LI status bar; tweeted – three hours worth of activity.
- *Out:*
  - ☐ 260 group members joined within 36 hours;
  - ☐ 80 new LI connections (within three days) as a direct result of raising awareness of my personal brand using new group;
  - ☐ many new signs up on my mailchimp list (potential customers); and
  - ☐ The number of seekers viewing my LI profile averaged 60 views and 220 searches per day for four days running.

- *And:* it was amplified, aka, retweeted, placed on other peeps' LI homepages regarding activity of individuals joining, discussing, posting news items, etc. on the group.
- *Relate:* numerous new affiliate/referral/potential client leads, particularly in relation to interest with regard to *the naked lawyer* e-book. The activity woke up existing contacts who got back in touch.

activity 4: Look up people and companies on LinkedIn

- Use the advanced search facility and look up your ideal lobsters and clients.

activity 5: Create your company profile

- Only relevant to partners/decision makers; and
- Can be relevant to an individual if you are a portfolio worker.

activity 6: Answer and ask a question

- Brand awareness;
- Market research;
- Proves you're credible, knowledgeable and helpful; and
- If your answer is fab, you may get ranked as 'best answer'.

Furthermore, here's a condensed version of the exercises and tips you may wish to carry out...

ROAR steps

- **Step 1:** Get yourself set up on LI, Twitter, FB, YouTube and a blog.
- **Step 2:** Integrate them all.
- **Step 3:** See 'easy like a Sunday morning' section again. Use your Microsoft Office calendar, contacts, tasks (or equivalent software) and sales spreadsheet. Create some templates.
- **Step 4:** See 'secret agent provocateur' section again. Note the list in relation to how to build your network fast, secret agent provocateur style!
- **Step 5:** Apply *everything* you learned and prepared in Volumes 1 through 5. Apply wwwwwh and prrrrrrr.

examples of really cool guys (lawyers) using SM well

- Julian Summerhayes – http://www.juliansummerhayes.com
- Andrew Sharpe – http://bh.linkedin.com/in/andrewsharpe
- Steve Kuncewicz – http://uk.linkedin.com/in/stevekuncewicz
- Nils Montan – http://www.linkedin.com/in/nilsmontan
- David Gabor – http://www.linkedin.com/pub/david-gabor/a/445/307
- Mitch Jackson – http://www.linkedin.com/in/activesuccess
- Anthony Verna – http://www.linkedin.com/in/anthonyverna
- Peter Groves – http://www.petergroves.co.uk
- Andrew Woolley – http://uk.linkedin.com/in/andrewwoolley
- Brian Inkster – http://uk.linkedin.com/in/brianinkster; http://www.inksters.com/coollawyers.aspx
- Donna Seyle – http://www.linkedin.com/in/donnaseyle; http://lawpracticestrategy.com
- Raymond McLennan – http://uk.linkedin.com/in/raymondmclennan; http://www.raymondmclennan.com
- Michelle Hynes-McIlroy – http://legaleaglemhm.wordpress.com; http://twitter.com/legaleagleMHM
- Chrissie Lightfoot – http://entrepreneurlawyer.co.uk

- **Step 6:** See 'esp' and 'go...ogle... permissively' sections again. Use keyword content in your SM and SN activity. Follow my tips. Consider a Google Adword campaign (if relevant/pertinent).
- **Step 7:** See *all* of the 'high five junkie!' section and carry out the tips, secrets and other stuff I did (and do).
- **Step 8:** See 'I must, I must, I must improve my lust' section again and carry out your daily, weekly and monthly lust.

ROAR tips

- Make time: devote 30 minutes each day to SM and SN activity – after a while it will become second nature. A habit – a good, healthy habit.
- Lay out a designated time to carry out your SM and SN activity – morning, noon or night perhaps?
- Use Microsoft Outlook, calendar, contacts and tasks (or an equivalent software package) to help organise, manage and analyse your activity and effectiveness.
- Use your sales spreadsheet to highlight, monitor, benchmark and analyse your SM and SN activity and results.
- Set yourself three to five priority activities each day.
- Share 'Brand,You'.
- Blow your horn every day.
- Be a secret agent provocateur.
- Be a permissive Googler: go, ogle.
- Fumble around.
- Improve your *lust*.

ROAR summation

social savvy legal beagle

Well, after reading and applying all this little lot I'm confident you'll be well armed and truly on your way to attracting more clients, referrals, sales, income, value, growth and success.

Just keep in mind that positivity jives, you need to behave like a secret agent provocateur, perform like a high five junkie, fumble around ROAR style, blow your horn every day and focus on improving your *lust!*

I'm sooooo looking forward to Volume 7 where the little private dancing Naked Lawyer in law law land will rendezvous at your beck and call and help you nurture your fuzz to get more buzz...

References

1. Chris Brogan, Social Media 101
2. 2010 ABA Technology Survey Report surveyed12,500 attorneys about technology use: http://abovethelaw.com/2010/09/aba-survey-lawyers-profiting-from-web-2-0
3. Julian Summerhayes reporting on Hubspot's latest report, 'The State of Inbound Marketing 2010' – a report based on a survey of 231 professionals involved in, or familiar with, their business' marketing strategy: http://www.solicitorsjournal.com/story.asp?storycode=16482
4. *Ibid.*
5. Five Social Media Predictions for 2010', *SiteProNews*, 11/01/10. http://www.sitepronews.com/2010/01/11/five-social-media-predictions-for-2010/?utm_source=feedburner&utm_medium=e-mail&utm_campaign=Feed percent3A+sitepronews percent2FICnA+percent28SiteProNews percent29
6. Christine Hueber, SM specialist http://www.linkedin.com/in/christinehueber; http://christinehueber.com; Lyndon Ogden, SEO specialist: http://www.seopackages.com; http://uk.linkedin.com/in/lyndonogden; and Rachel Henke, specialises in helping entrepreneurs and professionals create a profitable online marketing presence and publishes the popular 'Marketing & Mindset' free ezine: http://www.Rachelhenke.com/coaching
7. http://press.linkedin.com/about
8. http://www.businessinsider.com/twitter-stats-2010-4

Volume 7: nurturing fuzz to get more buzz

social savvy junkie

Ah-ha. Here we are again. Happy as can be... Hiya!

rendezvous

Little private dancing Naked Lawyer rendezvousing with you now from Volume 6, as arranged, to help you nurture your fuzz to get more buzz... Quick sharp recap eh? Empathise now. It's 2009 and I am:

- Living my Big Rocks;
- Practising EI;
- SWOT aware;
- Appreciating my Ethicability conundrum;
- Living my ME Code of Conduct;
- Making my Epitaph;
- Adopting my Rainmaker Mindset, Attitude and Motivation;
- Living my PEE Poor Work Ethic;
- Working on my ideal niches;
- Working my positioning, differentiation, USPs, PODs, and g-spots (target market(s));
- Blowing my horn every day as 'Brand,Me' (and 'Brand,Firm') in law law land;
- Making sure my Raving Referral Lobster Net-Kingdom offline and online have swung into action;
- Armed in SM savvy and practising SN nous and netiquette (see glossary);
- Continually updating my Formidable ME Strategy & Plan (FMSP); goals, mission, vision, target market identification, niches, personal brand, referral network and client pool building; and
- Winning new business.

Winter 2008 and spring 2009 were mainly about 'getting out and about' offline and online, giving and receiving referrals and winning new business. Traction was really beginning to show come summer 2009 (when I left my then employer on qualifying as a solicitor), and by autumn and winter 2009 – my newly qualified solicitor status (non-practising) and CEO of my own company era – the enquiries and new business generation and opportunities were flowing in and referrals of value were duly passed to practising solicitors. The ROAR model had gathered real momentum.

In this volume I am *not* going to go into 'what is marketing', 'what is sales', or all of the different kinds of 'how to market' and 'how to sell' gubbins. Why? Because:

- I don't have the space here;
- I have no desire to bore you to death;
- There's a plethora of material available in relation to the basics of marketing and sales per se which is all much of a much-ness (and really good stuff, I hasten to add);
- It's not directly relevant to the ROAR model; and
- I wish to focus your attention on this thing called *relationships*... oh, and *fuzz*...

When all is said and done, I believe wholeheartedly, from my own experience, that successful marketing and sales, in whatever shape, form or definition, is simply all about *relating* – reaching out and relating – ROAR style.

No doubt your firm will be doing all of the usual marketing and sales stuff, the likes of tactical marketing, promotions, advertising and PR, blah, blah, blah. But I'm going to share with you in this volume how YOU can add value, in the overall scheme of things, to your lobsters, clients, firm and those whom you serve, due to your 'Brand,You' and relationship building, leveraging and sustaining activities, culminating in your surviving and thriving in this opportune law law land...

Subject to YOUR very own ROAR model thorough application, of course. I can share my knowledge and experience with you. But I can't create the enquiries, leads and conversions for you. It's up to you to do that... and truly make all your hard work count.

relationship marketing and relationship sales – huh?

I'm going to reveal to you now my personal marketing, brand and sales learning, practice and evolution. It focuses on positively relating to, and pro-actively engaging with, lobsters and clients.

'Branding me', and 'marketing me', was all about 'selling me', aka, making the *relating* easier. I would like to point out that, in my experience, there is a definite overlap in relation to marketing, branding and selling... but the skill sets are quite distinct.

I've already shared with you how to create your 'Brand,You' (Volumes 2 through to 4) and how to market yourself offline and online (Volumes 5 and 6). Now I'm going to share with you how to sell yourself by revealing my secret about selling... aka, the sales process, along with what I believe is an old-school mantra described as 'closing' a sale, that is, achieving a referral and/ or a direct instruction from a new client, or existing client...

Simply put: if you've got your 'Brand,You' spot on, built your Raving Referral Lobster Net-Kingdom and potential client pool through continually marketing (nicheing) your 'Brand,You', and thereby have begun to attract an audience (a following), then selling and sales will naturally flow.

You may be scratching your head. What's this prancing Naked Lawyer on about now, you may be thinking. The secret... it really is all in your 'Brand,You'. Build it, and they will come. It happened... and continues to happen for me... I have every confidence it could happen for you too!

Work it, through your consistent and persistent marketing efforts offline and SM and SN activities online, and they will come faster. I'll explain how in a later section. Keep reading.

For now, I will simply say this. It's all about relationship marketing:

"Relationship Marketing... recognizes the long term value of customer relationships and extends communication beyond intrusive advertising and sales promotional messages...With the growth of the internet and mobile platforms, Relationship Marketing has continued to evolve and move forward as technology opens more collaborative and social communication channels... [it] extends to include Inbound Marketing efforts (a combination of search optimization and Strategic Content), PR, Social Media and Application Development...The overall goals are to find, attract, and win new clients, nurture and retain those the company already has, entice former clients back into the fold, and reduce the costs of marketing and client service."[1]

I have actually discovered and experienced that in today's topsy turvy digital era and perilously shaky law law land that you don't have to be able to sell to be an extraordinary rainmaker. You simply have to be an extraordinary lobster... once you've devised your 'Brand,You' and whilst doggedly *marketing* the [bleep] out of it!

Of course, you also need to apply the 80:20/G:R rule, with a SUUUCKS attitude, weird mindset, PEE Poor Work Ethic, c-c-c-courage with precision g-spot focus whilst high on two drugs – love (passion) and adrenalin. Remember?

To coin a new phrase or two (perhaps, but could be worth checking) I reckon what I'm actually talking about is 'unsales' or 'relationship sales'; I couldn't find a definition of 'unsales' or 'relationship sales' when I carried out a JFGI. Suffice to say, it exists. Well, I reckon it does now anyway. If I were to have a stab at defining 'unsales'/'relationship sales', I would proffer this:

"Unsales occurs when two authentic people who know, like, trust, understand, 'get' and share a commonality come together in a positive way for mutual benefit."

There is no need for the traditional old-school hard sell, you may be relieved to know. The very thought of this may horrify you... as it does me. 'I'm not a new or used car salesman, so don't treat me like one buster', is my cry. Agree? No offence intended btw if you're a car salesman reading The Naked Lawyer. Car salesmen suffer from the same public perception as we lawyers. Enough said. Anyhow, I'm confident you'll be using the unsales approach naturally by now too, no doubt.

So, let's explore this 'unsales' thing further shall we?

cannon ball fun

sales process

You may recall I mentioned in Volume 1 that *the naked lawyer* comprises three musketeer models, one of which is a sales model? You may also remember me saying that I looked upon clients needing legal advice pretty much like health club members. Yes?

Well, when I worked at Cannons Health & Fitness Limited in 2000-01, I was blessed to be educated, coached and trained in what I believe was then one of the best sales and marketing teams in the UK health club industry. The Academy training centre, and 'Cannons Train' – the professional development and structured programme laid down for the Cannons Group – was truly exceptional... and I believe, ahead of its time.

The sales process and management system is something which I carried with me into subsequent ventures, including the legal profession, albeit adapted and innovated to suit the current thinking at that particular time and for future new world thinking.

The nuts and bolts of the sales process were as follows, including my innovations:

1. Target market identification;
2. Lead generation – cultivate enquiries, find prospects;
3. Meet and greet – be nice, be authentic, listen, learn, enthuse;
4. Qualification – benefits focus;
5. Tour of club – features explained, choice;
6. Soft sales presentation – consultation, more benefits;
7. Ask – am I the right person to help you overcome your pain and/or achieve your goal?
8. Close – welcome!
9. Monitor and review – what else can I help you with?
10. Follow on – touch, touch, touch.

Qualification consisted of:

- Needs analysis – why do you need to join the health club?
- Behavioural style – understanding their values, beliefs, behaviours, patterns, etc.;
- Mirror and match – making the prospect feel comfortable by my mirroring and matching them;
- Pleasure v. pain – what will make you happy? What is causing you pain?
- What if – you don't do something about your pain?
- Tour of club – product/service features explained, choice; and
- Massive rapport – engagement; natural conversation; focus on THEM.

It was a Full On sales process and management system – qualitative and quantitative; a fully documented sales process and data capture CRM system, geared around the buyer's needs and understanding the potential member's goals at each step in the process.

before and after

The prime focus was on the benefits to be gained by the prospective member. By addressing their pain and providing a solution based on intricate 'qualification' questions, analysis and barrier crushing (aka, sales prevention), the prospective member simply came to the right conclusion based on what they were looking for. We were the right club and people to satisfy their needs, wants and desires.

Loads of gurus have written about 'features and benefits' with regard to the sales process. Recently Andy Bounds[2] has spoken of 'afters', aka, 'benefits' (I reckon it's the same thing, just a different way of saying it) and 'certainty'. Customers simply want a better future and they want to know you can help give them that. Simple.

Similarly, Scott Stratten has recently published *Unmarketing*[3] which is worth a peek, I reckon. His key message is fundamentally 'stop marketing' and 'start engaging', aka, build rapport, build relationships and trust. Unsales.

I reckon Cannons was certainly one of the early adopters and forerunners of unsales because its training and sales process was ultimately highly focused on the 'before' – stages 1 through 4 of the sales process. The relationship building with the customer had begun 'before' they even got to stage 10. I have come across many sales training advocates who believe, and state, that relationship building begins at stage 10. I disagree.

Relationship building is by no means a new concept. But *how* we go about doing it is... because if we're smart (which I'm sure we are), we constantly evolve and change our practices.

yes! yes!! yes!!!

The quality of the 'qualification' was at the heart of the matter. Getting rid of anything that could be a barrier to achieving completion of all of the ten sales process stages and getting the prospective member into a 'yes' frame of mind. Asking the kinds of questions that (s)he was going to say 'yes' to ultimately culminate in a sale. I simply helped the prospect come to the conclusion they were seeking ensuring they said, 'Yes, I want to join the club because you're the right person to help me achieve my goals.' Good for the prospect was good for the club. Done deal.

Similarly, by devising 'Brand,Me' in law law land, stages 1 through 5 of the sales process are already being taken care of due to everything I apply in Volumes 2 through

6 of *the naked lawyer*. The prospective client is more likely to be in a 'yes' frame of mind, as we have already begun to build a relationship by this time due to them getting to 'know, like, trust, understand, 'get' and share a commonality' with me.

Unsales closure... 'Am I the right lawyer for you?' 'Would you like me to help you with x,y,z?' 'Hell, yes', comes the reply if I've done my EI, nicheing, 'Brand,Me', raving Referral Lobster Net-Kingdom and SM and SN activity right.

choo choo cannons train

I had an absolute ball in my role at Cannons.

I thoroughly enjoyed my responsibilities in relation to membership sales and working alongside a wonderful group of hard-working people during the period May 2000-June 2001. As a team, I reckon we were absolutely first class. I had 'the time of my life'.

I joined Cannons to specialise in corporate development and innovation relating to online marketing, sales and strategy. My role at the 'mature' club, that is, very well established health club in a wealthy community in South Buckinghamshire, was Sales Manager (direct line-managed five of a team of 50) primarily responsible for sales and marketing, PR, staff recruitment and management in relation to the same (including contract of services and contracts for services).

I feel blessed and proud to share with you that because of Cannons Train (its marketing and sales education, coaching and training) I was able to play an instrumental part in our club team achieving 270 percent over performance in January 2001 – the most successful club in the Cannons private club group (UK) category, including new start clubs – due to marketing and sales innovations. In monetary terms, January 2001 membership sales and positive membership movement equated to approximately £500,000 membership income for the 12 months ahead from these new members alone though their joining fees and direct debit contracts.

It was a cracking sales process.

Needless to say, I simply applied this winning sales process and formula in law law land; adding innovative 'bits and bobs' of course, such as utilising new technologies, new world thinking and my own learning, development and experience as the years progressed. When going about the sales process in law law land I simply reflect upon all the references to 'health club' and 'members' above and replace the same with either 'law firm', 'legal advice' and 'new client'. I then practice the 'befores' and 'benefits', aka, 'afters' and hey presto... Unsales... with regard to providing legal advice and winning new clients. Yowza!

There is of course something else which is fundamental to the sales process. And that's something called effective *conversation* – 'conversation strategy' – and communication. But I'll look at this in Volume 8: talking dirty to a saint when I'm a pure little devil.

just do something!

I'd like you now just to sit back and reflect on the entire sales process that I've shared with you. Ask yourself, 'Do I presently operate in this manner?'

Think about building, leveraging and nurturing your existing and potential relationships – with lobsters, clients, suppliers, other professionals and colleagues.

massage oil, not snake oil

Returning now to my quip about car salesmen... I have my reasons. I don't know whether or not you've noticed but there seems to be a lot of 'consultants' around at the moment attempting to belly crawl their way into taking advantage of the current need for the legal profession to get a grip with SM and SN... Present prancing Naked Lawyer excepted of course – I prefer to dance. Not crawl.

I've seen some of the sales mumbo jumbo they've been bombarding your inbox with. I receive it too. Do they really think we're going to fall for all that push, push, push old-school mumbo jumbo? Absolute poppycock.

Beware the snake oil salesman. They suck! They're simply jumping on the sales and marketing SM bandwagon and insulting our intelligence. No respect. You know the type? Snake oil salesmen.

However, the smart ones really are worth listening to. Those who buy into the built to last relationship building, leveraging and sustaining school of thought. They're the ones who practise with massage oil. Mmmmmmmmmmmm

And they preach unsales.

bedside manner

Let's turn now to ethics and netiquette. Arguably, the legal profession is one of the most revered and respected of all the professions worldwide... and very much needed. Without it, we human beings would be in a right shambles – criminally, commercially and personally.

To be a real player in the profession, of the rainmaker lawyer kind, we must balance extraordinary service savvy demanded by the client with deference to the red-tape handed down by the regulators within it. We lawyers ought to be proud and honoured to serve our clients and strive for service excellence... always. We should hold ourselves out to give the highest standard possible.

Accordingly, the attributes a lawyer is supposed to have are – to act with integrity, pay close attention to detail, to be 'thorough' and to genuinely care. We have a duty of care – similar to a Hippocratic oath.

Wearing my entrepreneur hat, as a buyer of legal services and potential client of a lawyer, when using SM and when active on SN platforms, I would expect your lawyerly profile to reach out to me, be exquisite and impeccable – a FULL (100 percent) profile. I would like to feel that I should already be able to trust you (that's a given, right?), that I'm actually already getting to know you, understand you, 'get' you in relation to your interests, personality and specialisms. This is achievable for *all* lawyers.

Wearing my lawyer hat, my point is quite simple. It's not about me, the lawyer; it's about you, the reader. I would wish that I have made every effort to make it easy for you to understand how I can help you and why it would be beneficial for you to strike up a relationship with me.

Albeit it may not be permissible for certain lawyers to have recommendations in relation to their legal work from clients available to view online, due to the restrictions imposed by the rules of particular bar associations (or equivalent), you could acquire recommendations from referrers, suppliers, knowledge sharers, etc. whom you have assisted; where you have evidenced your positive character traits, for example.

Of course, from an ethical standpoint it's imperative we lawyers do not breach confidentiality, provide legal advice, or form lawyer client relationships (in the technical/administrative sense of the word) and disclose attorney client privilege, etc. online; a requisite of the Solicitors Code of Conduct in the UK and the Attorneys' Code of Ethics in the US (and the equivalent in other countries). When all is said and done it should be common sense to us lawyers not to press the professional suicide button.

Accordingly, I would like to think that we are sensible enough to know what is 'right' and 'wrong' in how we engage online, being guided from our own (individual) moral compasses, irrespective of the 'social guidance' available at our firm. Do you not agree?

just do something!

Take time out now to reflect back on Volumes 2 and 6 in relation to ethics, your ME Code of Conduct and online behaviour.

nurturing sales equity bank

Let me ask you a question. When you're getting 'salesy' stuff pushed at you do you like it? No? Well, don't do it to your receiver then.

You should have read enough of my stuff by now to realise that it's not about pushing, it's about pulling. Unsales (relationship sales) and extraordinary rainmaking is predominately about behaviour. It's about building an emotional equity bank with your lobsters, potential clients and existing clients. It's about engagement, involvement and giving... aka, a nurturing sales equity bank.

It works like this... Building a relationship is like building up your savings in a bank (or some other place which gives a higher return nowadays!). Stay with me, this is just an analogy after all. You have to keep putting money into the bank before you can withdraw anything. Correct? Similarly, you have to keep putting something into your relationships before you can draw (or expect) something back. If you don't build some equity then there'll be nothing there for you to pull on. Even if you don't expect anything; remember me sharing that with you in previous volumes?

80:20/G:R, remember? 80 percent giving; 20 percent receiving. Refresh: focus 80 percent of your marketing and sales activity, unsales (relationship building, time and effort in giving) to referrers and clients (THEM) and only 20 percent on self promotion.

Building an emotional equity bank means drawing on the four 'super networker' and 'super referrer' traits which I shared with you in Volume 5:

- Be a giver;
- Be a connector;
- Be a listener; and
- Be empathetic.

What's the lesson? In the wise words of two exceptional gurus:

"It's all a matter of engagement. How one engages is one thing. Why one engages is another. What you get out of the engagement is obviously the most important."[4]

"Go-getters...take the initiative and make things happen, rather than waiting around hoping for things to go their way. Go-getters get things done. In fact, everyone we know who is a genuine Go-Giver is also a powerful go-getter."[5]

just do something!

Start building your emotional equity bank. Or, work on it more!

what's all the fuzz about?

buzz fuzz buzz

Do you know the saying about sales, 'it's a numbers game'? Well, I agree. It is. However, I actually think it's evolved in the true sense of its meaning. What do I mean by this? Well, I reckon it's actually now, 'a fuzz game'. But it's still about numbers. It's also about reach.

I alluded to 'fuzz' in Volume 6, 'example of how peeps find me'. Fuzz is where all those requests to connect and sales enquiries came from. By people who I didn't know. Remember? How did they know about me? From what Bob Burg recently described as "gravitational pull of our influence which is our capacity to engender those know, like and trust feelings in others." That's why you and I have done all that hard ground work appertaining to Volumes 1 through 6...

We wish to attract the kind of niche lobsters and clients, the kind of synergistic people who are most likely to hear about us, the type of person who will naturally be drawn to us because, through shared connections and 'network noise', the process of 'know, like, trust, understand, 'get' and share commonality' is already taking place... without our knowing.

Bob wraps it up in a nutshell: "How do you find your greatest customers? You don't. They find you." Sooooooo true. I can testify to that! In fact, I'll share some examples with you in the 'mouse wrap'...

mouse wrap

hunting or gathering?

What do you think? Should you hunt for sales, or do you gather for sales? Me? Personally? I gather... then nurture.

Using the ROAR sales funnel, which I will share with you in Volume 9: touch touch and touch me again, I liken the sales process to a mouse trap... Not the kind that would hurt or kill the mousey though! I simply make reference to the process; and it's purely an analogy, OK? Shades of Tom & Jerry? Nope. You won't find me chasing around like a frazzled tom cat.

I aim to draw the mouse out of his hole with the promise of a Mars Bar scrap as bait slapped onto a welcoming spring-loaded massage oiled shiny trap; 'befores' and 'benefits'/ 'afters' style. Ok, it could be cheese bait, but I usually have more Mars Bars at the ready than cheese. It's the sweet tooth girly thing.

If I've done stages 1 and 2 of the unsales sales process correctly, and there's lots of buzz fuzz buzz happening, then little mousey will be curious you see. He'll come looking for the 'Brand,Me' essence and promise. Once he's in the trap, caught in my 'more rabbit than Sainsbury's' bunny conversation and we've started on the rapport, stages 3 and 4, the 'sale' is pretty much in the bag, or should I say – trap?

I'll share with you now a handful of examples of the kind of work I've won using the ROAR model...

lobster and client action

As mentioned previously, during my time as a trainee solicitor, I focused on developing and 'working' niches. One of these niches was targeting entrepreneurs: women entrepreneurs, young entrepreneurs and serial entrepreneurs. Another niche was employee share schemes.

Using this niche of a niche as an example (and approach) in relation to the kind of work I won, how and £value, for those in the firm whom I was then serving, directly as a result of applying absolutely everything I have shared with you so far in Volumes 1 through 7 (and what I am about to share with you in Volumes 8 through 12), I am happy to share with you the following select new client work wins:

- MBO deal – £15k value. Achieved off the back of attending an awards dinner and nurturing a relationship with an entrepreneur for several months prior to instruction.

- Business and asset sale – £12k value. Achieved as a result of a raving lobster.
- Numerous start-up ventures; various legal work requirements – £1-4k value each time. Achieved as a result of lobsters, fuzz and SM activity.
- Numerous existing trading companies; various commercial legal work – £1k+ value each time. Achieved from offline network event attendance, attending seminars, and nurturing a relationship with a synergistic professional services firm.
- Numerous employee share scheme instructions – average £1.5k value. Achieved as a result of attending BNI breakfast meetings, conferences, lobsters, fuzz, SM activity and nurturing a relationship with a synergistic professional services firm.

From the start of autumn 2009, since moving on from the firm and 'Brand,Me' – arguably moving from the 'introductory' to 'growth' stage – I continue to win numerous enquiries for commercial and personal legal work, predominantly through SM and SN activity and lobsters. I refer this work to practising solicitors and attorneys – ranging in the value of £1-6k figures.

just do something!

Look again at your sales spreadsheet. Are you referring to it constantly, updating and 'working' it? Make an effort everyday to do so. It will help in motivating yourself, and planning and carrying out your follow-on, which I will speak more with you about in Volumes 8 and 9.

a reason, a season or a lifetime

I'd like to leave you with something to think about until we dance again... Every person whom I come into contact with in either a professional or personal capacity I ask of myself the following. 'Have you come into my life for a reason, a season or a lifetime'? Why? I'm curious. I'm hungry to know. I desire to continually learn... And I enjoy building relationships, for however short or long they may last.

I engage in relationships, not knowing the answer to the above question, but I go about developing the relationship trying to figure out whether it is for a reason, a season or a lifetime. When I do figure out which one it is, I know what to do for each person, and realise what they have done for me... and for that, I am grateful.

'Are you a reason, a season, or a lifetime' is a poem of unknown origin. Here it is:

"When someone comes into your life for a REASON... it is usually to meet a need you have expressed. They have come to assist you through a difficulty, to provide you with guidance and support, to aid you physically, emotionally, or spiritually. They may seem like a godsend, and they are! They are there for the reason you need them to be. Then, without any wrongdoing on your part, or at an inconvenient time, this person will say or do something to bring the relationship to an end. Sometimes they die. Sometimes they walk away. Sometimes they act up and force you to take a stand. What we must realise is that our need has been met, our desires fulfilled, their work is done. The prayer you sent up has been answered. And now it is time to move on.

"Then people come into your life for a SEASON. Because your turn has come to share, grow and learn. They bring you an experience of peace, or make you laugh. They may teach you something you have never done. They usually give you an unbelievable amount of joy. Believe it! It is real! But, only for a season.

"Lifetime relationships teach you lifetime lessons: things you must build upon in order to have a solid emotional foundation. Your job is to accept the lesson, love the person, and put what you have learned to use in all other relationships and areas of your life. It is said that love is blind but friendship is clairvoyant. "

For those of you who are in my life (past and present), THANK YOU. You can probably hear my cogs turning!

after dark activity

izzy ziggy, let's get bizzy

Zig Ziglar said something along the lines of (not ad verbatim): 'You will get all you want in life if you help enough other people get what they want". It's time now to get buzz fuzz buzz busy nurturing your lobsters, potential clients and existing clients. Dance again with me now as we engage in some after dark nurturing activity...

naked lawyer activity – a study worth casing

During 2009 I put into practice what is now Volume 7 of *the naked lawyer*. As to what I did and for a real live case study in 'how to nurture your fuzz to get more buzz', simply read the story again. You can relive my activity by taking yourself through the same process.

Let me help you. Here's a condensed version of the key activities and exercises you may wish to carry out...

ROAR steps

Carry out the following exercises in the step sequence provided, on an ongoing basis.

- **Step 1**: Reflect on the entire sales process in the 'cannon ball fun' section. Think about building, leveraging and nurturing your existing and potential relationships – with lobsters, clients, suppliers, other professionals and colleagues.
- **Step 2**: Reflect back on Volumes 2 and 6 in relation to ethics, your ME Code of Conduct and online behaviour.
- **Step 3**: Start building your emotional equity bank. Or, work on it more!
- **Step 4**: Look at your sales spreadsheet. Are you referring to it constantly, updating and 'working' it? Make an effort everyday to do so. It will help in motivating yourself and planning and carrying out your follow-on.
- **Step 5**: For every person who you meet, ask yourself, 'Have you come into my life for a reason, a season or a lifetime?' When you do figure out which one it is, you will know what to do for each person, and realise what they have done for you.

ROAR tips

- Get fuzzy;
- Get bizzy;
- Get nurturing;
- Build equity;
- Think 'befores' and 'afters';
- 'Brand,You' fuzz focus;
- Market 'Brand,You' focus; and
- Unsales focus.

ROAR summation

JFK wisdom

To quote John F. Kennedy in his inaugural address speech in 1961: "Ask not what your country can do for you – ask what you can do for your country." Wonderful. This statement can be reformed and then applied to many things, I reckon.

For one thing, it just about sums up the concept of nurturing fuzz to get more buzz. Ask not what your referrers or clients can do for you, but what you can do for your referrers and clients. The thing that differentiates and separates extraordinary rainmaker lawyering is the *giving* by the lawyer. It's that genuine caring and volunteerism aspect.

So, go now. Nurture your fuzz... get more buzz!

References

1. http://en.wikipedia.org/wiki/Relationship_marketing
2. Bounds, Andy, *The Jelly Effect: How to Make communications Stick* (Chichester: Capstone Publishing Ltd., 2007).
3. Stratten, Scott, *Unmarketing*, 2010
4. Brogan, Social Media 101
5. Burg & Mann, *Go Givers Sell More*

Volume 8: talking dirty to a saint when I'm a pure little devil

nurturing fuzz to get more buzz

Hello again! Fuzzy private dancing Naked Lawyer here, at the ready to play Saints and Devils with you… D'ya fancy learning a little bit about how to talk dirty? If so, read on, MacDuff!

best fuzz forward

At the end of the previous volume, I said, 'Ask not what your referrers or clients can do for you, but what you can do for your referrers and clients.' 'Ask.' Asking means you are 'communicating'. How to 'market, brand and sell YOU!' successfully requires extraordinary communication. Period.

This volume is therefore dedicated to the subject of 'communication and behaviour', a fundamental element of the ROAR model, and how YOU add value through communicating your messages by capitalising on your strengths, talents and 'Brand,You'.

You will no doubt recall in Volume 2 that I introduced the concept of focusing on our strengths and talents in devising a niche and 'Brand,You', and reiterated that in Volume 3, using David Beckham as an example?

I also shared with you that I carried out a variety of paper-based and computer-based tests (self-assessments) to assist with identifying my strengths, talents and learning style and that I'd look at these again in a bit more detail in this volume.

Tom Rath's 'StrengthsFinder'[1], Dr Meredith Belbin's 'Self Perception Inventory'[2] and David Kolb's 'Learning Style Inventory'[3] are three of the self-assessments I carried out. I particularly wish to share the essence of these tests with you, together with The Focus Lifestyle and SRO module (explained in a later section), as I reckon they are fundamental to the way in which we communicate and behave and how we can be of most value to the receivers of our messages. Our 'unsales' messages in particular.

As ever, I'm going to share with you my story, but it's up to you to adapt it to your own circumstances. So, let's get on and put our best fuzz forward shall we?

dynamic three-way

strength focus and ROAR talent

The StrengthsFinder[4] assessment is based on a 40-year study of human strengths conducted by Gallup:[5]

"we created a language of the 34 most common talents and developed the Clifton StrengthsFinder assessment to help people discover and describe these talents."

Over a ten year period spanning the mid 1990s to mid 2000s, Gallup surveyed more than ten million people worldwide on the subject of employee engagement. One of the staggering outcomes was that *only* one third of the respondents reported that they 'strongly agreed' with the statement: 'At work, I have the opportunity to do what I do best everyday'. Not surprising then that the research revealed the following:

"If your manager primarily ignores you the chances of your being actively disengaged are 40 percent... If your manager primarily focuses on your strengths the chances of your being actively disengaged are 1 percent... [and] having a manager who focuses on your strengths decreases the odds of your being miserable on the job. It appears that the epidemic of active disengagement we see in workplaces every day could be a curable disease... if we can help the people around us develop their strengths."

In essence, we each possess the 34 talents but when we do the test, five core talents come to the fore and are identified as our prime talents. We are then provided with an explanation of our core talents, aka, strengths, and given ideas for action.

If shared with Boss Lawyer it effectively helps Boss Lawyer understand how best to engage us, place us and use us, so that Boss Lawyer is likely to get more productivity from us as we will be positively engaged in our jobs and roles as a result of being able to play to our strengths. If you love what you do and get to do it, every day, the chances are that we're all going to be happy; the client, Boss Lawyer (the firm), you, your family and of course (hopefully)... your lover. A win win for everyone, methinks.

But I reckon there's a mega difference between 'doing a job', 'having a career' and/or living a lifestyle where you get to do what you love doing every day which plays to your strengths and talents. So, I'd like to share with you a little story.

Back in the early 1990s when I was working at a health club – one of the three part-time jobs I was holding down to pay my way through university for the first time – I got chatting to one of the members of the club – Roy – with whom, over a period of time, I built up a solid professional relationship. As regular as clock-work three days during the week he'd come into the club in the morning, have a work-out and then finish up in the cafe-bar ordering a cup of tea and a slice or two of toast.

If he spotted me passing through carrying out my duties he would say, 'Come and sit with me, Chrissie, and keep me company. Don't worry about your boss, I'll tell him you're doing your job... you're looking after the members. It doesn't get much better than that.'

Roy, the chap in question, was none other than Chubby Brown.[6] What's a young innocent girl to do? Refuse Chubby? And so it was... I would enjoy sitting and being entertained by Chubby. At times I wasn't quite sure who was entertaining who as he playfully jibed me about my hairstyle together with 'geisha petiteness', as Chubby coined it. For the most part, our cafe-bar chats together consisted of his talking dirty to a saint when he was obviously a pure little devil.

Actually, I'm joking. I think that should be the other way around.

Still joking.

The Chubby Brown you see on stage is Chubby Brown the performer. Whilst in the club and when jibber-jabbering with members and staff he was always very respectful – a perfect gentlemen – very polite and never shared any of his, how should I put this politely, 'XXX rated stage material' in our presence.

As he got up to leave, his parting words on every occasion were always something along the lines of, 'Farewell, fair maiden, I must go now and practise my filth.' My parting thoughts smacked of, 'Ashes to ashes, dust to dust. If God won't have you the devil must!'[7]

Why am I sharing this story with you? Chubby Brown was a plumber, by trade. It was a skill that he learned, much like lawyering, I guess. Not sure which of the two trades pays more nowadays actually? But his strength and his natural talent manifested itself in his being a comedian. Chubby could have remained a plumber, 'doing a job', and made plumbing his career. But instead he made a lifestyle choice to play to his natural talents. Had he not recognised his talent and chosen to do something with it, the world would have been a much more miserable place without the smiles, fun and laughter that he has brought into many peoples' lives.

Not unlike myself, I figure. I could have remained swinging on my chair emblazoned, 'get your traditional corporate lawyer here' in a full-time 'job' and 'career'. But it wasn't playing to my strengths and natural talent... nor was it ticking the 'lifestyle' box and the dream I had for myself. Effectively in 2009, I just ticked along in law law land doing my technical law grinder's monkey job.

But I positively danced around in Client Territory and raving Referral Lobster Net-Kingdom playing to my strengths and talent, rainmaking whenever and wherever possible.

learning's a style thing

Kolb's Learning Style Inventory is basically a self-description test which is based on experimental learning theory. It is designed to measure your strengths and weaknesses as a learner. The Learning Style Inventory works on two levels:

- Level 1 – four-stage cycle:
  1. Concrete Experience – (CE);
  2. Reflective Observation – (RO);
  3. Abstract Conceptualization – (AC); and
  4. Active Experimentation – (AE).
- Level 2 – four-type definition of learning styles, each representing the combination of two preferred styles:
  1. Diverging (CE/RO);
  2. Assimilating (AC/RO);
  3. Converging (AC/AE); and
  4. Accommodating (CE/AE).

I figure it's important to understand and recognise these learning style types as they come into play in team dynamics...

dynamic 'Me,Ta'

Dr Meredith Belbin's Self Perception Inventory is the icing on the cake... Understanding and putting the strength, talent and learning-style combo into action – a dynamic three-way – culminates in effective communications when engaging one-to-one with colleagues, clients and lobsters within a team matrix. They're extremely effective in developing powerful teams. Teams within the firm, but also 'team firm, client and 'Brand,You'.'

If you can identify each individual lawyer's natural talents and strengths it is then easy to pull together a wickedly dynamic group of lawyers – each with complementary strengths, talents, skills, knowledge and experience – and capitalise on their uniqueness throughout a legal project.

Belbin's Self Perception Inventory helped me identify my role within a team in order to improve my strengths further, and that of the team, and ultimately the project outcome for the benefit of all parties. At least that's the theory.

After 20 years of research, Belbin discovered that there are nine distinct team roles. I'll share them with you now together with a brief description of what they mean:

1. *Plant:* imaginative; radical thinker; vital spark; chief source of ideas; offers solutions to problems; unorthodox.
2. *Resource Investigator:* the fixer; explorer of opportunities; develops contacts;

popular; six phones on the go; extrovert; likes to run with ideas.

3. *Co-ordinator:* team unifier; natural chairperson; clarifies goals; promotes decision making; highly disciplined.
4. *Shaper:* self elected task leader; highly strung; achievement orientated; like a challenge and getting results; seeks ways around obstacles.
5. *Monitor/Evaluator:* the rock; objective thinker; capable of deep analysis of data; detached; calm.
6. *Team Worker:* diplomatic; accommodating; promotes harmony; supportive.
7. *Implementer:* workhorse; conservative; organised; turns ideas into getting the job done.
8. *Completer:* conscientious; detail, deadline and follow through orientated; catches omissions.
9. *Specialist:* highly professional; driven; committed; desire to attain a specialised skill.

We will have a dominant role and a second or third perhaps.

I'm not going to bore you with the outcome of my test. You're very likely not interested in the slightest. Albeit those of you who know me can probably take a wild guess at the two or three prevalent roles! And, you can probably take a wild guess at the outcome of the test in relation to your likely role too.

Accordingly, I strongly recommend you take the test for yourself, as when you have carried it out you can share it with your Boss Lawyer so that (s)he can place, manage and lead you more effectively for the benefit of all concerned.

If you are Boss Lawyer, then it will help you understand yourself and your lawyers better so that you can place them in a team accordingly for the benefit of all. You might think you've got it pretty well sussed at present, but you may be pleasantly surprised how much better it could be if you took this process on board too.

I came across StrengthsFinder, the Self Perception Inventory and the Learning Style Inventory back in 1999-2000. I've been practising and preaching them ever since, in the leisure industry, the new media industry, my own companies and latterly in the legal profession. I reckon that part of my rainmaker success in various roles can be attributed to my application and understanding of each of the very same tests, processes, systems and methods, together with The Focus Lifestyle which I am about to share with you now in the following section.

Why? They work. Particularly when combined.

As I've said before, I felt it was important to know myself before I could possibly 'know my client' or colleagues. The Self Perception Inventory makes the next step – where it counts, big time. That is, in helping me identify my 'best fit' role within a team so that my strengths and talents are utilised to the max for the benefit of the client and ultimately Boss Lawyer and the firm.

Albeit we are all 'doing a job' in our 'careers' and the grinder's monkey technical law stuff, our roles within a team may differ because of how we fit into a team due to our unique strengths and talents.

Our role is the 'Me,Ta' I have spoken of previously. Extraordinary teams comprise teams of complementary 'Me,Ta's. Without identifying, knowing, understanding, positioning and nurturing each lawyer's 'Me,Ta', I believe it is simply *not* possible to achieve a truly extraordinary forceful 'Me,Ta' team, nor deliver extraordinary customer service excellence, which I will share with you in Volume 9: touch, touch and touch me again. IMHO.

I attempted to introduce the strengths finder, talent process and learning style inventories (together with the SRO model which I am about to share with you now in the following section) into the firm where I was training as a solicitor. Sadly, The Resistance pooh-poohed it. True to form, we lawyers were conservative and not impressed by all that 'fluffy stuff' (at that time). I came to the conclusion not to push it and to just get on and do it myself in my own rainmaking activity. I figured, 'Hey-ho, Chrissie',

"If you are losing a tug-of-war with a tiger, give him the rope before he gets to your arm. You can always buy a new rope." (Max Gunther)

Prrrrrrrrrrrrrrrrrrrrrrrr. Amur leopard style. Or is it Grrrrrrr? Roll over pussy-cat. I'm a lover not a fighter.

Glad I have my arms intact so that I can dance with you now...

just do something!

I highly recommend that you take the StrengthsFinder, Self Perception Inventory and Learning Style Inventory self-assessments. I have provided some web-links to assist you on your way. I'm confident you'll have a lot of fun in doing the tests. And, I'm even more confident they will help you 'know yourself' better, 'know your client' better, help you communicate better and even contribute towards your becoming (or improving on being) an extraordinary lover...

Oops, I meant extraordinary rainmaker lawyer, of course...

press send, receive jibber-jabber

You may recall I mentioned in Volume 1 that *the naked lawyer* comprises three musketeer models, one of which is a communications and behavioural model? You may also have noted that I use the term 'receiver' quite a bit. This is because I live The Focus Lifestyle which embraces the Focus Model and the SRO module as one of its five modules.[8] Dr Gary Russell[9], creator of 'the Focus family', has this to say (reproduced with his blessing):

"The Focus Lifestyle is a people process for the people age. In basic terms, it aligns people's thoughts, feelings and actions, activating human potential and maximizing performance. When engaged, The Focus Lifestyle will lift people beyond their own vision of capability. The underlying processes that create The Focus Lifestyle enable messages to be more effectively delivered and received, strengthening communication and interaction at work, home or play... It teaches us to embrace the energy within and encourages others to do the same. The Focus Lifestyle is made up of certain factors. Learning the significance of each factor and applying it to the way we think, feel and act allows a new paradigm for living to emerge."[10]

I'm only going to briefly share with you one of the factors, and this is the relationship of interaction defined as SRO, as it is pertinent to the ROAR model. SRO stands for:

- **S**ender
- **R**eceiver
- **O**utcome

The Sender is me/you and the Receiver is the client/lobster/colleague/whoever. The Receiver stands at the centre of the model. In the words of Gary Russell (again, reproduced with his blessing):

"Focus is truly client/receiver centred. Each receiver has receptors which we believe are built in components found in every human being. It is the activation of these receptors

that leads to successful outcomes...The Outcomes produced are reflected back to the Receiver, demonstrating the development of a mutually beneficial relationship."

The Outcome is therefore determined by the quality of the Sender's message with a client-centric, consumer-centric, customer-centric, Receiver-focus.

just shoot the messenger!

I came to realise that it's vital to understand SRO, learning styles, the strengths and talents of myself and others so that I can communicate much better with my lobsters, clients and colleagues. The quality of my messages sent to lobsters and clients in particular is crucial because they are both the Receivers of my message and the Senders of my message. They tell the 'Me,Tale'...

It's the fuzz stuff, remember? And fuzz matters. This is where the new clients come from where I least expect it. The success of creating a fuzz epidemic is hugely dependant on the engagement, involvement, interest, curiosity and motivational factors of the special group of people I have identified as raving referral lobsters. They have the 'gift of the gab' in Client Territory, Referral Lobster Net-Kingdom and law law land.

These are my message Receivers and Senders, and I am theirs. I tend to click with those who share the same learning style as me, obviously; but it's not about me. It's about THEM. It's about making my communication fit my Receiver. I might want reams of detail, but my Receiver may not. *Respect.*

This is why I figure it's of vital importance to understand my Receiver's learning style and they understand mine, so that effective communication can flow between the parties and a successful Outcome is achieved. This way, misunderstandings which occur between me and colleagues, clients and referrers can be avoided. Frustrations, trouble, arguments kick-off when I get this wrong.

At times, I feel like shooting the messenger. But, in fact, I should be shooting myself. Why? Permit me to explain... If a Receiver of my message has gone off on the wrong track, lost the plot, whatever, and the whole communication has obviously took a nose dive off Angel Falls, it's not their fault. I don't like the word 'fault'. It's negative, but I need to use it in this example. It's my fault, the Sender. The quality of my message in tailoring it to the Receiver's learning style, strengths and talent is in question.

If I press send, and the quality of my message sucks, then I can expect to receive jibber-jabber. Not good. If there's a breakdown, it's because I, the Sender, wasn't clear in the message/instruction I gave and/or it wasn't presented in the right style.

Conversely, it's my responsibility as Receiver of a message from a Sender (client, referrer, Boss Lawyer, colleague) to check that the message/instruction I received from the Sender was in fact the exact message they intended to send.

In essence, the buck stops with me. First. Last. Always. Just like being Receiver focused, lobster-centric and client-centric – first, last, always...

just do something!

Check out The Focus Lifestyle and the SRO module. Just have a read about it to get a flavour of what it's all about. It's up to you if you wish to dig a bit deeper. I provided you with a link previously.

stunning straplines

sexy eyes

Have you ever heard the saying, 'It's not what you say, it's how you say it'? Hogwash.

It really does matter *what* you say, and where, when, why, how and who to.

Let's take 'how to get people to read your stuff, your message' and then 'how to get them to fuzz about it' as an example, shall we? It doesn't matter whether your message is in an e-mail, on twitter, LinkedIn, in a blog, on your website, in a missive, part of a marketing/advertising/promotional campaign, one-to-one or to the masses etc. I'll share with you now, how I achieve it...

I begin with a *phwoar* headline. I mentioned the idea of devising an attention grabbing title/headline in Volume 6 in relation to our LinkedIn profiles, do you recall? I raise this because the key to successful attention grabbing is making sure the right people – my niche pool of people, my markets that hit the g-spot – see my messages and they are moved to do something, such as get in touch, converse or fuzz.

Why would I want to devise an attention grabbing headline? Because you, the Receiver, will decide whether or not to read the rest of my message based solely on how compelling my headline is. The aim, after all, of a headline is to get your attention. Period. Whatever flows from that, you are then master of.

We all suffer from message overload. We therefore scan stuff. As digital age internetterati we are notorious scanners. If I don't capture your imagination and cause you to be curious at 'scan' stage I haven't got a Scooby-Doo of a chance in convincing you to read any further.

This calls for secret agent provocateur measures... Stunning straplines... Sexy headlines... Of the kind that cause your sexy eyes to pop out on stalks. OK, this is a little extreme, and not always appropriate or true depending on the message or circumstance.

My point is simply that I aim to hook you with a headline which will have impact. I want my message to stick, and then, if my headline and message is sexy enough, you may wish to fuzz about it. The rule of thumb in the advertising world is that I can either grab your attention using a direct headline or an indirect headline.

An example of a direct headline: 'How to Market, Brand and Sell YOU!' That headline is as direct as it gets. You, the Receiver, know exactly what I'm selling you.

Examples of an indirect headline: 'The Naked Lawyer'; 'markets that hit the g-spot'; 'from sweet rose to crapbag'; 'my "Brand,Me" secret exposed'; 'super lawyer fish-nets'. Now, these headlines tap your curiosity, I hope, otherwise I've failed miserably in the main function of an indirect headline which is to be more mysterious, provocative and subtle in attracting your attention. I wish to compel you to want to know more and read further.

Through experience, trial and error, I note that my indirect headlines work best. I know this because when I analyse by my budurl 'click-through' data, the most popular links are those which contain stunning straplines – indirect headlines. I also receive more direct messages from readers via e-mail, LinkedIn, Twitter and Facebook and see an increased number of retweets and mentions on Twitter when I write compelling headlines.

The lesson: when I'm not able to be compelling by conveying my message in person (Sender), that is, making physical eye to eye contact with you (Receiver), I must find the most stunning way to achieve the same Outcome...

If eyes are the window to the soul, then stunning straplines are the key to the trap-door of the mind.

emotionally sticky

I'd like to make one final point in relation to stunning straplines. We are emotional creatures. We buy due to emotion, and we justify the purchase with logic. Pop something emotional, such as humour, into your headline. Do this and I'm confident you'll create a sure fire, hard-core, emotionally sticky message with real buzz impact.

just do something!

Have a go at creating direct and indirect headlines. Try them out in your offline and online activities. Don't forget to track and analyse the results using budurl.com, or a similar tool. This way you'll get a feel for what's working well for you.

going deep

dirty talk

You may recall in Volume 4 my sharing with you that a story is actually more powerful than a brand and if your brand begins to tell the tale then that's hot stuff. I also suggested that having the right brand invariably attracts the attention and interest of the right kind of lobster and client and inevitably helps with the initial introduction and conversation which naturally flows.

I actually have a 'conversation strategy'... I'll share a little of it with you shall I? Albeit I have not 'documented' the entire conversation strategy in detail that I find particularly effective in engaging lobsters and prospective clients (maybe I should), the secret lies in gearing any topic around SRO, which I've already shared with you. Oh... and the devil's in the 'Me,Tale'.

It's as simple as that. If I've got my niche and 'Brand,Me' right. It's about the 'Brand,Me', 'Me,Tale' and putting the Receiver, YOU, at the centre of it. In true Bryan Adams style, "Everything I do, I do it for you."[11]

Oh... and it comes down to my talking DIRTY with you, a saint no doubt, when I'm a pure little devil:

- **D**irect – I talk directly to YOU. In the first person. Every time.
- **I**mpact – I say something to grab your attention/interest which makes an impact.
- **R**apport – We get chatting, we start to build up a rapport and a relationship.
- **T**hem – We talk about YOU.
- **Y**es – I focus on making you feel good about yourself and guide you gently into a 'yes' frame of mind by asking you questions which I feel you will respond 'yes' to.

In essence, I focus on making our conversation a positive experience for YOU.

Now, you and/or your firm, may or may not have a 'conversation strategy'. That's OK. But that's not to say that you shouldn't consider devising one. The ambitious and progressive entrepreneurial lawyers, of the naked kind, are in fact 'conversing online' and winning new business as a result of such activity.

In the wise words of Robert Scoble:[12]

"the growth of the blogosphere... (is) also a profoundly human phenomenon, a way of expanding and, in some cases, reifying the ephemeral daily conversation that humans engage in."

It always amazes me how quickly I can build up a new relationship with a lobster or client purely from striking up a conversation online which can quickly move offline and continue back online again.

Furthermore, from initial conversation to sale (the unsale process) can take as little as a few hours. I've already shared this with you how in Volume 1, so I'm not going to waste your time (or mine) repeating it. Do of course feel free to check it out again; it's at the end of Volume 1 in the 'sneak preview volumes 2-12 'How to...'' section. I'd like to share with you one final point on talking dirty, particularly online, when you're not even part of the conversation. Intrigued? The point was made recently by Steve Kuncewicz, an entrepreneurial lawyer, of the naked kind, in a recent LinkedIn group post:[13]

"what we're talking about here is 'the conversation that's happening without you'... We've got no real choice but to start building better and more transparent relationships. You'd be surprised at how good commentary on your firm spreads across Twitter, and how it can elevate you into being a 'thought leader' very quickly."

Enough said.

chatty chatty bang bang

So, how come I manage to strike up conversations, build relationships and move through the unsales process so quickly? Answer: Rapport. Chatty chatty demeanour. What's all that about, really? Bonding.

And what's the secret? If I've got my 'Brand,Me' right, niche target audience, aka, g-spot strategy right, establishing rapport becomes much easier because (hopefully) you will already:

- Know, like, trust, understand, 'get' and share an interest with me; and/or
- Probably have shared a similar experience with me; and/or
- Have synergy, one way or another with me.

We're already starting to bond before we've even said anything, either face to face or via the keyboard.

The next step, building rapport through having an extraordinary conversation is all about the quality of the bonding and the positive experience I aim for you to achieve. And that's accomplished by my reaching out and relating, ROAR style, putting YOU at the centre of the conversation and my being:

- SRO focused;
- Pro-active;
- Enthusiastic;
- Confident;
- Positive;
- Authentic;
- Genuine;
- Curious – about YOU;
- Interested – in YOU;
- Attentive – listening and hearing YOUR 'Me,Tale'; and
- Of a sunny disposition – you should be able to feel my smile even if you can't see it.

All with a view to making YOU feel comfortable.

As Bob Burg recently tweeted:

"Perhaps the single greatest skill in sales is a highly developed sense of interest in the other person... You know you are prospecting correctly if your prospect is enjoying the conversation even more than you are."

Now, doesn't that just make you want to smile? Bob also shares this with us:

"The classic sales formula for a rapport building conversation is F-O-R-M, which stands for Family, Occupation, Recreation, and Message, the idea being that touching on these particular topics in a conversation is likely to turn up a common interest."[14]

Establishing rapport is a skill. It begins by cutting yourself a niche and devising your 'Brand,You'. We've done that, I hope. I find that establishing rapport is made a great deal easier by having a 'Brand,Me' because it's easy to find and pick up on the 'common interest' between myself and the Receiver. We're already in the right place because we both want to be there, we've chosen to be there, *because* we share a common interest.

The conversation gets started almost seamlessly. It already has legs. Bang bang sexy legs.

rapid traction, give me action!

Building rapport and gathering momentum along the unsales process is also a skill. It's a fundamental skill that can be learned. And that's where understanding and working your FORM comes into play.

People just love talking about their Big Rocks – their families, their leisure interests as well as their work interests. I do. I bet you do. Am I right?

Building rapport is all about putting stages 3 and 4 of the unsales process into action that I shared with you in Volume 7 – the meet, greet and qualification questions and focus. I ask a lot of questions. I listen a lot. I hear a lot. I learn a lot. About YOU. The Receiver.

I'm hungry to know about YOUR 'Me,Tale'. How else can I possibly help you, introduce you, fuzz about you and assist you in getting more business, if I don't take the time or interest to learn all I can about you; well, all that you're willing to share of course. I don't allow myself to break into my 'Me,Tale'... not in the establishing rapport and building rapport first conversation...

Being a woman, of the prancing Naked Lawyer kind I hasten to add, I may well have more bunny than Sainsbury's but I actually keep my 'Me,Tale' intact, wherever and whenever possible, until at least the second conversation date...

devilishly delightful second date

Our first date should've been all about YOU.

Oh, before I share with you what I'd like us to do on our second date I'd first like to make this point... We lawyers (in general, but not all) are pretty poor when it comes to *speedy* follow-up, follow through, follow-on. Call it whatever you like. Note the word *speedy*. The fact of the matter is, from my observations and experience, we're pretty good at getting out there to networking events (some, not all), offline and/or online, and putting ourselves about, but we're rather shoddy at the follow-on and making the return conversation date. Our effectiveness is questionable. IMHO. Simply put, if you follow-on, speedily, and do it well, you will stand out. Ultimately, you will win new business!

This is the difference between being an 'OK rainmaker lawyer' and an 'extraordinary rainmaker lawyer'. It can be *the* difference of winning a new client, lobster or professional friend... or grumbling at the loss of 'what could have been'. Fact. Make absolutely no mistake about it. I'll evidence this statement and share more with you on this subject in Volume 9: touch touch and touch me again.

The follow-on conversation, second meeting/date, is where I like to dig a bit deeper and be really helpful. By the time we will have spoken a second time I would hope that I may have already been able to connect you, at least, with someone who may be of benefit to you.

Our second conversation is still predominantly focused on YOU. However, inevitably, by this point, you may be curious as to my 'Me,Tale' and it is at this stage that I will happily share the same with you. This is where my communication skills come into play because having spent a great deal of time learning about you in our first conversation, I am already beginning to gauge your learning style, strengths and talents so that when I take the time to educate you about 'Brand,Me', 'Brand,

Product' and 'Brand,Firm', the message from me, the Sender, will be the one I intended for you, the Receiver, to receive.

What's the likely Outcome? The whole communication process is likely to be that much sweeter, the unsales process that much slicker and our relationship building off to a flying start making for a much more solid and fulfilling relationship of mutual benefit through time.

just do something!

Have a go now at devising your very own conversation strategy, taking everything into account that I've shared with you in the sections 'dirty talk', 'chatty chatty bang bang', 'rapid traction give me action!' and 'devilishly delightful second date'.

Think through the process carefully. Perhaps even look back through the content of previous volumes to help you.

You may of course wish to document it. The process, *not* the exact conversation you anticipate having... IMHO scripted conversations suck. I can't stand that shallow, lifeless, telesales clap-trap I'm subjected to. It's patently obvious it's scripted. It doesn't make me feel very special. Does it feel that way for you too?

Similarly, I wouldn't insult my lobsters, clients or prospects by subjecting them to such a robotic approach. I enjoy my conversations coming to life, which are representative of, and respectful to, the unique qualities of my Receiver. Think of it this way. If it was our first conversation, the nascent of our professional relationship is due the respect of a bespoke virgin conversation, surely? I wouldn't want it any other way. Would you?

But, it's your call. You're the master of your mutiny, you're the captain of your mother-ship and you're the daddy of your ambition. It's your choice.

saintly recording of the 'Me,Tale'

Question: what's a prancing Naked Lawyer to do with all this quality information gleaned from lobsters, clients and prospects? Answer: record it of course.

I was as fastidious and vigilant about making a detailed record of the highlights of the conversations – the key points of significance (referral, sales and marketing information) – as I was about recording client communications on the client file!

Where did I record the information? The rich data was stored in my sales spreadsheet and Outlook contacts, where I was building my mini CRM system. At the same time, I updated my Outlook calendar with a follow-on date and time. It's a great discipline and habit to form, as it provides the foundation for lots of 'touch, touch, touch' and extraordinary client care/service/experience, which I'll share with you in the following volume.

just do something!

If you're not already making a detailed record of the highlights of the conversations you're having with lobsters, clients and prospective clients, then begin the process now, or improve upon what you're already doing. Record the information in your sales spreadsheet and Outlook contacts. Update your Outlook calendar accordingly.

after dark activity

making headway

OK, saint. Or is it, devil? If you enjoyed reading the story and content in Volume 8 non-stop, and so haven't already had a bash at the 'just do something!' activities, it's time for you to start communicating and behaving in true DIRTY talk style...

Dance on... before I prod you with my pitch-fork...

naked lawyer activity – a study worth casing

During 2009 I put into practice what is now Volume 8 of *the naked lawyer*.

As to what I did and for a real live case study in how to talk dirty to a saint when you're a pure little devil, simply read the story again. You can relive my activity by taking yourself through the same process.

Let me help you. Here's a condensed version of the key activities and exercises you may wish to carry out...

ROAR steps

Carry out the following exercise in the step sequence provided.

- **Step 1:** Take the StrengthsFinder, Self Perception Inventory and Learning Style Inventory self-assessments. I have provided some web addresses to assist you on your way.
- **Step 2:** Check out The Focus Lifestyle and the SRO module. Just have a read about it to get a flavour of what it's all about. Once again, I have provided you with a web address.
- **Step 3:** Have a go at creating direct headlines and indirect headlines. Track and analyse the results using budurl.com, or a similar tool.
- **Step 4:** Devise your very own conversation strategy, taking everything into account that I shared with you in the sections: 'dirty talk', 'chatty chatty bang bang', 'rapid traction give me action!' and 'devilishly delightful second date'. Think through the process carefully. Look back through the content of previous volumes to help you. You may wish to document the process; but not the exact conversation you anticipate having.
- **Step 5:** Make a detailed record of the highlights of the conversations you're having with lobsters, clients and prospective clients. Begin the process now; or improve upon what you're already doing. Record the information in your sales spreadsheet, Outlook contacts and update your Outlook calendar to record a follow-on date and time.

ROAR tips

- Be Receiver orientated;
- Think client-centric first, last, always;
- Create stunning straplines;
- Be mysterious;
- Talk DIRTY;
- Be chatty chatty;
- Think bonding;
- Be attentive;
- Think bang bang sexy legs;
- Know your FORM;
- Pursue rapid traction; and
- Record the highlights.

ROAR summation

devilishly saintly communications

Having shared with you a few tips, hints and secrets on the subject of 'communication and behaviour' I hope by now that you are confident (or more confident) in communicating your messages with devilish finesse.

By now you should have your best fuzz forward, be capable of understanding, practising and enjoying a dynamic three-way by sending and receiving messages SRO style, fired up to continually create stunning straplines that are emotionally sticky.

I trust you are also now comfortable with DIRTY talk, chatty chatty bang bang and 'rapid traction, give me action!', are well up for a devilishly delightful second date and last, but not at all least, saintly recording a 'Me,Tale'.

I am absolutely delighted that you are now perfectly poised to make great headway in communicating your messages through truly capitalising on your 'Brand,You' together with all of your strengths and talents.

I am now your very proud and private dancing Naked Lawyer. Until we meet again, I salute you with my pitch-fork...

References

1. http://www.strengthsfinder.com/113647/Homepage.aspx
2. http://www.belbin.com/rte.asp?id=8
3. http://www.businessballs.com/kolblearningstyles.htm
4. Tom Rath, *StrengthsFinder 2.0* (New York: Gallup Press, 2007)
5. The Gallup Organization; a team of scientists led by the late father of Strengths Psychology – Donald O. Clifton.
6. Chubby Brown is a British stand-up comedian, notorious for his blue humour and XXX rated material. His 'real' name is Royston Vasey. http://www.chubbybrown.biz
7. A re-jig of the original lyrics, 'Ashes to ashes, dust to dust. If God won't have me the devil must', by Venom, Black Metal band.
8. Trademark. Gary Russell and the Focus Group's innovative philosophy and methodologies: http://www.focuslifestyle.org/main.shtml
9. Dr Gary Russell is the founder of The Focus Group, which created many of the communication, behavioural, talent and strengths concepts and formulas administered by Winning Profile. Gary works alongside Sir Clive Woodward at Winning Profile. Sir Clive has achieved great success in nearly every facet of the athletic world. After years of success on the rugby field, Sir Clive tried his hand at coaching, taking what had become a relatively defunct English Rugby programme and turning the team into world champions once again. He has been honoured numerous times for his achievements, most notably being knighted and recently named Director of Elite Performance for the British Olympic Association.
10. http://www.focuslifestyle.org/main.shtml
11. Bryan Adams (born Bryan Guy Adams, 5 November 1959) is the bestselling Canadian male recording artist of all time. As a rock singer and songwriter he has won dozens of awards including a win for Best Song Written Specifically for a Motion Picture or Television for *(Everything I Do) I Do It for You* in 1992. http://en.wikipedia.org/wiki/Bryan_Adams
12. Robert Scoble & Shel Israel *Naked Conversations: how blogs are changing the way businesses talk with customers* (New Jersey: John Wiley & Sons Inc., 2006)
13. Steve Kuncewicz http://uk.linkedin.com/in/stevekuncewicz. Law Society Gazette group on LinkedIn; thread 'What do Solicitors Practices really have to tweet about?': http://www.linkedin.com/groupItem?view=&gid=2078586&type=member&item=29270258&commentID=-1&qid=f0122c6b-22f9-4c6d-b092-98a8f8657b98&goback= percent2Egmp_2078586#lastComment
14. Burg & Mann, *Go-Givers Sell More*

Volume 9: touch, touch and touch me again

talking dirty to a saint when I'm a pure little devil

Welcome back! Are you behaving yourself? I am... for a change. Pitch-fork has been placed in the toy cupboard alongside the broom-stick... for now.

So, where are we up to? Fancy a quick recap? In 2009, I am:

- Living my Big Rocks;
- Practising EI;
- SWOT aware;
- Appreciating my Ethicability conundrum;
- Living my ME Code of Conduct;
- Making my Epitaph;
- Adopting my Rainmaker Mindset, Attitude and Motivation;
- Living my PEE Poor Work Ethic;
- Continually working on my ideal niches;
- Working my positioning, differentiation, USPs, PODs, and g-spots (target market(s));
- Blowing my horn every day as 'Brand,Me' (and 'Brand,Firm') in law law land;
- Making sure my Raving Referral Lobster Net-Kingdom offline and online is positively swinging;
- Armed in SM savvy and practising SN nous and netiquette, daily;
- Making lots of fuzz;
- Working up my unsales process 80:20/G:R;
- Practising devilish communication and behaviour techniques;
- Having fun devising stunning straplines and talking DIRTY;
- Establishing rapport;
- Building enduring extraordinary relationships;
- Continually updating my sales spreadsheet and Formidable ME Strategy & Plan (FMSP); and
- Winning new business.

Starting to come together, methinks, *big time!*

You may have noticed that I love the word 'extraordinary'. Extraordinary: "unusual or remarkable; out of the usual course".[1] It will no doubt come as no surprise to you therefore, that I am now going to share with you what I believe is 'extraordinary customer service' resulting in establishing and building extraordinary relationships.

It's another fundamental element of the ROAR model, and how YOU will set your stall out as a truly extraordinary rainmaker lawyer in the sexy eyes of your lobsters, clients and prospective clients.

Dance again with me now...

the ROAR unsales egg-timer

I'd like to share with you now the ROAR unsales egg-timer... It's a sales, customer service and referral process that I devised (in my own time), and used (and still do) whilst a trainee solicitor, which embraces all of the elements of the ROAR model. It's how lobsters, prospects and clients go from not knowing anything about me to being ready to give me (and 'the firm') their business, or more of their business. It's also how I continually endeavour to provide extraordinary customer service and take 'eggstra' special care of them.

Take a look at the ROAR unsales egg-timer. I trust it is pretty self explanatory? However, I will take a little time to explain that the numbers 1 through 10 correlate with the stages of the sales process I shared with you in Volume 7, and the entire process embraces every element of the ROAR model kicking in from as early as stage 1 and consistently permeating through every stage thereafter.

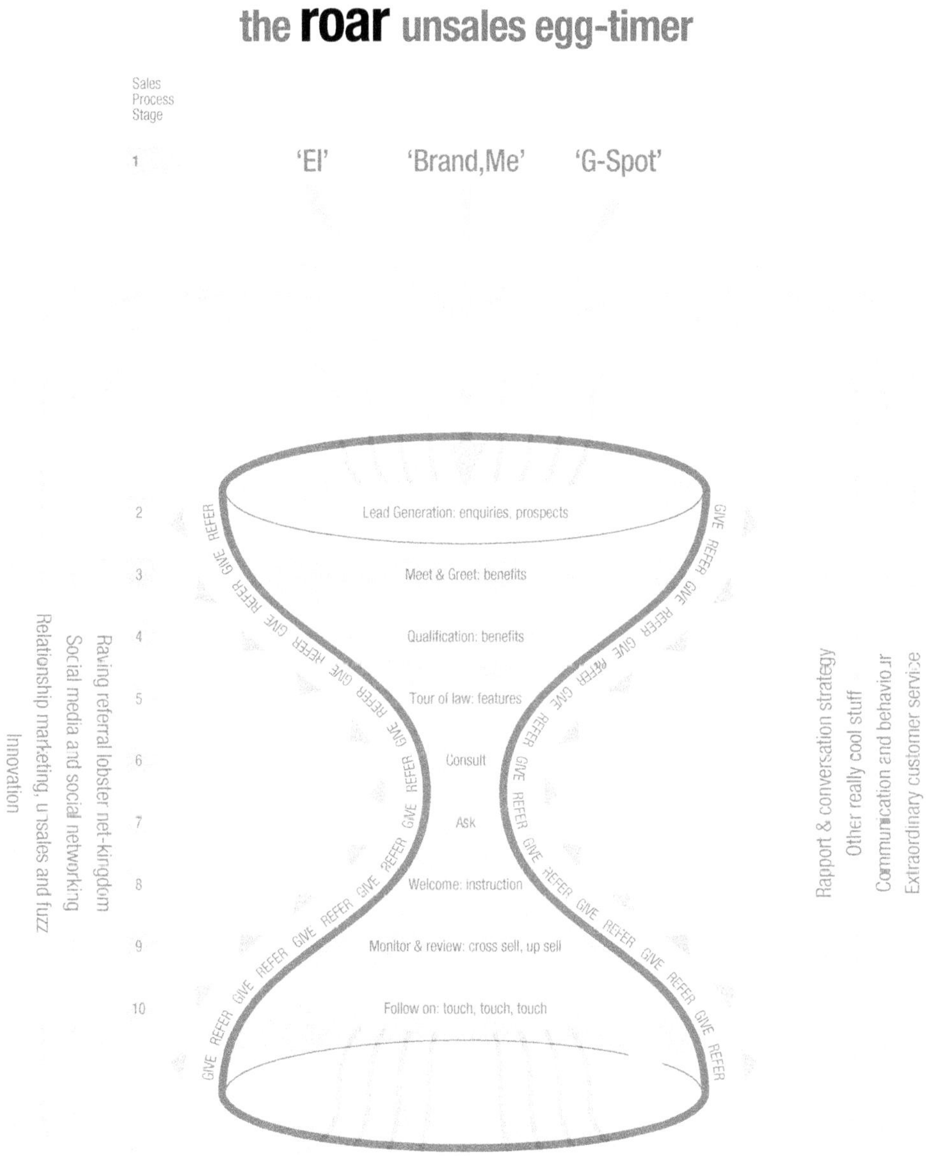

Figure 2: The ROAR unsales egg-timer

The key point is that a great deal of effort must go into stage 1 in order to achieve stage 2. Constant rapport is required throughout all of the stages and a massive effort is consistently required at stages 9 and 10.

just do something!

Take a little time to study and reflect on the ROAR unsales egg-timer diagram. You may wish to look back at previous volumes in relation to the ROAR elements, the sales process and the ideas which I have shared with you.

Pick me up again when you're ready.

we're engaged!

The art of extraordinary rainmaking and extraordinary customer service comes down to lots of engagement and involvement. Simply put: lots of touching... Touch points, as it's commonly known.

touch me quick

You may recall in Volume 8 I suggested that if you follow-on speedily, and do it well, you will stand out and ultimately win new business. If there is one 'take-away' message I would like you to note from this volume it is simply this...

Follow-on, follow-on, follow-on. *Fast.* With *passion, energy* and *enthusiasm* in your true PEE Poor Work Ethic fashion. Or, to put it another way in devilishly Naked Lawyer style... Touch, touch, and touch again.

Allow me to share with you now my touch process in relation to lobsters, prospects and clients...

touch #1: engagement.

I *follow-on speedily* from initial contact, whatever it is. Whether it's after attending an event, a direct enquiry via e-mail, telephone or missive, someone reaching out online via twitter, LinkedIn, a LinkedIn group conversation or even a 'shout-out' perhaps that I have noted from my Google dash-board or hootsuite.

With referrers, prospects and existing clients here's a snapshot of what I do:

- Send an IM/instant reply, on the platform received and/or an e-mail usually within an hour or so after 'the event' ('event' meaning any form of initial communication whether offline or online). Within this I create a bespoke and personal message including at least the following four phrases: 'delighted to meet you', 'thank you for taking the time to contact/speak/chat/meet with me', 'how can I be of help to you?' and 'can I introduce you to someone who may be of benefit to you perhaps?'
- Even if I attended a networking event on an evening, an awards dinner perhaps, and it wasn't a daft 'o' clock finish I would usually fire-up the laptop on returning home, fire-off the e-mail to my new contact(s) and add them to my CRM system...
- 'Work' my sales spreadsheet and mini-CRM system, aka, Outlook contacts and calendar.

frequent attention

touch #2: re-engagement.

LOTS of it, to avoid disengagement. On receiving a reply from my 'Follow On Speedily' initial e-mail I would then

- E-mail or call to offer an introduction and ask if they'd welcome me sending information and people of interest their way who could benefit THEM.
- Send snippets of information of likely interest to them; for example, likely Big

Rocks kind of stuff, information about their industry, interests, etc.

In my experience, lobsters, prospects and clients positively fall over themselves when I'm pro-active, available, present, genuinely interested in THEM, bending over backwards to find things of interest and benefit to THEM, helpful in generating new business for THEM and communicating regularly in order to 'move things along'.

Why? The reality is they don't expect me to be, and do, any of the above... In general as a profession, the perception, and in most cases the reality, of our reputation is such that we're an absolute shambles at doing that kind of stuff. Am I right? We lawyers can be as elusive as the Scarlet Pimpernel.

Needless to say, I made darn sure I was in contact with lobsters, prospects and clients on a regular basis to ensure that they didn't disengage. More to the point, by keeping in touch regularly and being helpful meant that I would probably be the first lawyer they would think of when the time came to do something about their need. The likelihood of them going anywhere else for their legal service was significantly reduced.

Lots of engaging, aka, touching helps to establish and build the relationship quickly which means that touch stage 3 can occur that much sooner too...

the only way is up... baby

touch #3: cross-sell and up-sell

I found that cross-selling and up-selling naturally flowed, largely due to the following:

- Building massive rapport and a solid relationship with a prospect and client within a short period of time (and colleagues).
- Spending the majority of my traineeship in the corporate department, which meant I had the pleasure of interacting with a lot of fellow colleagues in many different departments due to the nature of the corporate transactional work, which invariably required input from other departments; for example, employment, IP/commercial, property, trusts and insolvency. This meant I was blessed with the opportunity to 'know my colleagues' as Boss Lawyer ensured that I worked alongside a wide range of talented lawyers on a particular transaction each time. It helped with the natural referral process when I spotted the opportunities where I could pass work in the direction of a colleague and department, albeit my main contact didn't require any corporate work (at that time).
- Focusing on g-spots.
- The value adds of 'Brand,Me' and 'Brand,Firm'.
- Playing to my strengths and talents and dovetailing the firm's strengths.
- Devising and developing 'bundled products' for the identified niche markets; such as a start-up legal package for entrepreneurs which crossed the corporate and IP/commercial department.

The start-up legal package, aka, bundled products, was naturally advantageous to the prospect and/or client. It consisted of a handful of key corporate and commercial/IP 'day one' legal necessities. Albeit it had some legal basics, other corporate and commercial/IP legal work would naturally spin from it ... in a word – *up-sell*.

Plus, additional legal work would also spin out from the initial instruction such as employment, property and probate... in a word – *cross-sell*.

Similarly, cross-selling and up-selling in relation to the employee share scheme niche naturally flowed. I may have won an original piece of work which at first looked like a simple EMI share scheme, but off the back of it naturally fell a cross-option agreement such as wills and trusts work at times, depending on the circumstances and needs of the client.

I used to hum a little song to myself when I was buzzing and fuzzing around cross-selling and up-selling. You know the one? It goes something like this... "The only way is up... baby ... for you and me now".[2] Smoking !!!!!

just do something!

Start putting into action touch #1, touch #2 and touch #3 (if you're not already practising it). Remember the mantra: Follow-on, follow-on, follow-on. *Fast.* With *passion, energy* and *enthusiasm* in your true PEE Poor Work Ethic fashion.

Perhaps you could even think about devising some bundled products, and suggest them to Boss Lawyer.

i like retaining you

the secret of 'value' is 'valyou'

I maintain the view which I first raised in Volume 1: that extraordinary relationships and customer service will be the holy-grail at the heart of the successful super lawyer, and extraordinary rainmaker lawyer, for that matter. It's all about *giving*, remember? And being extraordinarily helpful, remember?

Why? Because I stand firmly by the courage of my conviction, from experience: that building an enduring *value* relationship with the client, utilising the 'fluffy soft-skills stuff' (some of which I have shared with you in *the naked lawyer*) combined with a total client-centric focus, is where the real value will be for the lawyer, law firm and consumer of today and the future.

That is, the trick (I find) is to stand in the clients', prospects' and lobsters' shoes, empathise, and *feel* their fear, their pain, their pockets (how short or deep) and to try and understand what value means to THEM. You have to take the focus totally off yourself and place it entirely on the receiver.

As an example of what value can mean to a customer/client I'd like to share with you a quick story. One evening after work, a few years ago, my good friend Dr Gary Russell and I were dining at a restaurant. We'd been at a workshop all day – very early start, intense activity all day, late finish – the usual kind of Full On event. Needless to say we were both rather hungry come 8pm and managed to munch our way through a fair amount of scrumptious food and full bodied red wine for the following two hours. As you do, after a tough, long and challenging day. Thirsty work! Anyhow, the food was lovely, the wine was perfect, the staff: friendly, helpful, energetic, enthusiastic and passionate about their service. All in all, everything was absolutely top notch.

At the end of the meal we were presented with the bill. Gary, being a gentleman, immediately scooped it up and scanned it. Oh, I forgot to mention that Gary is an American... He looked a little perplexed and said to me, "Chrissie, what's this?", pointing out a ten percent service charge already added into the total. I explained that it's a customary surcharge that some establishments in England automatically pop onto a bill. We indigenous men and women are probably used to this. But it's understandable for non-natives to be surprised. "Ah," he said, "no problem. I get it now. Pity though. I'd have willingly given a 20 percent tip if they hadn't already assumed ten percent."

The lessons:

- *Value* is what the customer places on something, not what the supplier thinks it is; and

- Extraordinary customer service only becomes extraordinary because the service is provided in PEE Poor Work Ethic style. Namely, with *passion, energy* and *enthusiasm*.

In essence, I suggest that the secret of value for us all, is VALYOU:

- **V**a Va Voom[3]
- **A**nd
- **L**ots of it
- Focused on **YOU**

VALYOU.
Perhaps you can now understand why I hold this view about value (VALYOU) and made the further suggestion in Volume 1 that LIC is where the true value lies. You may also recall me saying:

"what we need to ensure is that we can effectively communicate that LIC is what the consumer needs, wants and desires of us. Enter 'soft-skilling' to improve our powers of persuasion, communication, relationship building, conversation strategy, marketing, cross-selling, up-selling and selling per se."

Is it all beginning to fit together now?

wake up and smell the future

So, why do I reckon extraordinary customer service in the legal profession, and we lawyers providing the very same, is going to matter so much? Stuart Brown, a specialist in customer experience has this to say:[4]

"Whilst many good values and behaviours stand firm, the World around us is changing beyond recognition... and its people are now in a very different place. Gone are the days of certainty and contentment... abundance and frivolity. Instead, we live a life of global uncertainty, depleting resources and greater demands on our time - maybe as business people... or maybe as individuals and consumers... As businesses we need a greater awareness of what really matters. Not so much about what we do – but more significantly about how we do it and how that makes a positive contribution to our clients."

Jon Busby has this to add:[5]

"The market and consumers are liberated and they are using tools to find and solve but they still need people to refine and make those solutions precise to fit their needs... As Dorothy said to Toto in The Wizard Of Oz 'I have a feeling we're not in Kansas anymore. We must be over the rainbow'... Maybe you need to decide if you are a helpful witch or an unhelpful solicitor... Humans like help, humans like being helpful, humans recognise helpful people... a conversation with the solicitor. That is where the value is for the client, that is the comfort zone for the solicitor and that is where you can start to deploy an array of online and offline tools matched to the clients need."

I'd like now to refer back to Volumes 2 and 3.I trust it will be a wee memory jog to those of you who have already read the previous volumes, as I wish to reiterate the point about customer service excellence.

Using myself as an example, I'd like this opportunity now to put all that I have shared with you during Volumes 1 through to 9 into context... Flashback, it's 2009. The prancing Naked Lawyer in law law land is a trainee solicitor in a mid-tier law firm... I have a purpose, a belief, a cause. I want to help entrepreneurs. I want to do business with people who believe *why* I do *what* I do for THEM. This equates to my having a genuine passion for extraordinary service levels and to truly having their best interests at heart.

The secret to creating the lifestyle, job satisfaction and financial rewards that I craved was to focus on building a portfolio of business – rainmaking. I did this by matching my portfolio of skills, knowledge, experience, professional ethics, interests, strengths and talents to the needs, wants and desires of my (potential) clients.

It was about:

- Rainmaking;
- Being passionate about the application of the law and how it is of real value and help to the client as a solution to their problem;
- Being passionate about looking after the firm's existing clients and getting more new clients;
- Helping as many entrepreneurs as possible; and
- Delivering extraordinary customer service.

Accordingly, I am passionate about my dream, goals, mission and vision. My 'Brand,Me' positioning and differentiation embraced pioneering a totally client-centric, receiver orientated and extraordinary relationship approach, when others – colleagues and 'competitor lawyers', that is, all those lawyers who were not working at the firm where I was – were concentrating primarily on the billable hour technical law humdrum. I also focused heavily on providing a high-level of empathy and attention by getting closer to the client, when other lawyers were more reserved and primitive in their approach.

Which leads me nicely on to my next point... Empathy, and going the extra 10,000 miles.

the green mile

Have you seen the movie, *The Green Mile*? You know the one, it tells the tale of the encounter of Paul Edgecombe, a death row supervisor has (played by Tom Hanks), with an unusual inmate – John Coffey – who displays inexplicable healing and empathetic abilities?[6] Coffey is 'unusual'.

Where have we heard that word used as a descriptor before? Ah, yes, in connection with the word 'extraordinary'. Coffey stands out because he is unusual and because he is extraordinary. In effect, because he possesses a wonderful skill... a gift even... *empathy*. It's OK to be 'unusual'.

At the outset of *the naked lawyer* I stated "Home truth 5: Empathy will be one of the fundamental skills you must feel, experience and ultimately acquire."

In 2009 I set about emphasising my value adds, such as empathy, being pro-active and dynamic in finding new clients, connections, opportunities and innovating; that is, giving referrals, contacts, sharing industry knowledge, etc. to help the entrepreneurial client develop and grow their business, whilst other colleagues were mainly concerned with just getting the 'legal' job in and out.

Why did I do this? Because extraordinary rainmaking lawyering is all about LUST, remember? Continual:

- **L**inking
- **U**nderstanding
- **S**ocial Savvy
- **T**ouching...

of THEM... Lobsters, prospects and existing clients.

I was never too busy to re-engage (touch, touch, touch) with prospects, clients and lobsters when they least expected it, which inevitably made them feel valued, special and cared about. For example, it only took me ten seconds to fire off a quick e-mail every few days saying, "Apologies for the radio silence. Rest assured, I'm working away behind the scenes on your matter. I'll be in touch again shortly.". Indirectly I was actually saying, "You're on my mind and I haven't forgotten about you. Don't worry, I'm on with your stuff. You're important to me and I care what's happening here."

hot for the lot

I'll share with you now an example of new client work that I won due, in no small part, to empathising, being totally customer service excellence focused, applying a client-centric positive mindset and VALYOU approach together with commercial savvy and business nous. I intend to look at commercial savvy and business nous with you in Volume 11: yes! yes!! yes!!!

You may recall my sharing with you that I attended a breakfast networking meeting at daft 'o' clock every week. Well, at one such meeting there were many guests attending on that particular morning due to it being a special event laid on for visitors. The meeting therefore did not take its usual format, in so far as we members only had 20 seconds to stand up and say something (of impact) 'to the room'. There was also a flurry of activity at one point where we all had the opportunity to mix and mingle, shake hands, make eye contact, grab a business card, then leave. On returning to the office I immediately e-mailed all of my new contacts in #1 touch engagement style; adding the contacts to my mini-CRM system also. Speedy follow-on.

A few hours later I received an e-mail from one of the 'visitor' attendees in which he stated that he was impressed with my enthusiasm, passion and professionalism at the meeting and my entrepreneur and employee share scheme niche focus. He was particularly intrigued with my headline, 'Entrepreneur Lawyer – More Than A Lawyer'. Furthermore, he was 'bowled over' by my following up with an e-mail so quickly and offering to be of help with further business contacts within a matter of an hour or so. The upshot was that in the body of his e-mail he asked me to call him to discuss his placing some corporate legal work (an employee share scheme, for starters) with the firm.

At this point I added him to my sales spreadsheet as a 'hot' contact. I rang him immediately on reading the e-mail, discussed his requirements and then I shared the conversation and detail with Boss Lawyer. I called the prospect back and advised him of a fixed cost and likely duration of processing and finalising the matter. Whereupon 'the new client' instructed me, immediately.

The whole thing was turned around within a matter of weeks with constant touch, touch, touch. The new client was so pleased with the service and the work done by Boss Lawyer and myself, that he offered to pay in advance of the final dotting of i's and crossing of t's.

You're no doubt thinking that his request for the bill and paying early can't have been purely due to the service, surely? Well, not entirely, kind of. I suspected it was that he wanted the bill to fall within his company's VAT quarter and year end, so that the expenditure would fall in that year's company accounts and meaning he could reclaim the VAT quickly rather than wait another three months.

We raised an invoice accordingly, marrying the agreed fixed cost originally quoted. Albeit our new client did not have to pay immediately (usual payment terms 30 days, yarda yarda yarda) we received a cheque in total sum payment within a couple of days of posting the invoice. This was prior to finalising the matter which rumbled on another two weeks. When the cheque rolled in I remember Boss Lawyer smiling at me and commenting along the lines of, "Well done. We could do with more clients like your new client, Chrissie." To which I replied, "That's my intention for us."

I was also thinking 'not a bad result, Lightfoot' as I was cognisant of the words "I'll eat my dictaphone if you get any sales from that" which would no doubt be haunting The Resistance. Maybe it's the little devil in me, but I must confess I also thought, "Maybe you'd like to take my place and get up at 04.30 every Tuesday morning, get your AIG and hurtle down the motorway to a networking meeting starting at 06.00 for two hours and then fight in the traffic, park your car and run across the city to be at your desk for 09.00 so that colleagues aren't frowning at you?"

Was it worth it? YES.

It's called going the extra 10,000 miles. It's what makes the difference to your client, the firm, YOU and your future survival and thriving. It's the kind of thing that gets your 'Brand,You' essence and promise noticed and respected. It's the kind of thing that helps your reputation as an entrepreneurial lawyer of the naked kind grow. It's the kind of thing that fuels fuzz... globally. In a nutshell, it's the kind of stuff that attracts new clients, retains existing clients and gives clients and lobsters the confidence to keep referring prospects and more work your way.

I like engaging new clients and retaining existing clients. Do you?

just do something!

Just sit back and star gaze for a moment. Chill out. Think about how you prospect, treat referrers and serve clients. Can you recall extraordinary engagement, involvement and interaction where you won a new client and/or new instruction from an existing client? If so, note it down so that you can refer to it every time you lose a potential piece of work. Use it as a bench-mark for improvement purposes.

Do you know what your prospects and clients value? Have you asked them? If not, do so now!

Have you been working on 'empathy' since Volume 2? If so, that's great. If not, boo-hoo! Get cracking on it now!

Do you go the extra 10,000 miles? If so, that's wonderful. Carry on, do more. If not, then make today the day that you do.

i love maintaining you

at the law of attraction of law interface

I've mentioned my mini-CRM a few times now. As you're no doubt perfectly aware, CRM is a widely-implemented strategy for managing a company's interactions with clients and prospects. However, the process adopted by a law firm to handle its contact with its clients will vary from firm to firm. Some will be very sophisticated and some will not, meaning the level of detail recorded and data integrity may be questionable.

Similarly, we lawyers are somewhat disparate in our sales and marketing activity and even more so in our vigilance in using such a strategy, process and system to its best advantage, be it by continually recording information and activity, updating the database, etc.

As I've shared with you previously I'm a stickler for detail; I like to record highlights of conversations and keep my data and data-base bang up to date. It's why I created my own mini-CRM system by simply utilising Microsoft Outlook (contacts; tasks; calendar) together with my Excel spreadsheet and latterly the CRM system within LinkedIn, so I could import contacts expeditiously, manage and control the ROAR unsales egg-timer process. I did of course add all of my contacts to the firm's data-base also.

I'll share with you a quick summary of my CRM activity, which I carried out then as a trainee solicitor and continue to do now in my new role:

- I collect personal and business information on lobsters, prospects and clients.
- How do I collect it? Through conversations; business cards; other marketing collateral; PR.
- Where do I collect it? Offline and online interaction events.
- Where do I store it? As stated previously in my sales spreadsheet and Outlook contacts.
- What do I do with the data? Record the highlights.
- I have a repeatable follow-on activity plan...
- What is my frequency of communications?
    - Prospects: every week #2 touch style;
    - New clients: every week #2 and #3 touch style; and
    - Existing clients: every week #2 and #3 touch style.

The nature of my CRM system and activity was/is such that:

- It is totally receiver orientated, geared around the lobsters, prospects and clients needs, wants and desires.
- I know how many prospects and clients are at what stage of the ROAR sales process – meaning where they are at in the ROAR unsales egg-timer.
- I can work out my conversion rate, aka, closing percentage.
- Because I know my conversion rate I know how many prospects I need to fill the egg-timer each month to achieve the sales target that I have set myself.

I reckon CRM has become a social thing now – the social customer relationship management (SCRM) – which I'll talk a little bit about in Volume 10: continual stimulation.

'Brand,Me' communication game programme

During 2009, as I went about my Naked Lawyer rainmaking and relationship building activities utilising the ROAR unsales egg-timer process. I also had a 'Brand,Me' communication game plan...
It was a marketing and sales communications programme based on my communications objectives tailored specifically for my g-spot niche target markets in order to:

- Generate new leads/clients: I'd sort the leads based on the receiver's interest (into Hot, Warm, Cold, Dead categories; 'dead' meaning not a cat in hell's chance of a sale, not 'dead' as in tombstone) and follow on accordingly;
- Persuade the receiver to instruct me: factors coming into play strongly here were my USPs, PODs and 'Brand,Me' essence and promise;
- Inform: about new services such as the employee share scheme niche and Start-Up packages for entrepreneurs focusing on g-spots; and
- Remind: existing clients of other services the firm offers – cross-sell and up-sell.

just do something!

Have a look again at my CRM activity, the bullet points, and my communication game plan. You may wish to use them as a starter for ten to assist you in your own CRM structure, strategy and plan and creating your own communication game programme.

after dark activity

oi! touch me up more often, thank you

Right! Time to practise some of this touchy feely kind of stuff, methinks. Let's begin by taking your prancing private dancing Naked Lawyer by the hand and allow her to guide you in your after dark activities...

naked lawyer activity – a study worth casing

During 2009 I put into practice what is now Volume 9 of *the naked lawyer*. As to what I did and for a real live case study in how to touch, touch and touch your lobsters, prospects and clients so that they feel 'eggstra' special, and the ROAR style, simply read the story again. You can relive my activity by taking yourself through the same process.

Let me help you. Here's a condensed version of the key activities and exercises you may wish to carry out...

ROAR steps

Carry out the following exercise in the step sequence provided on an ongoing basis.

- **Step 1:** Study and reflect on the ROAR unsales egg-timer diagram. Look back at previous Volumes in relation to the ROAR elements, the sales process and the ideas which I have shared with you.
- **Step 2:** Start putting into action touch #1, touch #2 and touch #3 (if you're not already practising it). Remember the mantra: Follow-on, follow-on, follow-on. *Fast*. With *passion, energy* and *enthusiasm* in your true PEE Poor Work Ethic fashion. Think about devising some bundled products and suggest them to Boss Lawyer.
- **Step 3:** Think about how you prospect, treat referrers and serve clients. Can you recall extraordinary engagement, involvement and interaction where you won a new client and/or new instruction from an existing client? If so, note it down so that you can refer to it every time you lose a potential piece of work. Use it as a bench-mark for improvement purposes. Do you know what your prospects and clients value? Have you asked them? If not, do! Have you been working on your 'empathy' since Volume 2? If not get cracking on it. Do you go the extra 10,000 miles? If not, then make today the day that you do.
- **Step 4:** Look again at the 'i love maintaining you' section and in particular my CRM activity, the bullet points, and my communication game plan. Consider using them as a starter for ten to assist you in your own CRM structure, strategy and plan and creating your own communication game program.

ROAR tips

- Use the ROAR unsales egg-timer process;
- Be speedy with follow-on;
- Think engagement, re-engagement to avoid disengagement;
- Don't be a Scarlet Pimpernel;
- Think up-sell and cross-sell;
- Think about bundling products;
- Think Va-Va-Voom VALYOU;
- Go the extra 10,000 miles;
- Never be 'too busy' to avoid touching;
- Be hot for the lot;
- Like retain;
- Love maintain;
- Get jiggy with a CRM system;
- Have a communication game plan; and
- Strive to be extraordinary.

ROAR summation

it's all in the touch

I hope by now that you're getting a real feel for how the elements of the ROAR model are coming together in helping you market, brand and sell YOU!

Becoming an extraordinary rainmaker lawyer is partly accomplished through providing extraordinary customer service, which results in establishing and building extraordinary enduring relationships of value. Fundamentally, I reckon this is achieved by being a lover – not a fighter, a giver – not a taker.

One thing's for sure, if you want to win my business then I expect you to touch, touch and touch me again. Are you up to the challenge?!

Let's see shall we? The next volume is all about continual stimulation. Intrigued? Then take my hand again and join me now. Let's dance away to Volume 10, where I reveal the penultimate element of the ROAR model...

References

1. *The Concise Oxford Dictionary*, ed .Della Thompson (9th edn., Oxford, 1995)
2. *The Only Way Is Up*: a song written by George Jackson and Johnny Henderson, originally released as the title track to the 1982 album by soul singer Otis Clayy. It became a chart-topping single for Yazz and the Plastic Population in 1988. http://en.wikipedia.org/wiki/The_Only_Way_Is_Up
3. The term 'Va-Va-Voom', meaning 'life' or 'passion', spoken and acted by the professional footballer Thierry Henry, featured in the Renault Clio advertisements in which he popularised the term. http://en.wikipedia.org/w/index.php?title=Special percent3ASearch&search=va+va+voom
4. Director of Brand & Customer Experience at Osmosis Brand Communications: http://uk.linkedin.com/in/stuartbbrown
5. Jon Busby is a specialist advising law firms in client engagement through the use of technology: http://legal-two.com/?p=49527
6. *The Green Mile* is a 1999 film based on a 1996 serial novel written by Stephen King: http://en.wikipedia.org/wiki/The_Green_Mile

Volume 10: continual stimulation

touch, touch and touch me again

So, dance partner. Are we still holding hands? Are you seated comfortably in readiness for another enjoyable read? Are you ready to receive the penultimate element of the ROAR model? Are you prepared to be stimulated? Sit back, relax and let me take you there... Where? To a place far, far away from the daily grind...

Star-gaze for a moment... allow yourself to ease into the mood and moment... into OUR place... with your positive frame of mind... open... to engage with me... your very own private dancing Naked Lawyer...

innovation and stimulating LIC

Continual stimulation – 'innovation' – is the element that makes the ROAR model timeless. It's what arouses curiosity in lobsters, prospects and clients because it's what will make YOU exciting to know, like, trust, understand, 'get' and share commonality with. To 'innovate' means to, 'bring in new methods, ideas' and 'make changes.' It is the ability to successfully bring new ideas to the table and make changes for the better; in yourself, as you re-invent yourself, and in your business, aka, your line of work. It is the key business process that enables both YOU and your firm to compete effectively in the increasingly digital and competitive global environment.

The ROAR model in and of itself was, and is, an innovation within the legal profession. It's effectively a new idea – a method – in how to get more clients, sales, referrals, income, value, growth and success. Basically, it's a new idea in how to market and sell legal services for the benefit of many parties by focusing on the unique talents and strengths that reside within YOU, and not the entity you are a slave to. It's a model which helps you to keep re-inventing yourself and to make changes for the better.

Innovation is actually the reason I got into the profession. Do you remember me sharing this with you in Volume 1? If so, you may also recall it was partly due to the lack of innovation, well, certainly the speed of innovation and forward movement of the very same, in my reasoning for moving on from the firm where I did my training, having realised that a greater calling and more fulfilling role beckoned.

I found it incredibly sad, and frustrating, during my time as a trainee solicitor to discover that The Resistance (and the profession by and large) was/is mired in 'stare decisis'[1] in every respect. IMHO. There resides an extreme allergy to rocking the boat in any fashion. Anyone who dares to do so is simply persona non grata.[2]

Hey-ho. 'Que sera sera'[3], eh? Mind you, The Resistance ethos of 'just sit there and do as you're told' was *not* the way to go for me as I felt that I was destined to help bring about positive change, for myself and others. I know. I had envisioned it. I had seen it in my mind's eye – remember MindStore?

I reiterate my belief that I first shared with you in Volume 1: that continuous improvement and innovation is where our future survival and thriving resides. Inevitably this means 'change'. But, in law law land old habits die hard... if ever. Consequently, in these changing and challenging times we are witnessing polarity between the legal beagle sceptics and enthusiasts, in relation to embracing innovation in its various forms... inevitably...

Still, I wholeheartedly believe and advocate that the legal profession needs to welcome innovation, embrace radical change, reinvent customer service and work harder and smarter in light of the inevitable commoditisation and evolution of legal provision.

The ROAR model is simply one innovation that will either be pooh-poohed or championed. It's your choice. The ROAR approach is new, it's daring, it's risqué, it's fresh, it's innovative, it has a new way of looking at things, and in its own unique way it's kind of ground-breaking – certainly for the legal profession.

How I've chosen to deliver it, in the approach, style, tone, vernacular, format and structure which you are experiencing now, as *the naked lawyer* book, may or may not be to your particular taste. Nonetheless, it is a reflection of its teachings. And there's the rub.

Akin to the ROAR approach, in true entrepreneurial and Naked Lawyer style, it too is daring, risqué, fresh, innovative, has a new way of looking at things, and by presenting it in its own unique way, I truly hope I have achieved this aim...

Stimulation. That is, to arouse and excite YOU into thinking and acting differently – innovatively - in your drive for greater self improvement, development and fulfilment. I can't possibly do the subject of 'innovation' justice in this limited space so I'm probably going to dedicate a special Naked Lawyer book to this in due course. But for now, I'll give it my best shot and focus on the relevant bits appertaining to your needs, right here, right now...

innovate everything!

innovate what, why?

Why should we innovate? IMHO: We lawyers need to constantly innovate everything because the world is always innovating. Period. We lawyers need to get with the times, once and for all, as we've never before. We've always been lagging behind the rest of the world in pioneering spirit. Now, wouldn't that be a turn up for the books...

Wouldn't it be nice if we could only just keep pace with Client Territory? I'm not suggesting we lead the way in ground-breaking innovative world changing products and services, the likes of those invented by Mark Zuckerberg, Sergey Brin and Larry Page.[4] Not to say we couldn't, of course; we're certainly bright enough, creative enough and hard working enough. But, I suspect that the combination of our 'risk averse natures' and regulatory bodies will likely prevent us from pushing from the boat out.

However, duly note this. Mark Zuckerberg recently stated that over the next five years or so, social networking would make it possible to, 'pick any industry and rethink it', as internet experiences are redesigned to take into account social connections.[5]

Hmmm... social connections... social communications... social clients... social lawyers...

Let's take the legal industry shall we? Let's rethink the legal profession shall we? I'll share my thoughts with you in the following pages. Read on...

For now on, let's just take on board the idea and suggestion that we need to be continually re-inventing ourselves and our business processes as to how to market and sell 'Brand,Me', 'Brand,You' and 'Brand,Firm' by embracing continual stimulation, continual improvement and continual innovation. Does this remind you of something?

Ah yes. Extraordinary rainmaking. Extraordinary sex. Extraordinary lover. It's why I break all the rules, Chip Conley style and Tom Peters style. It's why I continually keep trying new stuff and re-inventing myself. Maybe you should try it too?

the ROAR model innovations

2009: returning to my prancing around in law law land story, albeit I was frustrated at the lack of pace of change and various barriers to progress that I was attempting to achieve at the firm where I worked, I didn't allow The Resistance to wear me down. In true Ivana Trump style I didn't get mad, I innovated everything.

I 'worked' the ROAR model to the max in my rainmaking activities and constantly innovated the Roar model elements as the sands of time, along with prospects and clients, filtered through the ROAR unsales egg-timer.

As time moved on, in relation to each of the ten elements of ROAR, new tools and new thinking developed in the world surrounding law law land. So, I simply jumped on board with them, tried the new stuff and kept riding the innovation wave in its prime. Surf's up!

For example, in relation to SM and SN (ROAR model element 5), throughout 2008 and 2009 there was a minority of 'social lawyer' early adopters with a majority of 'social lawyer' laggards. New apps and gizmos were/are being created all of the time to help make our use and experience of SM and SN more appealing and beneficial in our rainmaking activities.

Now, it's 2010. Facebook overtook Google earlier this year as the most popular US website. Accordingly, I figured it was only smart to consider this channel more seriously in my drive for business.

Twitter continues to innovate, having recently brought multimedia to the stream:

"It means each time you tweet a link to a video, for example, it will be embedded and play right in the Twitter stream. But that's not all.. Twitter has also partnered with Dailybooth, DeviantArt, Etsy, Flickr, Justin. TV, Kickstarter, Kiva, Photozou, Plixi (formerly TweetPhoto), Twitgoo, TwitPic, Twitvid, USTREAM, Vimeo, Yfrog, and YouTube to put content from the people you follow in the middle of your timeline."[6]

In a nutshell, I believe Twitter is all about focusing on the receiver of the message and the conversation and relationship between myself (the human being sender) and them (the human being receiver), person to person; meaning: lawyer to lobster, prospect and client. It's not about 'the firm' (an entity sender) to the receiver. It's us providing the receiver with focused information that is helpful, interesting, informative, intriguing and/or entertaining even, to THEM.

I've met some wonderful professionals, lobsters and clients (not the entity they work within) via Twitter in the UK and across the world. In my experience, the process has gone like this: referrers and clients have spotted my tweets on Twitter, then followed me to LinkedIn and/or Facebook and/or my blog/website, then requested to connect with me and contacted me, then we got involved in a discussion in a group, then we met (virtually, via Skype or face to face), then we 'did some business', aka, referrals, introductions and sales. Enough said, really. Albeit, one final point. A quote comes to mind: "You miss 100 percent of the shots you don't take."

I figured that if I wasn't using social media and social networking as a social communication channel to engage, get involved and share, I'd be missing one of the tricks of the decade... and possibly century.

The recent buzz as I write *the naked lawyer* (October 2010) is video blogging and focusing on video content (SEO and SSO friendly) to communicate our messages and attract and retain prospects and clients. In relation to extraordinary customer service (ROAR model element 8), we're witnessing the dynamics of a new decade due to continually evolving customer expectations. Ergo, we continually need to innovate and manage the customer experience we deliver.

Take a few moments to reflect on Figure 3.

I mentioned in the previous volume that CRM is now shifting to social CRM (SCRM). What I mean by this is simply that some channels are so sophisticated and innovative, for example, the LinkedIn Premium Account, that it's possible to store all of your customer relationship information 'in the cloud'. The benefit of this, of course, is that you can access it anywhere in the world from your digital device; you don't have to have it stored on your laptop/PC or firm's servers.

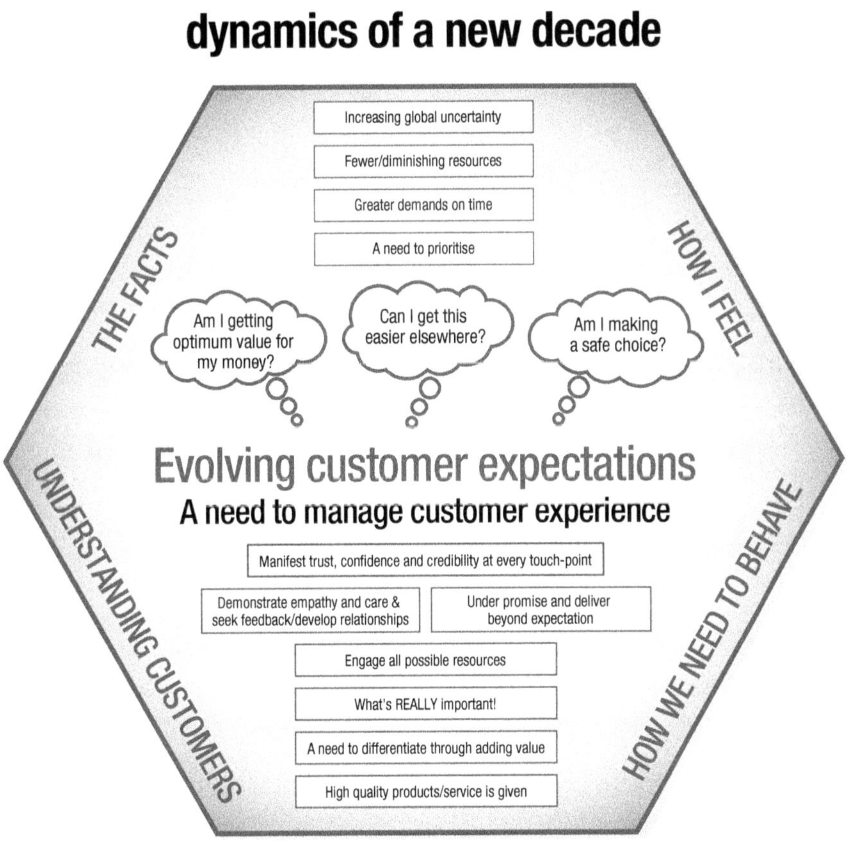

Figure 3: Dynamics of a new decade, © Stuart Brown[7]

It's great for delighting lobsters, prospects and/or clients as you can surprise them with the depth of knowledge and information you have stored on them, which you can utilise during conversations, so reflecting your interest in them. It also means that you can update your SCRM real-time as data integrity is continually restored.

innovating the business process

I read somewhere that innovation in business process involves:

- Avoiding commoditisation;
- Continually re-thinking your business around your core strength; and
- Moving up the food chain.

Most of us lawyers and our firms focus on matching and beating our competitor lawyers and law firms. Accordingly, our strategies no doubt tend to take on similar dimensions. What naturally happens therefore is head-to-head competition based largely on improvements in cost, quality or both.

But innovative firms and entrepreneurial lawyers break free from the maddening crowd by staking out new market space, namely, cutting a niche and creating products or services for which there are no direct competitors. An example of this is 'Brand,Me' cutting a niche focusing on entrepreneurs, devising the bundled product start-up legal package together with the entrepreneur team that plays to our unique strengths, talents, knowledge, skills and experience. The combination means value innovation in the making.

"This path to value innovation requires a different competitive mindset and systematic way of looking for opportunities. Instead of looking within the conventional boundaries that define how an industry competes, managers can look methodically across them. By so doing, they can find unoccupied territory that represents real value innovation. Rather than looking at competitors within their own industry, for example, managers can ask why customers make the trade-off between substitute products or services."[8]

If we lawyers compete on price, quality and niche, then arguably real value will reside in our LIC in a commoditised law law land.

trouble and strife
what's on my mind?

I don't know about you but there are a number of things that go through my mind on a daily basis in connection with my surviving and thriving in the present and the years to come. Is it like this for you too?

Many, many, many things rattled around in my Naked Lawyer grey cells in 2008 and 2009 whilst I was training to be a solicitor, and it remains so now in my new role supporting you in marketing, branding and selling YOU. I often think about what's troubling us lawyers most. It's because I can see the pain and the challenges. I can also feel the pain. It's real.

But I can also see the opportunities... that's real too...

"The downturn has removed the complacency and inertia to change that has affected the profession for years... The Legal Services Act is rewriting the rules of the law, and presents a shake up which some law firms will embrace and others will resist at their peril. There are less partner places to go round, and so the situation is getting tougher... (with) growing

disengagement of employees... Law firms need to pull their socks up and improve the priority they put on engagement and motivation or lawyers will vote with their feet and jump ship, men and women."[9]

I drew up a list some time ago identifying some of the things which concern, impact upon and/or liberate me, you, our profession and our clients in the present and future... for better or worse. I'll share them with you, shall I?

- LSA 2007;
- ABS;
- Regulation – more red tape;
- Technology;
- Trends – local to global;
- Entrenchment;
- Employee defection – talent drain;
- Employee loyalty – fickle and/or zip?
- How lawyers charge for legal services – fixed fee, hourly, retainer, value based, other?
- Luddite mentality – fear, ignorance or arrogance?
- What do we lawyers need to do to be successful now and in the future?
- What skills do we need more so?
- What working style options do we have – legal executive route or solicitor route toward partnership/directorship, virtual lawyering, collaboration networks, traditional firm morphing, new business set up (for example, Director format under ABS);
- Client loyalty – fickle and/or zip?
- Clients taking lawyers in-house more;
- Outsourcing;
- Price squeeze; and
- Legal purchasing options for the client – go to an established traditional law firm, use a virtual lawyer/virtual law firm, a solo niche practitioner, a new enterprise/newly formed provider perhaps (for example, a NewCo. which embraces an entrepreneurial ABS), or 'Tesco' type – may embrace legal, business, accountancy and finance services all under one roof, perhaps?

Hmmm. Are the above points trouble and strife?

Or, a welcome opportunity perhaps to embrace change, take up the mantle and innovate our profession into a new and improved product and service offering for the benefit of us all?

ABS, collaboration and virtual lawyering

One thing's for sure... with the arrival and expansion of ABS, collaborative law and virtual lawyering fuelled by economic, technological, digital and consumer trends (present and future) there's going to be a lot more choice going forward; lots of different alternative ways to working as a lawyer and providing legal advice and services.

Mirroring the very same, there are many options available for a prospect and/or client to purchase legal advice and services from the different kinds of lawyers. The latter ranging from traditionalist dinosaur technophobe to the social savvy, commercial savvy, entrepreneurial naked type. There are *many* entrepreneurial lawyers to be found; I mentioned a handful in Volume 6.

In addition, really cool lawyers in our uncool sector and entrepreneurs who lend a helping hand to the profession as well as being hot on collaboration and sexy in virtual lawyering who come to mind are: Donna Seyle, Jorge Colon, Mark Sheridan, David Gabor, Patricia Wheatley-Burt, Jaimie Field, Sonia Gallagher, Lisa Dimonte and Kathy DiLorenzo, to name just a few.[10] All worth checking out, I reckon, to see what they're up to and how they can help you, no doubt.

forward to a stimulating future

opportunity rocks: LIC, value and niche

Back in 2006 I presented Boss Lawyer with a book written by Ray Kurzweil[11], a celebrated futurist, in which he talks about a radical view of the future course of human development, including his portrayal that we will be living through an era in which our understanding of what it means to be human will be both enriched and challenged as humanity achieves inconceivable heights of intelligence, material progress and longevity, partially as a result of technological ingenuity and super-intelligence.

He speaks of technological change as exponential, and exponential growth in the rate of exponential growth. Yowza!

Take a moment now to reflect back on what I shared with you in Volume 2 with regard to Tom Peters's view on white collar work becoming disembowelled by 2020.

I'd like to share with you now Patrick Lamb's thinking on the future of the legal industry:

"The change the legal industry is experiencing is 'disruptive', meaning that it will improve our service in ways the market does not expect...Susskind and others are imagining a future for the profession where...clients will be the beneficiaries of these efficiencies...Disruptive change is inevitable. Indeed, it is happening now. The challenge for every lawyer and every law firm is whether one will shape one's future or merely hold on to the rollercoaster hoping not to get thrown off."[12]

Hear, hear!

I've already shared with you Susskind's view in relation to the commoditisation of (some) legal services and the use and impact of technology in law law land, see Volume 1 again.

Taking on board the predictions and views of numerous scholars, futurists and lawyers I would suggest that LIC will become our core tradable commodity of value, in the present and future, to ensure our survival. Accordingly, it will become even more imperative to specialise, niche and extol 'Brand,You'. Law firm corporate cosseting will be obsolete come 2020-25 I reckon, so you'd best have a few aces up your sleeve... Self-reliance, remember?

Continual innovation, re-invention and honing of your LIC – the Super Lawyer essence – in being able to truly ROAR, identify with, empathise and care about the client and his/her business and/or predicament (being human) will be fundamental in your success rate with regard to a lobster, prospect and/or client choosing YOU above another legal product or service alternative. This is why I am banging on about swotting up on your soft skills NOW, particularly those that will help you become an extraordinary rainmaker lawyer.

Why? Your LIC is what sits between your ears and is externalised in YOUR unique communication and behaviour. It is *not* something within the confines of the bricks and mortar of your law firm's walls. Clients choose YOU – the human being – *not* the law firm and *not* the legal department.

Remember this: the *value* of the firm lies in the customer list. Who creates the customer list? YOU do. The customer/client values YOUR LIC, and what (s)he perceives VALUE to be is determined by the client.

It's much more difficult to attract and retain a client nowadays which is why it's vital to provide value-added, the likes of 'Brand,You' encapsulating your specialisms, expertise, strengths and talents. Food for thought and a pause, perhaps for a moment, I reckon. Pick me up again when you're ready...

trends, challenges, ideas, choice and change

You may recall in Volume 3 that I shared some of my thoughts with regard to legal trends and whopper future trends. I'd like to delve into this subject a bit deeper here to give you some more food for thought. A few months ago I took part in a survey which focused on legal services and practice. I'll share the questions and my answers with you, shall I?

Question: What are the major global trends and developments that could influence the way businesses will use legal services?
Answer:

- Gen 'Y' comfort/ease with technology;
- Gen 'X' comfort/ease with technology;
- Gen 'X+1−1+1' comfort/ease with technology;
- Technological advancement;
- Digital platforms – social media and social networking;
- Real-time search;
- SSO;
- Web 2.0;
- Web 3.0;
- Web 4.0;
- Outsourcing & Insourcing;
- Niche focus/identification;
- Brand 'law firm' integrity/loyalty;
- 'Brand You' integrity/loyalty;
- Consumer sovereignty;
- Self-help;
- Green – Environment; and
- Economic recovery 'W' – pound foolish, penny wise syndrome.

Question: What major changes are you aware of within your country which will impact on the way legal services are used?
Answer:

- LSA 2007 (Tesco Law);
- ABS – alternative business structures;
- Layman can instruct a barrister direct (no need to go through a solicitor/law firm and/or clerk for that matter) – barrister v. solicitor face-off unless collaboration policy comes to fruition, that is, relaxation of red tape impeding barristers;
- Virtual law firms;
- 'The Virtual Lawyer';
- 'Brand You' lawyer emergence – law students, trainees, paralegals, legal executives; solicitors; barristers; attorneys; and
- Economic policy – TAX increases.

Question: What changes could you imagine taking place in the way clients pay for legal services?
Answer:

- Over the wire – clients will be comfortable with doing the initial work themselves, that is, pay in advance online to begin the legal process online by using self help technological systems; they'll be happy and willing to do part of the work to begin with to save on costs;
- Fixed price more prevalent and in demand;
- Values based more prevalent and
- in demand;
- Monthly retainer direct debit (like insurance payment); and
- With a 'loyalty card' (points) and/or vouchers and/or 'units' (like DubLi – bid/offer).

Question: How do you see the role of legal practitioners evolving?

Answer:

- Rise of the super lawyer v. paralegal check-out churn;
- Lawyerly Intellectual Capital v. pile 'em high sell 'em cheap; and
- In relation to corporate/commercial lawyering – Entrepreneurial lawyering; more than a lawyer, a business savvy consultant too.

Question: What changes could we see in the way legal practitioners are trained and rewarded?
Answer:

- Trained:
  - ☐ Offline and online virtually in 'soft skills' and not just 'hard' technical law skills, that is, inclusion of EI, rainmaking, commercial savvy and business acumen training. In law schools, law firms and by external consultants; and
  - ☐ In communication and behaviour – a people system.
- Rewarded:
  - ☐ Financial: Will depend on what type of practitioner/sector/level/ business structure/culture/goal. For example, will there be an exit strategy such as a trade sale/public listing? Share options/EMI scheme/EBT – permissible in the future perhaps?
  - ☐ Work/Life balance: sabbatical periods; home-working.

Question: What are the implications of these changes for how legal firms will be led, managed and structured in the future?
Answer:

- Even stronger leadership and management will be required;
- Greater EI by all individuals within 'the firm' will be necessary with a totally consumer-centric focus and delivery;
- Wherever possible, an inverse of the traditional hierarchical structure triangle; and
- A move toward horizontal structures where niche expertise and non-technical skills are valued and rewarded.

Question: What are the critical challenges facing the leaders of legal practices as they address the changes identified above – what personal capabilities will they need to address them?
Answer:

- Challenges:
  - ☐ A paradigm shift in thinking and behaviour;
  - ☐ Managing and leading through a Luddite v. Evangelist face-off;
  - ☐ Identifying latent talent, encouraging it to blossom and not to feel threatened by it – rather, to embrace it, in order to assist with succession planning;
  - ☐ Reducing churn: attracting, motivating, rewarding and retaining talented lawyers and other people (non-lawyers) within the firm;
  - ☐ Managing people and managing their expectations;
  - ☐ Soft skilling up;
  - ☐ Practical business experience for all – you can't teach business savvy, you have to live it and experience it;
  - ☐ Re-structuring;
  - ☐ Re-modelling;
  - ☐ Finding 'space'.

- Personal capabilities:
  - ☐ EI;

- ☐ Fear, ignorance and arrogance to be left at home – don't bring it to the office, thank you;
- ☐ Trust in your people – aka, 'let go', stop trying to 'control' everything and let the experts BE expert;
- ☐ Let go of the 'silo' mentality;[13]
- ☐ Dare to be innovative and entrepreneurial – dare to try new stuff – and encourage your people to do likewise;
- ☐ Celebrate success – focus on what people do right rather than what they do 'wrong'; get rid of the blame culture;
- ☐ Lead by example;
- ☐ Manage by example; and
- ☐ Innovate by example.

paradigm shift

Looking at paradigm shift a bit closer, how about these for a few ideas:

- Mindset: thinking differently, such as Rainmaking is purely about confidence...seduction...performance... delivery...and follow on. Whether you're a poor rainmaker or an extraordinary rainmaker will depend on your thoughts, feelings and actions. It goes something like this...
- Extraordinary rainmaking activity is definitely like extraordinary sex! Continual mind focus. Continual nurturing. Continual stimulation. Continual discovery. Continual delivery. Continual follow on. Continual improvement. Continual innovation. Continual research and development.
- LIC: Super Lawyer. Actually being able to truly relate and care about the client and his/her business and/or predicament is fundamental to what true lawyering and LIC is all about.
- What about introducing a people system perhaps? We have IT systems, financial systems, operational systems, sales systems, legal training systems, etc. What about a people system – a proper 'soft skills' professional development and structured programme in place from day one for all lawyers to partake in, as soon as they join the firm.
- A structured programme (akin to the Cannons Train which I spoke about in Volume 7), not something which is ad hoc and haphazard and paid lip service to, which will dovetail with an individual's desired career progression. I suggest it covers skills and tools that assist the lawyer in 'knowing him/herself', aka, Emotional Intelligence and learning the marketing, branding and sales process and management and leadership qualities. Plus, communicating and behaving differently – SRO module. Don't wait until associate level for all this gubbins! Start with paralegals and trainees.
- What about us lawyers becoming entrepreneurial and having business education and real life experience too?
- What about innovation in the business process? What about re-thinking your business around its core strength – the LIC of your lawyers. Niche, 'Brand,Me' and dovetail 'Brand,Firm' – bundle products to be devised with the 'Brand,Me' lawyer's strengths and talents. Not, 'we've got a strong team of lawyers in the corporate department and we can win corporate work', for example. Build on it more. Innovate. This paradigm shift may go some way to solving the problem associated with lack of employee motivation, productivity and retention, aka, talent drain. The profession is losing its top talent year

on year, particularly at associate level. Shocking. Stop the talent drain!

- What about innovating your sales process firm-wide by introducing the ROAR model and the ROAR unsales egg-timer process to all your lawyers? The ROAR model is an innovation. It's a new idea, a process in how to get more sales. It does one of the most powerful things – it creates new market space. It has the potential to do another more powerful thing: create market space in volume.
- What about innovating the management and leadership of yourself, your lawyers and your non-lawyers? So that ALL of your people are truly engaged and motivated; it will help free you up to grow and 'move on' yourself – succession planning.

Embrace the strengths and talents of your legatees. If you are the legatee, be bold, take control, stick your bootie in and use your newly acquired skills of persuasion to influence Boss Lawyer. Like saying, 'If you want me to free you up so you can have the lifestyle that you want then we have to work together. You need to 'let go' and loosen the 'control noose' in order to gain control and fulfil your own dream. You need to engage me, enthuse me and trust me'.

Remember Jack Black – 2000 – MindStore, which I shared with you in Volume 2 (not ad verbatim)?

"You will be a great leader if you have:

1. Oomph – bags of energy
2. A Positive Attitude – passionate self-belief
3. A Futurist mindset – goal, mission and vision
4. L&R Brainpower – a magical way of utilising both the left and right side of the brain where L = logic, knowledge, teaching; R = imagination, expansion, creativity.

and the degree and application to initiate and embrace innovation and change."

Then *be* the *leader* of your own mother-ship.

My final point is simply this: If you are a leader, a manager or a decision-maker in the legal profession (in particular), then I highly recommend you take a look at Patricia Wheatley-Burt's book[14] in which she reports on the present and future challenges, ideas, choices and change in relation to law firm management, leadership, succession planning and the relationship between legator and legatee.

Patricia delves much deeper and expands on some of the issues and ideas which I have merely highlighted in the above two sections. As ever, I shall leave you to decide on your next move. It's your choice, you are in control and only you can make the changes which you feel are right for you.

Who's the daddy of your ambition and who's the captain of your mother-ship?

after dark activity
positively stimulating

OK dance partner, time to let go of my hand and go stimulate yourself... This part you have to do on your own. Onward and upward...

naked lawyer activity – a study worth casing

During 2009, and on a continuous basis, I practised what I preached in what is now Volume 10 of *the naked lawyer*. As to what I did and for a real live case study in how to continually stimulate and innovate, simply read the story again. You can relive my activity by taking yourself through the same process.

Let me help you. Here's a condensed version of the key activities and exercises you may wish to carry out...

ROAR steps

Carry out the following exercise in the step sequence provided on an ongoing basis.

- **Step 1:** Check out a few books, LinkedIn groups perhaps, blogs, etc. on the subject of innovation. Just get a feel for what it's all about.
- **Step 2:** Study and reflect on the 'dynamics of a new decade' diagram in 'the ROAR model innovations' section.
- **Step 3:** Reflect on the bullet point list in the 'what's on my mind?' section. Do you share similar concerns? Do you see similar opportunities? What are you going to do about them? Innovate? Devise bundled products? Think. Then act.
- **Step 4:** Look again at the section 'opportunity rocks: LIC, value and niche'. Consider what you may wish to do for yourself to ensure your stimulating future. Refer back to Volumes 2, 3 and 4 to assist you in the process. Now, do it!
- **Step 5:** Ask yourself the questions in the section 'trends, challenges, ideas, choice and change'. I'm confident you will come up with different answers. Accordingly, what are you going to do, that is, what are going to innovate in order to capitalise on the trends and changes ahead? Think. Think. And then think some more. Take your time, and then begin to do something.
- **Step 6:** Consider the paradigm shift ideas that I shared with you in the final section. What additional ideas can you come up with that are pertinent to you; your personal development, your firm's, the legal profession and the legal industry generally? Feel free to use the ideas as a starter for ten.

Do check out Patricia Wheatley-Burt's book – no obligation to purchase. I merely draw your attention to it for you to consider the same.

ROAR tips

- Be innovative;
- Be stimulating;
- Think LIC;
- Think niche;
- Think value;
- Brainstorm regularly;
- Re-think your business process;
- Re-think your way of working;
- Re-think your way of managing and/ or leading;
- Be open to a paradigm shift;
- Take a few risks;
- Be bold;
- Embrace change; and
- Be the change that you want to see in the yourself and the profession.

ROAR summation

no rules here, we're innovating stuff

One of my favourite quotes of all time is:

"There ain't no rules around here, we're trying to accomplish something."
(Thomas Edison)

I hope by now that you will understand why 'innovation' is a key element in the ROAR model and fundamental to your continual personal and professional development. It's OK to take a few risks and make some mistakes along the way.

After all, in the wise words of George Bernard Shaw, "A life spent making mistakes is not only more honourable, but more useful than a life spent doing nothing." I personally subscribe to the line in the movie *Indecent Proposal*, in which Woody Harrelson (the actor) says, "A life without risk is like no life at all."

For The Resistance among you reading this Volume, I have only this to add... "Those who say it cannot be done, should not interrupt the person doing it." (Chinese proverb)

See you for again soon for some yes! yes!! yes!!!

References

1. A basic principle of the law whereby once a decision (a precedent) on a certain set of facts has been made, another Court of the same rank or lower, must apply that decision in cases presenting the same set of facts. http://www.duhaime.org/LegalDictionary/S/StareDecisis.aspx
2. Persona non grata: literally meaning 'an unwelcome person', is a legal term used in diplomacy that indicates a proscription against a person entering the country. http://en.wikipedia.org/wiki/Persona_non_grata
3. *Que Sera, Sera (Whatever Will Be, Will Be)* is a popular song, first published in 1956 and written by the Jay Livingston and Ray Evans songwriting team. It was introduced in Alfred Hitchcock's 1956 film *The Man Who Knew Too Much* with Doris Day in a leading role. Day's recording of the song for Columbia Records (catalogue number 40704) was a hit in both the United States and the United Kingdom. http://en.wikipedia.org/wiki/Que_Sera,_Sera_(Whatever_Will_Be,_Will_Be)
4. Sergey Brin and Larry Page are the founders of Google.
5. http://www.ft.com/cms/s/0/e983c280-dd68-11df-beb7-00144feabdc0.html?ftcamp=crm/e-mail/20101022/nbe/USMorningHeadlines/product
6. http://abovethelaw.com/2010/09/aba-survey-lawyers-profiting-from-web-2-0/
7. Stuart Brown is Director of Brand & Customer Experience at Osmosis Brand Communications: http://uk.linkedin.com/in/stuartbbrown
8. *Harvard Business Review on Innovation* (New York: Harvard Business Review, 2001)
9. Rachel Brushfield, director at Energise, The Talent Liberation Company, helping individuals and firms to liberate talent and fulfil their potential. Author of 'Locating The Skylight In The Glass Ceiling', *AWS Magazine*, Autumn 2010. http://uk.linkedin.com/in/energiseliberateyourtalent
10. http://www.linkedin.com/in/donnaseyle; http://www.linkedin.com/in/theonlinebar; http://www.linkedin.com/pub/marc-sheridan/17/7a4/1ab ; http://www.linkedin.com/pub/david-gabor/a/445/307; http://uk.linkedin.com/in/patriciawheatleyburt; http://www.linkedin.com/in/jaimiefield; http://www.linkedin.com/in/soniagallagher; http://www.linkedin.com/in/lisadimonte; http://www.linkedin.com/pub/kathy-dilorenzo/11/972/33b
11. Kurzweil, Ray, *The Singularity Is Near: When Humans Transcend Biology* (London: Penguin Books, 2005).
12. Lamb, Patrick, *Alternative Fee Arrangements: Value Fees and the Changing Legal Market* (London: Ark Group Ltd,, 2010).
13. Silo: air tight structure; pit or tower for the storage of grain. Silo mentality is in reference to 'tunnel vision' and operating within the confines of a department rather than the firm and its people as a whole.
14. Wheatley-Burt, Patricia,, *Leadership for Law Firms (after the Legal Services Act)* (London: Law Society, 2010)

Volume 11: yes! yes!! yes!!!

continual stimulation

Welcome again, my stimulated dance partner! Here's a penultimate big hug from your private dancing Naked Lawyer in law law land.

You will no doubt be pleased to know that we've broken the back of the ROAR model... 'yes! yes!! yes!!!' is the final piece of the ROAR model jigsaw.

In this volume I'm going to share with you some other really cool stuff that I reckon you may wish to consider. The information and musings may help you further (and quicker) along your way to becoming an extraordinary rainmaker lawyer. I'm not going to jibber-jabber on too much and I'm certainly not going to go over old ground...

You will find that this volume is going to be short and sweet, so that we can move swiftly on and wrap things up as quickly as possible in the final volume of *the naked lawyer*, Volume 12: XXX rated – tomorrow's lawyer.

other really cool stuff

Returning to my story, I'd like to share with you and highlight a few things which popped up during my journey...

continual improvement

growth matters

Professional development is a *big thing* in the business of law. You know this... So that we can deliver expert quality legal advice with the utmost client care foremost in mind, our profession requires us to keep abreast of the latest technical law, ethics and conduct rules as well as 'soft skills'.

We are, after all, tested on the very same each year in order to maintain a practising certificate, as we evidence accreditation of the required CPD hours. However, 'personal' development isn't a requirement by the SRA, nor is it regulated. That's up to me, and you, to regulate.

I actually believe that personal growth/ development and professional development are synonymous. I alluded to this concept in Volume 2, if you remember, when I advocated that we should get a grip on our EI and should be reading and learning about understanding business, understanding people, understanding trends and ultimately understanding the future, not just law. Continual improvement – this is where it's at.

As I pranced around in Client Territory, with raving referral lobsters, I was continually learning, continually developing, continually stimulated and continually improving... purely from the environment. By engaging and sharing with business people and getting involved in business activity, I was naturally evolving...

Personal and professional growth may happen, to a limited extent, when chained to a desk churning out black and white law, poring over law books and digesting LexisNexis et al. However, I learned and experienced that the real development stuff, both legal and business, happens beyond the confines of the ivory tower and law law land... that being where the clients are.

Continual improvement, not just in 'the law' but in *many* fields, disciplines and skill sets, is where the really cool stuff manifests that can make the all the difference to us becoming extraordinary rainmaker lawyers. This is where the magic happens, namely, where we take control of our careers and lives in our quest for greater knowledge and experience resulting in both personal and professional growth for the benefit of our clients.

tick-tock poppy-cock

The expectant and demanding requirement to continually 'make every six minutes count'[1] brought about by the corporate law firm mantra and culture, necessitated my operating efficiently and effectively... every day. No respite. This is law law land.

the naked lawyer, therefore, wouldn't be complete without my mentioning the ubiquitous subject of 'time management'. I already have though. Big Rocks, remember? PEE Poor Work Ethic, remember? Nevertheless. I shall add this. Managing my time and being efficient and effective in my daily life came down to the following:

- Getting up early;
- Getting organised and preparing the night before the next day was due to begin;
- Utilising my sales spreadsheet;
- Utilising Microsoft Outlook calendar and tasks to the fullest extent;
- Applying my SUUUCKS attitude;
- Living the PEE Poor Work Ethic;
- Balancing my Big Rocks; and
- Cultivating, managing and focusing my energy.

Volumes 2 and 5 revision, remember? And... duly note this, again... "what is this life if full of care, we have no time, to stand and stare".[2]

Here and then, between the tick-tock poppy-cock law law land billable hour madness, I was doggedly determined in factoring in some time for simply star gazing... After all, it's when I take the time to pause that I can free my mind from the day-to-day clutter allowing reflection, contemplation, absorption and my dreams to come to the fore. It's in moments spent doing this... simply doing nothing... simply just sitting or standing or lying... simply just staring... where new ideas and concepts come pouring in to flood the space.

Ultimately, it's where personal and professional growth happens, I reckon. Do you?

just do something!

Keep reading, not just law.

Keep an eye on your Big Rocks and manage your energy levels effectively.

Take time out to simply stand and stare. Do it now. Pause. Gaze. Reflect. Feel how it feels...

Pick me up again when you're ready...

continual savvy and nous

commercial savvy and business nous

I'd like to turn now to what I believe will set you apart as an extraordinary rainmaker lawyer from the maddening crowd legal pack. From my observations and experience as both a lawyer (when working alongside other lawyers and interacting with clients when providing legal advice) and an entrepreneur (when buying legal advice), I find that the exceptional lawyers are the ones who possess commercial savvy *and* business nous. They're the ones who are able to give the commercial client a *truly* commercial legal service because they can empathise; some have actually stood in the clients' shoes because they've ran a business themselves.

I recall Boss Lawyer returning to the fold one day after asking a client for some feedback in relation to the service he'd provided. Whilst the client was in most part highly complimentary and positive in the feedback, being delighted with the technical legal advice received, the area identified for improvement was of a 'non-legal' nature... sort of. The client actually said something along the lines of, "I'd like you to be more commercial," as reported by Boss Lawyer Partner.

Evidently, what law firm partners want in theory and practice from their junior lawyers – the mantras: 'business nous', 'business acumen' and 'commercial savvy', which are bandied around like candy-floss – cannot be learned from a text book, at law school or even in a law firm. They are learned and developed on the ground by getting our hands dirty at the coal face.

I know, from experience... As a business owner prior to entering the profession and from observing whilst a lawyer, it was patently obvious. I also reckon there is a difference between commercial savvy and business nous/acumen, so I'm going to take a few moments to talk about both of them.

'Savvy' is about 'knowing', 'shrewdness' and 'understanding'. Commercial savvy is simply commercial knowledge. 'Nous' is about common sense, aka, 'gumption'. Business nous is simply business gumption. 'Acumen' is about insight, aka, penetration. Business insight. Commercial insight.

It's one thing knowing, aka, understanding commerce, but it's an entirely different thing applying business gumption. Taking it a step further, legal advice containing business gumption and commercial savvy, is what the client is really after. It really is that simple. But it's not that simple to achieve without you and I, the lawyers, truly understanding commerce and acquiring business common sense.

Needless to say, to be a successful rainmaker lawyer requires both commercial savvy and business nous, I figure. It's something you learn through experience. I don't believe it can be truly learned from a text book or going on courses even. The text book and the course provides you with the theory, some knowledge and exposure. It's not enough. It's not practice.

For example, it's pretty much like learning law from a text book but realistically it means absolutely jack without you getting your hands dirty at the law firm coal face, by training and practising in the law. If your goal is to be an extraordinary rainmaker lawyer, a Super Lawyer even, then the biggest tip I can give you is get as much business experience/exposure as possible prior to entering the profession... or, whilst you're in it.

Go and work in an SME or corporation (outside of the legal profession) for a year or so and get a real feel for its culture, systems, operations, people and customer care/expectations/service.

If you're already in the profession as a junior lawyer, then perhaps you could consider getting your hands dirty by getting involved in a business which does not conflict with your lawyerly role – something in your 'leisure' time, maybe. You will find that many partners have their fingers in other business pies. Start your development now. Don't wait.

It may actually be an opportune time for you to consider a sabbatical from the profession perhaps? A business acquaintance recently shared with me a story about their lawyer friend who experienced the 'recession' of the late 1950s when he was already qualified and working as a solicitor in the UK – another time when many lawyers found the going tough. He took time out of the profession, went back to university, and qualified as an engineer. After several years working abroad in engineering, he came back to the UK and re-qualified (quite rapidly) as a member of the bar, specialising in IPR and contract law as it related to IP. Until he retired many years later, he was never out of well-paid work, much of it not formally at the bar but instead working directly for various global enterprises as a consultant. My friend made the point (from an entrepreneurial business person's perspective) that law as a qualification should now increasingly be seen as a necessary secondary qualification within business.

I agree. Do you? I also believe that business as a qualification should now increasingly be seen as a necessary secondary qualification within the law. What do you think?

I also agree with my friend in his belief that what businesses (such as law firms) increasingly need are people who have detailed or even expert legal knowledge which is ancillary to other skills and capabilities – such as IT, marketing, sales, accounting and/or an MBA, etc.

In essence, I'm an advocate of lawyers having more crossover skills, as this will help our understanding of and empathy with our future and existing clients, ultimately making us much better lawyers of benefit to those clients as we progress. Invariably this may make those of us with such crossover skills more valuable and marketable. Super lawyers. Super rainmaker lawyers.

As my entrepreneurial friend succinctly puts it:

"A single (and some might say narrow) specialisation such as the law is no longer sufficient, whilst the challenge of acquiring other skills and disciplines entirely unrelated to the law can be a huge stimulus to the individual's creativity and mindset. In some respects it no longer matters in which order the skills and capabilities are acquired; the important thing is to have more than one such set."

It's also important for choice, change and control. Who's driving the mother-ship and who's the daddy of your ambition?

I welcome law schools and colleges adding a curriculum on business 101 to help young lawyers in particular survive and thrive in the new economy.

But, when all is said and done, I figure you just can't beat getting your hands dirty when you're wet behind your business savvy ears. It's all part of life's rich tapestry... and a necessity for you and your future in law law land.

just do something!

Take a little time out now to ask yourself this: 'Do I possess commercial savvy AND business nous?' Answer, honestly. Perhaps you could ask the same question to a handful of clients? If you come to the conclusion that there's room for improvement then what are you going to do about it? When you figure the answer to that out, just do it!

the seduction of persuasion

I do not intend to go into all of the different kinds of skill sets that I believe you need to acquire in order to become an extraordinary rainmaker lawyer. I'm sure you can figure most of them out for yourself and go about acquiring them through time, dedication and perseverance. But I would like to share with you one of the most important skills that I learned (and continue to hone and practice) because it's helpful in many situations – in my work, at home, with my family, in my leisure life, etc.

I'm talking about the ability to be 'persuasive' and to 'influence'; for this skill can be instrumental in achieving my dreams, goals and vision. It's a necessary skill to be an extraordinary rainmaker lawyer. Fact. Period. No argument.

I learned about 'persuasion' whilst at Cannons; remember back to Volume 7 where I shared with you the 'cannon ball fun' sales process.

Well, permit me to share with you another little secret... To be a really exceptional rainmaker lawyer, it's the seduction of 'persuasion' that truly wins over lobsters and clients. I recommend that you get a grip on 'persuasion'. I'll share with you a few tactics now:

- Be a leader, not a follower – it's a herd thing.
- Be confident and comfortable when speaking; don't 'umm' and/or 'err' or use other 'filler' words or expressions. This kind of speech quirk will have the effect of making you less persuasive.
- Let time be your friend; choose the right moment to ask your receiver for something you suspect they may not be agreeable to. For example, people are more likely to say 'yes' when they're mentally tired.
- Mirror and match your recipient's movements, for example, leaning forward and using similar hand gestures. Be subtle though, by leaving a few seconds delay. Subconsciously the recipient will be more comfortable with you.
- Use 'emotional' words; reflect back to what I shared with you in Volume 8 about communication.
- Be an authority, an expert, on something; people are more likely to follow you and be persuaded by you – it's all about 'know, like, trust, understand, 'get' and share an interest', remember?

just do something!

Look up 'persuasion'. JFGI. I suggest you start learning all about it by reading tips from the 'experts'. Give it a go at your next networking event, offline or online. Then it's just a question of honing it. Not that it's any consolation, but... I'm still learning!

continual performance

Lots of 'soft skills' can be acquired through experience, embarking on educational courses and/or investing in either some coaching, training or consultancy. I put myself through the paces in 2000 whilst working in the leisure industry and took advantage of the Cannons Train development programme.

Nevertheless, it's a continual improvement thing with me so I feel it's important to continually update and/or upgrade my 'soft skills' with each new development in the different skill sets. From my experience of a variety of industries, as well as working alongside lawyers who are technically bright 'in the law' but limited in their 'out of law law land soft skills' exposure (particularly junior lawyers, I hasten to add), and my awareness and understanding of the present problems, stresses, strains, demands and future challenges for lawyers and the profession generally, I would advocate that business coaching, confidence coaching, stress management coaching, life coaching and happiness coaching are a handful of 'self-help' professional and personal development initiatives worthy of consideration for us lawyers.

built to perform

I've already rattled on about commercial savvy and business nous, so I don't intend to go there again. Phew... you're no doubt exhaling? Suffice to say there are a plethora of business coaches and business consultants who are available to assist us lawyers with our individual 'business' development and FMSP. Ask around, check out your contacts and connections in SM and SN and away you go. Find a business coach.

quietly confident

I've never had much of a problem walking into a business event and/or networking room on my own, not knowing anyone there and then approaching a complete stranger with a view to striking up a conversation. It's what I did whilst I was a trainee solicitor on many occasions. But most of us find this kind of thing difficult. Understandably.

I guess it's kind of a personality thing though. Well, it's actually all about *confidence*. Confidence is something you're going to need to possess if you expect to become an extraordinary rainmaker lawyer. It's certainly something that can be learned and honed if you question your confidence level.

You may recall me suggesting that rainmaking is purely about confidence... seduction... performance... delivery... and follow on. If you suspect that your confidence level could do with a boost, allow me to share with you my secret. The key to confidence is authenticity... and schmoozing people who you are likely to share commonality with. Now, perhaps you can see why we did all that work in Volumes 3, 4 and 5 on devising your niche and brand and identifying raving lobsters who will have synergy.

If you suffer from a lack of confidence, you're already beginning to win the battle because you can be confident that the environments in which you find yourself in are the kind you will naturally feel more at ease. Nonetheless, should you feel the need, there are many, many, many confidence coaches to choose from.

chill pill

Stress stress stress stress stress. Absolutely no way of avoiding this bad boy.

"I always remind my students to remember one thing: there are 8800 hours in a year. After you subtract work--say 4000+--the rest is yours. When you also add in the emphasis on business development, the distinction between work and play is almost meaningless... If you are required to produce billable hours of around 2000 to 3000+, which City and New York firms will ask for, then 4000+ may be an underestimate!"[3]

You may recall my mentioning the 'stress' issue a little in Volume 5, alluding to us lawyers working consistently at 100-125 percent capacity engaging in pill-popping, reduced to excessive alcohol in-take, manic depressive behaviour and suffering relationship breakdown as a result of chronic stress. *Please don't* let it get to this.

It's well to remember that if we're burnt out, not only are we lawyers bad for business, aka, the client and the firm, but we're actually doing ourselves and our families a lot of damage – health wise and relationship wise. Big Rocks, remember?

In my experience, service levels, aka, customer service excellence, customer relationship management, client care and marketing, sales, innovation and business development activity, dip considerably when we're stretched and stressed. Ironically, these are the very things that will help us and our firm to grow and hopefully pop out of the top of the 'W' recession that we are constantly warned about.

So, when I get stressed I simply focus on SUUUCKS and my PEE Poor Work Ethic. I star gaze, kick back and take a chill pill... It's a mindset thing. Remember my two drugs? Love (passion) and adrenalin (endorphins). Try and work on them. Love what you do by sticking to what you love with a SUUUCKS attitude and PEE Poor Work Ethic.

Oh, and star gazing is like wine for your soul and fish for your mind. Just do it! At least once in a wee while...

Nonetheless, if you do feel that you need a little help with your 'stress management', I'll be the first person to say 'it's good to talk'. There are many well qualified stress management coaches/consultants who can help you deal with 'fitting it all in'.

If you find yourself stressed, which you will, you *must* find what works for you in order to keep your sanity and everything together. A stress management coach may be the answer. Only you will know.

it's a wonderful life

One of my favourite movies of all time is *It's a wonderful life*.[4] I love life. I love living, not existing.

Harking back to Volume 2, I do well to remind myself of my FMSP and its component parts. I kind of 'life coached' myself back then, and still do. You have too, no doubt, if you've worked through the process.

I have a dream, a goal, a vision. You have too. I make choices, changes when deemed necessary and appropriate, and I take control of the direction I wish to take my life. You can too. I feel empowered... and life is wonderful. Is it for you?

No doubt you will not be surprised to hear that there are a plethora of life coaches/consultants at the ready should you need some assistance with your FMSP and EI kind of stuff.

smile smile smile

To cap it all off, if you really are so darned miserable, things in work and life are just so depressing and you feel like you desperately need some sunshine in your life, then listen up... You can "Pack up your troubles in your old kit-bag, and smile, smile, smile"[5] by hiring yourself a 'happiness coach'.

You may laugh. Chuckle, chuckle. Tee-hee. But, truly, there are such positively sunny coaches to be found who just may hold the key to helping you unlock your treasure trove of happiness which lies within you! That's if you can't manage it for yourself by digging deep and drawing on your positive mindset of course. If you need a little more help and guidance, then be comfortable in the knowing that it can be a wonderful life again...

'Yes' it can. 'Yes' it will be. Think 'Yes, I am going to live a wonderful life.' Yes! Yes!! Yes!!!

just do something!

If you feel that you could do with a little help in your professional and personal development to be a more effective rainmaker lawyer, then look into identifying the right business coach, confidence coach, stress management coach, life coach or happiness coach to help you on your way.[6]

after dark activity

yes means yes

Don't just think about it... do it! Just say 'yes' to:

- 'I am going to make a choice';
- 'I am going to make changes for the better'; and
- 'I am going to take control',

in my personal and professional life...

naked lawyer activity – a study worth casing

During 2009 I put into practice what is now Volume 11 of *the naked lawyer*. If you wish to know how to think, feel and act in the 'yes! yes!! yes!!!' style simply read this volume again. You can relive my thoughts and activities by taking yourself through the same process.

Let me help you. Here's a condensed version of the key activities and exercises you may wish to do...

ROAR steps

Carry out the following exercise in the step sequence provided on an ongoing basis.

- **Step 1:** Keep reading, not just law. Keep an eye on your Big Rocks and manage your energy levels effectively. Star gaze every now and then.
- **Step 2:** Ask yourself, 'Do I possess commercial savvy *and* business nous?' and ask the same question to a handful of clients. If there's room for improvement, what are you going to do about it? When you figure the answer to that out, just do it!
- **Step 3:** Look up 'persuasion'. JFGI. Learn about it by reading tips from the 'experts'. Give it a go at your next networking event, offline or online. Hone it.
- **Step 4:** If you feel that you could do with a little help in your professional and personal development to be a more effective rainmaker lawyer, then look into identifying the right business coach, confidence coach, stress management coach, life coach or happiness coach to help you on your way.
- **Step 5:** Pack up your troubles in your old kit-bag and smile, smile, smile.

ROAR tips

- Get up early;
- Get organised;
- Prepare for the day ahead the night before;
- Work on commercial savvy and business nous;
- Get some real business experience;
- Get a grip on the seduction of persuasion;
- Star gaze;
- Smile, smile, smile;
- Think Yes! Yes!! Yes!!! and
- Be happy.

ROAR summation

continual 'yes' mindset

I've just shared with you some other really cool stuff that may well help you on your way to becoming an extraordinary rainmaker lawyer.

How to market, brand and sell YOU ultimately requires a 'YES' mindset... unwavering, all the way. Have faith in yourself. You've just worked through what I hope has been a very thought provoking story and demanding series of after dark activities. You're a winner.

You just now need to truly believe that you can make your dream come true by piecing all of the ROAR elements together and continually putting it into practice.

Just think Yes! Yes!! Yes!!!

References

1. Mills, Catrin, *Making Every Six Minutes Count* (London: Ark Group Ltd., 2010)
2. A line from a poem by William Henry Davies: http://www.davidpbrown.co.uk/poetry/william-henry-davies.html
3. A comment by John Flood, Professor of Law and Sociology at University of Westminster, London, United Kingdom, on the Law Society Gazette group thread – 'What do Solicitors Practices really have to tweet about?', on LinkedIn.
4. *It's a Wonderful Life* is a 1946 American drama film based on the short story 'The Greatest Gift' written by Philip Van Doren

Stern. The film stars James Stewart in the character of George Bailey, a family man whose imminent suicide on Christmas Eve brings about the intervention of Clarence Odbody (George's guardian angel). Clarence shows George all the lives he has touched and the contributions he has made to his community. http://en.wikipedia.org/wiki/It percent27s_a_wonderful_life

5. *Pack Up Your Troubles in Your Old Kit-Bag, and Smile, Smile, Smile* is a World War I marching song, published in 1915 in London. It was written by George Henry Powell under the pseudonym of George Asaf, and set to music by his brother Felix Powell. It became very popular as one of a large number of music hall songs aimed at boosting and maintaining morale, recruiting for the forces, or defending Britain's war aims. http://en.wikipedia.org/wiki/Pack_Up_Your_Troubles_in_Your_Old_Kit-Bag
6. A handful of the kind of coaches who could help, for example:

   - Dr Richard Norris; leadership, performance and legacy coach: http://www.drrichardnorris.com
   - Ann Page; leadership, management and interpersonal skills coach: http://uk.linkedin.com/in/annpage; http://www.beyondthe brief.com
   - Michaela Hardwick; business development and personal performance coach: http://uk.linkedin.com/pub/michaela-hardwick/14/574/983; http://www.beyond-expectation.co.uk
   - Catrin Mills; personal development coach: http://uk.linkedin.com/in/catrinmills
   - Jules Wyman; confidence coach: http://uk.linkedin.com/pub/jules-wyman/4/608/552; http://www.positive-belief.co.uk
   - Jeni Purdie; happiness coach and life coach: http://uk.linkedin.com/pub/jeni-purdie/1/69/400; http://www.reachforstarfish.com
   - Adrian Jackman-Smith; business coach: http://uk.linkedin.com/in/adrianjs

Volume 12: XXX rated – tomorrow's lawyer

yes! yes!! yes!!!

I'm so excited! I just can't hide it... Your private dancing Naked Lawyer in law law land is smiling with you here and now, positively beaming with pride whilst prancing on the spot in utter delight, hugging and congratulating you as a result of your excellent achievement.

Well done! You made it... You survived! And... hopefully... thrived!

You made it through your first Entrepreneur Lawyer boot-camp. You experienced *the naked lawyer*... and... hopefully you've enjoyed dancing with me as you carried out your 'after dark activities'. Yes?

It's time to put this baby to bed, methinks. Would you like to dance with me, just one last time? Then join me now as we wrap things up together...

tomorrow's lawyer

So, maybe you're a lawyer and:

- Just starting out in the profession; or
- 'Powering through' monster-truck style, aka, going forward (you're ambitious and you're keen to progress); or
- Thinking, 'Get me the hell out of here!'

Whatever your circumstances are right now, hopefully I've managed to share with you some ideas, some skills, given you a few pointers and a number of things to be thinking about and doing which may be useful on your chosen life path.

You might not agree with the stuff I've said throughout. That's OK. A quote which tickles me springs to mind:

"Any clod can have the facts, but having opinions is an art." (Charles McCabe)

I confess. I love art. Naturally, I am opinionated. No surprises there, eh? But, I reckon that's OK because it's a typical trait of a lawyer (and an entrepreneur)... along with dealing with the facts, I hasten to add. *the naked lawyer* is, after all, me sharing my opinion, together with some facts. We're all entitled to this. And it's also why you and I may not agree on some of the content within *the naked lawyer*. Again, that's OK. I respect your opinion. Fact.

I've simply shared with you my story... my way... towards a more fulfilling and successful life, whatever I deem that to be for me. It's something that's worked, and continues to work, for me. And I figured I'd like to share it with you as I'd love you to experience the life which you dream of having too. The stuff that I have shared with you throughout the book just might work for you. Of course, you will go about it in your own unique way... with your own style and finesse...

However, placing hand on heart, IMHO, although I really do understand that many of us lawyers are uncomfortable with selling ourselves, I passionately, wholeheartedly, unreservedly and unquestionably believe that in this digital, consumer sovereign, highly competitive, human economy, self reliance decade (and century), that rainmaking is an activity that you simply cannot avoid.

I do believe that not only is it a skill that will enable you to survive, it will help you thrive, in business and life. As a legal colleague neatly puts it:

"Marketing (and sales) is a world away from the sober, deliberate, careful, fastidious, introverted work we lawyers are trained to do, and accustomed to doing...

"Rainmakers must be engaging, entertaining, gregarious, and extrovert, at least to a degree...There is no natural law that states that these two very different sets of qualities (lawyering and rainmaking) cannot exist in the same person. We lawyers must learn to switch between them as necessary...

"We are at our best when we are fully engaged with something, and any learning tool is only effective if it grabs our attention. If the naked lawyer *has compelled you to read it, and act on the 'after dark activities', then it has done its first, fundamental, most important marketing job."*[1]

The legal texts we are accustomed to (and arguably subjected to reading, through little choice of our own) rarely stimulate; they merely inform.

The professional skills of a lawyer – drafting, advocacy, interviewing techniques – may well be best conveyed in measured prose. But, the skills of the rainmaker are altogether different, and the task of forging a connection between them and the world of practice is a tough one – and still a relatively novel one. This is partly the reason why I chose to present *the naked lawyer* in an idiosyncratic way to approach this problem. It's a little light relief which may have stimulated you into laughing, smiling, crying or possibly even hurling a few rocks in my direction! EEK!! The style may not have been to your taste, but what ever is? That's OK.

At the very least, hopefully it has made you think about your practice, your clients, your prospects and lobsters, and most of all about YOU – your present and your future. Your dreams and the life you aspire to truly live. Hopefully it has both stimulated and challenged you in a way that no sober treatise on marketing or sales has ever done before. Hopefully it's turned your head around as far as relating to clients, prospects, lobsters and colleagues are concerned. Hopefully you may have had a eureka moment, a blinding revelation even about some important things that have gone wrong in your life and what and how you may be able to do something about it.

Perhaps your outlook is even a little different now compared with your thinking and behaviour prior to reading this book.

I sincerely hope that you found that The Naked Lawyer is much more than a lesson in marketing, branding and selling... I was aiming for it to be a manual for your life... Your FMSP will certainly help toward fulfilling your dream life.

But actually, there really isn't a blueprint right or wrong way in going forward, for it's really up to you what you do, why, where, when, how and who with. It's your choice. You are in control. You can change things if you want. You alone are the captain of your mother-ship and the daddy of your ambition.

ROAR nightcap

So, let's recap shall we? The box out summarises the key elements covered in each chapter of *the naked lawyer.*

If 'a picture paints a thousand words' then I'm about to save us a lot of time... Check out the ROAR odel diagram.

the naked lawyer Volumes 1-12	Element:
1: RIP – announcing the roar model	the present
2: wakey wakey rise and shine	emotional intelligence
3: slowly, slowly, catch a nichey	niche identification
4: getting under your skin	personal brand creation
5: raving referral lobsters rule!	referral network building
6: social savvy junkie	social media and social networking
7: nurturing fuzz to get more buzz	relationship marketing, unsales and fuzz
8: talking dirty to a saint when I'm a pure little devil	communication and behaviour
9: touch, touch and touch me again	extraordinary customer service
10: continual stimulation	innovation
11: yes! yes!! yes!!!	other really cool stuff
12: XXX rated – tomorrow's lawyer	the future

the **roar** model

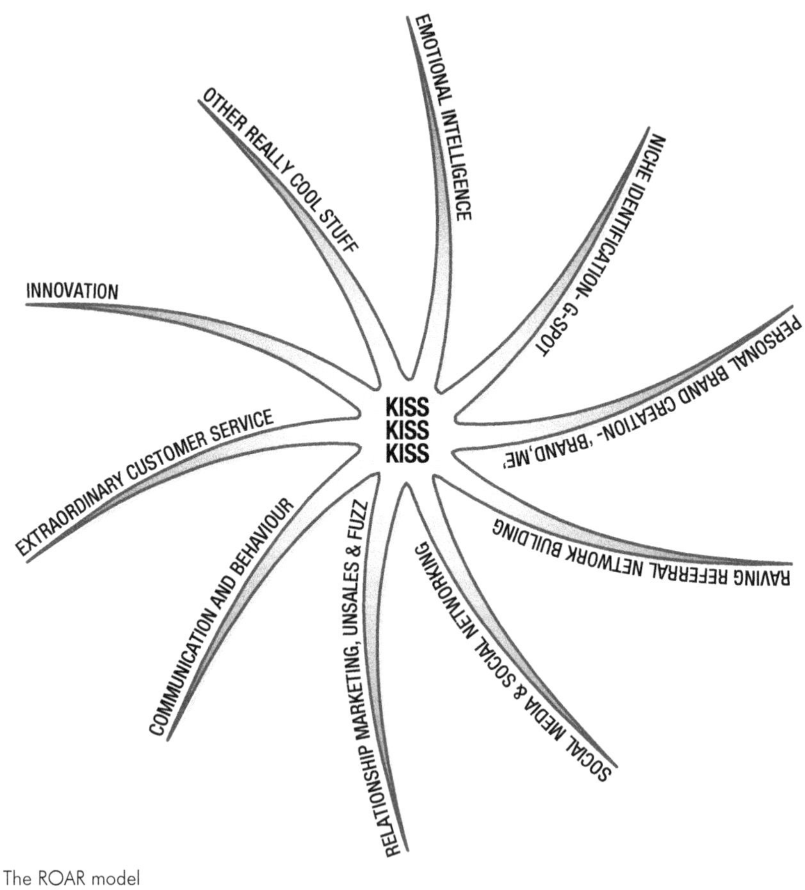

Figure 4: The ROAR model

I trust it is self explanatory. It's the model towards self-reliance, fulfilment, extraordinary rainmaking potential (and potentially extraordinary sex) and ultimately a solution in how to get more clients, sales, referrals, income, value, growth and success. Each element is fundamental to 'the big picture'. Miss one out, and the chances of your success will be reduced significantly.

XXX rated

after dark, before light

If you're up for making the transition from traditional lawyering to entrepreneurial lawyering, of the truly naked kind, then here is a summary of the key takeaways from Volumes 1-11 to assist you on your travels.

To step out of the dark and into the light:

- Live your Big Rocks;
- Develop and practise your EI;
- Be constantly SWOT aware;
- Appreciate your Ethicability conundrum;
- Live your ME Code of Conduct;
- Have pride of Epitaph;
- Adopt the Rainmaker Mindset, Attitude and Motivation ethos;
- Live your PEE Poor Work Ethic;
- Continually work on your ideal niches;
- Work your positioning, differentiation, USPs, PODs, and g-spots (target market(s));
- Blow your horn every day as 'Brand,Me' (and 'Brand,Firm');
- Rave with your raving Referral Lobster Net-Kingdom offline and online;
- Practise your SM savvy and SN nous and netiquette, daily;
- Make lots of FUZZ;
- Work up your unsales process 80:20/G:R;
- Practise devilish communication and behaviour techniques – SRO style;
- Have fun devising stunning straplines and talking DIRTY;
- Continually establish rapport;
- Continually build enduring extraordinary relationships;
- Continually strive to achieve customer service excellence;
- Use the ROAR unsales egg-timer;
- Practise touch #1, touch #2, touch #3 with speedy follow-on;
- Live your 'Brand,Me' communication game programme;
- Work your CRM system;
- Continually innovate your business process;
- Continually develop, innovate, hone and cherish your LIC;
- Have an open mind to paradigm shifts;
- Learn to apply commercial savvy and business nous to your legal work and dealings;
- Practise the seduction of persuasion;
- Draft in some external coaching/consultancy/training help where necessary; and
- Continually update your sales spreadsheet and Formidable ME Strategy & Plan (FMSP).

I am confident that if you do all of the above you will become a lawyer of tomorrow, today.

smorgasbord of quick fix tips

You will recall that we set out on our journey with my suggestion that 'sales begins by "buying" the salesperson – YOU'.

So, once again, here's a summary of *all* the ROAR tips I shared with you in Volumes 1-11 as to what you need to think and do so that lobsters, prospects and clients will buy YOU:

- Strive to be an extraordinary rainmaker by thinking 'extraordinary sex';
- Get a grip;
- Get personal;

- Get real;
- Speak up;
- Speak out;
- Find and be your true ME;
- Don't be afraid;
- Don't allow fear to interfere;
- Park ego firmly at the door;
- Give up waiting;
- Let go of resisting change;
- Be honest – with yourself and others;
- Be transparent;
- Just do it;
- It's time...;
- Respect everyone's uniqueness and individuality;
- Do not tolerate people who are attempting to mould you into something you are not;
- Be confident;
- Don't be afraid to stand alone;
- Celebrate your uniqueness;
- Be thorough – research deeply, slowly, methodically, systematically;
- Brainstorm! Think lots!
- Be creative;
- Be commercial;
- Be courageous;
- Don't wait;
- Don't stand still;
- Be sexy in your positioning;
- Be sexier in your differentiation;
- Be particular in pursuit of the g-spot;
- Say 'NO' to kneeling on the job;
- Use your initiative;
- Engage in fourplay;
- Get everything – brand stable;
- Be accommodating;
- Don't allow your role to define YOU;
- Get digging;
- Get surfing;
- Be authentic;
- Harmonise 'Brand,Me' and 'Brand,Firm';
- Be NUTS;
- Think domination!
- Share your brand ideas;
- Think emotional benefits;
- Think *big personality*;
- Think search engine optimisation;
- Think social search optimisation;
- Think brand reputation;
- Make 'Brand,Me' count!
- Take the plunge;
- Exit 'The Comfort Zone';
- Exit 'The Ivory Tower';
- Build multiple bridges;
- Strive to be accomplished in the four traits;
  - Be *giving;*
  - Be a *connector;*
  - Be a *listener;*
  - Be *empathetic;*
- Live your brand;
- Get your name *everywhere;*
- Rave about THEM;
- Be 80:20/G:R;
- Work your 'Me,Tale' off!
- Make time: devote 30 minutes each day to SM and SN activity – make it a habit;
- Lay out a designated time to carry out your SM and SN activity – morning, noon or night perhaps?
- Use Microsoft Outlook, calendar, contacts and tasks (or an equivalent software package) to help organise, manage and analyse your activity and effectiveness;
- Use your sales spreadsheet to highlight, monitor, benchmark and analyse your SM and SN activity and results;
- Set yourself three to five priority activities each day;
- Share 'Brand,You';
- Blow your horn every day;
- Be a secret agent provocateur;
- Be a permissive Googler: go, ogle;
- Fumble around;
- Improve your LUST;
- Get fuzzy;
- Get bizzy;
- Get nurturing;

- Build equity;
- Think 'befores' and 'afters';
- 'Brand,You' fuzz focus;
- Market 'Brand,You' focus;
- Unsales focus;
- Be Receiver orientated;
- Think client-centric first, last, always;
- Create stunning straplines;
- Be mysterious;
- Talk DIRTY;
- Be chatty chatty;
- Think bonding;
- Be attentive;
- Think bang bang sexy legs;
- Know your FORM;
- Pursue rapid traction;
- Record the highlights;
- Use the ROAR unsales egg-timer process;
- Be speedy with follow-on;
- Think engagement, re-engagement to avoid disengagement;
- Don't be a Scarlet Pimpernel;
- Think up-sell and cross-sell;
- Think about bundling products;
- Think Va-Va-Voom VALYOU;
- Go the extra 10,000 miles;
- Never be 'too busy' to avoid touching;
- Be hot for the lot;
- Like retain;
- Love maintain;
- Get jiggy with a CRM system;
- Have a communication game plan;
- Strive to be extraordinary;
- Be innovative;
- Be stimulating;
- Think LIC;
- Think niche;
- Think value;
- Re-think your business process;
- Re-think your way of working;
- Re-think your way of managing and/ or leading;
- Be open to a paradigm shift;
- Take a few risks;
- Be bold;
- Embrace change;
- Get up early;
- Get organised;
- Prepare for the day ahead the night before;
- Work on commercial savvy and business nous;
- Get some real business experience;
- Get a grip on the seduction of persuasion;
- Star gaze;
- Smile, smile, smile;
- Think Yes! Yes!! Yes!!!
- Be the change that you want to see in the yourself and the profession; and
- Be happy.

the future's... ?

Guess what hot shot? "The future ain't what it used to be" (Yogi Berra).

Given the aftermath of the global recession, the turmoil in the world of finance, the disruption in law law land, the increasing levels of customer service excellence demands and expectations from prospects and clients, coupled with the choice available to them as to *who* they wish to buy their legal products and services from (present and future), if the path you have chosen is to become a 'Tomorrow's Lawyer' then you'd better be prepared for a rough, tough and bumpy passage.

It's *not* going to be plain sailing, anymore. Period.

Just to stick the prancing dancing Naked Lawyer's bootilicious bootie in a bit more, if we take on board Tom Peters's views (see Volume 2 again) and Ray Kurzweil's predictions of a future in which we are moving toward 'singularity' – where humans transcend biology as a result of the combined effect of the revolution in genetics, nanotechnology and robotics (artificial intelligence)[2] – things are likely to get even tougher.

Ray's main concept is that our technological knowledge has been snowballing and that once strong artificial intelligence is achieved, it will become a runaway phenomenon of rapidly escalating super-intelligence. When we reach this point in time (predicted 2040 – 30 years from now) we will no longer recognise the world as we know it nor our place (and space) in it.

Certainly, we're in for a lot more *change*!

Are we talking about fact or fiction? I reckon *fact*.

Despite the outward lawyerly veil exuding confidence, most of us legal beagles are probably highly insecure right now in the present, let alone 'in the future'. We're probably a house of cards just waiting to crumble and fall. Some of you may no doubt be thinking, 'The sun is out... the sky is blue... there's not a cloud... to spoil the view... but it's raining... (doodle doodle doom)... raining in my heart.'[3]

You may recognise these lyrics from a song. I'm referencing it in relation to how all of you frustrated lawyers may be feeling right now. Whether you're frustrated as hell about trying to get into the profession, or whether you're in it and passionate to do well but feel as if you're being held back, or perhaps you're desperately depressed and you want to get the hell out... but feel stuck... this book and the lessons within it are for you.

For some of you, it may feel like a tornado is whipping around inside that legal beagle heart of yours.

We may be in for a double dip as far as the economy and recession is concerned. Even if this does not happen, the double-dip pessimist mongers say that, 'looking forwards the wider economic picture is not so bright'. Bottom line... doom and gloom. The feeling is that there will be no more boom for many years to come.

I've probably made you feel like jumping off the proverbial crumbling ivory tower roof (or equivalent), again. Jeronimoooooooooo! But hey, don't jump. Ever the eternal optimist I reckon there's still hope. We just have to find the strength and c-c-c-courage to persevere.

For a start, we shouldn't believe everything we read or hear. I believe there is hope because we have choice. We have options. For example, if you can't get through the 'no training contract here for you' brick wall, are struggling to duck around it by applying for a paralegal and/or legal executive position and having no success there either because law firms are hoarding any cash they have and are reluctant to take on more staff as the global economy faces continued uncertainty, then here's an idea...

Go and do something else with your life. For now, at least. While the economy and legal world is struggling and desperately trying to find its feet again and get itself on an even keel.

Reality check – there's an obvious over supply of law students, an obvious under supply of training contracts available (and/or paralegal positions available) and a pool of highly qualified and skilled 'give us a job' lawyers already in the market who were 'let go' in 2008-10, ever hopeful of reclaiming a rowing position on the good ship legal enterprise.

Taking another path may well mean less risk of racking up (more) debt. After all, there is no guarantee you will make it (or continue to make it) as a lawyer; some things may well be beyond your control. The saving grace is that there's always the chance you can come to the law (or return to it) later in life, as many lawyers have, successfully.

You may well find (like most people) that you will have more than one career during your working life. There's a whole range of exciting career paths for an intelligent, hard-working, ambitious person such as you. Remember, you are one of the top five percent in the world (as an educated professional). Even in a recession there are industries and niches doing rather well. Go seek and ye shall find... because it just may turn out that the dream you once believed as being the holy grail might actually turn out to be a paper cup.

If you don't believe me then go and talk to all those frustrated lawyers who remain in the profession and industry and all those who have since left, whether due to being shoved out of the nest or out of their own choosing.

Whether you're a paralegal, legal executive, assistant solicitor, associate solicitor, a senior associate, attorney, lawyer, partner or barrister you may well have already reached the point, mindset and realisation which Jim Rohn speaks of:

"Let others lead small lives, but not you. Let others argue over small things, but not you. Let others cry over small hurts, but not you. Let others leave their future in someone else's hands, but not you."[4]

Being unhappy in your job/career/role/life is akin to being unhappy in your marriage. When you've reached the point that there's more 'bad' than 'good' happening then you have to do something about it (for everyone's sake).

So, if the holy grail you may have once searched for and possibly even found at some point has most definitely turned into a paper cup, then how about these ideas:

1. Become a virtual lawyer – if you've got the network, contacts, collaborative relationships, wherewithal, personal marketing skills, personal sales skills... and guts, then go do it; or
2. Be a portfolio worker (be a lawyer and something else at the same time), for example, Tim Kevan: barrister (non-practising at present), *Guardian* law blogger, writer, author of *Law and Disorder*; Marci Alboher: lawyer, journalist, author and writing coach; Denise Nurse: lawyer and weather presenter (Sky News); Shireen Smith: lawyer, marketing and website business owner.[5] It might continue to rain in your heart as far as your lawyering role is concerned but the sunny joy the other roles bestow might actually be worth the juggling act; or
3. Go start a business. Hook up with an entrepreneur who will complement your skills and needs your connections, experience and level head. Together you could be a dynamic duo; the Batman & Robin of the new legal and business dynamic – although I suspect there could be a battle as to who drives the bat mobile.

There are plenty of entrepreneurs desperate to have esteemed professionals on board, who, dare I say it, already have finance lined up – their own or somebody else's – but need someone of your calibre and ability to add value to the team.

I have also read and heard of late that there are plenty of cash rich entrepreneurs (business angels) who would rather put their money behind a sound new business venture than invest it elsewhere in the present economic climate, as there's a chance that the yield will provide a much better ROI than sticking it in a bank or dabbling in the plum duck stock markets.

In my experience (as both a lawyer and an entrepreneur) some entrepreneurs have got all the ideas and whizzy gig oomph but no clue as to how to turn it into a viable business and make it work. They just might need us lawyers to bring that edge to the table that just may be the difference in their legacy.

It's worth remembering that great companies were born out of previous recessions – such as LexisNexis, Microsoft and Dell. And many lawyers who left the profession have made a great success of their new ventures (and careers and lifestyles).

Take a look at Philip Vecht. He's made an absolute fortune hanging advertisements in toilets. Reported as 'the lawyer who cleaned up with washroom adverts' in the *Sunday Times* in January this year, Vecht began his career as a commercial lawyer at Nabarros. After two years he got out of the profession and co-founded Admedia. In Vecht's own words, "it was terrifying." Surprisingly he wasn't referring to making the leap of faith into his new venture… it was with reference to the toils and challenges of making the business work and if he failed he "thought [he] would have to go back to being a lawyer". Turnover for 2010 is expected to be £7.5m.

I believe the world could probably do with less lawyers lawyering and more lawyers working in and on a business. It could be YOU.

You never know, this way ahead might actually just help the world get out of this long tail recession. There's already a plethora of lawyers in the world and a technological, digital, consumer sovereignty trend that will inevitably see the need, want and/or desire for even less.

Problems on the job (or search for a legal job) could lead you to begin a search for something better. But it may well not be the time for impulsive action. Only you will know what's right for you… where and when.

When all is said and done, if it's raining in your heart then you could do something about it. You have a choice. You could be master of your own mutiny. You are, after all, the captain of your mother-ship.

Of course, you will have to conduct a 360 degree personal talent, strengths, skills, knowledge, experience, fiscal, confidence and guts reality check. But you know how to do that now. And an honest one at that. You'd be a fool not to. After all, if you're going to walk the plank and jump into a stormy sea, then you'd better have all the bits 'n' bobs in the life raft to ensure your survival. Otherwise, you just might drown.

portfolio handbag: skills and careers

Fortunately, if you've been studious in reading and acting upon the activities suggested by *the naked lawyer*, you're likely to have some new and/or improved skills to act as arm bands; you're acquiring a portfolio handbag of skills that will stand you in good stead for whatever future you decide to pursue and lifestyle to sculpt.

If you become and/or remain a lawyer then my legal experience and business experience have led me to believe that for you to stay ahead of the 'competition' and to attract the entrepreneurial and business owner/decision maker clients of the past, present and future, you're going to have to deliver outstanding client service and develop extraordinary relationships…

You're going to have to ROAR to make your clients' grade. Building a portfolio of skills is a sure fire way of achieving this.

I reckon that the combination of commercial savvy, business nous, soft skills, rainmaking skills and technical law excellence will be a Godsend in order to capture the hearts and minds of lobsters, prospects, clients and colleagues.

So... If you want to achieve bottom line results then you're going to have to be prepared to be on the frontline with your 'Brand,Me':

- You might get shot;
- It may cost you an arm or a leg; or
- You could stick your neck out once too often and lose your head in the process,

but that's the price you just might have to pay to survive... and thrive!

Heck, you never know, learning and applying these new and improved skills may actually take you down a path you never thought you would find yourself. The experience may be quite serendipitous. You might even end up (like some lawyers) having a portfolio career...

What's a portfolio career? It's rejecting the old single profession model. It's like having a portfolio of investments and being a multi-trick pony. Rather than putting all of your eggs in one basket and being a one trick pony you spread the risk and increase the opportunity by diversifying... It's about discovering that maintaining a 'portfolio' of different careers can pay off in terms of time, money and quality of life. You scale back some of the time you spend on your 'main' career, to give you time and freedom to develop other strings to your bow and to pursue other interests.

The benefits of a portfolio career include:

- You decide when, how and on what you work;
- You get to develop, hone and use your portfolio skills across your different careers;
- You are CEO of your own bespoke career – you can structure work around your lifestyle;
- You get to pick and choose your attitude to work;
- You allow yourself the freedom to pursue something you feel close to (or drawn to);
- You make room for all the things you want to be in your life;
- You create the space to fulfil your dreams;
- You get the opportunity to make yourself feel happy and fulfilled; and
- You get to spread your well-honed handbag of skills across different roles bringing you increased security.

You get to live your life FULL ON.

Whatever the next step is that you decide to take,

- I dare you to be different...
- I dare you to leap out of your comfort zone...
- I dare you to make the transition from existing to living...
- I dare you to make the transition from having a 'job' or a 'career' to having an enriching lifestyle...
- I dare you to make the changes that will make you truly happy...

By marketing, branding and selling YOU it may just come to pass that you experience the fulfilling and happy life which you dream of.

Having conducted your 'after dark activities' from Volume 2, do you have your plan B, C and/or D at the ready? I ask because the future you thought you had, or might have, may have recently been washed away before your very eyes. Accordingly, it's up to you to create the future that you want for yourself.

I dare you to get off your butt, fulfil your dreams and make it count.

Here's my tip. Make it XXX rated...

sexily serendipitous, salubriously serene, socially savvy

Why XXX rated? You're no doubt aware of the original acronym 'KISS', meaning 'Keep It Simple Stupid'. Well, in true ROAR model style, I figured I would innovate 'KISS' and multiply it.

XXX = KISS KISS KISS

To be a successful Tomorrow's Lawyer and/or successful in business and/or life, I reckon I need to:

- KISS: Keep It Sexily Serendipitous;
- KISS: Keep it Salubriously Serene; and
- KISS: Keep It Socially Savvy.

The future, as I see it, for a Tomorrow's Lawyer, an entrepreneurial lawyer of the naked kind, such as YOU perhaps, will be all about XXX in the future YOU create.

Although I believe that every day is a blank page just waiting to be scribbled on, I make every effort to plant a firm 'X' 'X' 'X' on it.

Why? 'X' really does mark the spot...
'X' 'X' 'X' hits it and makes it count!

after dark activity

come away with me

I salute YOU. I raise my half full champagne glass to toast your present and future success...

I said at the outset of this journey (in Volume 1) that *the naked lawyer* is *not* going to be like the usual boring, dry-rot, scholastic, academic, management and marketing clap-trap tomes. There's a place for that – it's called the law school and law firm library.

I trust it has not been so. Accordingly... *Please do not confine me, the naked lawyer,* to a shelf in those places! Should you do so, I promise you this... I *will haunt you!* And... I will cause mischief beyond your comprehension... of a really prancing dancing stonky Naked Lawyer kind, because I am *not* meant to be positioned there amongst that dusty old stiff necked duty bound black and white lot!

I need to be dancing alongside you *every day*, as a kind of muse to continually inspire you, refresh you and comfort you – in the palm of your hand, laptop, briefcase or suitcase. Ooh, yes, that would be fun... I love to travel... "come away with me in the night" à la Norah Jones.[6] I hear you beckon. Yowza. Count me in!

naked lawyer activity – a study worth casing

As this is the final volume, I have only this to say in relation to the 'after dark activity'... Read and action all of *the naked lawyer*...

Albeit it is my legal beagle story, if you follow what I suggest throughout the book, it could be the wonderful beginning, or continuation of, your success story too...

ROAR steps

Do everything in *the naked lawyer* Volumes 1-11.

ROAR tips

Do everything in *the naked lawyer* Volumes 1-11.

ROAR quiz

Don't forget to check out the EntrepreneurLawyer website for the fun quiz and to see if carrying out the 'after dark activity' activities can count towards CPD accreditation (or its alternative).

ROAR summation

star gazer, dream maker

Prrrrrrr... Prrrrrrr... Prrrrrrr... And prance...

The Naked Lawyer wishes to say 'à bientôt', ask a final few questions and proffer one or two final thoughts... Having read and worked through *the naked lawyer* (hopefully all 12 volumes herein):

- Do you feel content? Inspired? Challenged? Motivated? Learned? Anything else?
- Do you feel confident that you can market, brand and sell YOU! Continually?
- Do you now think and feel that you are, or can become, an extraordinary rainmaker lawyer... an extraordinary lover? Think extraordinary sex!
- Are you XXX, ready to be rated?
- As Tomorrow's Lawyer, are you going to get more clients, sales, referrals, income, value, growth and success?

The answer ought to be a resounding... Yes! Yes!! Yes!!! Yes!!!! Yes!!!!!

If you *love* 'what you do' and '*why* you do it', it should continually give you the *courage* to be more than *what* and *who* you already are... You will achieve fulfilment... and your dream, no less.

Go now, make YOUR space. Make YOUR life count. You have, at YOUR fingertips and YOUR choosing, with the support of the ROAR model, the key to unlock the power within YOU to:

- Take control of those things that seemed so elusive in the past;
- Make those difficult choices that have niggled away for so long; and
- Dig deep for the courage and confidence to help you make all of the required changes,

in the quest to achieve YOUR dream life.

Whilst buzzing and fuzzing in your drive for success, whatever you perceive that to be, please don't forget to stand and stare sometimes... Be a star gazer... whilst a dream maker. If anything, it just might save you from losing the plot at times.

One of my key messages throughout *the naked lawyer* and which lies at the heart of the ROAR model is to *give, give, give* and then *give* some more, without expecting anything in return. I stand by it. Or, perhaps I should say, I prance by it.

Accordingly, I would deem it a privilege and an honour to be your new friend... whether it turns out to be for a reason, a season, or a lifetime.

I wish to thank you for being present throughout our journey together in experiencing *the naked lawyer*.

"When one teaches, two learn."
(Robert A. Heinlein)

Heck... hang the schmaltzy stuff... I've had a lot of fun. I'd love to think you have too!

And so, my parting wisdom... well, actually, it's Mark Twain's, but I subscribe to it...

"Whenever you find yourself on the side of the majority, it is time to pause and reflect."

Go star gaze, dream maker...

References

1. Peter Groves, IP Lawyer, London, England: http://www.petergroves.co.uk
2. Ray Kurzweil, The Singularity Is Near. Ray Kurzweil is one of the world's leading inventors, thinkers, and futurists, with a twenty-year track record of accurate predictions. He has been called 'the ultimate thinking machine' by *Forbes* magazine, the 'rightful heir to Thomas Edison' by *Inc.* magazine (and selected as one of the top entrepreneurs) and 'the restless genius' by The Wall Street Journal.
3. Status Quo lyrics: http://www.tsrocks.com/s/status_quo_texts/raining_in_my_heart.html
4. Quote by Jim Rohn: personal development and motivational guru. http://www.jimrohn.com
5. Sources: *Director* magazine October 2009 and *NatWest Sense* magazine 2009
6. *Come away with me*: a song by Norah Jones (vocals and piano); BMI

afterword

what's next pussycat?

meet the team

I'd like to introduce you to the experts who work alongside me:

- Gary Russell – Winning Profile;
- David Clarkson and Stuart Brown – Osmosis Brand Communications; and
- Richard Day and Chris Marshall – Onstate.

get in touch

If you enjoyed reading *the naked lawyer* and in particular if you followed the 'ROAR steps' throughout Volumes 1 to 11 and 'gave it your best shot', I'd love to hear how you're getting along.

Should you decide to sign up for the E-ntrepreneur Bullet newsletter (found on the EntrepreneurLawyer website) you will have the opportunity to enjoy 15 minutes FREE consultation with me via Skype in relation to *the naked lawyer.* My Skype handle: chrissie.lightfoot

Please do feel moved to ping me...

I'd be delighted to have the opportunity to begin building an enduring professional relationship with you.

If you'd like to do likewise, then please contact, connect, link, join, follow and get involved in one (or all) of the following ways:

- E-mail: chrissie@entrepreneurlawyer.co.uk
- Website: http://entrepreneurlawyer.co.uk
- Blog: http://entrepreneurlawyer.co.uk/blog
- LinkedIn: http://uk.linkedin.com/in/chrissielightfoot
- Twitter: http://twitter.com/thenakedlawyer
- Facebook: http://www.facebook.com/EntrepreneurLawyer
- Law Society Gazette 'In Business' Blog: http://www.lawgazette.co.uk/blogs/in-business-blog/the-end-lawyers-pah-this-time-039super-lawyer039
- LinkedIn Group – The Entrepreneur Lawyer Relationship Sales Network: http://www.linkedin.com/groups?about=&gid=2874570&trk=anet_ug_grppro

Feel free to let colleagues and/or friends know about *the naked lawyer* if you believe it will be of interest, benefit and/or value to them.

I also welcome you to link to the EntrepreneurLawyer website – http://entrepreneurlawyer.co.uk – if you find the information in *the naked lawyer* valuable and believe your website and users would benefit from it.

get naked

the naked lawyer book – all 12 volumes which contain the full ROAR model – is the sum total of my life's knowledge, experience, skills and talent that I have shared unreservedly with those of you who wish to take control of your career, business and life in a positive way.

I hope you found it enlightening and it brought, and continues to bring you, many hours and years of both professional and personal, development, success and fun...

Please do keep in touch with me on your travels and life journey... and remember...
Be happy!

Warmest regards

Chrissie Lightfoot

The Entrepreneur Lawyer (of the naked kind)

glossary

ABS	Alternative Business Structures
AIG	Ass In Gear
Blawg	Blog by a lawyer, usually with a legal angle
Btw	By The Way
CRM	Customer Relationship Management
DM	Direct Message
EBITDA	Earnings Before Interest Tax Depreciation and Amortisation
EBT	Employee Benefit Trust
EI	Emotional Intelligence
EMI	Enterprise Management Incentive
ESP	Extraordinary Search Power
FB	Facebook
Gen X	Generation X. The generation born after the baby boom ended
Gen Y	Generation Y. The generation described as the demographic cohort following Gen X; birth dates ranging somewhere from the mid-1970s to the early 2000s
Granular	Granulated structure
HR	Human Resource
IFA	Independent Financial Advisor
IM	Instant Messaging
IMHO	In My Humble Opinion
IPR	Intellectual Property Rights
JFGI	Just ****ing Google It
LI	LinkedIn
LIC	Lawyerly Intellectual Capital
LOL	Laugh Out Loud
LSA	Legal Services Act 2007
LTR	Long Term Relationship
MBO	Management Buy Out
Netiquette	Netiquette – internet etiquette – is a set of social conventions that facilitate interaction over networks, ranging from Usenet and mailing lists to blogs and forums.
Pantone	In reference to the colour system, the Pantone Matching System, a proprietary color space used in the printing industry
Peeps	Web term used to describe people
POD	Points Of Difference
ROI	Return On Investment

ROTF	Roll On The Floor
SCRM	Social Customer Relationship Management
Semantic Web	Semantic Web is a group of methods and technologies to allow machines to understand the meaning – or semantics – of information on the World Wide Web.
SEO	Search Engine Optimisation
SM	Social Media
SME	Small/Medium Sized Enterprise
SN	Social Networking
SSO	Social Search Optimisation
USP	Unique Selling Point
Web 1.0	Web 1.0 is a retronym that refers to the state of the World Wide Web, and website design style used before the advent of the Web 2.0 phenomenon. Web 1.0 began with the release of the WWW to the public in the 1990s and is the general term that has described the Web before the bursting of the Dot-com bubble in 2001
Web 2.0	Web 2.0 has been the term used to describe the current web design, business models and branding methods of sites on the World Wide Web since 2004(ish)
Web 3.0	Web 3.0 is about the Semantic Web and personalisation. Focusing on the computer elements, it's where the computer is generating new information, rather than humans.
Web 4.0	The next frontier in WWW evolution
WOM	Word Of Mouth
YT	YouTube

inspiration

books

Abramson, B., *Digital Phoenix: Why the Information Economy Collapsed and How It Will Rise Again* (Cambridge, Mass.: MIT Press, 2005)

Anderson, Chris, *The Long Tail: How Endless Choice is Creating Unlimited Demand* (London: Random House, 2006)

Anderson, Chris, *The Long Tail: Why the Future of Business Is Selling Less of More* (London: Random House, 2006)

Bakan, Joel, *The Corporation: The Pathological Pursuit of Profit and Power* (London: Constable, 2004)

Blanchard, Ken and Bowles, Sheldon, *Gung Ho! Turn on the people in any organization* (New York: William Morrow and Company, Inc., 1998)

Blanchard, Ken, *Whale Done! The Power Of Positive Relationships* (New York: The Free Press, 2002)

Bounds, Andy, *The Jelly Effect: How To make Communications Stick* (Chichester: Capstone Publishing Ltd., 2007)

Bounds, Deirdre, *Fulfilled: A Personal Revolution In 7 Steps* (Harlow: Pearson Education, 2009)

Brogan, Chris, *Social Media 101: Tactics and Tips to Develop Your Business Online* (New Jersey: John Wiley & Sons Inc., 2010)

Brown, Rebel, *Defy Gravity: propel your business to high-velocity growth* (Austin, Texas: Greenleaf Book Group Press, 2010)

Bryan, Lowell et al, *Race For The World: Strategies To Build A Great Global Firm* (Boston, Mass.: HBR Press, 1999)

Buckingham, Marcus and Clifton, Donald, *Now, Discover Your Strengths* (New York: The Free Press, 2001)

Burg, Bob, *Endless Referrals: Network Your Everyday Contacts Into Sales* (3rd ed., New York: McGraw-Hill Books, 2006)

Burg, Bob and Mann, John D., *Go-Givers Sell More* (London: Penguin Books, 2010)

Carnegie, Dale, *How To Win Friends & Influence People* (Ebury Press, 1998)

Carr, Nicholas, *The Digital Enterprise: How To Reshape Your Business For A Connected World* (Boston, Mass.: HBR Press 1999)

Christensen, Clayton, *The Innovator's Dilemma: When New technologies Cause Great Firms To Fail* (Boston, Mass.: HBR Press, 1997)

Christensen, Clayton and Raynor, Michael, *The Innovators Solution: Creating And Sustaining Successful Growth* (Boston, Mass.: HBR Press, 2003)

Clark, J. and Critcher, C., *The Devil Makes Work: Leisure in Capitalist Britain* (London: The MacMillan Press Ltd., 1993)

Collins, James and Porras, Jerry, *Built To Last: Successful Habits of Visionary Companies* (London: Random House Business Books, 2000)

Collins, Jim, *Good To Great: why some companies make the leap... and others don't* (London: Random House Business Books, 2001)

Conley, Chip, *The Rebel Rules: Daring To Be Yourself In Business* (New York: Simon & Schuster, 2001)

Covey, Stephen R., *The 7 Habits of Highly Effective People* (New York: Simon & Schuster, 2004)

Croslin, David, *Innovate The Future: A Radical Approach to IT Innovation* (New York: Prentice Hall, 2010)

Csikszentmihalyi, Mihaly, Flow – *The Psychology of Happiness* (London: Rider, 1992)

Csikszentmihalyi, Mihaly, *Beyond Boredom and Anxiety* (San Francisco: Jossey-Bass, 1975)

Fagerberg, Jan et al., *The Oxford Handbook Of Innovation* (Oxford: OUP, 2005)

Fisher, William, *Promises To Keep: Technology, Law, and the Future of Entertainment* (California: Stanford University Press, 2004)

Gates, Bill, *Business @ The Speed Of Thought: Using A Digital Nervous System* (London: Penguin Books, 1999)

Gawer, Annabelle & Cusumano, Michael, *Platform Leadership: How Intel, Microsoft and Cisco drive Industry Innovation* (Boston, Mass.: HBR Press, 2002)

Gladwell, Malcolm, *The Tipping Point: How Little Things Can Make a Big Difference* (New York: Little Brown & Company, 2000)

Godin, Seth, *Permission Marketing* (New York: Simon & Schuster, 1999)

Godin, Seth, *Meatball Sundae: How New Marketing Is Transforming The Business World* (London: Piatkus Books, 2007)

Goleman, Daniel, *Emotional Intelligence: why it can matter more than IQ* (London: Bloomsbury Publishing, 1996)

Hamel, Gary, *Leading The Revolution* (Boston, Mass.: HBR Press, 2000)

Handy, Charles, *Understanding Organisations* (4th ed., London: Penguin Books, 1993)

Handy, Charles, *The Empty Raincoat: Making Sense Of The Future* (London: Hutchinson, 1994)

Handy, Charles, *The Elephant and the Flea* (London: Hutchinson, 2001)

Harvard Business Review, *Harvard Business Review on Innovation*, (New York: Harvard Business Review, 2001)

Harvey-Jones, John, *Trouble Shooter* (London: BBC Books, 1990)

Harvey-Jones, John, *Trouble Shooter 2* (London: Penguin Books, 1992)

Harvey-Jones, John, *Making It Happen: Reflections On Leadership* (London: Harper Collins,1988)

Haserot, Phyllis, *The Rainmaking Machine: Marketing Planning, Strategies and Management for Law Firms* (New York: Garland Law Publishing, 1989)

Hughes, Mark, *Buzz Marketing: Get People To Talk About Your Stuff* (London: Penguin Books, 2005)

Johnson, Spencer, *Who Moved My Cheese? An amazing way to deal with change in your work and in your life* (New York: G.P. Putman's Sons, 1998)

Kotler, Philip et al., *Marketing Moves: A New Approach to Profits, Growth, and Renewal* (Boston, Mass.: HBR Press, 2002)

Kurzweil, Ray, *The Singularity Is Near: When Humans Transcend Biology* (London: Penguin Books, 2005)

Lamb, Patrick, *Alternative Fee Arrangements: Value Fees and the Changing Legal Market* (London: Ark Group, 2010)

Lessig, Lawrence, *The Future Of Ideas: The Fate Of The Commons In A Connected World* (New York: Vintage Books, 2002)

Lessig, Lawrence, *Free Culture: The Nature And Future Of Creativity* (New York: Penguin Books, 2004)

Levinson, Jay & Rubin, Charles, *Guerrilla Marketing On The Internet* (London: Piatkus, 1995)

Lightfoot, Chrissie, nee Burak, 'Relative Work, Relative Leisure: Women Entrepreneurs in the 1990s', BA (Hons) Leisure Studies Degree (Leeds Metropolitan University, 1996)

Locke, Christopher, *Gonzo Marketing: Winning Through Worst Practices* (Oxford: Capstone Publishing Ltd., 2001)

Lundin, Stephen et al., *Fish! A Remarkable way to boost morale and improve results* (New York: Hyperion, 2000)

Maltz, Maxwell, *Psycho-Cybernetics* (New Jersey: Prentice Hall, 1960)

Maslow, Abraham H., *Motivation And Personality* (New York: Harper, 1954)

McKenna, Regis, *Total Access: Giving Customers What They Want In An Anytime, Anywhere World,* (Boston, Mass.: HBR Press, 2002)

McKeown, Max, *The Truth About Innovation: A Small Book About Big Ideas* (Harlow: Pearson, 2008)

Mills, Catrin, *Making Every Six Minutes Count* (London: Ark Group Ltd., 2010)

Moss-Kanter, Rosabeth, *The Change Masters: Corporate Entrepreneurs At Work* (London: Routledge, 1984)

Murray, Will, *Brand Storm: A tale of passion, betrayal, and revenge* (London: Prentice Hall, 2000)

Peters, Tom & Barletta, Martha, *Trends: recognize, analyze, capitalize* (New York: DK Publishing, Inc., 2005)

Peters, Tom, *The Brand You 50: Fifty ways to transform yourself from an "employee" into a brand that shouts distinction, commitment, and passion!* (New York: Alfred A. Knopf, Inc., 1999)

Peters, Tom, *Thriving On Chaos: Handbook For A Management Revolution* (London: Pan Books Ltd., 1989)

Peters, Thomas & Waterman, Robert, *In Search Of Excellence: Lessons from America's Best-Run Companies* (New York: Harper & Row, 1982)

Pink, Daniel, *A Whole New Mind: How To Thrive In The New Conceptual Age* (London: Cyan Books, 2006)

Prahalad, C.K & Krishnan, M.S., *The New Age Of Innovation: Driving Co-Created Value Through Global Networks* (New York: McGraw-Hill Books, 2008)

Purdie, Jeni, *Life Coaching For Dummies,* (2nd ed., Chichester: John Wiley & Sons Ltd., 2010)

Rath, Tom, *StrengthsFinder 2.0* (New York: Gallup Press, 2007)

Rath, Tom & Clifton, Donald, *How Full Is Your Bucket?* (New York: Gallup Press, 2004)

Rath, Tom & Conchie, Barry, *Strengths Based Leadership* (New York: Gallup Press, 2008)

Redfield, James, *The Celestine Prophecy* (London: Bantam Books, 1994)

Russell, Gary, *Big Rocks: balancing life & work* (Sausalito, Calif.: Lifestyle Press, 2005)

Scoble, Robert & Israel, Shel, *Naked Conversations: how blogs are changing the way businesses talk with customers* (New Jersey: John Wiley & Sons, Inc., 2006)

Semler, Ricardo, *Maverick!* (Sydney: Random House Business Books, 2001)

Semler, Ricardo, *The Seven-Day Weekend: A Better way To Work In The 21st Century* (Sydney: Random House Business Books, 2003)

Silver, Cole, *How To Create Wealth and Freedom in Your Law Practice: 101 powerful client development and retention strategies for attorneys* (New York: The Silver Group Ltd., 2009)

Steare, Roger, *Ethicability: how to decide what's right and find the courage to do it* (3rd ed., York: Roger Steare Consulting Ltd., 2009)

Stratten, Scott, *Unmarketing: stop marketing, start engaging* (New Jersey: John Wiley & Sons, Inc., 2010)

Susskind, Richard, *The Future of Law: Facing the Challenges of Information Technology* (Oxford: Clarendon Press, 1996)

Susskind, Richard, *The Future of Law: Transforming the Law – Essays on Technology, Justice and the Legal Marketplace* (Oxford: OUP, 2000)

Susskind, Richard, *The End Of Lawyers? Rethinking The Nature of Legal Services* (Oxford: OUP, 2008)

Templar, Richard, *The Rules Of Work* (2nd ed., Harlow: Pearson Education Ltd., 2010)

Terrett, A. and Monaghan, I., 'The Internet – An Introduction for Lawyers' in Edwards, L. and Waelde, C., *Law and the Internet: A framework for electronic commerce* (Portland, Oreg.: Hart Publishing, 2002)

Thompson, Della, *The Concise Oxford Dictionary* (9th ed., Oxford: OUP,1995)

Treasury Independent Average, *Forecasts for the UK Economy*, Treasury Independent Average, Crown copyright material (August 2005)

Tupman, Simon, *Why Lawyers Should Eat Bananas* (Byron Bay: Simon Tupman Presentations Pty Ltd., 2000)

Watkins, John, *An Insider's Guide On Hiring A Business Attorney: And How To make the Relationship Work* (Atlanta: Ocelot Atlanta LLC., 2010)

Welch, John F., *Jack: Straight From The Gut* (New York: Warner Books, Inc., 2001)

Wheatley-Burt, Patricia, *Leadership for Law Firm (after the Legal Services Act)* (London: The Law Society of England & Wales, December 2010), ISBN: 978 1 85328 697 1; The Law Society bookshop, DX 742330 Sudbury 5, PO Box 99, Sudbury, Suffolk, CO10 2SN.

Wright, Jeremy, *Blog Marketing: The Revolutionary New Way to Increase Sales, Build Your Brand and Get Exceptional Results* (New York: McGraw-Hill Books, 2006)

Zeng, Ming & Williamson, Peter, *Dragons At Your Door: How Chinese Cost Innovation Is Disrupting Global Competition* (Boston, Mass.: HBR Press, 2007)

articles, journals and reports

Badenoch & Clark, 'Professional Talent Spotlight – August 2010: Recruitment market commentary', August 2010

Berners-Lee, Tim, 'The World Wide Web - Past, Present and Future', *Journal of Digital Information*, Article No. 1, Volume 1 Issue 1, 17 July 2006

BlizzardInternet.com, http://newsletter.blizzardinternet.com/the-internet-future-is-closer-than-you-think/2006/08/14

Boswell, W., 'A Short History of the Internet', part of *The New York Times Company*, http://websearch.about.com/od/whatistheinternet/a/historyinternet.htm

Boswell, W., 'The World Wide Web and The Internet – Not The Same Thing', part of *The New York Times Company* http://websearch.about.com/od/whatistheinternet/a/worldwideweb.htm

Braithwaite, Tim, 'My Video leads next generation of upstarts', *Financial Times*, 5 September 2006, p30

Braithwaite, Tim, 'Companies learn value of blogging', *Financial Times*, 17 July 2006

Carroll, Jim, '10 big trends for the legal profession', 14 December 2005, http://www.jimcarroll.com/weblog/archives/000712.html

Cerf, V., 'The Future of the Internet', interview by Jennifer Robinson, *Gallup Management Journal*, 13 April 2006, http://gmj.gallup.com/content/default.asp?ci=22348

Chicago-Kent College of Law, http://www.kentlaw.edu/cyberlaw/resources/whatis.html

Content Wire.com , 'FRESH PICKS: Law Profession Gets to Grip with Knowledge', 21 Aug 2006, http://www.content-wire.com/FreshPicks/Index.cfm?ccs=86&cs=4253

Daily Mail, 'Coutts seeks suitably rich females for LTR', *Daily Mail*, 28 August 2006, p51

Daniel, Dianne, 'Networks of the future', 21 August 2006, http://www.computerworld.com/action/article.do?command=viewArticleBasic&taxonomyId=16&articleId=9002591

Director Magazine, 'Talking Semantics', *Director Magazine*, September 2006, pp66-68

Evan Carmichael & Associates, 'Cashing in on Blogs: How Entrepreneurs Are Profiting From The Online Craze', 15 September 2006, http://openpr.com/news/11274/CASHING-IN-ON-BLOGS-How-Entrepreneurs-Are-Profiting-From-The-Online-Craze.html

Financial Times, 'Apple and NBC enter the digital video race', *Financial Times*, 13 September 2006, p25

Garrote, I.J., 'Linking and Framing: A Comparative Law Approach', *European Intellectual Property Review*, 2002 24(4), pp184-198

Gartenberg, Michael, 'Technology now defines the business', 10 August 2006, http://www.computerworld.com.au/index.php/id;61559839;fp;4;fpid;1398720840

Grande, Carlos, 'Consumer content on the internet increases', *Financial Times*, 15 September 2006

Hobson, Neville, 'Pay Attention To Gartner's Hype Cycle', 11 August 2006, http://www.webpronews.com/blogtalk/blogtalk/wpn-58-20060811PayAttentiontoGartnersHypeCycle.html

Hornsby, William, 'Improving the Delivery of Affordable Legal Services Through the Internet: A Blueprint for the Shift to a Digital Paradigm', ABA Standing Committee on the Delivery of Legal Services, http://www.abanet.org/legalservices/delivery/deltech.html

Horowitz, A. S., 'How to get to the top of search-engine results', *The Wall Street Journal, Start Up Journal – centre for entrepreneurs,* 14 August 2006, http://www.startupjournal.com/ecommerce/ecommerce/20060814-horowitz.html?sjcontent=mail

Keynote, 'The Legal Services Market: Executive Summary', http://www.keynote.co.uk/kn2k1/13712_02//doc_4.htm?uni=1155561027

Keynote, 'The Legal Services Market: The Future', http://www.keynote.co.uk/kn2k1/13712_02//doc_4.htm?uni=1155560649

Lightfoot, Chrissie, 'Understanding and Exploiting Opportunities in relation to the Future of the Law in the Digital Age: research, ideation, business model and development concepts – proposals for consideration', Leeds, 2006

Martin, James, 'Gurgle, gurgle ...Google', *The Sunday Times, News Review,* 24 September 2006

Maslow, Abraham H., 'A Theory of Human Motivation', *Psychology Review,* 1943

Miniwatts Marketing Group, 'Internet Growth And Stats: Today's road to eCommerce and global trade', *Miniwatts Marketing Group*, 10 April 2006, http://www.allaboutmarketresearch.com/internet.htm

Miniwatts Marketing Group 'Internet Users By Language', *Miniwatts Marketing Group,* 2006, http://www.internetworldstats.com/stats7.htm

Miniwatts Marketing Group 'Internet Usage in European Union: Internet User Statistics & Population for the 25 European Union countries and regions', *Miniwatts Marketing Group*, 2006, http://www.internetworldstats.com/stats9.htm

Nerds2.0.1 wiring the world , 'The Future of the Internet: A Bigger Pipe', http://www.pbs.org/opb/nerds2.0.1/wiring_world/future.html

Netcraft.com, 'Total Sites Across All Domains August 1995 - April 2006' *Netcraft News* – Web Server Survey, 6 April 2006

Netscape, 'The net in a nutshell', *Netscape*, http://wp.netscape.com/netcenter/newnet/whatis.html

Peters, Andy, 'Lawyers Stop Bowing Before Billable Hour: Firms use advanced software to encourage alternative billing arrangements', *Fulton County Daily Report*, 8 September 2006, http://www.law.com/jsp/legaltechnology/pubArticleLT.jsp?id=1157629871529

PR.com, 'Domain Name Law Minus the Lawyers', *PR.com*, http://www.pr.com/press-release/17411

PricewaterhouseCoopers, 'UK Economic Outlook July 2006', *PwC*, July 2006

PRLeap.com, 24 September 2006, http://www.prleap.com/pr/49226

Projections Database, Government Actuary's Department

PRweb.com, 'New PR Firm is First to Combine Traditional, Digital Methods for Boomer Marketing', *PR Web*, http://www.prweb.com/releases/2006/9/prweb440547.htm;

Rachman, G., 'Apostles of the blogosphere may just be political pooters', *Financial Times*, 26 September 2006, p21

Roulac, Stephen, 'Learning How To Break Away To Get Alpha Results', Global CEO, 2008

SEOChat.com, 'The Future of Search', *SEOChat.com*, http://www.seochat.com/c/a/Search-Engine-News/The-Future-of-Search

SiteProNews, 'Five Social Media Predictions for 2010, *SiteProNews*, 11 January 2010, http://www.sitepronews.com/2010/01/11/five-social-media-predictions-for-2010/?utm_source=feedburner&utm_medium=e-mail&utm_campaign=Feed percent3A+sitepronews percent2FICnA+ percent28SiteProNews percent29

Sloan, P. and Kaihla, P., 'Blogging for big bucks', *Business 2.0 Magazine*, 22 August 2006, http://money.cnn.com/2006/08/21/technology/bloggingdollars0822.biz2

Sunday Times, 'Grey, female and loaded', *Sunday Times,* 13 August 2006

Sunday Times, 'Britain and world set for hard landing', *Sunday Times,* 16 July 2006

The Law Society, 'An e-Strategy for the Law Society', *The Law Society,* February 2005

Thirdage Inc., 'Tech Terms: Cyberspace', http://www.thirdage.com/cgi-bin/glosdb.cgi?glos_name=tech&action=view&term_name=Cyberspace

Thirdage Inc., 'Tech Terms: Internet', http://www.thirdage.com/cgi-bin/glosdb.cgi?glos_name=tech&action=view&term_name=Internet

Thirdage Inc., 'Tech Terms: WWW', http://www.thirdage.com/cgi-bin/glosdb.cgi?glos_name=tech&action=view&term_name=WWW;

TimesUnion.com, 'Turn trends into business advantages',TimesUnion.com, 8 August 2006 http://timesunion.com/AspStories/story.asp?storyID=506509&category=BUSINESS&newsdate=8/8/2006

Ward, Andrew, 'Coke and Apple in iTunes move', *Financial Times*, 2 August 2006, p22

Webber, Gary, 'Put A Brand On Your Work', *Fast Company*, 2000

Webopedia.com, 'The Difference between the Internet and the World Wide Web', *Jupitermedia Corporation*, http://www.webopedia.com/DidYouKnow/Internet/2002/Web_vs_Internet.asp

WebProNews.com, http://www.webpronews.com/blogtalk/blogtalk/wpn-58-20060912ProfessionalBloggingEffectiveOutsourcing.html

Wright, Greg, 'Building a Thriving Legal Market', *Yorkshire Today*, 19 September 2006, http://www.yorkshiretoday.co.uk/ViewArticle2.aspx?SectionID=1299&ArticleID=1775336

websites, links and people of interest

The Naked Lawyer and EntrepreneurLawyer stuff

http://www.entrepreneurlawyer.co.uk

http://www.youtube.com/TheNakedLawyer

http://www.youtube.com/EntrepreneurLawyer

http://www.linkedin.com/in/chrissielightfoot

http://www.twitter.com/TheNakedLawyer

http://www.twitter.com/EntrepreneurLaw

http://www.facebook.com/EntrepreneurLawyer

http://budurl.com/TNL1

http://budurl.com/mutiny

http://budurl.com/SNzenLaw

http://budurl.com/ItsABoxOfFrogs

LinkedIn stuff

http://uk.linkedin.com/in/raymondmclennan

http://www.linkedin.com/in/soniagallagher

http://uk.linkedin.com/in/juliansummerhayes

http://uk.linkedin.com/in/annpage

http://uk.linkedin.com/pub/michaela-hardwick/14/574/983

http://uk.linkedin.com/in/catrinmills

http://uk.linkedin.com/pub/jules-wyman/4/608/552

http://uk.linkedin.com/pub/jeni-purdie/1/69/400

http://uk.linkedin.com/in/adrianjs

http://uk.linkedin.com/in/stuartbbrown

http://www.linkedin.com/in/christinehueber

http://www.linkedin.com/in/donnaseyle

http://www.linkedin.com/pub/marc-sheridan/17/7a4/1ab

http://www.linkedin.com/pub/david-gabor/a/445/307

http://uk.linkedin.com/in/patriciawheatleyburt

http://www.linkedin.com/in/jaimiefield

http://www.linkedin.com/in/lisadimonte

http://uk.linkedin.com/in/petergroves81

http://www.linkedin.com/in/anthonyverna

http://uk.linkedin.com/in/stevekuncewicz

http://www.linkedin.com/pub/kathy-dilorenzo/11/972/33b

http://www.linkedin.com/in/theonlinebar

http://br.linkedin.com/in/nilsmontan

http://uk.linkedin.com/in/lyndonogden

http://press.linkedin.com/about

http://www.linkedin.com/groupItem?view=&gid=2078586&type=member&item=29270258&commentID=-1&qid=f0122c6b-22f9-4c6d-b092-98a8f8657b98&goback= percent2Egmp_2078586#lastComment

http://www.linkedin.com/groupItem?view=&srchtype=discussedNews&gid=145854&item=24909662&type=member&trk=EML anet qa ttle-cnhOon0JumNFomgJt7dBpSBA

http://uk.linkedin.com/in/energiseliberateyourtalent

Wikipedia stuff

http://en.wikipedia.org/wiki/Entrepreneur

http://en.wikipedia.org/wiki/Bryan_Adams

http://en.wikipedia.org/wiki/The_Only_Way_Is_Up

http://en.wikipedia.org/w/index.php?title=Special percent3ASearch&search=va+va+voom

http://en.wikipedia.org/wiki/The_Green_Mile

http://en.wikipedia.org/wiki/Persona_non_grata

http://en.wikipedia.org/wiki/Que_Sera,_Sera_(Whatever_Will_Be,_Will_Be)

http://en.wikipedia.org/wiki/It percent27s_a_wonderful_life http://en.wikipedia.org/wiki/Pack_Up_Your_Troubles_in_Your_Old_Kit-Bag

http://en.wikipedia.org/wiki/What percent27s_New_Pussycat percent3F_(song)

http://en.wikipedia.org/wiki/The_sound_of_music

http://en.wikipedia.org/wiki/Better_Days

http://en.wikipedia.org/wiki/South_Pacific_(musical)
http://en.wikipedia.org/wiki/Yuppie
http://en.wikipedia.org/wiki/DINKY
http://en.wikipedia.org/wiki/Soylent_Green
http://en.wikipedia.org/wiki/William_Gibson
http://en.wikipedia.org/wiki/Deepak_Chopra
http://en.wikipedia.org/wiki/Carpe_diem
http://en.wikipedia.org/wiki/Amur_Leopard

General stuff

http://www.petergroves.co.uk
http://www.Rachelhenke.com/coaching
http://lawpracticestrategy.com
http://www.raymondmclennan.com
http://legaleaglemhm.wordpress.com
http://twitter.com/legaleagleMHM
http://legal-two.com/?p=49527
http://www.beyond-expectation.co.uk
http://www.positive-belief.co.uk
http://www.reachforstarfish.com
http://www.beyondthebrief.com
http://www.solicitorsjournal.com/story.asp?storycode=16482
http://www.sitepronews.com/2010/01/11/five-social-media-predictions-for-2010/?utm_source=feedburner&utm_medium=e-mail&utm_campaign=Feed percent3A+sitepronews percent2FICnA+ percent28SiteProNews percent29
http://www.mpmagazine.com/Publication.asp?pubid=FFD595B7-F234-45EF-A421-9115C8933D5A
http://www.amazon.co.uk/Legal-Issues-Web-Social-Media/dp/1906355959/ref=sr_1_1?ie=UTF8&s=books&qid=1288687299&sr=8-1
http://www.informaworld.com/smpp/content~db=all~content=a713767054
http://www.wisegeek.com/what-is-a-bean-counter.htm
http://darmano.typepad.com/logic_emotion/2010/09/how-be-an-effective-corporate-ambassador.html
http://www.enotes.com/shakespeare-quotes/what-s-name-that-which-we-call-rose
http://www.kloog.co.uk/index.php/home/marketing-expert/marketing-tips
http://easily.co.uk
http://www.godaddy.com
http://darmano.typepad.com/logic_emotion/2010/09/how-be-an-effective-corporate-ambassador.html
http://www.personalbrandingblog.com
http://abovethelaw.com/2010/09/aba-survey-lawyers-profiting-from-web-2-0
http://www.sitepronews.com/2010/01/11/five-social-media-predictions-for-2010/?utm_source=feedburner&utm_medium=e-mail&utm_campaign=Feed percent3A+sitepronews percent2FICnA+ percent28SiteProNews percent29
http://christinehueber.com
http://www.seopackages.com

http://www.businessinsider.com/twitter-stats-2010-4

http://www.davidpbrown.co.uk/poetry/william-henry-davies.html

http://www.strengthsfinder.com/113647/Homepage.aspxhttp://www.belbin.com/rte.asp?id=8

http://www.businessballs.com/kolblearningstyles.htm

http://www.chubbybrown.biz

http://www.focuslifestyle.org/main.shtml

http://www.duhaime.org/LegalDictionary/S/StareDecisis.aspx http://www.ft.com/cms/s/0/e983c280-dd68-11df-beb7-00144feabdc0.html?ftcamp=crm/e-mail/20101022/nbe/USMorningHeadlines/product

http://abovethelaw.com/2010/09/aba-survey-lawyers-profiting-from-web-2-0/

http://hootsuite.com

http://tweetulater.com

http://budurl.com

http://hashable.com

http://twitter.com

http://facebook.com

http://linkedin.com

http://youtube.com

www.ingramcontent.com/pod-product-compliance
Ingram Content Group UK Ltd.
Pitfield, Milton Keynes, MK11 3LW, UK
UKHW050231160926
8657IPUK00008B/190

9 781907 787300